WRITING INSTRUCTION ACROSS THE DISCIPLINES

Also Available

Best Practices in Writing Instruction, Third Edition
Edited by Steve Graham, Charles A. MacArthur, and Michael A. Hebert

Handbook of Writing Research, Third Edition
Edited by Charles A. MacArthur, Steve Graham, and Jill Fitzgerald

Writing and Reading Connections: Bridging Research and Practice
Edited by Zoi A. Philippakos and Steve Graham

Writing Instruction Across the Disciplines

Evidence-Based Practices in Grades 6–12

edited by
Steve Graham
Carol Booth Olson
Tanya Baker

ASSOCIATE EDITORS
Huy Q. Chung
Undarmaa Maamuujav
Jacob Steiss

THE GUILFORD PRESS
New York London

A Division of Guilford Publications, Inc.
www.guilford.com

Printed in the United States of America

This book is printed on acid-free paper.

For product and safety concerns within the EU, please contact *GPSR@taylorandfrancis.com,* Taylor & Francis Verlag GmbH, Kaufingerstraße 24, 80331 München, Germany.

Last digit is print number: 9 8 7 6 5 4 3 2 1

Library of Congress Cataloging-in-Publication Data is available from the publisher.

ISBN 978-1-4625-5911-4 (paperback)
ISBN 978-1-4625-5912-1 (cloth)

About the Editors

Steve Graham, EdD, is a Regents Professor and the Warner Professor in the Division of Leadership and Innovation at Mary Lou Fulton Teachers College, Arizona State University. Since the 1980s, he has studied how writing develops, how to teach it effectively, and how it can be used to support reading and learning. Dr. Graham's research involves typically developing writers and students with special needs in both elementary and secondary schools, with much of this research occurring in classrooms in urban schools. He is a recipient of the Thorndike Career Achievement Award from Division 15 of the American Psychological Association, the William S. Gray Citation of Merit from the International Literacy Association, and the Exemplary Research in Teaching and Teacher Education Award from Division K of the American Educational Research Association, among other awards. He is coauthor of three influential Carnegie Corporation reports on writing and coauthor or coeditor of several books.

Carol Booth Olson, PhD, is Professor Emerita in the School of Education at the University of California, Irvine (UCI). She was founding Director of the UCI Writing Project and served in that capacity for 42 years. Dr. Olson's research focuses on improving academic writing outcomes for all learners, especially culturally and linguistically diverse students in low-socioeconomic-status, high-needs middle and high schools. She served as Director and Principal Investigator of the WRITE Center at UCI and Principal Investigator of the Pathway to Academic Success Project, a professional development intervention that takes a cognitive strategies approach to teaching text-based argument writing in secondary school.

Tanya Baker, EdD, is Executive Director of the National Writing Project and has more than 25 years of experience working in education in and outside of schools. She has worked with many funders and partners to build and manage national programs that connect educators to work together on areas of interest and problems of practice. Dr. Baker served as Co-Principal Investigator of the WRITE Center at the School of Education at UCI. She strives throughout her work to design learning experiences that begin with a presumption of competence and are relentlessly collaborative and deeply joyful.

Associate Editors

Huy Q. Chung, PhD, is Director of Research and Project Scientist for the UCI Writing Project. Previously, he served in the same roles for the Pathway to Academic Success Project and the WRITE Center. All three projects focus on the professional development of teachers of literacy, particularly in enhancing teachers' pedagogical content knowledge around writing. Dr. Chung's research commitments particularly focus on English language arts teachers' appropriation of evidence-based practices, across the career span, to support multilingual learners. He has taught college courses on children's literature in the elementary classroom, advanced writing for education science majors, secondary literacy across the disciplines for MAT students, and improvement science methodology for doctoral students. He is also a former middle school humanities teacher. He has published in leading journals of education research and practice.

Undarmaa (Undraa) Maamuujav, PhD, teaches in the College of Education at Butler University in Indianapolis. Prior to joining Butler University, she was a research scientist in the School of Education at UCI, working for the Pathway to Academic Success Project. She also served on the leadership team of the national WRITE Center, funded by the Institute of Education Sciences, for secondary students' writing development. Dr. Maamuujav's work centers around improving writing and disciplinary literacy skills of students both at secondary and postsecondary levels. She is coauthor of the book *Academic Languaging and Historical Thinking: Cultivating Students' Language Skills for Argument Writing*. She has taught a variety of undergraduate and graduate courses focused on writing and literacy for over 20 years.

Jacob Steiss, PhD, is a postdoctoral fellow in the College of Education at the University of Missouri–Saint Louis. A former English language arts and social studies teacher, he helped design and facilitate professional learning for novice and experienced teachers as part of the WRITE Center. In addition to helping educators improve their literacy instruction, he has published qualitative and quantitative research to improve knowledge of student writing, how disciplinary thinking develops, and how teachers' beliefs and practices affect student learning. Dr. Steiss is coauthor of the book *Academic Languaging and Historical Thinking: Cultivating Students' Language Skills for Argument Writing.*

Contributors

Tanya Baker, EdD, National Writing Project, Berkeley, California

Kaitlin Bundock, PhD, Department of Special Education and Rehabilitation Counseling, Utah State University, Logan, Utah

Huy Q. Chung, PhD, School of Education, University of California, Irvine, Irvine, California

Penelope Collins, PhD, School of Education, University of California, Irvine, Irvine, California

Tricia Ebarvia, MSE, Greene Street Friends School, Philadelphia, Pennsylvania

Nicole Gilbertson, PhD, Teacher Academy, School of Education, University of California, Irvine, Irvine, California

Steve Graham, PhD, Mary Lou Fulton College for Teaching and Learning Innovation, Arizona State University, Tempe, Arizona

Brian Hand, PhD, College of Education, University of Iowa, Iowa City, Iowa

Young-Suk Grace Kim, EdD, School of Education, University of California, Irvine, Irvine, California

Penny Kittle, MAT, Plymouth State University, North Conway, New Hampshire

Sharlene A. Kiuhara, PhD, Department of Special Education, University of Utah, Salt Lake City, Utah

Jenell Krishnan, PhD, WestEd, Santa Ana, California

Catherine Lammert, PhD, Department of Teacher Education, Texas Tech University, Lubbock, Texas

Carol D. Lee, PhD, Northwestern University, Evanston, Illinois

Undarmaa Maamuujav, PhD, College of Education, Butler University, Indianapolis, Indiana

Chauncey Monte-Sano, PhD, Marsal Family School of Education, University of Michigan, Ann Arbor, Michigan

Debra Myhil, PhD, Graduate School of Education, University of Exeter, Exeter, Devon, United Kingdom

Carol Booth Olson, PhD, School of Education, University of California, Irvine, Irvine, California

Kimberly N. Parker, PhD, Crimson Summer Academy, Harvard University, Cambridge, Massachusetts

Amber B. Ray, PhD, Department of Special Education, University of Illinois Urbana–Champaign, Champaign, Illinois

Nancy Romance, PhD, Florida Atlantic University, Boca Raton, Florida

Mary J. Schleppegrell, PhD, Marsal Family School of Education, University of Michigan Ann Arbor, Ann Arbor, Michigan

Jacob Steiss, PhD, College of Education, University of Missouri–Saint Louis, Saint Louis, Missouri

Tamara P. Tate, PhD, School of Education, University of California, Irvine, Irvine, California

Alison F. Warren, PhD, College of Education, University of Iowa, Iowa City, Iowa

Mark Warschauer, PhD, School of Education, University of California, Irvine, Irvine, California

Acknowledgments

From March of 2019 through March of 2025, the School of Education at the University of California, Irvine, received grant funding from the Institute of Education Sciences (IES) of the U.S. Department of Education to establish and operate the WRITE Center, a research and development center dedicated to improving academic writing outcomes for students at the secondary level.

One of the many contributions the WRITE Center made to the field of writing research was our 2023 meta-analysis of writing treatments for students in grades 6 through 12, which identified evidence-based practices in writing instruction across the disciplines. It included over 400 writing treatment–control comparisons containing one or more writing measures that assessed written products, writing skills, writing processes, writing beliefs, and writing knowledge. This book builds upon the meta-analysis to focus not only on *what* evidence-based practices to teach but also *how* to integrate them into secondary classrooms in the disciplines of language arts, history, mathematics, and science.

Contributors to this book include members of the WRITE Center research team and our Advisory Board, as well as experts featured in our many webinars for classroom teachers, doctoral students, researchers, and policymakers.

We want to express our gratitude to IES for their support of the WRITE Center. We continue to believe in the power of educational research to generate the scientific knowledge necessary to provide high quality evidence-based instruction for all learners.

STEVE GRAHAM	CAROL BOOTH OLSON	TANYA BAKER
Co-Principal Investigator, WRITE Center	Director and Principal Investigator, WRITE Center	Co-Principal Investigator, WRITE Center

Contents

PART II. WRITING IN THE DISCIPLINES

PART III. WRITING IN A DIGITAL WORLD

Introduction

EVIDENCE-BASED PRACTICES FOR TEACHING WRITING

Steve Graham and Young-Suk Grace Kim

In 2019, the Institute of Education Sciences established the WRITE (Writing Research to Improve Teaching and Evaluation) Center to improve academic writing outcomes for secondary students. One of the projects undertaken by the Center was a comprehensive meta-analysis of writing intervention research with students in grades 6 to 12 (Graham et al., 2023), updating the *Writing Next* meta-analysis published in 2007 (Graham & Perin, 2007a, 2007b). Both the 2023 meta-analysis and *Writing Next* identified evidence-based practices for teaching writing tested in true experiments (random assignment) and quasi-experiments (no random assignment). The two primary differences between the more current and the prior meta-analysis are that the 2023 review included studies that assessed any aspect of writing (*Writing Next* only included studies assessing writing quality), and quasi-experiments had to include pretest data in the more recent review so that study outcomes could be adjusted for preexisting writing differences. While *Writing Next* included 123 studies, the 2023 meta-analysis involved 357 papers that yielded 406 independent writing treatment and control comparisons, providing a richer evidentiary base for identifying evidence-based writing practices.

The primary purpose for conducting the 2023 meta-analysis was to provide secondary teachers, both English language arts teachers as well as content-area teachers, with tools for improving students' writing and making writing more integral to secondary teachers' daily instructional practices. The assumption underlying this objective was that writing procedures shown to be effective in multiple research studies are likely to be effective in individual teachers' classrooms. Of course, there is no absolute guarantee that this is the case. So, we encourage teachers who apply instructional procedures described in this book to monitor the success of these techniques with their students. This way, secondary teachers can make informed decisions about which of these instructional procedures work for their students.

So why is a book needed that identifies evidence-based practices in writing and provides secondary teachers with guidance on how to implement these procedures? Most importantly, the writing of secondary students is not what it should be. On the last national assessment of students' writing in the United States, two-thirds of grades 8 to 12 students did not write well enough for grade-level success (National Center for Education Statistics, 2012). The scores on this writing assessment were even lower for boys, students with disabilities, and students who were Black, Hispanic, and American Indian/Alaskan Native. While there are many possible reasons for this, an important contributing factor was the lack of writing and writing instruction in many secondary schools. While some teachers and schools do an incredible job of teaching writing, secondary students in most classrooms do little writing, and little time is devoted to teaching them how to write, with increasingly less attention devoted to writing in social studies, science, and mathematics (Applebee & Langer, 2011; Drew et al., 2017; Gillespie et al., 2014; Ray et al., 2016). If secondary students are to receive the writing instruction they deserve and need, teachers need to know and use writing practices with a proven record of success. Further, the teaching of writing needs to be the responsibility of all secondary teachers.

With these goals in mind, the WRITE Center drew upon its collective resources to create this book. Scholars and doctoral students who carried out the Center's objectives, as well as consultants and affiliates who participated in activities hosted by the Center, generously contributed chapters to this publication. The book presents writing practices aligned with the 2023 meta-analysis conducted by the WRITE Center (Graham et al., 2023), focusing on evidence-based practices in writing that are applicable across the disciplines (e.g., culturally sustaining practices, teaching sentence construction and grammar, teaching writing strategies for writing, reading, and critical thinking) as well as within specific disciplines (e.g., social studies, science, and mathematics). The book also addresses the increasingly digital nature of writing, with chapters devoted to writing and generative artificial intelligence, multimodal writing, and new media literacies.

The intended audience for the book is all secondary teachers across subject areas and anyone who plans or aspires to teach middle and high school students. We think schools that desire to align their writing instruction across the disciplines will find the book to be useful too. Each chapter provides practical information and recommendations for teaching writing and opens with a set of questions designed to guide the reader and ends with possible action steps for classroom implementation. Chapters address how the evidence-based and best practices presented can be implemented in the classroom, while at the same time addressing how these procedures address the linguistic and cultural diversity common in American classrooms.

With this in mind, we open this introduction with the following four guiding questions:

GUIDING QUESTIONS

1. Why is it important to teach writing to students in grades 6 to 12?
2. Why should we use evidence-based practices to teach writing?
3. What does science tell us about effective writing instruction?
4. How can teachers use this book to guide their writing instruction in their discipline?

Why Writing Is Important

Writing emerged at least 5,000 years ago when Sumerians used wedge-shaped symbols produced with a reed stylus on a moist clay tablet to record commodities such as number of animals or goods possessed (Cook, 2003). From this humble start, writing has undergone multiple transformations. This includes a parade of ever-evolving tools for producing writing, including styluses made of bones, reeds, and brushes, as well as reed, quill, metal, fountain, ball-point, felt-tip, and roller-based pens. The pencil joined this cavalcade of tools in the 1790s, with the typewriter patented in 1868 and personal computers making their debut in the early 1970s. It also includes a variety of different tokens for conveying meaning, some of which are still used and some that are not (Robinson, 2022). These tokens range from pictures, pictograms, and rebus symbols to cuneiform, hieroglyphs, Mayan glyphs, runes, Chinese characters, and various alphabets and syllabaries. You can also throw in shorthand, scientific symbols, musical notations, numbers, and road signs. Writing is a continually evolving system for conveying information. In this decade alone, machines now produce meaningful text that only humans could create in the past.

As writing tools and tokens evolved, so did its purposes. Our signature identifies who we are, while autobiographies, biographies, obituaries, and funerary inscriptions describe who we were. Writing allows us to sustain personal connections with family, friends, and colleagues across space and time. It can create a sense of purpose and heritage that extends beyond our immediate circle of loved ones, friends, and acquaintances. The adoption of a standard system of writing in China 2,300 years ago, for example, promoted a sense of national unity (Swedlow, 1999), just as documents like the Constitution and Bill of Rights define what it means to be an American.

Writing not only connects people, but it can persuade them as well. Thomas Paine roused revolutionary sentiment in colonial America with his pamphlet *Common Sense*. *Narrative of the Life of Frederick Douglass, an American Slave* served as a catalyst for antislavery beliefs in 19th-century America, laying the groundwork for the war between the North and South. Henry David Thoreau's essay "Resistance to Civil Government," published in 1848, provided a rationale to resist governmental demands that promote injustice, influencing the actions of freedom fighters from Mahatma Gandhi to Martin Luther King. In fact, the persuasive power of writing is so strong that governments ban "subversive" texts and jail the offending authors.

The power of writing is also evident in its use as a repository for storing and sharing ideas. A wealth of information can be accessed by consulting books, magazines, newspaper articles, scientific reports, travel guides, websites, product labels, and encyclopedias: to name just some of the written sources that serve as the archives for human knowledge. Writing makes it possible for these and other ideas to flow from one person to another through a host of channels, including emails, memos, tweets, blogs, blueprints, personal correspondences, faxes, PowerPoint, multimodal presentations, religious texts, and government documents. Many of the things we take for granted today, like a modern transportation system, would disappear if writing no longer existed. For example, blueprints and plans for building cars and trucks would not exist, and rules and directions for traveling the roadways that did exist would need to be relatively simple because they could exist in memory only.

Another purpose of writing is illustrated in the declaration by the master of horror, Stephen King (who modeled it after a quote from Robert Bloch): "I write such gross stuff [because] I have the heart of a small boy—and I keep it in a jar on my desk." For Mr. King, novelists and poets, and everyday people, writing provides a venue for creating imaginary worlds and exploring ideas. It provides an outlet for artistic expression, creativity, and self-expression, as writers craft the stories that entertain, inspire, and capture who we are, who we were, and who we will be.

The power of writing is so strong as to be therapeutic. We can lessen physiological and psychological pain when we write about our feelings, loneliness, and traumas (Smyth, 1998). Exploring these experiences through writing helps us better understand and process difficult emotions, lowers blood pressure, lessens stress and anxiety, provides emotional release, and reduces symptoms of depression.

Writing is an essential tool for learning. We demonstrate what we know about a topic when we write about it, but more importantly writing about material read, seen, or heard enhances learning (Graham et al., 2020). The permanence of writing makes ideas available for evaluation and review. The explicitness of writing encourages the creation of connections between ideas. The active nature of writing fosters the exploration of unexamined assumptions about ideas. The value writing brings to learning was captured by E. M. Forster, who observed, "How do I know what I think until I see what I say?"

Although writing and reading are not identical processes, the knowledge drawn on when reading overlaps with the knowledge drawn on when writing (Fitzgerald & Shanahan, 2000; Kim, 2020). For instance, knowledge of how letters, sounds, and meaning connect informs the reading and spelling of words. Similarly, knowledge about the functions and purposes of different types of texts helps writers construct written messages and readers interpret them. As a result of this reciprocal relationship, teaching writing improves reading skills (Graham & Hebert, 2011).

While thinking can occur without writing, writing is thinking. Thinking involves a variety of cognitive skills, including analysis, evaluation, interpretation, inference, reasoning, problem solving, creativity, and communication (Baehr, 2013). When writers create text, they engage in these same thinking processes. This can be illustrated by considering two basic aspects of writing: deciding what information to include in text and how it is presented (Graham, 2018). As writers gather possible content for writing, they subject this information to analysis, evaluation, interpretation, and inference. This is necessary in order to determine which ideas are useful and which ones are not. Writers engage in these same thinking processes as well as reasoning, problem solving, creativity, and communication as they determine which of the surviving ideas will take center stage, how ideas are connected one to another, and how to craft the text so it is interesting and comprehensible to the intended audience.

Finally, look around—it is obvious that writing is a ubiquitous part of our existence. We are constantly writing to each other using digital devices, including smartphones that convert our oral messages to written ones. Through these digital devices, writing has become a common part of our home, social, civic, and work lives. Because writing is a powerful tool and one of the greatest inventions of all time, students who do not learn to write well cannot draw fully on its strengths. These students are less likely to realize their educational, personal, and occupational potential. The good news is that effective practices for teaching writing are available; they just need to be applied in the classroom with more regularity (Graham, 2019).

Why We Use Evidence-Based Practices

A surprising equation underlying teaching in schools around the world is that instructional practices repeatedly shown by research to be effective are applied infrequently, but practices with little to no scientific support are quite common (Cook et al., 2012). If secondary students are to receive the writing instruction they need and deserve, this equation must be reversed, with evidence-based practices implemented as a matter of course.

Our assumption that evidence-based practices need to become commonplace should not be interpreted as a refutation of teachers and the knowledge they acquire as a result of teaching writing. The reset recommended here presumes that teachers should apply the best evidence available to make conscious, informed, and judicious decisions when teaching writing. The advantage of routinely applying evidenced-based practices is that they have a proven track record of success established under rigorous testing procedures (see "Evidence-Based Practices"). Even so, the use of such procedures involves weighing the benefits, limitations, and even possible harm that might ensue as a consequence of implementing or not implementing them. If the effects of evidence-based practices are to be maximized, we believe teachers must contextualize knowledge gained from research with the knowledge they have acquired about their students, classroom, and the teaching of writing. It is also important to recognize that research on writing instruction can best be described as an incomplete portrait. The evidence-based practices currently available do not cover all aspects of teaching writing, and some of the untested writing practices teachers apply today will become evidence-based practices tomorrow (Graham & Harris, 2014). Thus, the reset we envision, where evidence-based writing practices become widespread and ordinary, places a premium on using teaching practices identified as effective through high-quality research, without dismissing or denigrating teachers' knowledge.

Teaching Lore

The most common instructional practices teachers apply in the classroom are based on teaching lore (Schwartz, 1995). This refers to the understandings, knowledge, and feelings acquired through designing instruction, implementing it, and/or reflecting on its success or failure. Teaching lore is customarily based on insights teachers obtain from instructional practices they develop and apply, practices they saw other teachers implement, practices teachers experienced as students themselves, and practices promoted by others as effective (Graham & Harris, 2014). This final source of teaching lore involves practices included in commercial materials as well as advice proffered by experts. The distinguishing factor for all of these forms of teacher lore is that the effectiveness of the recommended or applied instructional practices was not tested scientifically. Basing writing instruction solely or even mostly on teaching lore is risky for the following reasons.

First, it is quite challenging to separate the "wheat from the chaff" in determining what aspects of teaching lore account for assumed or even observed improvements in students' writing. For example, teachers do many things as they teach writing, making it difficult to single out one or more practices that are conclusively responsible for changes in students' writing. The practices that teachers or experts identify as being responsible for the desired change may be accurate, but it is also possible they are not correct or they are only correct for some students. Teachers, writing experts, and those who study teachers in action are not immune to selective bias, as they can overestimate the effects of instructional practices, identifying ingredients as effective that are consistent with their philosophical views about writing and learning.

Second, the data used to support writing practices based on teaching lore is often limited and sometimes completely absent. Even when evidence is provided by teachers or writing experts, it typically takes the form of testimonials or purposefully selected examples of success (see Smagorinski, 1987). This makes it difficult for teachers to determine who actually benefits from the proffered instructional practice.

Third, the teaching lore a teacher acquires as a result of learning by teaching is based on that teacher's singular experiences. In such a circumstance, it is not possible to be sure if specific teaching practices deemed effective by one teacher will be effective with other teachers and their students. Consequently, the reliability, validity, and generalizability of instructional writing practices based on teaching lore are uncertain.

Evidence-Based Practices

An alternative to teaching lore is the use of evidence derived from high-quality instructional research as a means for identifying effective writing practices. Beginning in the late 20th century, disciplines as diverse as medicine, economics, and agriculture advocated the use of evidence-based practices (Slavin, 2002). Practitioners in these fields used untested, ineffective, and sometimes harmful practices based on lore, theory, or both (Chalmers, 2005). To develop norms for effective practices, fields like medicine promoted the application of procedures whose effectiveness was supported by scientific evidence. A similar process is now occurring in writing and education more broadly (Graham & Harris, 2014).

The gold standard for scientifically testing the effectiveness of a writing practice is a randomized controlled design (RCD). In RCD studies, students, classrooms, schools, or districts are randomly assigned to a targeted writing treatment and a control condition. Such studies include procedures (e.g., randomization, control group) for increasing confidence that the tested writing treatment, as opposed to a rival explanation, is responsible for observed changes in students' writing.

Quasi-experiments (QEs) can also provide a reasonable estimate that a tested writing treatment is responsible for changes in writing performance. In QE studies, students, classrooms, schools, or districts are not randomly assigned to the targeted writing treatment and control conditions. A QE provides a weaker test of a writing treatment than an RCD. Because students are not randomly assigned in a QE, they may differ in multiple ways. This threat can be addressed, at least in part, by matching treatment and control students at the start of a QE study, establishing that their writing performance is equivalent, or using statistical procedures such as controlling for possible pretest differences in writing.

Mechanisms in these two designs that enhance internal validity (i.e., confidence that can be placed in a cause-and-effect relationship), such as randomization (RCD) or the inclusion of a control group (RCD and QE), do not ensure the outcomes from a single study are generalizable. This requires repeated replications of the observed findings across multiple studies.

Evidence from RCDs and QEs, when replicated, provides a more trustworthy approach for identifying effective writing practices than knowledge gained through teaching lore. Practices repeatedly demonstrated to be effective in such investigations provide direct evidence on whether (a) a writing practice produced the desired impact (i.e., effectiveness), (b) observed outcomes are replicable across students and situations (representativeness and generalizability), and confidence can be placed in the findings via statistical analyses (reliability).

Meta-Analysis

Meta-analysis is a systematic method of review used to summarize the direction (positive or negative) and magnitude of effects obtained in quantitative investigations, such as RCDs and QEs. With this approach, the outcomes from each investigation are converted to a common and comparable quantitative metric (i.e., effect size) that can be aggregated across studies. Effect sizes (ESs) for a specific measure in RCD or QE studies are computed as follows (assuming pretest performance is tested). One, the pretest mean for the writing treatment is subtracted from the posttest mean, resulting in an adjusted posttest mean for treatment. This same procedure is applied with the control condition. Two, the resulting adjusted posttest mean for the control condition is subtracted from the adjusted posttest mean for the writing treatment. Three, the differences between the adjusted posttest means are divided by the variability in posttest scores for both conditions. If the resulting ES is positive, then the writing treatment had a more positive effect than the control condition on this particular measure. If the ES is negative, then the control condition had a more positive effect. The magnitude of an ES, positive or negative, is determined by its size. As a general rule of thumb, an ES of 0.25 is small, 0.50 medium, and 0.80 large (Lipsey & Wilson, 2001).

As noted earlier in this introduction, the primary source of evidence that served as the underpinning for this book came from a meta-analysis conducted by the WRITE Center. This review examined the effectiveness of 23 different writing practices (Graham et al., 2023). It only included RCD and QE studies. QEs had to include a pretest, so possible prestudy differences were controlled. An overall effect was not computed for a writing practice unless there were at least four studies examining its effectiveness. For each writing practice tested in four or more investigations, statistical analysis was used to determine if the overall effect was greater than no effect. With a single exception (increasing amount of student writing), we only present writing practices that statistically enhanced students' writing performance.

While the WRITE Center meta-analysis (Graham et al., 2023) served as the primary framework for this book, we also drew on several other sources for the 11 recommendations for teaching presented in this chapter. This included meta-analyses examining the effects of writing about science, social studies, and mathematics content on learning this material (Graham et al., 2020), writing about material read and writing instructional effects on learning to read (Graham & Hebert, 2011), reading and reading instruction effects on learning to write (Graham, Liu, Bartlett, et al., 2018), and the effects of combined writing and reading instruction (Graham, Liu, Aitken, et al., 2018). Our recommendations for teaching writing also drew on a meta-synthesis of the writing practices employed by exceptional literacy teachers (Graham et al., 2015) as well as recommended best practices for teaching writing to diverse learners (Aronson & Laughter, 2016; Gay, 2000).

What Science Tells Us about Effective Writing Instruction

If teachers know *why writing is important*, we think they will invest the time and energy needed to develop excellent writing instruction for secondary students. If teachers understand *how writing develops*, we believe they will teach writing in a flexible and reasonable manner. If teachers possess *effective tools for teaching writing*, we maintain they have the know-how to maximize their students' success as writers.

Hopefully, we made it clear at the beginning of this introduction *why writing is important*. Although our understanding of *how writing develops* is still a work in progress, we know the road to becoming a competent writer is paved by the contexts in which writing occurs and changes in students' writing skills, strategies, knowledge, and motivation over time (Graham, 2006).

In terms of context, writing and the teaching of writing take place in multiple communities (Graham, 2018). These communities shape the teaching of writing. For example, the main purpose of writing in a high school biology class may focus exclusively on using writing as a tool for learning, whereas a high school English class focused on Shakespeare may use writing as a tool for critiquing the Bard's prose as well as a tool for students to produce their own narratives. In addition to such purposes, writing communities acquire specific norms for writing, writing identities, values and motivations for writing, preferred audiences, favored writing tools, sanctioned approaches to writing, common writing collaborations, established social interactions, and a collective writing history. Students' success in writing communities, like the ones they encounter at school, depends in part on how successful they are at learning how the community operates and their commitment to its goals and operation.

Writing is not just a social activity, however, as it involves the use of a variety of cognitive and affective processes. Writing is a self-sustaining and goal-directed activity requiring the skillful management of the constraints imposed by the writing topic, intentions of the writer, the writing environment, as well as the processes, knowledge, and skills involved in composing text (Zimmerman & Reisemberg, 1997). Writers must juggle and master a dizzying array of writing skills, knowledge, and processes. While writing, they draw on knowledge about the writing topic and genre(s) of the writing task. They apply strategies for planning, drafting, revising, editing, and publishing text. They transform and transcribe ideas into sentences that convey their intended meaning. With the rapid development of new ways of composing, including the creation of multimodal texts and the potential use of AI as a writing partner, this process has become even more demanding cognitively. Finally, the use of these various cognitive processes depends on a variety of beliefs held by writers. This includes beliefs about (1) the value and utility of writing, (2) writing competence, (3) reasons for engaging in writing, (4) writing success or failure, (5) writing identities, and (6) the communities in which writing takes place (Graham, 2018). These beliefs fuel whether one engages in writing, how much effort is allocated, and what cognitive resources are deployed when writing.

Context as well as the cognitive and affective resources of students and teachers shape and constrain how writing is taught in middle and high school classes (Graham, 2018, 2023). Collectively, the recommendations provided in this chapter address both of these viewpoints. The writing practices identified in these 11 recommendations provide a framework for teaching writing to secondary students by identifying instructional practices that advance critical writing skills, strategies, processes, knowledge, and motivations. While Recommendations 10 and 11 are not based on outcomes from RCDs and QEs, they address critical issues in creating a writing community in which all students thrive. This includes creating a writing context that is supportive as well as culturally responsive and relevant. The examples included in these two recommendations are drawn from the qualitative study of exceptional literacy teachers (Graham et al., 2015) and best practices in culturally responsive instruction (Aronson & Laughter, 2016; Gay, 2000). Finally, for all evidence-based writing practices identified in the following section, the ESs are provided.

What Science Tells Us about Teaching Writing

Based on what the scientific study of writing, we offer 11 recommendations for teaching writing to students in grades 6 to 12. These recommendations are applicable within specific disciplines and across them.

Recommendation 1: Writing Is Essential to Teaching Writing

One recommended avenue for becoming a better writer is to write frequently. This appealing homily assumes that if students have more opportunities to write, they will become better writers. Unfortunately, the evidence from the meta-analysis conducted by the WRITE Center (Graham et al., 2023) did not support this contention. While the impact of increasing how much students wrote was positive (ES = 0.14), it was so small it did not produce meaningful writing gains. Even so, many of the following writing practices identified as effective involved writing. For instance, as students learned writing strategies for planning, drafting, and revising text, they practiced using them while writing. Likewise, effective writing practices such as goal setting, feedback, inquiry, and prewriting procedures were tested and applied as students engaged in one or more writing processes. While writing in and of itself did not make students better writers, it was central to the learning and use of multiple writing practices that do lead to improvement.

Recommendation 2: Write Across the Curriculum

Writing about content presented in class increases students' exposure to this material and acts as a rehearsal strategy. Writing about such content can further prompt elaboration, as students adjust prior understandings of this content to new understandings evoked by writing about it. Writing also fosters *explicitness*, as students determine which information is most important; *integration*, as they organize ideas into a coherent whole; *active involvement*, as they decide how selected information is to be treated; *transformation*, as they translate ideas into their own words; and *reflection*, as the permanence of writing makes it possible for them to review, reexamine, connect, critique, and construct new understandings.

While increasing how much students write did not make them better writers (see Recommendation 1), writing about materials presented in social studies, science, and mathematics facilitated learning of the material being studied (ES = 0.30; Graham et al., 2020). The types of writing that were tested included argumentation, summarization, learning logs, personalizing information, creating a report, sharing information about a topic on the web, and producing a story about the information to be learned.

Writing can also enhance understanding of content material read (ES = 0.50 for researcher-designed tests and 0.37 for norm-referenced tests; Graham & Hebert, 2011). Effective practices included using writing to answer questions, make notes, or summarize material read, as well as writing arguments, stories, and explanations about this information. Teaching students how to apply these types of writing practices can make them even more effective. For instance, teaching students how to summarize material presented in class enhanced students' ability to apply this skill (ES = 0.49; Graham et al., 2023).

Recommendation 3: Support Students as They Write

Writing involves five interactive and reciprocal production processes (Graham, 2018). They are conceptualization (creating mental or physical representations of the writing task as well as what to say and how to say it), ideation (acquiring content for writing from long-term memory or external resources), translation (converting ideas for writing into acceptable sentences conveying the writer's intentions), transcribing (turning words and sentences into print or digital text), and reconceptualization (changes applied to any of the decisions made in the four production processes described earlier). Providing students with support as they engage in these processes is one way to enhance their writing.

The WRITE Center meta-analysis identified the following five effective writing practices for supporting students as they compose (Graham et al., 2023). One practice involved goal setting (ES = 0.44), which included teachers setting goals for students' writing (e.g., refute a specific number of counterarguments in a persuasive text). A second effective writing practice was the application of prewriting procedures (ES = 049). This includes activities designed to help students acquire, cull, and organize possible information for text, including small group discussion about the writing topic, reading text to gain information, gathering writing ideas from the internet, brainstorming possible writing content, and using graphic organizers to generate and organize writing ideas. Inquiry was the third most effective way to support students' writing (ES = 0.92). Inquiry was characterized by activities designed to help students generate information for a specific writing task by analyzing immediate and concrete data. An example includes students analyzing different but related concepts to determine how they were similar and diverged in order to write about them.

A fourth writing practice that effectively supported students as they wrote was peer-assistance (ES = 0.51). Peer-assistance involved the following types of activities: (1) peer-tutoring, (2) cooperative learning writing activities, and (3) students working together to plan, draft, edit, and/or revise text. The fifth effective writing practice for supporting students as they composed was providing them with feedback about their compositions (ES = 0.34). Examples of feedback include written comments on papers, assessments guided by rubrics, and evaluations of students' writing based on specific criteria (e.g., clarity, completeness).

Recommendation 4: Teach Writing Strategies

Writing strategies involve the mental and sometimes physical operations writers use to plan, draft, monitor, evaluate, revise, and edit their text. They are heuristics for carrying out one or more of the production processes involved in writing (see Recommendation 3). Some writing strategies like brainstorming can be applied to any writing task, whereas other writing strategies are more genre or topic specific, such as a strategy where students produce as many reasons as possible to support each side of an argument, decide which position they want to defend, reexamine the reasons already generated to decide which ones will be included and refuted in their essay, and continue planning as they write. In both cases, writing strategies provide a schema for directing and coordinating mental and physical operations when writing. The WRITE Center meta-analysis (Graham et al., 2023) found that teaching writing strategies improved secondary students' writing (ES = 0.76).

Recommendation 5: Teach Creativity and Critical Thinking for Writing

Teaching students to be more creative and critical thinkers should help them become better writers. Creative students are more likely to generate novel ideas or solutions for text, whereas students who think more critically are likely to analyze and evaluate what they write. The WRITE Center meta-analysis (Graham et al., 2023) provided support for both of these propositions (ES for teaching creativity and critical thinking studies combined = 0.27). An example of effective creativity instruction involved teaching students how to use similes, metaphors, and analogies when writing. An example of effective critical thinking instruction was teaching students to use questions to help them think more analytically about what they write.

Recommendation 6: Teach Foundational Writing Skills

To write effectively, students must learn how to translate ideas for writing into sentences that represent their intentions, thus creating sentences that are comprehensible to readers. This involves deciding on a suitable sentence structure where ideas are presented in a grammatically correct manner and clarifying the relationships among ideas where necessary (e.g., which idea is subordinate). While translating ideas into sentences requires thinking and conscious decision making, helping students become effective sentence constructors, who use grammar correctly and intelligently, should make it easier for them to apply these foundational writing skills. Consistent with this proposition, teaching students how to create more complex sentences improves their writing (ES = 0.73; Graham et al., 2023) as does teaching grammar (ES = 0.77; Graham et al., 2023). An example of effective sentence instruction is sentence combining, where the teacher models how to combine simpler sentences into more complex ones, and students practice mastering these combinations. An example of effective grammar instruction involves treating grammar as a metacognitive process. For instance, students learn how to make grammatical choices that influence text meaning, as is the case when deciding which modal verb best indicates the writer's degree of certainty with an assertion made in persuasive text.

Once students translate ideas into words or sentences, they must transcribe them into print or digital text where words are spelled correctly. For some secondary students, spelling can still be problematic (Graham & Santangelo, 2014), and the WRITE Center review (Graham et al., 2023) found that teaching spelling can improve secondary students' writing (ES = 0.53). An example of effective spelling instruction for these students involves teaching the spelling of Germanic, Latin, and Greek words and roots as well as common prefixes and suffixes.

Recommendation 7: Enhance Students' Writing Knowledge

Good writing is dependent on a variety of different types of knowledge possessed by writers (Graham, 2018). This includes knowledge of language, writing topics, audiences, characteristics of good writing, writing genres, and the context in which writing is produced. Writers with a richer knowledge base should have more personal resources to access, allowing them to produce better text. This assumption was supported by our meta-analysis (Graham et al., 2023), demonstrating that writing practices designed to increase one or more aspects of writing knowledge resulted in higher-quality text.

One of these effective writing practices included analyzing and emulating model text (ES = 0.46), as illustrated by providing students with examples of well-constructed text to analyze and emulate in their own writing, as well as emulating models of how to provide useful feedback. A second effective writing practice for enhancing writing knowledge was teaching students about the purposes of specific types of text, the basic elements of such text, and how these elements can be organized (ES = 0.39). A third effective writing practice involved observation (ES = 0.41). Examples of effective observation activities were observing others as they read and react to a written text, as well as observing how others carry out specific writing assignments.

Recommendation 8: Apply 21st-Century Writing Tools

Much of the writing done in schools today depends on 18th-century writing tools—paper, pencil, and pen. In contrast, writing outside school primarily involves digital tools (Graham, 2019). This is unfortunate, as newer digital tools provide writers with multiple advantages over writing by hand. For example, when using a word processor, it is easier to move, remove, add, or change text. Likewise, the development of more sophisticated word processing programs, referred to here as "word processing plus programs," provides even more affordances, including features to facilitate planning, provide feedback, create multimodal text, and increase motivation (e.g., gaming features). Computers can also provide interactive and personalized writing instruction, and the advent of programs like ChatGPT create a new reality where computers can act as writing partners.

While it is too soon to know how artificial intelligence programs such as ChatGPT will impact students' development as writers, secondary students benefit when 21st-century writing tools are used for writing or the teaching of writing (Graham et al., 2023). Secondary students demonstrate improvement when writing with word processing (ES = 0.22) or word processing plus programs (ES = 0.44). Computer-assisted instruction also enhanced their writing performance (ES = 0.32). An example of an effective word processing plus program was a multimedia word processor that allows students to produce compositions with text, sound, graphics, and videos. An example of an effective computer-assisted intervention was a computer program that provided individualized instruction in punctuation, capitalization, spelling, usage, and sentence construction.

Recommendation 9: Connect Writing and Reading Instruction

The knowledge students draw on when writing overlaps with the knowledge they draw on when reading (Fitzgerald & Shanahan, 2000; Kim, 2020). This includes general knowledge used to acquire ideas for writing and to understand what is read. It involves metaknowledge about the functions and purposes of text used to construct written messages and interpret text. It entails pragmatic knowledge about text features, words, syntax, and usage used to encode words and construct text, as well as decode words and comprehend text. Finally, it encompasses procedural knowledge that writers and readers use to set goals, access information, pose questions, predict, summarize, visualize, and analyze. Consequently, increasing the breadth and depth of these knowledge bases in reading should result in better writing, and vice versa.

This proposition was supported by the findings from several meta-analyses. Teaching writing to secondary students improved their writing in the WRITE Center review (ES = 0.22; Graham et al., 2023), whereas teaching writing improved reading (ESs ranged from 0.22 to 0.66 depending on the reading skill assessed) in an earlier meta-analysis by Graham and Hebert (2011). Similarly, teaching reading improved writing (ES = 0.35) in a meta-analysis by Graham, Liu, Bartlett, et al. (2018), whereas both writing (ES = 0.37) and reading (ES = 0.33) were improved when instruction in each was allocated a similar amount of time (Graham, Liu, Aitken, et al., 2018).

Recommendation 10: Create a Supportive Writing Community

Writing is hard work, and learning to write well is even harder. If students view a classroom as an unfriendly, high-risk, or unsupportive place, they are less likely to put forth their best efforts or to take the risks necessary to advance as a writer. As a result, it is especially important to develop classroom writing environments that are supportive, pleasant, interesting, and nonthreatening. This requires that teachers support students and students support each other when writing and learning to write. This approach was evident in the classrooms of highly effective literacy teachers (Graham et al., 2015). These teachers:

- were enthusiastic about writing and teaching writing, creating a stimulating mood during writing time;
- made writing visible by encouraging students to share what they wrote with peers and others, as well as publishing students' writing in anthologies, books, or other classroom collections;
- created a positive environment where students were encouraged to try hard, believe the writing skills and strategies taught would permit them to write well, and attribute their writing successes to effort and the writing skills they were learning;
- provided just enough support so that students were successful but encouraged them to act in a self-regulated fashion, doing as much as they can on their own.
- kept students engaged by involving them in thoughtful activities (such as gathering information for their composition) versus less thoughtful activities (such as completing a workbook page); and
- created classroom routines that promoted positive interactions among students, with students working together as they composed text.

Many of these same and other instructional practices are evident in the process approach to writing (ES = 0.65; Graham et al., 2023). This includes the following supportive and motivating procedures: writing for real audiences; encouraging ownership and personal responsibility for one's writing; promoting high levels of student interactions, creating a positive and pleasant writing environment; and encouraging self-evaluation and reflection. Instructional procedures such as those identified earlier can help teachers build a writing community where purposes and audiences for writing are established, writing is valued, a classroom identity for writing is established, students are motivated to write, writing collaborations and social interactions are positive, and a collective writing history develops over time.

Recommendation 11: Create a Culturally Responsive and Relevant Writing Classroom

Classrooms in schools in America have become increasingly diverse, populated with students from many different cultures, English-language proficiencies, and writing capabilities. If we are to maximize these students' writing success in the language arts, science, social studies, math, and other content classrooms, we need to ensure that instruction promotes what we refer to as the three *R*s: Respect, Relevance, and Responsiveness. Best practices for promoting these objectives (Aronson & Laughter, 2016; Gay, 2000) include:

- learning about students' cultures and background;
- respecting and reinforcing cultural differences;
- appreciating differences in communication styles;
- recognizing and combating one's own personal biases;
- assigning writing tasks that involve equity and social issues, connect to students' family and community, and concern topics students view as important;
- encouraging students to propose their own topics for writing;
- creating diverse groups where students write and work together;
- setting high but realistic expectations for all students, encouraging them to surpass previous efforts and accomplishments;
- adapting writing assignments and instruction so they are appropriate to the interests and needs of all students; and
- seeking feedback from all students to determine if their needs and interests are addressed.

The procedures identified earlier can help teachers build an environment where all students view themselves as valued and respected writing community members. They provide mechanisms for connecting students' classroom writing with family, community, and pressing social issues. Just as importantly, they stress that all students are capable but recognize each student as a unique individual with different assets and needs.

How Teachers Can Use This Book to Guide Writing Instruction in Their Disciplines

The 11 recommendations noted previously, which were based on evidence-based and best practices in writing, provide the foundation for the chapters in this book. In each chapter, the authors share practical and research-supported practices for teaching writing. This includes procedures for teaching writing across disciplines as well as within specific disciplines. Collectively, these chapters provide a rich tapestry on which to build an effective writing program.

The book is divided into three parts. Part I, "Writing Instruction Across the Disciplines," includes five chapters. Each chapter examines a specific approach to teaching writing that can be applied across disciplines. This includes chapters on teaching strategies for integrating writing, reading, and critical thinking (Olson et al., in this volume); culturally sustaining writing practices (Ebarvia & Parker, in this volume); teaching argumentative writing to support college readiness (Baker, in this volume); self-regulated strategy development (Ray & Graham, in this volume); and teaching grammar and sentence skills (Myhill, in this volume). These chapters illustrate scientifically validated writing practices and describe how they can be applied across content areas.

Part II, "Writing in the Disciplines," applies a different approach, illustrating scientifically validated practices for teaching writing in specific disciplines. This includes chapters on teaching narrative and poetry writing in the language arts (Kittle, in this volume), teaching argumentative writing in language arts (Lee, in this volume), writing in social studies (Monte-Sano & Scheppegrell, in this volume), strategies for teaching counterarguments in history (Baker et al., in this volume), strategies for writing in science (Romance, in this volume), writing and learning in science (Lammert et al., in this volume), and writing to improve learning in mathematics (Kiuhara & Bundock, in this volume). While each of these seven chapters is discipline specific, they include instructional writing practices that can be applied across disciplines.

Part III, "Writing in a Digital World," contains two chapters. The writing practices presented in each of them can be applied across disciplines. These chapters focus on leveraging generative AI to improve writing (Warschauer & Tate, in this volume) and multimodal writing (Krishnan et al., in this volume).

The evidence-based practices presented in these chapters provide a wealth of teaching strategies you can apply in your own classroom. Even more importantly, they can be applied by teachers in your school across the curriculum in a unified manner. We believe that such an alignment is the best way to maximize the impact of writing instruction.

ACTION STEPS

As you consider the information presented in this chapter and the book more broadly, we encourage you to consider actualizing one or all of the following actions (or ones of your own choosing):

- Identify writing practices presented in this book that can be applied in your class.
- Develop a plan for implementing these practices in your class.
- Work with other teachers and school administrators to use this book to develop a framework for coordinating writing instruction across grades and disciplines.
- Adopt and adapt the evidence-based practices presented in this book to create a respectful, relevant, culturally responsive classroom that engages all learners and promotes their success as writers.

REFERENCES

Applebee, A., & Langer, J. (2011). A snapshot of writing instruction in middle schools and high schools. *English Journal, 100*, 14–27.

Aronson, B., & Laughter, J. (2016). The theory and practice of culturally relevant education: A synthesis of research across content areas. *Review of Educational Research, 86*(1), 163–206.

Baehr, J. (2013). Educating for the intellectual virtues. *Journal of Philosophy of Education, 47*(2), 248–262.

Chalmers, I. (2005). If evidence-informed policy works in practice, does it matter if it doesn't work in theory? *Evidence & Policy, 1*(2), 227–242.

Cook, B., Smith, G., & Tankersley, M. (2012). Evidence-based practices in education. In K. R. Harris, S. Graham, & T. Urdan (Eds.), *APA educational psychology handbook* (Vol. 1, pp. 495–527). American Psychological Association.

Cook, M. (2003). *A brief history of the human race.* Norton.

Drew, S., Olinghouse, N., Luby-Faggella, M., & Welsh, M. (2017). Framework for disciplinary writing in science grades 6–12: A national survey. *Journal of Educational Psychology, 109*, 935–955.

Fitzgerald, J., & Shanahan, T. (2000). Reading and writing relations and their development. *Educational Psychologist, 35*(1), 39–50.

Gay, G. (2000). *Culturally responsive teaching: Theory, research, and practice.* Teachers College Press.

Gillespie, A., Graham, S., Kiuhara, S., & Hebert, M. (2014). High school teachers' use of writing to support students' learning: A national survey. *Reading & Writing: An Interdisciplinary Journal, 27*, 1043–1072.

Graham, S. (2006). Writing. In P. Alexander & P. Winne (Eds.), *Handbook of educational psychology* (pp. 457–478). Erlbaum.

Graham, S. (2018). The writer(s)-within-community model of writing. *Educational Psychologist, 53*, 258–279.

Graham, S. (2019). Changing how writing is taught. *Review of Research in Education, 43*, 277–303.

Graham, S. (2023). Writer(s)-within-community model of writing as a lens for studying the teaching of writing. In R. Horrowitz (Ed.), *The Routledge handbook of international research on writing* (Vol. II, pp. 337–350). Routledge.

Graham, S., & Harris, K. R. (2014). Conducting high quality writing intervention research: Twelve recommendations. *Journal of Writing Research, 6*(2), 89–123.

Graham, S., Harris, K. R., & Santangelo, T. (2015). Research-based writing practices and the Common Core: Meta-analysis and meta-synthesis. *Elementary School Journal, 115*, 498–522.

Graham, S., & Hebert, M. (2011). Writing-to-read: A meta-analysis of the impact of writing and writing instruction on reading. *Harvard Educational Review, 81*, 710–744.

Graham, S., Kim, Y., Cao, Y., Lee, W., Tate, T., Collins, T., . . . Olson, C. (2023). A meta-analysis of writing treatments for students in grades 6 to 12. *Journal of Educational Psychology, 115*, 1004–1027.

Graham, S., Kiuhara, S., & MacKay, M. (2020). The effects of writing on learning in science, social studies, and mathematics: A meta-analysis. *Review of Educational Research, 90*, 179–226.

Graham, S., Liu, K., Aitken, A., Ng, C., Bartlett, B., Harris, K. R., & Holzapel, J. (2018). Balancing reading and writing instruction: A meta-analysis. *Reading Research Quarterly, 53*, 279–304.

Graham, S., Liu, K., Bartlett, B., Ng, C., Harris, K. R., Aitken, A., . . . Talukdar, J. (2018). Reading for writing: A meta-analysis of the impact of reading and reading instruction on writing. *Review of Educational Research, 88*, 243–284.

Graham, S., & Perin, D. (2007a). A meta-analysis of writing instruction for adolescent students. *Journal of Educational Psychology, 99*, 445–476.

Graham, S., & Perin, D. (2007b). *Writing next: Effective strategies to improve writing of adolescent middle and high school.* Alliance for Excellence in Education. Commissioned by the Carnegie Corporation of New York.

Graham, S., & Santangelo, T. (2014). Does spelling instruction make students better spellers, readers, and writers? A meta-analytic review. *Reading & Writing: An Interdisciplinary Journal, 27*, 1703–1743.

Kim, Y.-S. G. (2020). Interactive dynamic literacy model: An integrative theoretical framework for reading and writing relations. In R. Alves, T. Limpo, & M. Joshi (Eds.), *Reading–writing connections: Towards integrative literacy science* (pp. 11–34). Springer.

Lipsey, M., & Wilson, D. (2001). *Practical meta-analysis.* Sage.

National Center for Education Statistics. (2012). *The nation's report card: Writing 2011* (NCES 2012-470). U.S. Department of Education, Institute of Education Sciences.

Ray, A., Graham, S., Houston, J., & Harris, K. R. (2016). Teachers' use of writing to support students' learning in middle school: A national survey in the United States. *Reading & Writing: An International Journal, 29*, 1039–1068.

Robinson, A. (2022). *The story of writing: Alphabets, hieroglyphs, and pictograms*. Thames & Hudson.

Schwartz, G. (1995). Teacher lore. *Action in Teacher Education, XV11*, 76–78.

Slavin, R. (2002). Evidence-based education policies: Transforming educational practices and research. *Educational Researcher, 31*(7), 15–21.

Smagorinski, P. (1987). Graves revisited: A look at the methods and conclusions of the New Hampshire study. *Written Communication, 4*(4), 331–342.

Smyth, J. (1998). Written emotional expression: Effect sizes, outcome types, and moderating variables. *Journal of Consulting and Clinical Psychology, 66*, 174–184.

Swedlow, J. (1999). The power of writing. *National Geographic, 196*, 110–132.

Zimmerman, B., & Reisemberg, R. (1997). Becoming a self-regulated writer: A social cognitive perspective. *Contemporary Educational Psychology, 22*, 73–101.

PART I

WRITING INSTRUCTION ACROSS THE DISCIPLINES

Chapter 1

Strategies for Teaching Writing to Foster Critical Thinking Across the Disciplines

Carol Booth Olson, Undarmaa Maamuujav,
and Huy Q. Chung

Learning to write across different disciplines for different purposes is a complex process that requires critical thinking, disciplinary knowledge, and rhetorical problem solving. Teaching writing in a way that fosters these higher-order analytical skills is equally challenging. To ensure students write effectively across different disciplines, teachers need to use a variety of strategies to foster critical thinking and to scaffold instruction to help students navigate the complexity of writing across disciplines and genres. This chapter provides instructional guidance and practical strategies to support students' writing and literacy development across various disciplines. The following questions guide the content of the chapter:

GUIDING QUESTIONS

1. Why teach writing and reading strategies across the disciplines?
2. What types of writing are frequently taught in the disciplines?
3. How can teachers use writing-to-learn strategies across the disciplines to promote critical thinking?
4. How can teachers integrate writing-to-learn strategies into more extended process writing assignments?
5. What action steps can teachers take to integrate writing into their content-area instruction?

Why Teach Writing and Reading Across the Disciplines?

Writing plays a central role in students' skill development in the areas of academic language, disciplinary knowledge, and critical thinking (Graham et al., 2020). The significance of writing across different disciplines is emphasized by Graham and Perin (2007), who assert that writing effectively in various contexts is "not just an option for young people—it is a necessity" because it is "a predictor of academic success and a basic requirement for participation in civic life and in the global economy" (p. 3). Moreover, the importance of writing as a job requirement has grown as labor increasingly involves transforming knowledge into a usable, shareable form (Bazerman et al., 2017). To sum up, students' success in college and beyond depends heavily on their ability to write and communicate well in disciplinary contexts (Council of Writing Program Administrators et al., 2011).

Despite its importance for academic and career success, writing is one of the most challenging skills to develop. The act of writing is complex and multidimensional. It involves multiple processes related to cognitive and affective factors and is shaped by the rhetorical situations in which it takes place (Bazerman et al., 2017). Developing proficiency in writing across the disciplines requires students to communicate with diverse audiences across different content areas (Zawacki & Rogers, 2012). The differences in disciplinary literacy and distinct rhetorical situations add to the complexity and the multidimensionality of writing as students need to develop specialized knowledge and skills to communicate effectively within each discipline. This means writing in a literature class is different from writing in a history or a science class. For example, "Historians study past events through an examination of primary documents and secondary sources; whereas scientists analyze, especially, exacting experimental and observational evidence and logic" (Shanahan & Shanahan, 2012, p. 12). Thus, students need to understand the nature of inquiry in the discipline, details of relevant genres, and what constitutes "evidence" across disciplines.

To better support students in writing across different disciplines, it is crucial to take a cross-curricular approach that promotes sustained writing support, clear objectives and expectations for writing development, and consistent and conscientious effort to improve students' writing skills across classes and content areas. Thus, all teachers need to develop strategies to address the challenges students face in their writing. Such an instructional agenda is critical in a contemporary educational context where a growing number of multilingual learners and marginalized students are striving to become better writers and communicators (Zawacki & Rogers, 2012).

An important pedagogical question, then, is how teachers across the disciplines in a secondary education context can support diverse students with different literacy needs, backgrounds, and experiences to become proficient writers who are well versed in the specialized language and conventions of writing across various disciplines. The IES Practice Guide *Teaching Secondary Students to Write Effectively* recommends integrating reading and writing in all disciplines as one of the most beneficial approaches to helping students develop writing skills across the curriculum in diverse contexts (Graham et al., 2016). Research indicates that using writing as a learning tool during reading instruction leads to better reading outcomes (Graham & Hebert, 2010). At the same time, using reading as a learning tool for elaborating on ideas leads to better writing outcomes (Tierney & Shanahan, 1991).

When taught together, reading and writing engage students in a greater use and variety of cognitive strategies than do reading and writing taught separately (Tierney & Shanahan, 1991, p. 272). This exposure to and practice of cognitive strategies promotes and enhances critical thinking. Hence, the IES Practice Guide also recommends, "Teaching students to use cognitive strategies is one way to develop their strategic thinking skills, ultimately helping them to write more effectively" (Graham et al., 2016, p. 9). Cognitive strategies are acts of mind, or thinking tools, such as planning and goal setting, tapping prior knowledge, making connections, monitoring, forming interpretations, reflecting and relating, evaluating, and so forth; research indicates readers and writers use these tools to construct meaning (Olson, 2011). Numerous reports from policy centers and blue-ribbon panels "implicate poor understanding of cognitive strategies as the primary reason why adolescents struggle with reading and writing" (Conley, 2008, p. 84). Further, research conducted over the past 15 years on the content of college courses and instructor expectations indicates that cognitive strategy use is the key to college and career readiness (Conley, 2013).

Although Graham and Perin (2007) note the dearth of experimental studies conducted with low-achieving writers from low-income families in inner-city settings, and especially with low English-language proficiency, evidence also exists of the positive impact of cognitive strategy instruction on the literacy of English learners (ELs). Short and Fitzsimmons (2007) hypothesize that strategy instruction is especially effective for ELs with an intermediate level of English proficiency because it provides them with an explicit focus on language, increases their exposure to academic texts, makes the texts they read comprehensible, gives them multiple opportunities to affirm or correct their understanding and use of language, assists them in retrieving new language features and in using these features for academic purposes, and provides them with the means of learning language outside of class. In short, explicitly teaching strategic reading and writing behaviors to ELs can help them engage with complex texts and convey those interpretations in well-reasoned essays with compelling claims, judged to be higher in quality and displaying more depth of interpretation and better idea organization (Fitzgerald, 2017; Olson et al., 2023).

Judith Langer (2011) maintains that generalized cognitive strategies are actually critical thinking moves that everyone can access when solving problems. However, domain-specific cognitive strategies help students to be disciplinary critical thinkers and "to learn to think and act—and eventually know—in disciplinary ways" (Langer, 2011, p. 43). A growing body of research indicates that taking a cognitive strategies approach to literacy in the disciplines can have a positive impact on middle and high school students' ability to construct meaning from and with texts (De la Paz et al., 2014; Nokes et al., 2007; Fang, 2006; Spence et al., 1995). In the sections that follow, we will provide specific activities teachers can implement in the classroom to integrate writing and reading instruction to promote students' cognitive strategy use and foster critical thinking. These activities will reinforce students' ability to learn content within the disciplines and help develop their disciplinary thinking while offering opportunities to practice and improve their academic writing.

What Types of Writing Are Frequently Taught in the Disciplines?

In any typical secondary school setting, students take at least five different subject matter classes each term, with each class demanding different types of writing assignments from students. In their English language arts class, they might be expected to analyze a short story or a poem, while in social studies, they might be asked to summarize or explain the causes of a historical event. In mathematics class, they use theorems to prove geometric truths, while in physics class, they use angles and the formula for velocity to predict the trajectory of a small marble as they launch it off a ramp and then submit a lab report about it. This all goes to say that students are expected to understand these many genres of writing and communicate them effectively in their daily classes. And although students write more in English language arts than in any other class, they write more for their other subjects combined than they do for English (Applebee & Langer, 2011).

A genre or writing type is a specific category of writing with an identifiable form and function (Coffin, 2013). For example, a narrative tells a story, either real or imagined, that is designed to entertain, inform, or instruct; it follows an event sequence with a beginning, middle, and end.

It can be written from multiple points of view and contains rich, descriptive language. Informational writing, the conveying of factual information about a nonfiction topic, uses more objective language than a narrative. It often involves the synthesis of information from multiple sources, uses textual structures like description, sequence, compare/contrast, cause and effect, and problem/solution as organizational devices and may include textual features like maps, timelines, photos, and graphs to clarify the written text. Argument writing involves not only delivering factual information but also presenting reasoned opinions supported by evidence from sources. It often acknowledges opposing positions on an issue and offers rebuttal.

The Common Core State Standards (CCSS) state, "To be college- and career-ready writers, students must take task, purpose, and audience into careful consideration, choosing words, information, structures, and formats deliberately" (National Governors Association, 2010, p. 23, Appendix A). In other words, students need to learn how to appropriately respond to the multitude of writing situations they will encounter throughout their lives. For example, the CCSS describes the different purposes for argument writing across three disciplines as follows:

> In English language arts, students make claims about the worth or meaning of a literary work or works. They defend their interpretations or judgments with evidence from the text(s) they are writing about. In history/social studies, students analyze evidence from multiple primary and secondary sources to advance a claim that is best supported by the evidence, and they argue for a historically or empirically situated interpretation. In science, students make claims in the form of statements or conclusions that answer questions or address problems. Using data in a scientifically acceptable form, students marshal evidence and draw on their understanding of scientific concepts to argue in support of their claims. (National Governors Association, 2010, p. 23, Appendix A)

The common thread across English, history/social studies, and science is the use of data/evidence from primary and secondary sources to come to conclusions or form interpretations. Each discipline has its own purposes, discourse, and conventions when it comes to constructing arguments.

As students advance through the grade levels, there is less emphasis on reading and writing about literary narratives and more focus on informational texts. For instance, 12th graders are expected to read 70% informational texts and 30% literary texts across all of their classes (U.S. Department of Education, 2009) and engage in writing tasks for the purposes of persuasion (40%) and explanation (40%) more than to convey experiences (20%) (U.S. Department of Education, 2012). Thus, the more exposure students at all grade levels have to different genres, the better prepared they will be.

In *Envisioning Knowledge,* Judith Langer (2011) argues that in order to develop students' critical thinking, it is important to conceptualize, analyze, compare, synthesize, evaluate, justify, and theorize as readers and writers. These acts of mind encourage students to move beyond reporting factual knowledge to transforming this knowledge (Bereiter & Scardamalia, 1987) and communicating it using the accepted conventions of each respective discipline. Every disciplinary classroom can provide opportunities for students to engage in these ways of thinking through writing and reading tasks.

The English language arts curriculum in U.S. secondary schools emphasizes four widely encompassing genres: narrative, literary analysis, informational, and argumentative. It is in an English class where students are introduced to myriad literary texts, including fiction (e.g., fantasy, fables, science fiction) as well as nonfiction texts such as news reports, feature articles, and biographies. Each of these genres has its own conventions or "universally accepted forms" that need to be taught. The social sciences have also developed certain writing genres unique to their discipline, particularly for synthesizing evidence from multiple sources to defend a claim. Document-based questions (DBQs) are widely assigned in history classes and challenge students to use the given texts to respond to an essential question. Applebee and Langer (2011) surveyed history teachers and found that they valued their students' abilities to write: explanations, critical analyses, application of concepts to new situations, analyses and syntheses of multiple texts, responses and interpretations of sources, summaries, and definitions of concepts or terms.

The written genres found in science classrooms reflect the standards of the discipline, such as "making observations, experimenting, developing claims based on evidence, and communicating those findings to a larger community" (Nachowitz, 2013, p. 94). Moreover, the way these findings are shared must meet the expectations of the scientific community in order to be considered valid and reliable, which reflects how knowledge is developed in the discipline. Similarly, math has its own language (Nasir et al., 2008). Students are taught to read numbers, signs, and symbols in math classes a certain way and sometimes in a certain order. Their ability to make sense of problem sets and word problems and also their ability to interpret graphs, tables, and charts is contingent on their knowledge of the content and language (Fang, 2012). The genres that are often present in assignments for students are working on problem sets, interpreting the language of word problems, elaborating on and defending mathematical proofs using theorems (especially in geometry), and taking notes that help them review procedural methods while developing mathematical reasoning and problem-solving skills. When it comes to writing in mathematics classrooms, the predominant genre is asking students to write "the justification for why a particular mathematical statement is true or a conclusion is accurate" (Mastroianni, 2013, p. 91). This genre challenges students to defend their conclusions and to translate symbols into words.

Barone and Eisner (2004) believe that the written genres in visual and performing arts (VAPA) "tended toward the literary or quasi-literary, employing formats associated with, for example, poetry, critical essays, plays, novels, biographies or autobiographies, and collections of life stories" (p. 97). They also note that arts-based writing utilizes language in particular ways that are "evocative, contextual, and vernacular" (p. 97). Writing in VAPA courses promotes the idea of both form and function as a way to communicate ideas, themes, and creativity.

This brief summary of the different forms, functions, and expectations of written communication across the disciplines is by no means exhaustive. However, it is evident that some of these genres cut across different domains, whereas others have their own unique place in the curriculum and are what experts utilize in the "real world." Table 1.1 presents the different genres assigned in typical secondary classrooms across the United States.

These genres and types of writing across various disciplines provide students with opportunities to develop habits of mind unique to each discipline but also ways to transfer their learning from one discipline to the next (Ritchart, 2015).

How Can Teachers Use Writing-to-Learn Strategies Across the Disciplines to Promote Critical Thinking?

Provided in the following section is a range of expressive writing-to-learn strategies teachers across the disciplines can implement in their classrooms to help students interact with a text and each other in order to construct meaning. That is, they are designed to serve as a "tool for learning rather than as a means to display acquired knowledge" (Applebee, 1981, p. 10). The concept of expressive writing to learn comes from James Britton and colleagues (1975), who conducted a foundational study on the development of writing abilities in secondary school. In their 3-year study of 65 secondary schools in England, they identified three types of writing (or what they called "function" categories) that students were asked to undertake: transactional writing to inform or instruct, poetic writing to create and imagine, and expressive writing to learn and discover. Tom Newkirk (2009) has identified expressive writing-to-learn

TABLE 1.1. Genres and Types of Writing Across Disciplines by the Three Purposes of Writing

Content	Research and reports	Arguments	Narratives
English	• Annotated bibliography • Book reports	• Opinion editorial • Literary analysis	• Autobiography • Short story • Biographies • Poems • Plays
Math	• Solutions • Problem sets	• Proofs	• Math story
Science	• Lab reports • Problem sets	• Problem solution	• Observations
Social science	• Timelines • Annotations • Headnotes • Footnotes	• Change and continuity • Cause and effect • DBQ	• Point of view • Family history
VAPA	• Review	• Critiques	• Performer biography
Any subject	• Emails • Instructions • Lists • Memos • Exposition • Research paper • Short responses	• Business letter	• Anecdotes • Testimonials • Journals • Reflections

Note. Based on the 22 writing tasks Kiuhara and colleagues outlined in their 2009 study.

strategies as "maybe one of the best ideas of all" because rather than just using writing to show what one has learned, expressive writing enables students to "expose their thinking" (p. 7), thus creating "a provisional first draft of ideas" (Britton et al., 1975, p. 145). Several of the strategies we showcase have been developed by the Pathway to Academic Success Project, a comprehensive writing intervention that takes a cognitive strategies approach to developing students' text-based argument writing. This intervention has been shown to enhance writing outcomes for all secondary students, but particularly for students of culturally diverse backgrounds and ELs (Olson et al., 2017, 2023). These strategies often involve brief responses that are usually ungraded, making them easy for teachers in the disciplines to integrate into their instruction in order to help students engage in inquiry, analyze and form interpretations, plan and goal set, focus on self-assessment, and revise ideas and reflect. They can also serve as prewriting for more extended writing assignments.

Writing to Motivate Students to Engage in Inquiry

In response to the CCSS, many states have renewed interest in promoting an inquiry stance in the classroom (Beach et al., 2015) to enhance the connection between reading and writing skills. However, in reality, conducting high-level research and analysis in order to produce engaging, complex written responses to such inquiries is challenging for many students. Students also cite the lack of connection between the curriculum and their own interests as a reason why they do not commit to reading complex texts or responding in equally complex ways (Daniels et al., 2015). To increase interest and motivation and provide students with multiple entry points into the curriculum, offering them low-stakes writing-to-learn strategies and getting students to use cognitive strategies can enhance their investment in reading and writing and reinforce their learning and retention of content (Ainsworth, 2010). In Graham and colleagues' (2023) meta-analysis of writing treatments of students in grades 6–12, engaging students in inquiry resulted in statistically significant effect sizes for all writing outcomes. Strategies that can be used to engage in inquiry should have features that promote curiosity and provide room for student interpretation. In the following sections, we highlight two writing exercises that will engage students in cognitive strategy use to foster inquiry.

See/Think/Wonder

This activity encourages students to make careful observations and form thoughtful interpretations of any visual media. By prompting students to slow down their thinking and contemplate, teachers can stimulate students' curiosity and set the stage for inquiry. To engage students in the See/Think/Wonder strategy, teachers select an image (e.g., a piece of art, photograph, video clip) that can be analyzed in depth. During instruction, teachers display the image on the board or pass out copies to their students. While students are observing the visual media, teachers can ask their students to respond to the following questions: (1) What do you see? What details stand out to you? (2) What do you think is happening? (3) What evidence can you provide? and (4) What makes you wonder, and does this raise any questions for you?

After the designated time, students respond to the questions in their journals or share their thoughts in paired or whole-class discussions. Figure 1.1 is a See/Think/Wonder response from a secondary history classroom after they watched a video clip about the internment of Japanese American citizens during World War II.

Having students first visualize and notice what they see ("I see . . . ") from the newsreel before making interpretations allows students to

Watch this 1943 newsreel and type your observations.
Watch about 4 minutes of it.

I see . . .

- A man explaining what's happening to the Japanese Americans
- Shows images of where they would be relocated
- Shows government officials and bank owners helping the Japanese before they were sent to the camps
- "Cheerfully," "wholeheartedly," said loyal Japanese who felt it was necessary for the better of America

I think . . .

- Uses words like *mass migration* and *relocation* to make the internment camps sound less harsh and more positive

I wonder . . .

- How did Japanese Americans feel after realizing the American government sugarcoated what was happening?

FIGURE 1.1. A See/Think/Wonder response about the internment of Japanese American citizens.

participate in a low-stakes activity; summarizing or monitoring their understanding of what they hear and see has no right or wrong answer. Then, as they start to form interpretations and evaluate ("I think . . .") what they have noticed, their interest in asking questions and seeking out answers about self-generated questions ("I wonder . . .") increases. Self-generated observations and questions motivate students to launch a deeper inquiry into a topic of study because they are genuinely interested in learning.

Note Taking/Note Making

Note Taking/Note Making is a strategy to encourage students to think critically about what they are learning—to question, sort through, puzzle over, clarify, solve problems, or comment on information. It allows them to think aloud on paper as they make observations about notes they are making about their subject or topic of study. Teachers can instruct students to make a T-chart and, in the left-hand column of a piece of paper, record what they are learning (e.g., take lecture notes, record the results of experiments, work through the steps of a problem, copy down a passage of text, etc.). In the right-hand column, students take notes that record their thoughts, questions, reactions, and conjectures about the reading and/or activity they are engaging in. The note-making column (i.e., the right-hand column) may be cognitive, affective, or a mixture of the two. Figure 1.2 is a sample T-chart of a student's observation about flipping coins and the ratio of heads to tails.

Being metacognitive and trying to make sense of notes in this activity is also highly engaging for students because they are given opportunities

Note taking	**Note making**
1. What is the ratio of heads to the total number of flips after the first 25 flips? *H/F: 14/25* What is the ratio for tails? *T/F: 11/25*	1. Heads seem to fall more often than tails.
2. What is the ratio of heads to the total number of flips after the first 50 flips? *H/F: 22/50* What is the ratio for tails? *T/F: 28/50*	2. Now, tails are occurring more often than heads.
3. What is the ratio of heads to the total number of flips in the second fifty flips? *H/F: 27/50* What is the ratio for tails? *T/F: 23/50*	3. The ratio is even close to .5, although heads came up more often than tails.
4. What is the overall ratio of heads to the total number of flips after 100 flips? *H/F: 49/100* What is the ratio for tails? *T/F:51/100*	4. The more we flipped, the more even the ratio got.
5. What can you predict about future flips?	5. Maybe in the next round, the result would be in favor of heads. However, if we keep doing it, the ratio will eventually come out as 1:2.
What theory can you conclude from your note taking and note making? *As the number of flips increases, the ratio of heads and the ratio of tails to the total number of flips comes closer and closer to being 50% for each. In other words, there is a 1 out of 2 chance that either side will come up.*	

FIGURE 1.2. Sample note-taking/note-making response.

to revise meaning, reflect and relate, and even evaluate what they are thinking as they continue to problem solve through an iterative process. The act of asking questions and summarizing their overall interpretation of what they see in their notes also provides an opportunity for students to engage in using expressive writing to begin to form a theory around the topic of study. This type of problem solving also motivates students as they construct meaning to formulate an answer.

Writing to Read, Analyze, and Form Interpretations

The CCSS, and other state standards, prioritize the ability to "read closely to determine what the text says explicitly and to make logical inferences from it" (p. 10) and to "write arguments to support claims in an analysis of substantive topics or texts, using valid reasoning and relevant and sufficient evidence" (National Governors Association, 2010, p. 18). To meet these standards, students must move from reading and literally understanding what the text says to analyzing what the text means and forming thoughtful interpretations as well as transition from summary or "knowledge telling" in writing to "knowledge transformation" (Bereiter & Scardamalia, 1987). As mentioned previously, writing about reading can improve reading comprehension, foster critical thinking, and deepen disciplinary content knowledge (Graham et al., 2016).

Cognitive Strategy Bookmarks

Another way to integrate reading and writing to motivate students to become more interpretive readers and analytical writers is to use Cognitive Strategy Bookmarks. Prior to introducing students to these bookmarks, the teacher will need to introduce the concept of a cognitive strategy. To make this comprehensible, the teacher might say:

> "We are going to learn about what experienced readers and writers do when they make meaning out of words. They use something called cognitive strategies. 'Cognitive' means thinking and 'strategies' are tools people use to solve a problem. So, a cognitive strategy is a thinking tool. Inside your head, you have a lot of cognitive strategies or thinking tools that you use to make sense of what you read and write. It's almost like there's a little voice inside your head that talks to you while you're reading and writing. It tells you when you're confused or when you understand something. It helps you to make pictures in your head or to decide to reread something before going forward." (in Olson, 2011, p. 22)

The teacher can then pass out the bookmarks for students to use while annotating a text. Sentence starters such as "At first I thought ______, but now I" or "This is relevant to my life because ______" give students a point of departure and invite them to expand upon their thinking. Note that domain-specific cognitive strategies can be added to bookmarks for different disciplines, and general strategies can be adapted. For example, adopting an alignment in English language arts can be renamed "historical perspective taking" in history (see Figure 1.3) and making predictions can become "hypothesizing" in science. Students can use their Cognitive Strategy Bookmarks to annotate the texts they are reading. To engage students in deeper critical thinking, they can be asked to keep Reader Response Logs, in which they select key passages, identify the cognitive strategy they are using, and write about the meaning of what they have just read.

Cognitive Strategy Bookmarks can also be used by students in writing groups to respond to each other's writing. Sentence starters like "A golden line for me is . . . " or "I really got into the story when . . . ," shared either orally or in writing, can help enable peers to assist the writer in determining if they have communicated their message effectively as well as give them ideas for revision. The effect size for strategy instruction for writing quality was among the highest in Graham and colleagues' (2023) meta-analysis on what works in secondary writing instruction.

Say, Mean, Matter

Say, Mean, Matter is another pedagogical strategy that helps students think out loud on paper, explore ideas, form interpretations, draw conclusions, and express opinions. This strategy can be used in a variety of subject areas to facilitate students' construction of meaning from the texts they are reading. It is effective for all grade levels and students—from ELs to honors students—and can be applied to interpret academic texts, fiction, and visual material as well. It is also a powerful prewriting strategy for text-based argument writing. The Say, Mean, Matter strategy is designed to focus students' reading and/or examination of a text first on literally what the text *says*, followed by what is important about the text (or what it *means*) and then on why the passage or visual is significant within the text as a whole and/or beyond the context of the text itself—in other words, why it *matters*. Generally, students use this strategy with a trifold graphic organizer that allows them to plot their interpretations of the text and see the levels of meaning it provides.

- *Say*. The "Say" column includes important quotations or unclear passages, sentences, or phrases from the reading. Initially, as students

Cognitive Strategies Sentence Starters

Planning and Goal Setting
- My purpose is . . .
- My top priority is . . .
- I will accomplish my goal by . . .

Tapping Prior Knowledge
- I already know that . . .
- This reminds me of . . .
- This relates to . . .

Asking Questions
- I wonder why . . .
- What if . . .
- How come . . .

Making Predictions
- I bet that . . .
- I think . . .
- If __________, then . . .

Visualizing
- I can picture . . .
- In my mind I see . . .
- If this were a movie . . .

Making Connections
- This reminds me of . . .
- I experienced this once when . . .
- I can relate to this because . . .

Summarizing
- The basic gist is . . .
- The key information is . . .
- In a nutshell, this says that . . .

Adopting an Alignment
- The character I most identify with is . . .
- I really got into the story when . . .
- I can relate to this author because . . .

Forming Interpretations
- What this means to me is . . .
- I think this represents . . .
- The idea I'm getting is . . .

Monitoring
- I got lost here because . . .
- I need to reread the part where . . .
- I know I'm on the right track because . . .

Clarifying
- To understand better, I need to know more about . . .
- Something that I still not clear is . . .
- I'm guessing that this means __________, but I need to . . .

Revising Meaning
- At first I thought __________, but now I . . .
- My latest thought about this is . . .
- I'm getting a different picture here because . . .

Analyzing the Author's Craft
- A golden line for me is . . .
- This word/phrase stands out for me because . . .
- I like how the author uses __________ to show . . .

Reflecting and Relating
- So, the big idea is . . .
- The conclusion I'm drawing is . . .
- This is relevant to my life because . . . .

Evaluating
- I like/don't like __________ because . . .
- My opinion is __________ because . . .
- The most important message is __________ because . . .

FIGURE 1.3. Two content-area versions of the Cognitive Strategies Bookmark with sentence starters (ELA above; history/social studies on facing page).

Cognitive Strategies Sentence Starters

Planning and Goal Setting
- My purpose [for reading this source] is . . .
- My top priority is . . .
- I will accomplish my goal by . . .

Sourcing
- Because this author was ___________, I think they wrote/created this to . . .
- Because this source is ___________ and created in ___________, I think . . .
- This source is reliable/unreliable because . . .

Tapping Prior Knowledge
- I already know that . . .
- This relates to . . .
- During this time, people were concerned with . . .

Asking Questions
- I wonder why . . .
- Why did the author write this? Who was the audience?
- Why did ___________ happen?

Making Predictions/Hypothesizing
- I bet that . . .
- Because ___________, I think . . .
- If ___________, then . . .

Visualizing
- I can picture . . .
- In my mind I see . . .
- If this were a movie . . .

Making Connections
- This reminds me of . . .
- I can relate this to my life or to another historical period because . . .
- I think this person was influenced by . . .

Historical Contextualization/Perspective Taking
- At the time this was written/created, people were concerned with . . .
- From ___________'s perspective, I can understand . . .
- Given the historical context, I think _________ really matters because . . .

Summarizing
- The basic idea of this source is . . .
- The key information is . . .
- In a nutshell, this says that . . .

Forming Interpretations
- This helps us understand ___________ because . . .
- Given these sources, one potential interpretation is . . .
- This is significant because . . .

Corroboration
- I need to check another source because . . .
- Another source that confirms/challenges my understanding of this historical event is . . .
- Although this says ___________, other pieces of evidence show . . .

Analyzing the Author's Craft
- The phrase ___________ helped me understand . . .
- The author uses ___________ language in order to . . .
- A significant phrase related to the historical question is . . .

Monitoring
- I got lost here because . . .
- I know I'm on the right track because . . .
- I need to check another source because . . .

Clarifying
- To understand, I need to know more about . . .
- Something that is still not clear is . . .
- I'm guessing this means ___________, but I need to . . .

Revising Understanding
- At first, I thought ___________, but now I think . . .
- My latest idea about this is . . .
- I'm getting a different picture here because . . .

Reflecting and Relating
- What this tells me about the question is . . .
- So what this tells me about history is . . .
- This is relevant to my life because . . .

Evaluating
- I think this is/is not relevant because . . .
- This argument is effective/ineffective because . . .
- The best evidence to support my interpretation is ___________ and ___________ because . . .

FIGURE 1.3. *(continued)*

learn to use this strategy, the teacher provides the text passage. Later, as students continue analyzing this text or other texts, they choose passages or visuals that stand out or confuse them. The "Say" column addresses any of these questions: *What does the text say? (quote and/or paraphrase) What happened? Who is speaking to whom?*

• *Mean.* The "Mean" column requires students to read between the lines, going beyond the literal analysis of what the text is saying. Students must consider first what the text says and then determine what meaning it has for the reader or viewer. The "Mean" column addresses any of these questions: *What does the text mean? What does the text say between the lines? What does the author mean?*

• *Matter.* The "Matter" column is the most abstract and difficult for students. Students reflect on the text to determine the significance of the quotation to the whole of the text, to themselves, to others, and/or to other texts beyond this one. The "Matter" column addresses any of these questions: *Why does it matter to me or others? Why is this important? What is the significance to the text as a whole? Me? Society? The world?*

Figure 1.4 illustrates a Say, Mean, Matter response to a passage from Abraham Lincoln's Gettysburg Address.

Say	**Mean**	**Matter**
"Four score and seven years ago our fathers brought forth on this continent a new nation, conceived in liberty, and dedicated to the proposition that all men are created equal." (November 19, 1863) *It says our country was founded based on the concepts of liberty and equality.*	*Lincoln uses biblical language to reference the Declaration of Independence, signed 87 years before, reminding his audience at the Gettysburg Civil War Cemetery that the United States was created in the pursuit of liberty for all men—men who are all created equal. His speech ties the abolition of slavery to the principles on which the nation was conceived.*	*By referencing both the Bible and the Declaration of Independence, Lincoln is signaling that if his audience trusts the words in those documents, then they should trust his words as well. His objective is to motivate them to demonstrate "increased devotion to that cause" for which these soldiers died, the cause of freedom and equality. These are noble goals that we are still struggling to achieve today.*

FIGURE 1.4. Say, Mean, Matter response to Abraham Lincoln's Gettysburg Address.

In terms of cognitive strategy use, Say, Mean, Matter moves from summary to interpretation to reflecting, relating, and evaluating. Once students have completed the deep reading for this strategy, they can use their notes to structure and write an evidence-based argument essay. The Say, Mean, Matter graphic organizer keeps track of details from the text and provides practice in interpreting and commenting on the text. The paper's claim derives from the "Matter" column, supported by quotations from the "Say" column. The "Mean" column provides commentary and explanation for the quotations.

Writing to Plan and Goal Set

An important characteristic of strategic readers and writers is that they plan and set goals. Goal setting involves creating steps to engage in specific behaviors, and this is most effective when goals are specific, reasonably challenging, and proximal (Locket et al., 1981). In terms of teaching students strategies for improving their writing, the inclusion of planning, goal setting, and self-assessment improves the quality of students' writing (Graham et al., 2012).

DO/WHAT Chart

One of the first challenges that students encounter when beginning to write in any discipline is making sense of the prompt. How students conceive of and define the problem of writing has been shown to have a tremendous effect on the writing they produce. To help students navigate prompts and determine what they are being asked to do, they can be taught a planning and goal-setting strategy that involves the creation of a DO/WHAT chart, which enables them to deconstruct a prompt and create a roadmap for composing.

To create a DO/WHAT chart, students use green and blue highlighters to mark all of the verbs in the prompt that instruct a student to DO something in green and underline the task words that tell the student WHAT to do in blue. For example, in English language arts, students often have to write (green) an essay (blue) and make (green) a claim (blue) about the main point, lesson, or message of the text. Students then transfer those words onto a T-chart below the prompt. This activity helps the students to clarify and visualize what is expected, plan and goal set, organize information, and evaluate the criteria for a successful response to the prompt. Figure 1.5 illustrates a prompt and a DO/WHAT chart for an assignment in environmental chemistry. (Note: DO words in this prompt are bracketed, and WHAT words are underlined.)

Writing Situation/Essential Question:

Wildfires are a form of chemical reaction and are more frequent or severe now than they were a hundred years ago. Why are wildfires in Tustin, California, worse now than they were 100 years ago?

Tustin 1918	Tustin 2018

Writing Prompt:

First, [identify] at least three differences between Tustin today and Tustin 100 years ago based on the pictures above or what you already know. Then, [describe] at least three causes of wildfires. [Consider] how the differences or primary factors you identified and the causes of wildfires are related. [Draw] a scientific model to show how the primary factors and causes of wildfires are related. [Use] your model to [explain] why wildfires are worse now in Tustin than they were 100 years ago.

DO	WHAT
Identify	at least three differences
Describe	at least three causes
Consider	how primary factors and causes are related
Draw	a scientific model
Use	your model
Explain	why wildfires are worse

FIGURE 1.5. Environmental chemistry prompt. Writing prompt reprinted by permission of Professor Hosun Kang. Copyright © 2023 John Wiley and Sons. Reprinted by permission.

Self-Assessment and Goal-Setting Checklist and Revision Planner

Involving students at the draft stage in assessing the quality of their own written words and making plans for revision can improve their writing (Chung et al., 2021). In any discipline, students can be given a Self-Assessment and Goal-Setting Checklist. After completing a DO/WHAT chart to ensure that they understood the writing task, students can read their initial draft and check off the appropriate box for each question about their written text. For example:

Does the writing present a clear claim?

- The writing presents a clear claim in the introduction that responds to the essential questions.
- The writing attempts a claim, but the claim is not in the introduction and/or the claim is not clear.
- The writing does not present a claim.

Students then use this checklist to fill out a Goal-Setting Revision Planner form in which they indicate the following: "What I did well on my initial writing draft; what I didn't do well, was challenged by, or I didn't do as well in my initial draft" (on the left) and "When I revise, I will do the following:" (on the right). After students revise, they can submit a Revised Writing Reflection to the teacher in which they discuss the revisions they made based on their self-assessment, what they are most proud of in their revised draft, and what strategies helped them the most when they revised their paper. Goal setting was found to have a positive statistically significant effect on writing outcomes in the meta-analysis of writing treatments for students in grades 6–12 (Graham et al., 2023); however, effects were not detected for self-feedback.

Writing to Review/Revise Ideas and Reflect

Research-based strategies that engage students in revising their understanding and reflecting on both the writing process and the product are another way to scaffold students' writing development and promote critical thinking skills (Graham et al., 2023). Revising understanding and reflecting on learning are self-regulated strategies that experienced readers and writers use for meaning making (Harris & Graham, 2016). A 2023 meta-analysis of writing treatments at the secondary level (Graham et al., 2023) found that self-regulated strategies and the cognitive strategies approach that engages students in monitoring, evaluating, revising, and reflecting on their writing have statistically significant positive effects on secondary students' writing outcomes.

When students are provided with an opportunity to revise and reflect on their writing, they develop critical thinking skills. Hence, the IES Practice Guide *Teaching Secondary Students to Write Effectively* (Graham et al., 2016) recommends using "a Model–Practice–Reflect instructional cycle to teach writing strategies" (p. 19). The guide states that "reflection activities enable students to carry out the evaluation component of the writing process, and deepen their understanding of their writing effectiveness and how well they accomplished their goals and executed their strategy" (p. 23). Through reflection, students also monitor their progress, discover ways to improve their writing, and evaluate whether the strategies help (or do not help) them to complete the task. The following two strategies—color coding and the STAR revision strategy—effectively engage students in revision and reflection processes.

Color-Coding Strategy

Color coding is a revision strategy used for analytical or argumentative writing. The goal of color coding is to move students beyond retelling and summary to analysis, interpretation, and commentary. As Bereiter and Scardamalia (1987) point out, inexperienced writers use a simplified version of the idea-generation process that they call *knowledge telling*, which consists of retrieving information from long-term memory and converting the writing task into simply regurgitating what is known about a topic. More expert writers, on the other hand, engage in a complex composing process known as *knowledge transformation*, in which they analyze the writing task in accordance with rhetorical purposes. One way to help students move from knowledge telling to knowledge transformation is to help them make their thinking visible using color coding.

In English language arts in which students engage in analytical writing (i.e., literary analysis), teachers first designate three colors for the types of assertions that comprise a literary analysis. The first color is *yellow* for plot summary. Plot summary is yellow because it's like the sun and reiterates what is obvious and known in a text. It makes things as plain as day. We need some plot summary to orient our reader to the facts, but we don't need to retell the entire story. The second color is *blue* for commentary or reasoning. Commentary is like the ocean because the writer goes beneath the surface of things to look at the deeper meaning and to offer opinions, interpretations, insights, and "aha" moments. The third color is *green* for supporting detail or evidence. Supporting detail and evidence bring together the facts of the text (yellow) with your interpretation of it (blue). It is what glues together plot summary and commentary.

The color-coding technique can be flexibly adapted depending on the genre of writing in a specific content area. For example, in history classes that engage students in argumentative writing in which students synthesize multiple sources and include counterarguments to acknowledge an alternative point of view, the color-coding technique can be adapted to include the rhetorical moves that are involved in developing historical argumentation (see Figure 1.6).

When students apply the color-coding technique to evaluate their writing, the coded draft becomes a guide for revision because they can

Summary	Evidence	Reasoning	Counterargument
Yellow	Green	Blue	Pink
Background to event/issue; Retelling what happened	Examples; Details supporting claim; Quotes from sources and paraphrases	Deeper thinking/ analysis; Interpretations/ reasoning; Conclusions; The So What?; Insight and opinions	Acknowledgment of counterargument; Reasons addressing/refuting counterargument

FIGURE 1.6. Color-coding technique adapted for history.

see whether they have simply summarized or have gone further and woven other rhetorical moves such as evidence, commentary/reasoning, and counterclaims into their writing. The color coding is followed by a self-reflection and revision planner asking students to identify the strengths of their writing, the areas where they need to improve, and specific steps for revising. Such a planned revision process that engages students in self-assessment and reflection not only has a positive effect on students' self-efficacy but also improves their overall writing quality (Chung et al., 2021).

STAR Revision Strategy

The STAR revision strategy (Gallagher, 2006) can help students guide their revision process and make meaningful changes that will enhance the quality of their drafts. The strategy can be used with any writing genre (e.g., narrative, informational, persuasive, argumentative) in any discipline. The four letters represent the four steps of the STAR strategy, which are as follows:

S: Substitute overused words with precise words, weak verbs with strong verbs, weak adjectives with strong adjectives, and common or general nouns with proper or specific nouns.

T: Take out unnecessary repetition, irrelevant information, or information that belongs elsewhere.

A: Add details, description, new information, figurative language, clarification of meaning, or expanded ideas.

R: Rearrange information for a more logical flow.

After students learn and use this strategy during the revision process of their writing, teachers can have students reflect on their use of the STAR strategy by asking them to think about and share how this strategy helped them (or failed to help them) in their revision process.

Since it is a strategy for the revision process of writing, the STAR strategy is used after students have written their drafts. It focuses on both global macro-level aspects of writing, such as organization and development of ideas, and micro-level linguistic features, such as word choice and sentence construction. Overall, students can follow the STAR strategy to revise and reorganize their papers for logical flow and expand their ideas. Teachers can use the STAR strategy frequently with any writing assignment students engage in.

How Can Teachers Integrate Writing-to-Learn Strategies into More Extended Process Writing?

Research indicates that writing-to-learn strategies like writing summaries, taking structured notes and concept mapping, and generating short answers after reading a segment of text can improve student learning; however, writing extended texts involving analysis and interpretation has an even more powerful impact (Graham & Hebert, 2010). Since engaging in expressive writing-to-learn strategies can help students make their thinking visible, these strategies can be carefully scaffolded into more extended process writing to enhance the end product. Let's look at one example of how a teacher might incorporate writing-to-learn strategies into an extended process writing task.

The Saturation Research Paper

The Saturation Research Paper integrates the disciplines of English language arts and history as students research and immerse themselves in a famous historical figure: First, they select a significant event in that historical figure's life, assuming their persona and speaking in their voice; then the student weaves together factual information and narrative techniques to dramatize the event, showing and not just telling why it was significant.

The teacher begins by guiding students through a mentor text (e.g., a sample Saturation Research Paper written about Harriet Tubman or Anne Frank), stopping to engage students in using their Cognitive Strategy Bookmarks to respond to the author's craft moves to consider how suspense is created, examine the way factual information is interwoven and documented; then the student visualizes the scene, analyzes the central message, and reflects on and relates its relevance today. Using a DO/WHAT chart, students then deconstruct the prompt and create a roadmap for composing. After clustering a range of historical figures (e.g., Vincent van Gogh, Cesar Chavez, Albert Einstein, the Dalai Lama, Martin Luther King Jr.), students select the person, begin preliminary research to ensure that enough factual source material is available, and present a Saturation Research Paper proposal in which they identify the person they will research, explain the event they will dramatize and why it is significant, outline the writing strategies they will use to bring the event to life, and indicate at least three sources to consult during research. After participating in mini-lessons on documenting sources, writing dialogue, interior monologue, showing not telling, and flashback, students create a storyboard of the key scenes they will dramatize.

In addition to providing models of what is expected and extending multiple opportunities to practice, one of the key principles of instructional scaffolding is to break up tasks in order to concentrate the student's attention on "something manageable" (Bruner, 1978, p. 254). Students who are accustomed to writing impersonal expository reports may find historical fiction to be unfamiliar territory. To get into the persona of their chosen historical figure and to strategize about how to get started may be challenging and involve several preliminary attempts. Asking students to write and share an opening scene that sets the stage for their significant event can help ensure the paper is off to a good start and provide motivation to make revisions during the composition stage rather than waiting for a complete final draft. Figure 1.7 presents a sample of an opening scene written about Neil Armstrong.

In groups of four, students can use job cards to respond to each other's writing (see Figure 1.8). Reader #1 responds to the questions: *Does the writer have your attention? What hooked you, or what would draw you further into the scene?* Reader #2 addresses the questions: *Do you feel like you are there? Which of the author's craft moves helped you to visualize the scene or what would make the piece more vivid?* Reader #3 considers: *Has the writer chosen an interesting historical figure and a significant event to dramatize? What do you think the writer's paper is going to focus on?* Giving students feedback early in the writing process and a chance to make changes or additions they are pleased with can enable them to continue writing with a greater sense of confidence.

Once an initial draft is complete, students work in pairs to respond to each other's papers, give the paper a provisional score (not shared with the teacher) of their draft in progress, and fill out a Saturation Research Paper Sharing Sheet to provide suggestions for improvements. Students then use the STAR strategy to Substitute, Take things out, Add, or Rearrange elements of their paper to make it more compelling. Finally, the papers are mounted on posterboard, illustrated, and displayed around the classroom. During a gallery walk, classmates read each other's final drafts and celebrate the work done by posting kind comments.

Scaffolding writing-to-learn strategies for extended process writing is part of many comprehensive writing programs, such as the Pathway to Academic Success Project. The effectiveness of this type of process writing approach was identified in a meta-analysis of secondary writing treatments (Graham et al., 2023) to have a positive impact on all writing measures but especially writing quality. Unfortunately, research suggests that the amount of extended process writing students engage in "remains distressingly low," especially for "the kinds of writing where students might be expected to engage with the discipline-specific arguments and evidence called for by the Common Core Standards" (Applebee & Langer, 2011, p. 16).

July 16, 1969

"This is Apollo/Saturn Launch Control," NASA commentator Jack King booms, "We are now less than 16 minutes away from planned liftoff for Apollo 11" (Barbree, 2014, p. 214). *This is it!* I think to myself, *the culmination of America's race with the Russians to put a man on the moon.* Adrenaline courses through my body but I steady my hands and give my crewmates Buzz Aldrin and Mike Collins a big thumbs up.

Methodically, we go through our checklist one more time: liftoff configuration, boost insertion, booster separations, launch emergency procedures. Then, after testing systems for power transfer from Saturn to Columbia and Eagle, we arm the destruct system, and the access to the walkway leading to Apollo swings back out of the way. Last but not least, I place my hand on the abort handle (Woods et al., 2019b). *We definitely won't be needing this today,* I assure myself.

"Houston. This is Apollo," I report. "Our transfer is completed on internal power. All the second stage tanks are now pressurized. It's green all the way."

"Roger that, Apollo. We've passed the six minute mark. Now 5 minutes 52 seconds and counting, and we're on time for our planned lift-off at 32 minutes past the hour."

As I wait, the butterflies in my stomach quell as a deep calm washes over me. I think of my ten year step-by-step journey to this moment: from my selection to the Space Soonest Program, to joining the NASA Astronaut Corps, to serving as back-up for Gemini 5, then becoming the first American civilian in space in Gemini 8, and now commander of Apollo 11. Deke Slayton says he picked me because I'm the best man for the job and have earned this, hands down. *I won't let you down, Deke.*

Written by Carol Booth Olson.

FIGURE 1.7. Opening scene on Neil Armstrong.

FIGURE 1.8. Ninth-grade students at Cerritos High School use job cards to share their opening scenes with each other and their teacher Marianne Stewart.

What Action Steps Do Teachers Take to Integrate Writing into Their Content-Area Instruction?

One of the most important pedagogical decisions teachers have to make is to determine how much time they need to devote to delivering the content of their discipline, particularly in middle and high school settings. At the same time, one of the greatest returns on a teacher's investment in the classroom is teaching writing, especially when students are provided with opportunities to write within and across disciplines because writing is such a powerful tool for learning.

In previous sections of this chapter, we have provided a wide array of writing-to-learn strategies that can be used to cultivate disciplinary literacy. Strategies such as See/Think/Wonder and Note Taking/ Note Making encourage students to visualize, make predictions, form interpretations, and solve problems in the act of constructing meaning. Strategies like the Cognitive Strategy Bookmarks and Say, Mean, Matter are used to help students transition from knowledge telling to knowledge transformation (Bereiter & Scardamalia, 1987) as they read and respond. The DO/WHAT chart, Self-Assessment and Goal-Setting Checklist, and Goal-Setting Revision Planner are particularly useful for planning and goal setting for composing texts. The color-coding technique and the STAR revision strategy encourage students to study the author's craft and revise meaning as they revise their initial drafts. Each particular strategy provides opportunities for students to apply their critical thinking in determining next steps throughout the reading and writing process. The Saturation Research Paper serves as an example of an extended writing exercise that fosters critical thinking because artfully blending the elements of both narrative and informational writing takes skill and practice, especially as students select a historical figure, incorporate dialogue, and set the scene of a particular event. Across all of these strategies, students are developing their declarative, procedural, and conditional knowledge (Paris et al., 1991) of writing strategies and genres, enabling them to become confident and competent readers and writers across the disciplines.

ACTION STEPS

In order to integrate these strategies—and others that you may have accumulated throughout your professional experiences—into your content-area instruction, consider the following action steps:

- Explain to your students *why* you are doing *what* you are doing. Emphasize the importance of writing in every discipline. Research shows that when you write about your reading, not only does your reading improve, but your command of the content increases as well.
- Start with small, ungraded writing-to-learn strategies that help students understand what they are learning better and become accustomed to using writing as a tool for learning in each discipline.
- Think about more extended writing assignments; work backward to scaffold writing-to-learn strategies that help make the task more manageable.
- Write to learn for yourself, and create your own models of writing to share with students in the context of your discipline.
- Share strategies that work with your colleagues in professional learning communities to foster collaboration across classes and disciplines.
- Have students share what they are writing in your class and in other content-area classes to capitalize on shared knowledge; this will help students build specific, disciplinary knowledge and cross-curricular writing ability.

As you implement these action steps and integrate writing into your instruction, keep in mind that "the benefits of writing across disciplines extend beyond the writing itself—writing can improve reading comprehension, critical thinking, and disciplinary content knowledge"

(Graham et al., 2016, p. 32), all of which help students to prepare for college and careers.

REFERENCES

Ainsworth, L. (2010). *Rigorous curriculum design: How to create curricular units of study that align standards, instruction, and assessment.* Lead+ Learn Press.

Applebee, A. N. (1981). *Writing in the secondary school: English and the content areas.* NCTE Research Report No. 21. National Council of Teachers of English.

Applebee, A. N., & Langer, J. A. (2011). A snapshot of writing instruction in middle schools and high schools. *English Journal, 100*(6), 14–27.

Barone, T., & Eisner, E. (2004). *Arts-based educational research.* Sage.

Bazerman, C., Applebee, A. N., Berninger, V. W., Brandt, D., Graham, S., Matsuda, P. K., . . . Schleppegrell, M. (2017). Taking the long view on writing development. *Research in the Teaching of English, 51*(3), 351–360.

Beach, R., Webb, A., & Thein, A. H. (2015). *Teaching to exceed the English Language Arts Common Core State Standards: A critical inquiry approach for 6–12 classrooms.* Routledge.

Bereiter, C., & Scardamalia, M. (1987). Knowledge telling and knowledge transforming in written composition. *Advances in Applied Psycholinguistics, 2*, 142–175.

Britton, J. Burgess, T. Martin, N., McLeod, A., & Rosen, H. (1975). *The development of writing abilities (11–18).* National Council of Teachers of English.

Bruner, J. (1978). The role of dialogue in language acquisition. In A. Sinclair, R. J. Jarvella, & W. J. Levell (Eds.), *The child's conception of language* (pp. 241–256). Springer.

Chung, H. Q., Chen, V., & Olson, C. B. (2021). The impact of self-assessment, planning and goal setting, and reflection before and after revision on student self-efficacy and writing performance. *Reading and Writing, 34*(7), 1885–1913.

Coffin, C. (2013). Theoretical approaches to written language. In A. Burns & C. Coffin (Eds.), *Analyzing English in a global context: A reader* (pp. 93–121). Routledge.

Conley, D. T. (2013). *Getting ready for college, careers, and the Common Core: What every educator needs to know.* Jossey-Bass.

Conley, M. W. (2008). Cognitive strategy instruction for adolescents: What we know about the promise, what we don't know about the potential. *Harvard Educational Review, 78*, 84–106.

Council of Writing Program Administrators, National Council of Teachers of English, & National Writing Project. (2011). *Framework for success in postsecondary writing.* Creative Commons. *http://wpacouncil.org/aws/CWPA/asset_manager/get_file/350201?ver=7548*

Daniels, E., Hamby, J., & Chen, R. J. (2015). Reading writing reciprocity: Inquiry in the classroom: Focusing on authentic teaching and learning experiences aids the development of young adolescents' literary lives. *Middle School Journal, 46*(4), 9–16.

De La Paz, S., Felton, M., Monte-Sano, C., Croninger, R., Jackson, C., Deogracias, J. S., & Hoffman, B. P. (2014). Developing historical reading and writing with adolescent readers: Effects on student learning. *Theory & Research in Social Education, 42*(2), 228–274.

Fang, Z. (2006). The language demands of science reading in middle school. *International Journal of Science Education, 28*(5), 491–520.

Fang, Z. (2012). Language correlates of disciplinary literacy. *Topics in Language Disorders, 32*(1), 19–34.

Fitzgerald, J. (2017). How practice-based research informs adolescent English language learners' composing and compositions. In K. A. Hinchman & D. A. Appelman (Eds.), *Adolescent literacies: A handbook of practice-based research* (pp. 357–378). Guilford Press.

Gallagher, K. (2006). *Teaching adolescent writers.* Stenhouse.

Graham, S., Bruch, J., Fitzgerald, J., Friedrich, L. D., Furgeson, J., Greene, K., . . . Smither Wulsin, C. (2016). *Teaching secondary students to write effectively. Educator's Practice Guide* (NCEE 2017-4002). What Works Clearinghouse.

Graham, S., & Hebert, M. (2010). *Writing to read: Evidence for how writing can improve reading: A report from Carnegie Corporation of New York.* Alliance for Excellent Education.

Graham, S., Kim, Y. S., Cao, Y., Lee, W., Tate, T., Collins, P., . . . Olson, C. B. (2023). A meta-analysis of writing treatments for students in grades 6 to 12. *Journal of Educational Psychology, 115*(7), 1004–1027.

Graham, S., Kiuhara, S. A., & MacKay, M. (2020). The effects of writing on learning in science, social studies, and mathematics: A meta-analysis. *Review of Educational Research, 90*, 179–226.

Graham, S., Kiuhara, S. A., McKeown, D., & Harris, K. R. (2012). A meta-analysis of writing instruction for students in the elementary grades. *Journal of Educational Psychology, 104*, 879–896.

Graham, S., & Perin, D. (2007). *Writing next: Effective strategies to improve writing of adolescents in middle and high schools—A report to Carnegie Corporation of New York.* Alliance for Excellent Education.

Harris, K. R., & Graham, S. (2016). Self-regulated strategy development: Theoretical bases, critical instructional elements, and future research. In R. Fidalgo, K. R. Harris, & M. Braaksma (Eds.), *Design principles for teaching effective writing* (pp. 119–151). Brill.

Kiuhara, S. A., Graham, S., & Hawken, L. S. (2009). Teaching writing to high school students: A national survey. *Journal of Educational Psychology, 101*(1), 136–160.

Langer, J. (2011). *Envisioning knowledge: Building literacy in the academic disciplines.* Teachers College Press.

Locket, E., Shaw, K., Saari, L., & Latham, G. (1981). Goal setting and task performance: 1969–1980. *Psychological Bulletin, 90*, 125–152.

Mastroianni, M. (2013). Writing in mathematics. In A. Applebee, J. Langer, K. C. Wilcox, M. Nachowitz, M. P. Mastroianni, & C. Dawson (Eds.), *Writing instruction that works: Proven methods for middle and high school classrooms* (pp. 71–93). Teachers College Press.

Nachowitz, N. (2013). Writing in science. In A. Applebee, J. Langer, K. C. Wilcox, M. Nachowitz, M. P. Mastroianni, & C. Dawson (Eds.), *Writing instruction that works: Proven methods for middle and high school classrooms* (pp. 94–110). Teachers College Press.

Nasir, N. I. S., Hand, V., & Taylor, E. V. (2008). Culture and mathematics in school: Boundaries between "cultural" and "domain" knowledge in the mathematics classroom and beyond. *Review of Research in Education, 32*(1), 187–240.

National Governors Association. (2010). *Common Core State Standards for English language arts and literacy in history/social studies, science, and technical subjects.* Center for Best Practices & Council of Chief State School Officers.

Newkirk, T. (2009). *Holding on to good ideas in a time of bad ones: Six literacy principles worth fighting for.* Heinemann.

Nokes, J. D., Dole, J. A., & Hacker, D. J. (2007). Teaching high school students to use heuristics while reading historical texts. *Journal of Educational Psychology, 99*(3), 492.

Olson, C. B. (2011). *The reading/writing connection: Strategies for teaching and learning in the secondary classroom* (3rd ed.). Pearson.

Olson, C. B., Maamuujav, U., Steiss, J., & Chung, H. Q. (2023). Examining the impact of a cognitive strategies approach on the argument writing of mainstreamed English learners in secondary school. *Written Communication, 40*(2), 373–416.

Olson, C. B., Matuchniak, T., Chung, H. Q., Stumpf, R. A., & Farkas, G. (2017). Reducing achievement gaps in academic writing for Latino secondary students and English learners. *Journal of Educational Psychology, 109*(1), 1–21.

Paris, S. G., Wasik, B. A., & Turner, J. C. (1991). The development of strategic readers. In R. Barr, M. Kamil, P. B. Mosenthal, & P. D. Pearson (Eds.), *Handbook of reading research* (Vol. II, pp. 609–640). Longman.

Ritchart, R. (2015). *Creating cultures of thinking: The 8 forces we must muster to truly transform our schools.* Wiley.

Shanahan, T., & Shanahan, C. (2012). What is disciplinary literacy and why does it matter? *Topics in Language Disorders, 32*(1), 7–18.

Short, D., & Fitzsimmons, S. (2007). *Double the work: Challenges and solutions to acquiring language and academic literacy for adolescent English language learners—A report to Carnegie Corporation of New York.* Alliance for Excellent Education.

Spence, D. J., Yore, L. D., & Williams, R. L. (1995). *Explicit science reading instruction in grade 7: Metacognitive awareness, metacognitive self-management, and science reading comprehension.* Paper presented at the National Association for Research in Science Teaching annual meeting.

Tierney, R. J., & Shanahan, T. (1991). *Research on the reading–writing relationship: Interactions, transactions, and outcomes*. Lawrence Erlbaum Associates.

U.S. Department of Education. (2009). *The nation's report card: Reading 2009* (NCES 2010-458). Institute of Education Sciences, National Center for Education Statistics.

U.S. Department of Education. (2012). *The nation's report card: Writing 2011* (NCES 2012–470). Institute of Education Sciences, National Center for Education Statistics.

Zawacki, T. M., & Rogers, P. M. (2012). *Writing across the curriculum: A critical sourcebook*. Bedford.

Chapter 2
Culturally Sustaining Writing Practices

Tricia Ebarvia and Kimberly N. Parker

We have been writing in some capacity for much of our lives—as children, students, learners, parents, colleagues, literacy activists, and published authors. As educators, our belief in doing what we ask our students to do has led us to write alongside our students in writing workshops, open up space for conversations about craft, and interrogate our own positionality as teachers. Shifts away from more "traditional," direct instruction and toward culturally sustaining approaches to teaching in general have led us to create space in classrooms where children and youth know that their words are valued and that they have control over the decisions they make as writers. In short, they need to know that their voices matter—to themselves and in the world.

We believe that writing workshop is essential to the practice of writing. For us, there is no other way for young people to learn how to write effectively. We make this claim after spending our formative years of learning to teach writing while shedding our own outdated beliefs about what writing is (too many formulas!) and experimenting with a range of writing that responds to purpose, audience, and genre. While learning how to write, we've had thoughtful discussions about the ways that writing is taught in various educational settings; often, those in urban schools, and/or in settings with children who rarely have access to robust writing opportunities, have the poorest writing instruction, while those in suburban and well-resourced settings have broader options.

However, regardless of the specific context, in our experience and based on our work with teachers across the country, we know that by the time students reach high school, writing workshop is rare in English language arts (ELA) classrooms. This is unfortunate, as some of our most powerful work with students has come within a classroom writing workshop setting. There, because of the beliefs that undergird the practices, young writers learn, through regular practice, feedback, and collaboration, how to articulate their thoughts in ways that make sense to them. In this chapter, we establish a framework for a culturally sustaining writing workshop. By interrogating definitions of power and culture within writing workshops and then affirming the theoretical foundations of culturally sustaining pedagogy (CSP), we look closely at why traditional writing instruction needs culturally sustaining writing practices and, more specifically, culturally sustaining writing workshops. We include practices and resources that enable culturally sustaining writing workshops to be applicable to a range of disciplines and grade levels. We argue for culturally sustaining writing workshops as an important practice that should ground secondary writing instruction and what that can look like for a range of students. We explore four essential guiding questions:

GUIDING QUESTIONS

1. How does our positionality as individuals and educators influence how we approach writing instruction and conceive of culturally sustaining pedagogies?
2. What is culturally sustaining writing instruction?
3. Why are culturally sustaining writing practices important?
4. How can we promote culturally sustaining practices through the workshop model?

Positionality

Before we continue, we preface our discussion with an acknowledgment of our own positionality as individuals and educators. We believe it is important to name the ways in which our personal identities and experiences have informed our thinking. Teaching is not a neutral act. At its core, teaching is about the learning that can happen between teacher and students and students with one another based on the relationships they build with each other every day.

Professionally, we have nearly 50 combined years of experience in education between us. Most of our experience has been in high school classrooms. In addition, each of us has facilitated and led professional workshops for teachers, working side by side with educators to embed culturally relevant, responsive, and sustaining pedagogies (more on the distinctions between those terms ahead). We are two of the four cofounders of #DisruptTexts, a collective online movement that advocates for an equitable, inclusive curriculum and a pedagogy that values and amplifies the work of marginalized groups, especially Black and Brown communities. In addition to teaching public high school, Tricia is currently a school leader in an independent school that serves students in grades PreK–8, while Kim is the director of a college access program for students from low-income families at a large, private university. Together, our experiences in education consist of teaching a broad span of learners, from our youngest 4-year-olds to adult learners in graduate programs.

Our professional experiences have informed how we think about our work as educators and as teachers of young writers. However, we also believe that our *personal* identities and experiences—both in and out of school—have been just as critical and inform how we have taught writing in the past as well as the present and how we will continue to teach writing in the future. Like all ideas we hold about schooling, our beliefs about what constitutes "good" writing are *socially constructed*. The schools we attended, the expectations our teachers had for us as writers, the criteria they used to judge the quality of our writing, the state-mandated tests that determined whether we were proficient or basic writers, the feedback we received or didn't receive, the types of writing assignments we were given—these and countless other factors shaped our ideas about what "good" writing is and whether or not we ourselves were "good" writers.

Furthermore, our identities as students of color who attended many predominantly White institutions throughout our lives have also impacted our experiences as students and as writers. As the daughter of Filipino immigrant parents, I (Tricia) was taught to respect my teachers—nearly all of whom were White—and follow their guidance, with little room for questioning if what I was learning was good, bad, right, or wrong. As someone whose cultural and racial background already marked me as different from my peers, I did my best to fit in by excelling academically. Raised in a predominantly White suburb, I had few opportunities to write personal narratives, and although I filled journal after journal in the safety of my home, I never saw myself as a writer. In school, I not only never questioned what my teachers defined as "good" writing, I internalized these ideas and used them when I became a teacher, passing these same ideas to my students.

I (Kim) grew up working class on a farm in Kentucky, raised by my grandparents. While we are currently in the process of tracing our exact lineage, given Kentucky's history as a state of enslavement of African Americans, I'm fairly certain my ancestors were enslaved, likely within, or even on, the place where I was raised. I had Black teachers throughout my K–12 experience, many of whom encouraged me to write my thoughts in various genres and to a range of audiences. I did have lots of formulaic writing instruction; in fact, that was most of my writing experience. The dominant way of learning to write was through the five-paragraph essay, which I mastered sometime in middle school, and I'm pretty sure I used until I got to college and a professor expanded my abilities in a freshman English seminar. While I had occasional opportunities to write for audiences of my choice (which I can count on one hand, now that I remember it), most of the time I wrote for the teacher. I was expected to draft at home (rarely in class) and can't remember ever seeing mentor texts.

Although we had different experiences, each of us walked away from school with some shared and limited beliefs about writing. Among the beliefs about writing we internalized:

- Writing is primarily assigned by a teacher.
- Serious writing (writing that "counts") is only done in school and about topics learned about directly and explicitly in classes.
- Our abilities as a writer were defined by our final grade on any assignment.
- There were clear "right" and "wrong" ways of writing.

How we see ourselves as teachers of young people—the power we hold, the responsibilities we carry—informs every decision we make. As we will see in this chapter, to teach writing from a culturally sustaining lens, we must understand not only the cultural backgrounds that our students bring to our classrooms but also the cultures of schooling that we ourselves have experienced. When we are not reflective and critical about the identities we as teachers bring into the classroom, we risk not understanding how these identities may impact our students, perhaps in harmful ways.

Finally, we also come to this chapter as both writers and *practitioners* of writing instruction. While we consider ourselves scholars, we are not traditional academics or academic researchers. Our work has been largely informed by the thousands of hours we have spent side by side with students in classrooms, as full-time K–12 teachers in a variety of contexts. Our work as practitioners has given us many opportunities to get to know students, their families, and communities, in the intimate, complicated, and joyful ways that come from a teacher's day-to-day work. As such, we hope that this chapter offers a brief primer not just on what culturally sustaining writing practices are, but also some practical shifts that fellow teacher-practitioners can make in their classrooms tomorrow.

Invitation for Reflection

- Think back to your own experiences in school. How did your own teachers define "good" writing?
- What beliefs about what writing did you internalize as a student? How?
- How were your beliefs about writing confirmed, challenged, or changed when you began teaching?

Traditional Writing Instruction

As we strive toward a vision of writing instruction that is rooted in culturally sustaining pedagogies, we begin briefly by considering what writing instruction in the secondary classroom generally looks like. Although we know that no two classrooms are identical, based on our own experiences and our work with teachers across the country, we know some practices continue to persist in many secondary writing classrooms. For the purposes of this chapter, we categorize these practices as characteristics of "traditional" writing instruction:

- All students write and respond to the same teacher-created prompt.
- Writing is focused on analysis of a text (i.e., literary analysis).
- Writing is generally taught as a formula (e.g., five-paragraph essay).
- Writing is taught as "objective" with little use of personal voice.
- The teacher is either the only or primary audience of student writing.

In short, in "traditional" writing instruction, the teacher holds most, if not all, the authority; the teacher acts as the ultimate arbiter and gatekeeper of what qualifies as "good" writing. Writing is assigned, often to be completed at home, then turned in to a teacher who uses a predetermined rubric (with criteria set by the school, district, or state) to evaluate the student's writing. A teacher may provide some feedback during writing, but what matters the most is the final product and grade.

Although we grew up and went to school in different contexts, our experiences in school with traditional writing instruction were similar. And for much of our early careers, it was also the approach that we adopted as teachers.

The longer we taught, however, the more we realized that traditional writing practices weren't really working for our students. We were assigning writing but not teaching it. Students followed directions but struggled to develop voice and agency. Students learned to organize their writing using the formulas and templates we provided but often at the expense of developing their ideas. In *Why They Can't Write: Killing the 5-Paragraph Essay*, John Warner (2018) argues that most of the writing students are asked to undertake in school is not genuine writing so much as it is an *imitation* of writing. This was our experience as well.

The one-size-fits-all approach to teaching writing was, in some ways, easier and more convenient for us as teachers. We set the requirements, conditions, and criteria for good writing, and students either "got it" or they didn't. Detailed rubrics and checklists made the labor of grading so many essays more efficient. "Good" writers were the students who complied, who could follow the "paint by number" approach to writing. Students who couldn't (or refused to) assimilate their ideas and voices into the templates and models we provided were "struggling" writers. This was a *deficit*-minded approach to teaching writing that focused on what students *couldn't* do. This approach places the blame on students for what they *fail to do* rather than examine the conditions, methods, and practices that we, as teachers, did (or didn't do) to support their success.

While we had the best intentions ("This is how I was taught and it worked for me!"), we unfortunately taught this way for far too long. Then came writing workshop.

Invitation for Reflection

- What feels familiar, new, or challenging in the way that traditional writing instruction is described?
- How did you teach writing when you began your career? What have you noticed has worked and not worked for students? What shifts have you made or would you like to make?

Considering Context and Culture

Writing is one of the most powerful ways that young people in school can develop their voices, and being able to exercise one's voice is a fundamental right in a justice-centered society.

Writing workshop provides the space for students to develop and exercise their voice. That said, we also recognize its limitations. After all, like any tool or framework, components of writing workshop can also be leveraged in negative ways, especially in school systems that have largely underserved and mistreated Black and Brown students and other historically marginalized groups. Unfortunately, this applies to most schools in the United States. Therefore, no approach to teaching writing—whether it is a teacher-directed traditional approach or a student-centered workshop model—can be effective if it doesn't also take into consideration the context and *culture* in which it is enacted.

What is culture? Whenever any group of people comes together—whether they form informal organizations, institutions, religious congregations, art classes, school communities, clubs, study groups, or sports teams, and many others—they create a culture. Culture can be defined as a "social system of meaning and custom that is developed by a group of people to assure its adaptation and survival. These groups are distinguished by a set of unspoken rules that shape values, beliefs, habits, patterns of thinking, behaviors and styles of communication" (Institute for Democratic Renewal and Project Change Anti-Racism Initiative, 2000, p. 32). More simply, culture consists of the shared and common beliefs, models for living, and practices by a group of people (Muhammed, 2019).

Although cultures created in different groups vary, a larger shared culture (or imposed, depending on your point of view) exists on a societal level. In the United States, this "dominant" culture can be described as White dominant or White supremacy culture. Applying this to writing instruction, we can ask ourselves what "shared and common beliefs, models for living, and practices" do we share as educators about the teaching of writing? Furthermore, and perhaps more critically, how are these shared and common beliefs and practices informed by the larger context of White dominant or White supremacist culture?

Tema Okun (2021) drafted a list of characteristics of White supremacy, and among them are several that directly inform how schools teach writing: perfectionism, objectivism, either/or thinking, and quantity over quality, to name a few. For example, although we know that there is no "perfect" in writing, too many students focus on getting things "perfect," and both students and teachers set unrealistic expectations about their writing. Similarly, despite teachers' or states' efforts to create detailed rubrics and standards that give the illusion of objectivism, in practice we know that assessing student writing is an inherently subjective practice. Either/or thinking—that there is a "right" or "wrong" way of doing things—narrows the scope of possibilities for writing in terms of craft, voice, genre, and countless other ways. Prioritizing quantity over quality can lead students to equate writing more with writing better when there are many instances in which saying less may be more succinct and effective.

In each of their different ways, characteristics of White supremacy culture effectively limit and restrict the full range of possibilities for student expression in writing. For Black and Brown students who bring cultural assets from their families, communities, and histories that stand in contrast to White dominant culture, writing instruction in school has the added impact of silencing or erasing these assets. In *Craft in the Real World*, Matthew Salesses points out how "writers of color in a workshop where the craft values are implicitly White, or LGBT writers in a workshop where the craft values are straight and cis, or women writers in a workshop where the craft values are patriarchal, and so on, are regularly told to 'know the rules before they can break them.' They are rarely told that these rules are more than 'just craft' or 'pure craft,' that rules are always cultural. The spread of craft starts to feel and work like colonization" (2021, p. 10). Acknowledging, actively noticing, and then interrupting the ways that White supremacy culture may negatively impact teachers' and students' beliefs and practices related to writing is critical to our work as educators.

Invitation for Reflection

- How are your students' cultures, backgrounds, communities, and histories affirmed or marginalized in school?
- Read Okun's (2021) scholarship on White supremacy culture. How do you see any of these characteristics manifesting in school and then specifically in how writing is taught in schools?

Possibilities of Writing Workshop

Writing workshop is the antithesis to the model of traditional writing instruction. In 2009, I (Tricia) attended my first summer writing institute hosted at the local site of the National Writing Project in my area. During this 4-week intensive institute, teachers learn about the writing workshop model by participating *as writers*. Over the course of the institute, my fellow participants and I wrote *and wrote and wrote*. We wrote personal essays, narratives, arguments, poetry, and other genres. We wrote in our notebooks and on our laptops. We shared our writing with each other in small groups and then gave and received feedback from our peers. We read mentor texts to inspire new ideas for more writing. We studied craft moves that we could make our own. For the first time, I understood that there could be a different, more effective, authentic, and even joyous way to teach writing. The institute allowed me to experience how writing *in community with others*—not for a grade and not to a checklist—could be empowering for all writers.

We see writing workshop as a reversal of the power dynamics that are rooted in traditional writing instruction that emphasizes the teacher as the primary authority of what defines "good" writing and all that comes with it. Instead of a teacher's primary role being a "sage on the stage," in a writing workshop, a teacher's primary role is *supportive rather than directive*. Furthermore, in a writing workshop, a teacher is *also a writer*; students see the teacher as a more *experienced* writer versus an *expert* writer. This distinction is an important one. The latter emphasizes authority and power while the former emphasizes wisdom and knowledge. This is not to dismiss the professional expertise that teachers certainly have, but we cannot mistake our *experiences teaching writing* with an *expertise as writers*.

Although there are many variations and interpretations of writing workshop among teachers, we see the following as key components:

- study of craft through mini-lessons and close reading of mentor texts
- sharing, co-writing, and modeling by teacher and peers
- multiple opportunities for feedback through the writing process
- time for revision and/or reflection about the choices writers make
- shared and transparent criteria about measures of success
- guided and/or independent time to write during class

The last component—time—is critical. It is both the bare minimum and essential component that makes all the other pieces of workshop possible. Too often, we have heard young people (and many adults) claim that they aren't "good" writers or that writing isn't "their thing." At some point in their school experience, this was the message they internalized from teachers, peers, or standardized testing. But our experience as teachers has taught us that there is no such thing as "good" or "bad" writers. Instead, there are writers who have had more or less opportunities to study, practice, and play with the craft of writing. There is no substitute for time spent writing. Writing is thinking, and thinking—especially deep, critical thinking—takes time.

The National Council of Teachers of English (NCTE) affirms many of our practices and beliefs about writing as outlined in its policy statement "Understanding and Teaching Writing: Guiding Principles" (2018). We appreciate the important summary: "When learners have in-depth writing experiences, they have opportunities to spend time, work from multiple drafts, and see how their writing and thinking have changed over time" (n.p.). These experiences are much more possible when centered in a culturally sustaining writing workshop.

Invitation for Reflection

- What is your own experience with writing workshop, as both a student and teacher?
- What elements of writing workshop resonate with your work with students? Which feel challenging? Why?

Culturally Relevant Teaching, Culturally Responsive Teaching, and Culturally Sustaining Pedagogy

In this section, we trace the distinctions between culturally relevant teaching, culturally responsive teaching, and CSP. This is not a comprehensive review; rather, this section introduces these frameworks while encouraging educators to seek out the robust research surrounding their implementation to further supplement their understanding.

Culturally Relevant Teaching

Gloria Ladson-Billings (1995) originated the framework of culturally relevant teaching. CRT has three principles that undergird it, all with the intention of creating a culture of high achievement and success for African American students. Ladson-Billings (2014) has remixed and updated CRT to respond to the ways culture has changed. However, at its core, CRT has always had three components that an educator must practice to be considered a culturally relevant practitioner. In summary, these three necessary parts are academic success, cultural competence, and critical consciousness. What some practitioners forget is that all three parts must function for a practice to be considered culturally relevant. Often, the development of critical consciousness is lacking; however, supporting students in the development of insight, challenging assumptions and boundaries, and formulating their own solutions to problems is an important component of CRT that works with the others. Educators, too, must develop their own critical consciousness if they hope to help their students.

Culturally Responsive Teaching

Geneva Gay (2021) defines culturally responsive teaching as a complex process of *doing*. Gay extends Ladson-Billings's framework into processes that impact all aspects of instruction. She explains:

> Operationally, it is more a multidimensional methodological enterprise than mere curriculum content inclusion. While improving the academic

> achievement of students of color is a fundamental part of culturally responsive education, it is more inclusive than that. Other key components include cultural affirmation, socio-emotional well-being, interpersonal relations, and political efficacy on individual and institutional levels. Therefore, virtually every aspect of the educational enterprise should be amenable to and held accountable for implementing culturally responsive education for students of color. (2021, p. 212)

Thus, culturally relevant teaching offers a framework for supporting students, especially students of color and others who have been systematically denied quality access to liberatory education, while culturally responsive teaching offers more details about *how* educators can incorporate practices.

Culturally Sustaining Pedagogy

Paris (2012) originated CSP, reasoning:

> Our pedagogies [must] be more than responsive of or relevant to the cultural experiences and practices of young people—it requires that they support young people in sustaining the cultural and linguistic competence of their communities while simultaneously offering access to dominant cultural competence. Culturally sustaining pedagogy, then, has as its explicit goal supporting multilingualism and multiculturalism in practice and perspective for students and teachers. That is, culturally sustaining pedagogy seeks to perpetuate and foster—to sustain—linguistic, literate, and cultural pluralism as part of the democratic project of schooling. (p. 95)

What Paris contends is the both/and nature of CSP: that it recognize, center, and affirm what young people already have, culturally, linguistically, and so forth, *and* that practices honor and build on what students enter our writing classrooms with. CSP, like culturally relevant and culturally responsive teaching, is assets and strengths based, with the aim of ensuring our classrooms are places where all of what students bring serves as the foundation of how we conceptualize our instruction.

Invitation for Reflection

- Where are the intersections and divergences between culturally relevant teaching, culturally responsive teaching, and CSP in your own literacy practices?
- Where are there opportunities to make sure your current practices are fully aligned with CSP?

Toward a Culturally Sustaining Practice in Writing Workshop

Writing workshop provides a powerful model for teaching writing for all students, and as mentioned previously, no approach to teaching writing is complete without considering the context and culture of the students and communities we serve in schools. In their position statement on "Understanding and Teaching Writing: Guiding Principles," the NCTE (2018) asserts that "writers bring multiliteracies, and they bring cultural and linguistic assets to whatever they do" (n.p.). Although this might seem an obvious point, because of standardized tests, district mandates, and other one-size-fits-all approaches, student writing is viewed through a deficit versus asset lens. Instead, we argue that taking a culturally sustaining stance and applying it to writing requires that we recognize and celebrate the "funds of knowledge" our students bring with them into any writing task. *Funds of knowledge* refers to the historically accumulated and culturally developed bodies of knowledge and skills essential for household or individual functioning and well-being (Moll et al., 2006).

In our view, culturally sustaining writing practices begin with writing workshop but extend beyond it by centering some key understandings:

1. Writing is tied to the personal and social identities of the writer.
2. Writing is an equity-centered process.
3. Writing is justice oriented, centering voice, power, and freedom.
4. Writing occurs in, with, and among community.

Writing Is Tied to the Personal and Social Identities of the Writer

Writing can be one of the most empowering or disempowering things we ask students to do in school. For many, if not all, students, writing isn't just an academic task but a personal one tied to their many identities. Teaching writing through a CSP lens means understanding that students do not leave aspects of their identities at the door when they enter our classrooms. Instead, students bring with them the many diverse, complex identities that make them who they are: their personal identities such as their beliefs, likes, dislikes, hobbies, passions, talents, as well as their social identities such as race, gender, family background, ethnicity, abilities, languages, socioeconomics, nationalities, among others. In a CSP writing classroom, students know that they are invited to bring whatever parts of their identities they choose to when they are writing.

To do this well, teachers must intentionally embed opportunities for students to explore their identities and do so in ways that feel protected. For example, teachers might consider having students reflect on the complexities of their many identities through a structured identity inventory (Ebarvia, 2023, pp. 93–94) that asks students to explore how their social identities impact their lives. While *personal* identities include individual opinions, perspectives, experiences, interests, and passions, *social* identities refer to the identities individuals may have (although not necessarily choose) based on the different social groups they belong to. Social identities may include race, gender, sexual orientation, social class, language, nationality/immigration status, ability, religion/spiritual practice, and age. In an identity inventory, students are invited to consider how their different social identities impact the ways in which they navigate the world; depending on the context, some social identities might confer advantages while others present disadvantages. By asking students to reflect on how their social identities intersect with one another, creating unique advantages or disadvantages in any given situation, students develop a deeper appreciation for the complexities of both their own and others' experiences. Although identities such as race and gender are *socially constructed*, each student's experience with any of their identities is personal. As such, although teachers can and should invite students to reflect and write about their many identities, students should not be expected or required to share with others. Indeed, in some cases, it may be unsafe to do so.

In addition, even small amounts of daily writing in a writer's notebook each day can build a habit of self-reflection. Teachers can choose low-stakes writing prompts that invite students to write about their interests, passions, and experiences and then to share some of that writing with a peer or small group. For example, students may be invited to write about:

- lists of their favorite places, foods, books, TV shows, movies, songs, and so forth;
- a favorite moment from the last 24 hours;
- a list of things they are grateful for;
- the most recent dream they can remember having;
- a personal motto or belief that is important to them;
- a value or a list of the most important values they have learned from their families, friends, or communities;
- the people, places, or things that hold special meaning in their lives;
- a piece of advice that they struggle to follow but know that they should;
- the most important qualities they look for in a friend;
- the strengths they bring to their friendships and relationships;
- a goal or dream for the future;

- an indelible moment that changed the way they saw themselves or the world;
- a time they were challenged in an unexpected way;
- a timeline of significant moments in their lives;
- a list of traditions related to their culture or family practices; and
- their response to a brief text, such as a poem, excerpt from a novel or short story, or current event article.

Because the possibilities for writing are vast, teachers can consider how to integrate the rich variety of experiences and backgrounds students bring to class and that exist in their communities. Sometimes, what students write about in their notebooks are seeds for longer essays or other pieces of writing in the future, but sometimes that writing stays in their notebooks. Low-stakes daily writing and sharing out help to build the necessary foundation of trust that will be required as students are invited to share longer pieces later in the year.

Although we believe writing workshop works best when power is ceded to students, we know the powerful role that the teacher has in facilitating the workshop environment. Writing requires vulnerability. Teachers can model this vulnerability by sharing their own writing and, as much as possible, writing *alongside* students at every step of the process. At the beginning of the year, a teacher might write a letter to their students, sharing about both themselves and the year ahead. Students, in turn, may write their own letter to the teacher. During the year, teachers might share their own drafts of writing, modeling for students not only what writing-in-progress might look like but also modeling what it looks like when their writer identity intersects with other personal or social identities they hold. For example, one simple protocol for this type of sharing is the following framing: "As someone who [name an identity, experience, or background], this piece of writing is . . . because . . . "

Writing opens students up to being judged for their ideas and how they express them, and teachers can serve as models for how to be in partnership with a writer and provide feedback through conferring. We recommend a *listen-centered* stance when conferring with students, asking students to talk about their ideas while the teacher's role is to listen and ask questions to better support students' ideas while being careful not to impose our own ideas for what students should or should not do next. In a CSP writing classroom, the teacher positions themselves as *a reader* (one of many different readers) versus a *judge* of student writing. This positionality is critical to ensuring the trust and confidence necessary for students to be able to bring the fullness and richness of their many identities to the writing process.

Honoring the identities and experiences that students bring to writing also requires that teachers intentionally create opportunities for students to see themselves—and others—in the mentor texts used to teach craft and voice. Teachers can begin doing an audit of the mentor texts they currently use when teaching writing, keeping in mind that mentor texts can be diverse in many different and important ways: the identities and background experiences of the authors, the content and ideas expressed, and the ways in which style and voice are conveyed. The mentor texts that teachers offer as models of craft send the message to students not only about *whose writing is worthy of study* but also *what topics are worthy of writing* (Chavez, 2021). The following are some questions teachers can consider when choosing mentor texts (Ebarvia, 2023):

1. What are the identities of my students in my class?
2. Does this speak to the diverse identities of the students in my classroom? In the school? In the community?
3. Is the text written by someone from within that identity group(s) or an outsider?
4. Can this provide meaningful insight to students about identities with which they are unfamiliar?
5. In what ways can this text help to develop a positive social identity for my students?
6. How can this text challenge incomplete or harmful dominant narratives about different identities?
7. Does this writer treat their subject with complexity and nuance and avoid stereotypes?
8. In what ways could students be potentially and negatively spotlighted in their identities if I use this text? How can I mitigate any harm associated with stereotype threat (Steele & Aronson, 1995)?
9. What craft moves can I teach using this?
10. What does this text not do or include that I will have to supplement with another mentor text? What counternarratives will my students need after this text?

The mentor texts that teachers choose are an invitation for students to see what is possible in their own writing. Students may not always be willing to write about particular aspects of their identities and experiences, nor should they be expected to. But as teachers, we can create the necessary space in our classrooms to invite them to explore the richness and complexity of who they are.

Writing Is an Equity-Centered Process

The National Equity Project (n.d.) defines educational equity as when "each child receives what they need to develop to their full academic and social potential." We also know that historically particular students have not been allowed to fulfill their potential; those students are often Black, Indigenous, Latiné, students with disabilities, students from low-income backgrounds, multilingual learners, and so forth. These students are often denied robust writing opportunities that can include writing workshop.

A culturally sustaining writing workshop understands that students have different needs and that those needs might be tied to the identities and experiences they have. Those identities and experiences also might be ones the writer does not want to share within the classroom, and an equity-centered process recognizes and respects such a decision.

Flexibility is also central to a culturally sustaining writing workshop. Teachers draw on a range of mentor texts that vary in genre, length, and audience to provide students with robust examples of a type of writing. For example, even during a task that can be viewed as narrow, the college essay/personal statement, students can read and learn from different types of personal writing: spoken word poetry, lists, rants, and graphic memoir essays, for example. If a teacher knows students' interests and writing needs, providing writers with a range of texts that demonstrate the many ways they can approach a topic is an invitation to write in ways that students feel more able to achieve success.

While writing workshops regularly offer writers opportunities to share their work, a culturally sustaining writing workshop gives students flexible opportunities to share writing with their peers. Sharing might also be within pairs or triads rather than a whole group. Students might also suggest their own ideas for sharing their writing that could expand their audience. Some students might need more time to feel comfortable with sharing their writing. Enabling them to decide what they feel comfortable sharing—and when and what they choose to share—allows students control over their writing and over how they want to share it with the world. In our experience, we've found that when a student eventually decides to share what they've written with their peers or in other spaces, they become confident in the power of voice and their ability to reach others through their writing.

Because White supremacy culture advances the notion that there is often a single and "right" way of doing things—a "right" way for students to write, speak, act, present, respond, and engage in class that's considered acceptable in schools—it's imperative that teachers intentionally and consistently provide students opportunities to see that there are many valid ways to be a writer in the world. This means understanding that because of these differences, students' needs will be different, and our work as educators is to create a classroom space that meets them.

Writing Is Justice Oriented, Centering Voice, Power, and Freedom

We have always believed in the power of writing to address injustice, to create new ways of thinking, and to create worlds of possibility. Often, we return to Baldwin's articulation of writing's purpose, "You write in order to change the world" (in Romano, 1979, n.p.). If students can write powerfully, they can demonstrate what matters to them, in ways that matter to them. Because BIPOC and other students have so often been told their writing doesn't matter, insisting on culturally sustaining writing workshops, especially in classrooms and other places where they are initially lacking, is a first step toward justice. What occurs in those spaces is the next step. Young people live in the world. They are aware of political and social issues. They navigate intersections of identities. They face inordinate pressures exacerbated by social media. And, yet, young people are also activists. Believers. Doers. World builders. They bring all of these identities into our classrooms, and writing needs to be responsive.

A *justice-oriented* approach in teaching writing means that we center students' voices, provide opportunities for students to exercise power, and create a space in our classrooms free of racism, sexism, classism, homophobia, transphobia, xenophobia, ableism, and all the other forms of systemic oppression. A *justice-centered* approach means that teachers are actively conscious of the historic injustices that have impacted different communities. Teachers using a CSP approach consistently seek to understand how these injustices impact the students in their classrooms who belong to these communities. Teachers using a CSP start with the premise that *injustice exists* and that teachers play an important role in addressing and repairing this injustice. Note that this is markedly different from a "color-blind" approach, in which students are simply treated "the same" without regard to the ways in which students' experiences and cultural assets (as well as those of their families and communities) may have been misrepresented, marginalized, or erased.

Teachers can center students' voices in many different ways, such as offering students as much choice as possible in their writing. Teachers may help students to "try out" different voices in their writing pieces as a way to help students find the voice—or voices—that feel most authentic to who they are and their purpose for writing. Teachers convey the message to students that a strong voice is not something writers have or don't have; instead, all students have a voice (if not many voices), and writing workshop is a place where students can experiment, play, and develop their voice. It is not for teachers to impose a standard voice onto students' writing; instead, teachers can help students to understand that voice is the result of all the craft decisions that they make when they write. The study of diverse and well-chosen mentor texts is critical in this endeavor, as is providing students with choices about what mentor texts they would like to study that might support them at whatever stage of writing they are in. These texts might include excerpts from memoirs such as Nicole Chung's *All You Ever Know* (2018), Ta-Nehisi Coates's *Between the World and Me* (2015), and Michelle Zauner's *Crying in H-Mart* (2021), but also print and spoken word poetry such as Ariana Brown's "Ode to Thrift Stores" (2018), Amir Safi's "Ode to DJ Khaled" (2017), Jose Olivarez's "Mexican American Disambiguation" (2018), and Jamaal May's "There Are Birds Here" (2016).

Students exercise power in a CSP writing workshop throughout the entire process. When students enter a CSP writing workshop, they determine what they need at their particular stage of the writing process: Do they need to explore more mentor texts for inspiration? Do they need a quiet place to sit and draft? Do they need a listening ear from a peer to get feedback on a particular area of their writing? Or do they need to check in with the teacher? Teachers trust that students can make these decisions on their own or at least need practice and experience making these decisions for themselves.

When students get feedback from their peers about their writing, feedback is framed intentionally as *response* based versus correction focused or advice centered. Consider the difference between these two approaches. In a correction-focused or advice-centered approach, teachers might give students a checklist of editing tasks to be completed, such as checking for an attention grabber or identifying the thesis statement and marking evidence. The role of peers is to "correct" the writer when they see something missing or wrong in what the writer has done, where "wrong" is defined by what the teacher has indicated on the checklist. In a CSP writing workshop, feedback from peers is, instead, *response based*. Students provide feedback by describing their responses to each other's writing. Students may give advice, but the advice is not corrective, and the advice may vary from student to student. Because each of their peers may have a different response, the writer is empowered with the choice to consider how they will act on the different responses and advice from their peers. In *Antiracist Writing Workshop,* Felicia Rose Chavez (2021) argues that this type of feedback model can empower the writer to moderate their own workshop while participants rally in service of the writer's vision.

The writer, as the author, holds the authority to take what responses and advice are most useful for them.

A CSP writing workshop actively pushes back against the ways in which the experiences of Black and Brown communities have been misrepresented, marginalized, and erased. In a CSP workshop, students know that they have the right *to write*, that writing is a form of self-expression that is rooted in freedom. Students read and study the work and legacy of Black and Brown writers who came before them, who used their own voices to fight for their own freedoms. CSP writing teachers also consistently question the writing practices they enact in their classrooms, identifying the ways that structures and systems might have a negative impact on different students, even if that impact is unintentional. For example, asking students to write narratives about specific aspects of their family histories will have a different and possibly negative impact on some students, depending on their identities and experiences. Knowing this, teachers can make adjustments and frame writing as invitations rather than requirements.

Writing Occurs in, with, and among Community

A writing workshop is a shared community of practice that is intentionally created. It is in community with others that students draft, revise, offer and receive feedback, and share their work and turn what is oftentimes thought of as a solitary endeavor (writing) into a socially constructed one that offers support. We have both benefited from being members of writing communities. Those groups have pushed us to rethink our work, to process criticism and feedback, and to celebrate progress. A culturally sustaining writing workshop offers the same for students.

Writing in community requires a nuanced understanding of the members of the community. This information can be learned through writing conferences, surveys, and class meetings whose purpose is to build students' understanding of each other while also thinking about the organizational structures needed for the community to thrive. Students might create a visual biography as a way of introducing themselves to their peers (Ebarvia, 2023, p. 103), or they might interview each other with a series of "getting to know you" questions (Ebarvia, 2023, p. 71). Teachers might facilitate any number of team-building activities that help to surface the importance of encouragement, support, and patience. During these conversations, writing teachers should also surface discussions of communities that were unwelcoming and/or where harm happened as ways of collaborating with students to think about how to make their writing community a transformative one.

Being prepared to navigate conflict and to enact restorative measures when harm happens is imperative for an equity-centered writing community. Students need practice learning how to share their perspectives productively and how to navigate conflict. Oftentimes, rather than speak up, students will remain silent because they fear retribution or that their ideas will not be received. Our current political climate can also make teachers reluctant to support students. However, in a culturally sustaining writing workshop, through mini-lessons and regular practice, students and teachers can first consider the ways they want to be together in a community that enables all members to thrive and share. Then, through ongoing collaborative work—which can include shared agreements that are regularly revisited and revised as well as role-playing situations (actual and imagined that arise when people disagree)—students can gain experience with conflict and learn how to remain engaged.

Writing communities can be deeply relational places if time is taken to thoughtfully consider who is in the community and the identities that students and teachers bring with them. Thinking through power dynamics, especially as related to race, gender, ability, and sexual orientation, and the ways that these identities have been historically marginalized and silenced is also important for establishing community expectations that center their needs. Also, recognizing that communities are places where conflict happens and helping students know what to do when that happens helps all to understand the expectations of what a fully functioning community can offer. With those structures in place, students can feel more confident offering and accepting feedback, asking for help, and feeling valued for their work as writers.

To build community and the capacity for critical feedback during the writing process, students need intentional and regular practice in talking with one another—and varied ways to do so. Turn-and-talk can be an effective and low-stakes strategy many teachers use, but teachers must also consider the complexities of group conversations where students have to share the floor and listen actively. Just as teachers provide scaffolds for reading and writing, in a CSP writing workshop where productive talk is necessary, teachers can also scaffold classroom discussions, especially listening protocols that help students practice what effective listening looks, sounds, and feels like for themselves and each other. Tools like equity maps, progressive discussions, and critical listening dyads (Ebarvia, 2023, pp. 174–191) can help teachers identify patterns in how students talk and engage with one another. By the time they reach our classrooms, too many students are accustomed to *not* being listened to. CSP writing teachers are cognizant of these dominant conversational dynamics and work to interrupt them.

Classroom Close-Up

We reject the idea that there can be any one-size-fits-all strategy to culturally sustaining writing practices. As we've outlined, a CSP approach to writing workshop has overarching features, but each of these must be tailored to the specific strengths and needs of students, classrooms, schools, and communities. The following is a brief description of a high school classroom engaging in a CSP workshop, drawn from an amalgam of our own teaching experiences.

Context

In this particular class, students are currently working on a personal essay about a meaningful object in their lives. It is one of the first longer pieces of writing in the school year, and students are working on several different writing skills at once: developing narrative voice, writing with detail, and connecting the concrete to the abstract, to name a few. After engaging with several mentor texts—such as Li-Young Lee's poem "The Weight of Sweetness" (1986), Gary Soto's short essay "The Jacket" (1986), and student essays from the *New York Times* collection "What Students Are Saying About Objects of Comfort" (Learning Network, 2020)—and doing some informal writing and brainstorming in their writer's notebooks, the teacher has invited students to write about a meaningful object in their own lives, using the following prompt:

> "Consider the material objects in your life—things you own, perhaps given to you, perhaps you earned. Of these things, which are most valuable to you? Don't think of it in terms of monetary value, but consider its personal value to you. Another way to think about this: if you could only save one thing among your possessions, what would it be?
>
> "That said, a meaningful object might be meaningful for less-than-positive reasons. Consider something that you wish you didn't own or have. What is that tension about?
>
> "Choose an object and write about it. Tell the story of how you came to have this object and what meaning it's had for you in your life in the past, present, and/or future. How does this object reflect personal or social identities and experiences that are important to you?"

Start of Class (10 Minutes)

As students walk into the classroom, there are three key areas they attend to. These areas have been previously established as part of the ritual and routine of their writing workshop classroom.

First, on the side board is a sign with the prompt, "What are you working on today?" Several large pieces of chart paper line the walls. These charts display a table with a list of students' names with the days of the week written across the top. In the row with their name and under the appropriate date column, students jot down what writing task or goal they are working on during writing workshop that day. With a brief glance, the teacher and students can all quickly see what everyone in the classroom community has been working on. Some students are reading more mentor texts, others are working on a "down" (first) draft, some are working on revision, and others are getting peer feedback. The work students are doing is reflective of the diverse needs and goals of each writer. As students enter the room, the teacher greets and chats individually with students, checking in on what support might be needed for that day.

Second, another area on a whiteboard serves as a priority list check-in with the "Need Help?!" title at the top. There are two columns beneath this: "Today" and "Today or tomorrow." The purpose of this list is for students to indicate their level of need to confer with the teacher. As students walk in, the teacher reminds students, "Don't forget, if you're stuck or need some feedback sooner versus later, be sure to sign up under the 'Need Help' " board. On any given day, a few students might sign up, which helps the teacher prioritize which students to confer with during writing workshop time.

Finally, the third area is a slide projected at the front of the room with today's notebook writing prompt. Once seated at their desks, students open up their writer's notebooks and spend the first few minutes of class responding to the prompt. Generally, the prompt is brief and varies from day to day, depending on what goals the teacher or students have for writing that particular day or for their current unit of study. Sometimes, the prompt is to read an excerpt from a text projected on the board and to write a personal response. Other times, students might be asked to brainstorm a list related or unrelated to a text they're reading (e.g., a ranked list of the most important supporting characters in a book they are reading, or a list of the places they'd like to visit before a certain age). Writing prompts might also include essential questions (e.g., *What does it mean to be a good friend? What is the most important job in the world? What's the difference between fairness and justice?*).

Because students are working on writing about a meaningful object, today's writing prompt asks students to reread an excerpt from Gary Soto's essay "The Jacket" (1986) in which the author uses vivid details and personification to describe a jacket he loathed as a child. A few craft-related questions are posted next to the excerpt to help guide students' thinking: *What do you notice about the diction Soto uses to describe the jacket? What is Soto's attitude toward the jacket, and how do you know? How does Soto engage the reader's five senses?* Students take about 10 minutes to settle in and respond to the notebook prompt.

Mini-Lesson (10 Minutes)

After students have had time to reread and respond to the excerpt, the teacher invites them to talk with each other about what they noticed in Soto's writing. After a minute or so, the teacher asks them to describe Soto's writing using just one word. Going around the room, students take turns sharing their one word before the class engages in an open discussion about Soto's writing. Then either the teacher or a student writes a list of the class's observations on a chart paper. This anchor chart is posted somewhere in the classroom as another resource for students to reference as they are writing.

Workshop Time (20–30 Minutes)

The workshop time is the bulk of the class period and allows students the flexibility to work on whatever their current writing tasks are (and which they indicated when they signed into class). Again, the work students are doing reflects the diverse needs and goals of each writer. A visitor observing the classroom might see some or all of the following:

- Several students are sitting at their individual desks, typing on their laptops. These students are actively engaged in producing more original writing (getting their ideas down on the page) or they are revising what they have already written or some combination of both. Some students have their notebooks open and reference the ideas in their notebooks as they write. Some or all may have headphones on, listening to music or white noise or whatever helps them with focus.
- Some students are reading additional mentor texts, either on paper or on their laptops. Students browse the dedicated "mentor texts station" that the teacher has set up with several copies of different mentor texts, curated for this particular writing assignment. Or students might visit a dedicated online resource of mentor texts, curated by the teacher and/or students, that they can browse digitally. The mentor texts are diverse in voice, form, and genre and are intentionally representative of a wide variety of life experiences.
- Two smaller groups of students have formed, with two to three students in each group. In these groups, students are giving or getting feedback about each other's writing. They are using a peer response protocol that empowers them to center the writer's goals, offering

constructive feedback. One student reads his essay about the watch he inherited from his grandfather. After listening, one of his peers wonders aloud, "I wonder why this watch was special to your grandfather? Is there another story in the family?" Another peer prompts, "Maybe you could tell a story that shows your relationship with your grandfather." The students exchange sticky notes with their feedback, annotate their drafts, or write additional ideas in their notebooks.

- With teacher permission, two students are on a "walk and talk." Together, they walk side by side in the hallway or outside, where they take turns talking about their writing so far: What are they writing about? What's going well? Where are they stuck? What overarching message or idea or impression do they want to give their reader? This is an organic, generative option that allows students to move their bodies as they think through their writing.
- The teacher is at their desk, conferring with students who have requested to meet. These individual conferences might last anywhere from 3 to 8 minutes, depending on what each student needs.

Wrap-Up (5 Minutes)

The last few minutes of class offer students the opportunity to come back together to share their learning and make plans for the next day. This could be a very quick share of one sentence from their writing or just one word to describe how their writing is going. The teacher might also provide a prompt for reflection. Students might respond in their notebooks or turn and talk with a peer. A few examples follow:

- What elements of my identity feel important as I write about this object? What is something new I am learning about myself, this object, and any connections to my identities or my culture(s)?
- What's something I might be missing in this piece of writing?
- What perspective(s) have I yet to explore?
- What am I assuming about my reader?
- What does my reader need to know to connect with this piece of writing?
- If I could only add one more thing to this piece, what is it and why is it important?
- Where do I need to go next with this piece of writing?
- What will I work on tomorrow?
- What is something I still want to try?
- What other related ideas are coming up for me that I might want to explore later or in another piece of writing?

Invitation for Reflection

- Whi ch understandings outlined here currently exist in your writing workshop? Which ones might you want to put into practice?
- How might your own personal and social identities impact the way you enact a CSP writing workshop approach?
- What characteristics of a CSP writing workshop—*Writing is tied to the personal and social identities of the writer; writing is an equity-centered process; writing is justice oriented, centering voice, power, and freedom; writing occurs with, in, and among community*—do you notice in the classroom close-up?
- How can you prepare students for the routines and rituals described in the classroom close-up? What adaptations and adjustments would you make your own students and community?

The Role of Assessment in CSP Writing Workshop

We can apply the same core principles of CSP writing workshop outlined earlier to writing assessments. For example, we know that how students respond to feedback and assessment of their writing is closely tied to their personal and social identities. Assessments, whether they are formative or summative, must center on what different students need as writers. A justice-centered approach to writing assessment means that teachers must recognize that most if not all school-based assessments have been, historically, embedded in deficit-lens approaches that are the antithesis of a CSP writing workshop model. Finally, traditional frameworks of writing assessment, especially those given on standardized tests (i.e., text-dependent analyses or TDAs), are high-stakes, performance-based, isolated tasks, and as such, they undermine the sense of community and collaboration that is at the foundation of a CSP writing workshop approach. We argue against any one-size-fits-all approach whenever possible. We recommend learning more about the writing assessment strategies from scholars such as Asao Inoue (2015), John Warner (2018), Maja Wilson (2017), who each advocate for the type of student-centered assessment strategies that align with a CSP writing workshop approach.

Writing assessment can be highly subjective, varying from teacher to teacher, and thus highly susceptible to potential biases that teachers hold about students. To minimize the impact of bias, teachers can be transparent with students about how their writing may be assessed. Clarity about what criteria are being used and why can also engender trust; whenever possible, students take an active role in defining these criteria and how their writing is assessed. In a CSP writing workshop, assessment is never "one-and-done," individual, discrete evaluations. Instead, writing assessment is framed as a dynamic and growing portfolio where each piece of writing contributes to a student's larger body of work. Furthermore, rather than focus solely on a single teacher's assessment of a student's writing, students also regularly self-assess their own work with mutually agreed-upon criteria. In a CSP writing workshop, teachers confer with students not only during the writing process but also when assessing a piece of writing when it is completed. Teachers and students sit and talk about where a particular piece of writing succeeded or fell short of the student's purpose. Growth versus mastery is prioritized and celebrated.

Final Thoughts and Action Steps

In this chapter, we have attempted to argue for an equity-centered approach to writing that creates possibilities for students who have been too often marginalized. Culturally sustaining writing instruction can help educators to understand students' broad abilities and leverage those in writing workshop classrooms. It's time to move beyond tradition, as that adherence to form and style has too often created barriers for young people with much to say and not nearly enough support to help them become the brilliant writers they are. Culturally sustaining writing instruction offers us a way forward if we embrace its potential and think about the benefits for a wide range of students who have much to say and contribute to the world.

ACTION STEPS

In closing, we offer these action steps:

- Consider how your positionality as an individual and as an educator influences how you approach writing instruction in your classroom. Being able to name the ways in which your personal identity and experiences have informed you can help you expand your thinking.
- Revisit what worked and didn't work for you in how you were taught to write and explore what shifts you have made or would like to make as a teacher.
- Involve your students in identity work to create a safe space and build community within your classroom.

- Integrate writing workshop into your instructional repertoire to become more of a "guide on the side" than a "sage on the stage."
- Incorporate culturally sustaining practices to create an equity-centered curriculum where students see themselves reflected in the texts they read and write.
- Take an asset-based approach to teaching that honors students' abilities and leverages them to enhance motivation and learning.

REFERENCES

Brown, A. (2018). *Ode to thrift stores* [Video]. YouTube. *www.youtube.com/watch?v=PFZJoU44uOo&ab_channel=ButtonPoetry*

Chavez, F. (2021). *Antiracist writing workshop: How to decolonize the creative classroom.* Haymarket Books.

Chung, N. (2018). *All you can ever know.* Catapult.

Coates, T. (2015). *Between the world and me.* Spiegel & Grau.

Ebarvia, T. (2023). *Get free: Antibias literacy instruction for stronger readers, writers, and thinkers.* Corwin.

Gay, G. (2021). Culturally responsive teaching: Ideas, actions, and effects. In R. Milner & K. Lomotey (Eds.), *Handbook of urban education* (pp. 212–233). Routledge.

Inoue, A. B. (2015). *Antiracist writing assessment ecologies: Teaching and assessing writing for a socially just future.* The WAC Clearinghouse; Parlor Press.

Institute for Democratic Renewal and Project Change Anti-Racism Initiative. (2000). A community builder's "dictionary." In *A community builder's tool kit* (pp. 32–33). *https://static1.squarespace.com/static/536ce727e4b0a03c478b38e4/t/55a82f25e4b065c79de1b19c/1437085477559/15+Tools+for+Creating+Healthy%2C+Productive+Interracial-Multicultural+Communities-+A+Community+Builder%27s+Tool+Kit.pdf*

Ladson-Billings, G. (1995). Toward a theory of culturally relevant pedagogy. *American Educational Research Journal, 32*(3), 465–491.

Ladson-Billings, G. (2014). Culturally relevant pedagogy 2.0: a.k.a. The remix. *Harvard Educational Review, 84*(1), 74–84.

Learning Network. (2020, October 22). What students are saying about objects of comfort. *The New York Times. www.nytimes.com/2020/10/22/learning/what-students-are-saying-about-objects-of-comfort-lessons-from-tv-and-political-divisions.html.*

Lee, L. (1986). *The weight of sweetness.* Academy of American Poets. *https://poets.org/poem/weight-sweetness*

May, J. (2016). *There are birds here.* Poetry Foundation. *www.poetryfoundation.org/poetrymagazine/poems/56764/there-are-birds-here*

Moll, L., Amanti, C., & Gonzales, N. (2006). *Funds of knowledge: Theorizing practices in households, communities, and classrooms.* Taylor and Francis.

Muhammad, G. (2019). *Cultivating genius.* Scholastic.

National Council of Teachers of English. (2018). *Understanding and teaching writing: guiding principles. https://ncte.org/statement/teachingcomposition*

National Equity Project. (n.d.). *Educational equity definition. www.nationalequityproject.org/education-equity-definition*

Okun, T. (2021). *White supremacy culture characteristics* [Online post]. White Supremacy Culture. *www.whitesupremacyculture.info/characteristics.html*

Olivarez, J. (2018). *Citizen illegal.* Haymarket.

Paris, D. (2012, April). Culturally sustaining pedagogy: A needed change in stance, terminology, and practice. *Educational Researcher, 41*(93), 93–97.

Romano, J. (1979, September 23). James Baldwin writing and talking. *The New York Times. www.nytimes.com/1979/09/23/archives/james-baldwin-writing-and-talking-baldwin-baldwin-authors-query.html.*

Safi, A. (2017). *Ode to DJ Khaled* [Video]. YouTube. *www.youtube.com/watch?v=PFZJoU44uOo&ab_channel=ButtonPoetry.*

Salesses, M. (2021). *Craft in the real world: Rethinking fiction writing and workshopping.* Penguin Random House.

Soto, G. (1986). The jacket. In *The effects of Knut Hamsun on a Fresno boy.* Persea.

Steele, C., & Aronson, J. (1995). Stereotype threat and the intellectual test performance of African Americans. *Journal of Personality and Social Psychology, 69*(5), 797–811.

Warner, J. (2018). *Why they can't write: Killing the 5-paragraph essay.* Johns Hopkins University Press.

Wilson, W. (2017). *Rethinking writing assessment.* Heinemann.

Zauner, M. (2021). *Crying in H Mart.* Knopf.

Chapter 3

Teaching Argument Writing to Support Secondary Students for College Readiness and Beyond

Tanya Baker

There are many reasons to teach secondary students how to write arguments. For instance, many Americans today are concerned about polarized public discourse. The rise of social media has made it easy for us to only hear the voices of people who agree with us, and if we are not careful, we can find ourselves in a sort of "echo chamber" where we are fed content that often is an increasingly radical version of what we believe (Grant, 2021). Since the COVID-19 pandemic, we have seen a rise in rates of anxiety and depression in young people. Rates of school absenteeism have risen and engagement with school, even when students are present, is at an all-time low (Powell et al., 2021). One reason for these statistics may be that young people are wondering why they are engaged in learning that seems irrelevant to the significant problems they are living with today: pandemics, climate change, and loneliness to name a few. Argument writing is a way that schools can engage students in talking and writing about the things they care about the most, making school relevant and engaging once again.

At the National Writing Project (NWP), we have seen that giving students the opportunity to write about issues of interest to them, as well as the skills to do so thoughtfully and with maturity, has reinvigorated classrooms and even whole schools. Young people armed with the skills to write arguments, and the invitation to do so in a civic-minded way, see writing as an action they can take that makes a difference in the world. As this chapter will illustrate, students in College, Career, and Community Writers Program (C3WP) classrooms see school as a place to develop, vet, and elaborate on their own ideas.

Engaging students in writing civic arguments does not come at the expense of academic work but rather serves students by helping them develop skills that are necessary for college, for the workplace, and for participation in civic life. As George Hillocks (2011) tells us, "Argument is not simply a dispute, as when people disagree with one another or yell at each other. Argument is about making a case in support of a claim in everyday affairs–in science, in policy making, in courtrooms, and so forth" (p. 1). In other words, both in school and outside the classroom, students should engage in a civil exchange guided by the use of logic and compelling evidence. This chapter sets out to help teachers develop classroom practices that support students to develop the habits of mind and skills necessary to write better arguments and, further, to succeed in college and beyond. Readers may want to consider the following guiding questions as they make their way through the chapter:

GUIDING QUESTIONS

1. Why is writing arguments so difficult for student writers and what has proven helpful in overcoming these difficulties?
2. How can we help students develop transferable skills and practices that build over the course of a year?
3. How can we help students take up iterative reading and writing practices that develop argument literacy and build knowledge about a topic over time?
4. How can we help students move beyond the five-paragraph essay structure so that they can make intentional writerly decisions regarding the structure and organization of their arguments?
5. How can our instruction help students prepare for college success while also helping them be successful right now?

Why Is Writing Arguments So Difficult for Student Writers and What Has Proven Helpful?

Despite concern that has been expressed for 50 years, at least since the infamous *Newsweek* cover story "Why Johnny Can't Write" (1975), writing outcomes in secondary education continue to be weak, especially in rural and economically disadvantaged schools. The most recent publicly available National Assessment of Educational Progress (NAEP) data show that only 27% of 8th- and 12th-grade students' writing was rated proficient or above. Writing achievement is weakest for low-income students; for example, 67% of 8th-grade students scoring below the 25th percentile were eligible for free or reduced-price lunch (National Center for Education Statistics, 2012).

Internationally benchmarked assessments paint a similar picture of weak English language arts (ELA) outcomes. The Partnership for Assessment of Readiness for College and Careers' ELA assessment results for 2014–2015, which include a focus on writing, show that 38.5% of 6th graders; 41.6% of 8th graders, and 38.1% of 10th graders, respectively, met or exceeded expectations. These assessments, which place greater weight on students' writing than previous ELA assessments, "appear more sensitive to instructional differences between teachers, especially in middle school grades" (Kane et al., 2016, p. 3). In other words, good teaching can impact these poor outcomes.

Researchers report particular challenges that students face in argument writing, including (1) developing warrants that explain why or how their evidence supports their claims, (2) adapting writing to various purposes and audiences, and (3) acknowledging and refuting potential criticisms of their positions (Ferretti & Lewis, 2019; Kuhn, 2005).

Despite what we know about writing outcomes for young people, writing continues to be the "neglected R" of K–12 education. A gap continues to exist between the educational goals outlined in college- and career-ready standards and the capacity on the ground for teachers and students alike to engage with argument—especially in schools that serve students with the highest need. While at least one study of Common Core implementation suggests that teachers are beginning to *assign* more writing (Kane et al., 2016), the current amount and focus of writing instruction remains inadequate to meet today's more demanding expectations. A RAND survey of its nationally representative teacher panel revealed that only 20% of elementary and 47% of secondary ELA teachers engage their students in writing arguments to support claims through analyses of substantive topics daily, almost daily, or often. Of even greater concern, many teachers never engage students in the type of short or sustained research projects central to academic writing in college (20% of secondary ELA; 32% of elementary teachers) (Opfer et al., 2016, pp. 68–69). Unfortunately, this recent documentation of a slim focus on writing instruction is consistent with earlier national research (Applebee & Langer, 2011; Graham et al., 2012; Graham & Perin, 2007). Given the importance of writing to success in college as well as on new internationally benchmarked assessments, policy analysts at Harvard's Center for Education Policy Research recommend identifying "effective interventions designed to help teachers with writing instruction" (Kane et al., 2016, p. 25).

The NWP's C3WP, an effective, standards-aligned approach to supporting teachers in improving how they teach argument writing, is one such effective intervention. The work discussed in this chapter was developed as part of C3WP. Designed by NWP teacher leaders to improve students' argument writing by supporting teachers in skill-based instructional practices and formative assessment, C3WP focuses instruction on those parts of argument writing students struggle with the most: developing nuanced claims, weighing evidence, developing reasoning that connects evidence and claims, adapting to different purposes and audiences, and acknowledging and refuting potential criticism. As a professional development program, C3WP has three components:

1. *Intensive professional development to support classroom implementation.* Teachers in the three randomized controlled trials that studied C3WP received approximately 40 hours of professional development, emphasizing support for classroom enactment of C3WP instructional resources via demonstration lessons, coplanning, coteaching, coaching, and the use of a C3WP formative assessment tool.
2. *Instructional resources that focus on key skills for argument writing.* Each resource includes a four- to six-day sequence of activities focusing on a specific skill or practice in argument writing (e.g., selecting and annotating evidence in source material) and a set of texts that represent multiple points of view on a complex, engaging topic.
3. *Formative assessment to focus analysis and inform next steps.* C3WP formative assessment tools focus teachers' analysis of student work on the key skills targeted by the instructional resources. The tools are designed to support teachers to identify what their students can already do with argument writing and where they need additional teaching.

Three randomized control trials have found positive and statistically significant effects on student writing achievement. The size, scale, rigor, and independence of these three studies make for a strong evidence base to support C3WP's effectiveness in improving students' writing achievement at scale and in diverse contexts (Arshan & Park, 2021). In the following sections, I unpack some key ideas about the teaching of argument writing embedded in C3WP.

How Can We Help Students Develop Transferable Skills and Practices That Build over the Course of a Year?

Just as you would not expect a student athlete to excel at her sport after going to 1 week of practice and playing in a single game, we cannot expect students to improve as writers by receiving instruction on a particular genre or mode of writing once during the year and then writing a single example text. Rather, we need to provide students with many opportunities not just for low-stakes practice but also for creating particular kinds of texts across a school year. In the next section I describe four strategies embedded in C3WP that support students in developing transferable skills and practices that build argument writing efficacy over the course of a year: keeping a writer's notebook, engaging in routine argument writing, enacting cycles of instruction, and implementing formative assessment, feedback, and reflection.

Writer's Notebook

Throughout my teaching career and work at the NWP, I have had the opportunity to work with thousands of students, hundreds of teachers, and scores of professional writers and other professionals who use writing as part of their work. Across all these people, one strategy that pops up in many places is keeping a writer's notebook. My teaching mentor carried index cards in his shirt pocket and would regularly take one out to jot down an idea for a book he was working on, something smart that a student said, or notes about a lesson plan that went off the rails, all so that he could put that writing to good use at the end of the day. This month (July of 2024) I have noticed a number of Olympic athletes who keep their performance journals close by, including a high jumper who returned to and wrote in her journal after each attempted jump. All the other activities and cycles of instruction that are shared throughout this

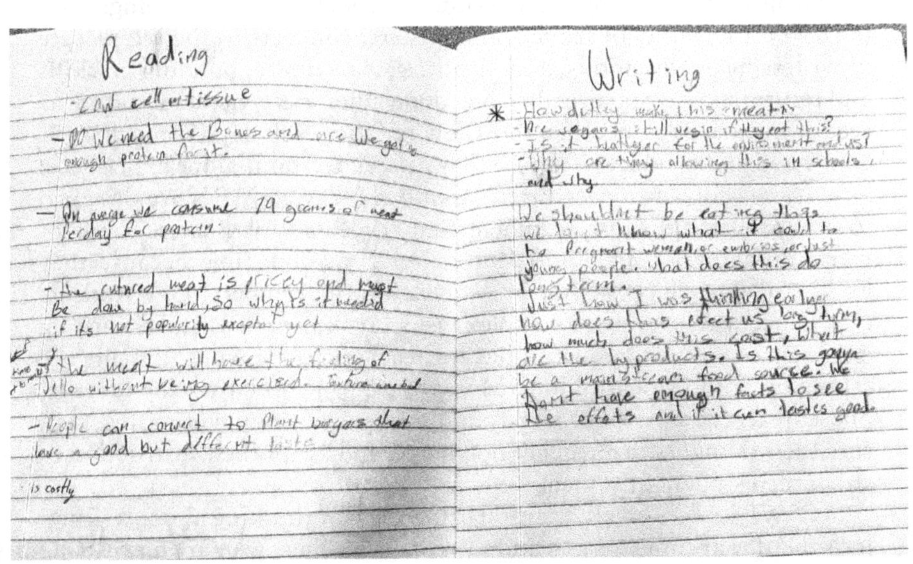

FIGURE 3.1. C3WP student writer's notebook.

chapter are built on the assumption that each student writer will keep all of their exercises and first draft writing in a writer's notebook (see Figure 3.1). This practice offers student writers the opportunity to keep everything in one place, to track starts and stops, to notice the development of their thinking, to see their growth over time, and to remember and track the strategies that they learn for improving their academic reading and writing.

Routine Argument Writing

As any good athletic coach would do to help students create the habits of mind and practices to excel at their sport, we need to create a culture in which students see how powerful, engaging, and, indeed, fun argument writing can be. We need to help them see arguments not only of literary analysis, or historical reasoning, but the potential for constructing arguments about what surrounds them in their lives. So, for classrooms where argument writing has never been explicitly taught, C3WP teacher leaders created a layer of instruction called routine argument writing to provide daily low-stakes practice opportunities for students to help them understand the genre of argument writing.

Routine argument writing can be considered another form of the "bell ringer," the 5 minutes of warm-up writing that might take place at the beginning of a class period while a teacher takes attendance or checks in with individual students. However, C3WP designers note that if daily argument writing leverages the writing students are already doing; capitalizes on the habits of readers and writers; connects to the big picture of writers' lives, situations, and identities; is recursive, building on skills and returning to work already being done; and/or is generative, acting as seeds for work to come, then those few minutes each day are much more connected and productive than if they are each a stand-alone experience.

These short, sequenced writing-into-the-day activities are designed to build toward a short argument that students write. These kinds of warm-up activities make efficient use of classroom time because they build students' fluency and, by sequencing the prompts, give students experience with ever more complex tasks. Also, these low-stakes writing experiences provide opportunities for teachers to see what students are taking up without scaffolding. Moreover, during and after the drafting phase, teachers can notice trends and patterns of argument moves, capture their thoughts in a teacher notebook, and adapt their instruction to strengthen student argument writing.

C3WP leaders created several categories for thinking about writing-into-the-day argument ideas and to support teachers who are just getting started with routine argument writing (see Figure 3.2).

Arguments in Students' Lives: Help students recognize that they are already surrounded by arguments in their own lives, so they begin to see themselves as argument makers. One way this might look is to leverage the kinds of generative writing you might have students already do in their writing notebooks. For example, you might already have students create writing topic lists, write their schedule for a day, create a list of "I Believe" statements, or even respond to prompts in their notebooks. Each one of these, and many more, can become argument topics. Then, with a little bit of writing time, students are writing seed arguments and practicing claims and reasons. The goal is to help students notice that they already live in a world of argument.
Arguments in the World: Surround students with the arguments in the world so they begin to notice that they already live in and participate in many arguments throughout their day. Even more important, they begin to notice that they have a response to them. One way this might look is by exposing students to the arguments that surround them in newspaper headlines, advertisements, PSAs, songs, Twitter feeds, and even cups from fast food restaurants. With all of these, students can notice what argument is being made and how it is being made, and then, with a little bit of writing, they are taking part in the arguments with their own response. This practice is leveraging the idea that writers notice arguments and respond to them.
Oral Arguments: Capitalize on time and the idea of oral composing as practice for writing by having students practice making arguments through mini-speeches. These speeches take little time and help students internalize the elements of argument, such as a claim, a focused topic, reasons, and evidence. Quick argument speeches can cover a range of topics from the usefulness of a spirit assembly to a response to a short, written debate. Even better, they can help students practice text support and internal text structures or help students practice elements of written arguments like a line of reasoning, engaging introductions, or useful conclusions.
Arguments in Response to a Single Source: Move students into longer arguments in the world by using short (one- to two-page) articles. With these articles, students practice reading strategies and habits of reading arguments by noticing claims, reasons, evidence, counterclaims, and structure. Then, with a bit of writing, students begin to practice the habits of writers as they find lines and ideas worth responding to, make claims based on what they read, and respond with support from or in reference to the text. Reading and responding to a single text could happen in one day or stretch across a week and could simply live in a writer's notebook until it is time to choose one and revise for publication.

(continued)

FIGURE 3.2. Categories of thinking and planning routine argument writing.

Arguments in Response to a Text Pair or Text Trio:
Introduce students to multiple perspectives in authentic arguments by stretching a pair or trio of texts (videos, infographics, articles) centered on the same topic across a week or multiple days. This daily argument writing helps students practice the hard skills of noticing various perspectives, beyond pro and con, and juggling more than one source in writing. One way this process might look is through layering. Each day, students read a new piece of text in the series and add to their reading and writing with information they gather each day. This writing has multiple uses as students can practice creating claims, using source material, choosing appropriate internal text structures, and synthesizing information, and as they write, they are making lots of decisions about organization, source material, and even revision.

FIGURE 3.2. *(continued)*

Cycles of Instruction

It is important to differentiate between simply assigning more writing and actually teaching students how to develop skills and strategies that will help them across rhetorical situations. C3WP is characterized by cycles of instruction (see Figure 3.3) in which teachers attend to what students have mastered, as well as where they need more instruction, models, and/or practice to master or level up. With the support of local NWP coaches, teachers receiving professional development in this program completed at least four cycles of C3WP instruction across a single academic year. Each cycle of instruction, which might last four to six class periods or sometimes longer, focuses on developing a new skill or practice, while also reiterating practices and skills learned in previous cycles. Teachers choose the next assignment sequence based on an analysis of student work. Therefore, in a C3WP classroom, students learn about making claims early in the year, and have at least four opportunities throughout the year to practice making ever more sophisticated, nuanced claims, while at the same time layering on new practices and skills in each new opportunity to practice argument writing. Teachers become practiced at using student writing as evidence of the just-right next step in instruction.

Formative Assessment, Feedback, and Reflection

One finding of the latest meta-analysis on the teaching of writing (Graham et al., 2023) shows that feedback, including peer response, is important for promoting student agency over their own writing and learning, and that when students are guided to use that feedback to set

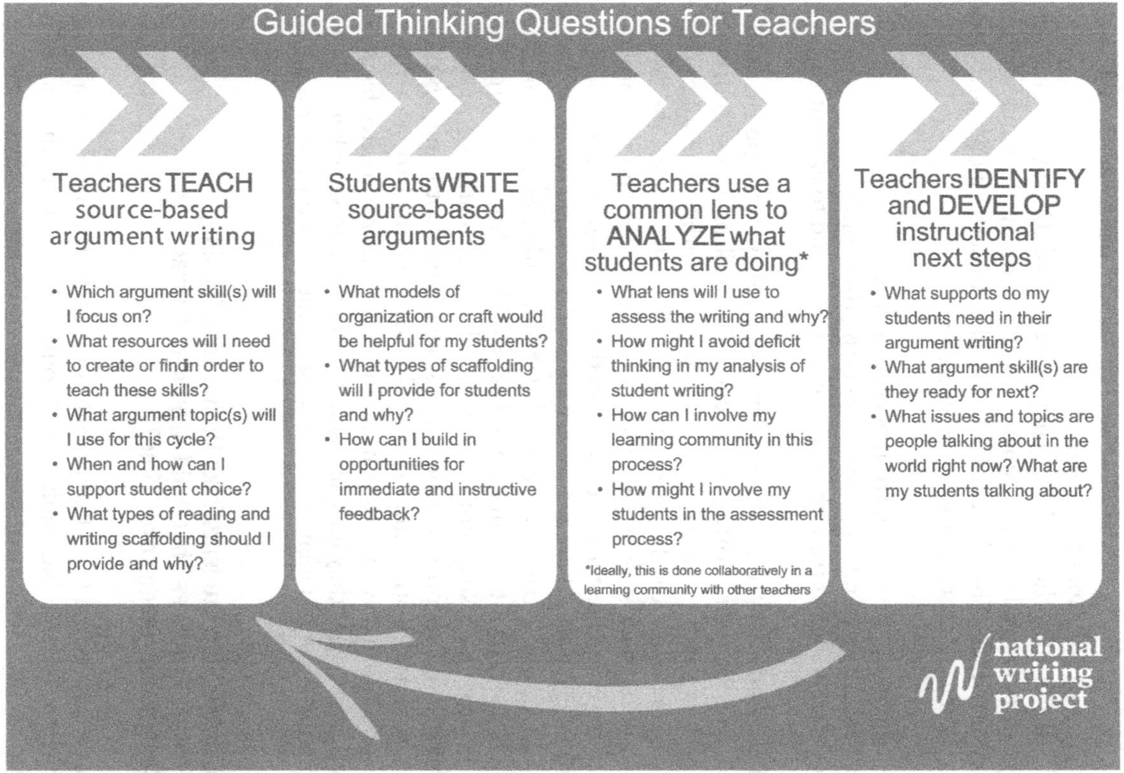

Guided Thinking Questions for Teachers

Teachers TEACH source-based argument writing

- Which argument skill(s) will I focus on?
- What resources will I need to create or findin order to teach these skills?
- What argument topic(s) will I use for this cycle?
- When and how can I support student choice?
- What types of reading and writing scaffolding should I provide and why?

Students WRITE source-based arguments

- What models of organization or craft would be helpful for my students?
- What types of scaffolding will I provide for students and why?
- How can I build in opportunities for immediate and instructive feedback?

Teachers use a common lens to ANALYZE what students are doing*

- What lens will I use to assess the writing and why?
- How might I avoid deficit thinking in my analysis of student writing?
- How can I involve my learning community in this process?
- How might I involve my students in the assessment process?

*Ideally, this is done collaboratively in a learning community with other teachers

Teachers IDENTIFY and DEVELOP instructional next steps

- What supports do my students need in their argument writing?
- What argument skill(s) are they ready for next?
- What issues and topics are people talking about in the world right now? What are my students talking about?

national writing project

FIGURE 3.3. Planning a cycle of instruction.

goals for themselves as writers, the impact of feedback is increased. Practice alone is necessary but insufficient for improvement. Whitney and her colleagues (2019) argue that it is reflection on learning and feedback that moves a writer beyond mere writing experience to actually having learned something about writing.

C3WP utilizes the Student Using Sources Tool (UST; see Figure 3.4) to support peer- and self-assessment and reflection on the feedback that the tool provides. The Student UST provides a peer response structure for source-based argument writing wherein:

- Student writers learn from peer response.
- Student respondents learn from using the tool.
- Teachers learn from the way students respond to each other.

The Student UST guides students through peer response and/or self-analysis of their written arguments. The tool prompts students to respond to a small number of skills or "moves," rather than all possible revisions and edits. Used consistently across the school year, the Student UST supports student agency for writing and learning. This tool provides a common language for the classroom that will help reinforce key elements of source-based argument writing; outlines expectations for what an effective source-based argument might look like; focuses classroom formative assessment on a small number of skills or "moves" in argument writing; provides a snapshot of where students currently are in writing arguments; and supports teachers and students in identifying next steps for revision and instruction. This tool is not designed to be a rubric; rather it is a formative assessment tool to help students receive feedback and reflect on what they have learned. It helps them to see where they are and supports them in identifying what steps they can take for revision.

How Can We Help Students Take Up Iterative Reading and Writing Practices That Build Argument Literacy and Content Knowledge over Time?

A central idea of the C3WP approach is to teach students to think of an argument as an ongoing, multivoiced conversation, rather than a yes/no pro/con debate. Because of that stance toward argument, we invite students to read first, to develop and revise their claims as they know more, to think of sources as "voices" with ideas and opinions on the question or topic they are investigating, and to be thoughtful and respectful about how they use those sources in their own arguments, whether they are forwarding particular ideas or countering them. The activities in this

College, Career, and Community Writer's Program
Student Using Sources Tool

_____ (Check one) _____ Peer Response _____ Self-Review

Writer's Name: ____________________ **Draft number:** ____________

Responder's Name: ____________________ **Date/Class period:** ____________

1. **Read through the entire piece of writing.** ☐ ***Check when complete***
2. **Read the piece of writing a second time. As you reread, annotate or highlight the claim(s), source material, and commentary.** ☐ ***Check when complete***
3. **Does the writing present a claim?**
   _____ The writing presents a claim that is nuanced, debatable, and defensible.
   _____ The writing presents a claim that is debatable and defensible.
   _____ The writing attempts a claim and/or presents a summary statement about source material but that statement is not debatable.
   _____ The writing does not present a claim.
4. **Does the writing include information from other sources?**
   _____ The writing includes three or more sources to support the claim.
   _____ The writing includes two sources to support the claim.
   _____ The writing includes one source to support the claim.
   _____ The writing includes no source material to support the claim.
5. **Does the writing include source material to present multiple perspectives?**
   _____ The writing includes source material to present multiple perspectives.
   _____ The writing includes source material to present pro and con perspectives.
   _____ The writing includes source material to present a single perspective.
   _____ The writing does not include source material.
6. **Can you tell the difference between writing that belongs to the writer and writing that comes from source material?**
   _____ The writing consistently includes quotation marks, signal phrases, or clear paraphrasing to indicate the use of source material.
   _____ The writing sometimes includes quotation marks, signal phrases, or paraphrasing to indicate the use of source material.
   _____ The writing's use of quotation marks, signal phrases, and/or paraphrasing is unclear.
   _____ The writing does not use source material.

(continued)

FIGURE 3.4. Student using sources tool.

7. Does the writing characterize the credibility of the sources?

_____ The writing consistently characterizes the credibility of the sources.

_____ The writing sometimes characterizes the credibility of the sources.

_____ The writing does not attempt to characterize the credibility of the sources.

_____ The writing does not use sources.

8. Does the writing's commentary connect the source material to the claim?

_____ The commentary consistently includes analysis that shows how the source material connects to and supports the claim.

_____ The commentary sometimes includes analysis that shows how the source material connects to and supports the claim.

_____ The commentary summarizes the source material and/or offers little analysis to connect to the claim.

_____ The writing contains no commentary on source material.

9. Does the organization of the writing contribute to the overall structure of the argument?

_____ The writing is thoughtfully organized and the ideas are logically connected. I can easily follow the structure of the argument.

_____ The writing is mostly organized. I can mostly follow the structure of the argument, but I am sometimes confused.

_____ The writing is somewhat organized. I am often confused by the structure of the argument.

_____ The structure of the argument is unclear.

10. Does the writing use source material for any of the following purposes?

Circle all that apply.

Illustrating–*Using specific examples from the text to support the claim*

Authorizing–*Referring to an "expert" to support the claim*

Extending–*Putting your own "spin" on terms and ideas you take from other texts*

Countering–*"Pushing back" against the text in some way (e.g., disagree with it, challenge something it says, or interpret it differently)*

None of the above

NEXT STEPS for REVISION:

Based on your reading and your responses above, identify the one or two revisions that will improve this argument the most. Consider the claim, use of source material, and commentary.

FIGURE 3.4. *(continued)*

section illustrate this key idea and show examples of the kind of instructional supports that help students develop warrants and acknowledge and refute potential criticism of their own ideas.

Layering Reading and Writing to Arrive at a Claim

Often in school students are asked to think of issues in a pro or con, two-sided way. Yet, issues in the world have multiple perspectives that are not always clearly pro or con. As we learn more about a topic and research varying perspectives, our opinions often shift and evolve. Therefore, in C3WP, rather than asking students to write a claim first and then search for evidence to back it up, we take a content-first approach that invites students to consider multiple perspectives *before* arriving at a claim. Students work through layers of reading, reflective writing, and critical thinking to explore their own changing opinions. Figure 3.5 suggests a sequence to support students in beginning to think critically about the idea of homework before landing on a claim they would like to make on that topic.

This layering of texts can continue with as many texts as you like, depending on time, student interest, and skills you want students to practice. Eventually, after thinking and layer writing through a set of texts, students are ready to write their own claim about the topic. After working through several texts, students will have gathered a lot of textual evidence and written their own commentary. When this writing is pieced together, students have a rough draft of an essay in which they can start tracing the development of their thinking toward their own claim. This first draft can be developed further as students make choices in developing their reasoning or thinking about an organizational structure.

Developing Moves with Evidence

Students are often told that they are required to "use evidence" to support their claim, and sometimes are taught the Toulminian idea that arguments must be made up of claims, evidence (backing), and warrants. However, instruction is usually less specific about *how* writers do this. What does a writer *do* in order to *use evidence?*

C3WP developed instructional materials for this purpose based on Joseph Harris's (2006) book *Rewriting: How to Do Things with Texts.* Harris's ideas about working with the words of other people expand students' ideas about *how* and *why* to cite other people's texts. His overall argument is that citation is an action that a writer can take. While many students see quoting as finding the right quotation to support their claim, Harris divides quoting into two broad categories: "forwarding" and "countering." Harris defines these actions or "moves" that the

Input (reading or viewing)	Output (writing in notebooks and/or discussion)
Start with a quick-write to a short text* or just a word. *Example:* The single word *homework*	This first writing is to acknowledge that we come to an idea with a gut claim, feeling, or belief. After writing for a couple of minutes, students can share with a partner.
Add a text to build more interest and background. This beginning text could be a short excerpt, picture, infographic, or brief video. *Example:* A graphic about how much homework students are assigned on a daily basis	Provide a reading strategy/tool for students as they read the text. They may jot down a statistic, fact, or opinion. Using the "They Say/I Say" concept form, students can add on to their initial writing with some sentence templates, first giving credit to the text: • According to . . . • This makes me think/wonder . . . • In my experience . . . • I agree/disagree because . . . • At first I thought ___________, but now . . .
Add another text to expand the conversation. *Example:* An opinion piece, argument, or informational article about homework	After reading, annotating, and discussing, return to the writing. Students add to their writing with new information from the text as it relates to the topic and where their thinking currently stands. Additional sentence templates: • As the article says, . . . • Now I am thinking . . . • I'm wondering . . . • Just as I was thinking earlier . . .
Add another text with a different perspective. *Example:* An opinion piece, argument, or informational article about homework	Students add to their writing with new information and expand upon how ideas are being supported, changed, challenged, or extended. Additional sentence templates: • Although the article states, . . . • Now I am wondering . . . • I used to think ___________, but now . . . • I understand . . . However, . . .

FIGURE 3.5. Layered reading and writing assignment: an example.

writer makes this way: "In forwarding a text, you extend its uses; in countering a text, you note its limits" (p. 38).

Harris (2006, p. 39) further divides "forwarding" into different purposes:

- Illustrating: When you look to other texts for examples of a point you want to make
- Authorizing: When you invoke the expertise or status of other writers to support your thinking
- Extending: When you put your own spin on the terms or concepts that you take from other texts

Because learning how to make moves with text is often a new idea for students, writing project teacher leaders developed clear, focused lessons that isolate these moves and include four pedagogical moves: naming the move that the student is trying to make; explaining why a writer would do this, providing an example of that move from a published text, and providing scaffolding language that can both signal to a student reader that an author is making that move with text and also provide scaffolding for student writers as they try on that move. Figure 3.6 provides an example of this structured direct instruction on the concept of illustrating.

Harris (2006) defines "countering" as developing "a new line of thinking in response to the limits of other texts" (p. 57). This definition, as well as his careful unpacking of the idea, highlights the best use of disagreement, and opposes a point/counterpoint understanding of countering. Instead, when writers counter other texts, they do so not to tear down an opponent but rather in order to advance their own point of view. Note that in these moves, Harris stresses the constructive nature of countering.

As with forwarding, Harris (2006, p. 57) subdivides countering into different moves:

- Arguing the other side: Showing the usefulness of a term or idea that a writer has criticized or noting problems with one that she or he has argued for.
- Uncovering values: Surfacing of a word or concept for analysis that a text has left undefined or unexamined.
- Dissenting: Identifying a shared line of thought on an issue in order to note its limits.

Figure 3.7 provides an overview of direct instruction on countering, similar to the framework offered for how to teach illustrating.

We recommend offering student readers a lot of opportunities to learn about the moves that writers make in argument writing by analyzing many examples. When engaging students in analyzing an author's moves within a text, the goal is to help learners see quoting as *part of* an action that is indicated by surrounding words and phrases. Some prompts that writing project teachers have found useful in supporting students in analyzing examples are as follows:

- Highlight the quote in each example.
- Look carefully at the signal phrase and the sentences surrounding the quote.
- Circle the key words the writer uses to indicate the "move" he or she is making.
- Discuss: Do any of the examples show more than one move?

Similarly, C3WP supports many isolated, low-stakes opportunities for student writers to practice these moves in the service of developing

Based on Harris's *Rewriting: How to Do Things with Texts*			
The move	**Why to use it**	**Example** Note: authors often use more than one move with a single quote	**Some language for making the move**
Illustrating When you look to other texts for examples of a point you want to make.	Illustrating further clarifies your point and provides greater explanation; use illustration to define a critical concept or idea.	Another issue with global warming is it makes natural disasters more severe. There are more greenhouse gases in the atmosphere, and that is affecting the severity of storms. In the article "Global Warming Increases the Frequency and Severity of Natural Disasters," it says, "A recent study in Nature, for instance, found that the extra greenhouse gases that humans are putting into the air are driving heavier rainfall patterns in the Northern hemisphere. A warmer planet means more water vapor in the atmosphere, which in turn makes storms stronger."	Demonstrates A famous example of Often seen in Explains Affirms Illustrates Reinforces

FIGURE 3.6. How to teach illustrating.

Based on Harris's *Rewriting: How to Do Things with Texts*			
The move	**Why to use it**	**Example** Note: Authors often use more than one move with a single quote.	**Some language for making the move**
Countering When you develop a new line of thinking in response to the limits of other texts.	Countering happens when you have considered another perspective offered in a text but you see potential to push back on limitations such as the logic, use of evidence, or credibility of the text.	Some argue zoos are good for conservation. For example, a zoo helps "save some species from extinction" (Lewis). Even though that is true, it does not help enough. In fact "approximately 8700 species are represented in zoos around the world and just 117 have reintroduction programs" (Vox). If only a small percentage of animals in zoos get released, what happens to others that don't get released?	Yes, but To some degree It is not sufficient to say On the other hand Although she/he makes a good point

FIGURE 3.7. How to teach countering.

completed arguments. C3WP teachers offer the following tips for practicing the Harris moves:

- Keep it short. Choose a text that students can access and find something to say quickly.
- Be sure to model and write some examples together as a class early on.
- Choose just one piece of evidence and try out different moves with it.
- Encourage students to try out the full range of moves, rather than always using the same move.

How Can We Help Students Make Intentional Writerly Decisions About the Structure and Organization of Their Arguments?

Similar to the way that students are taught to include and cite evidence, they are also often told that they need to organize their arguments. In secondary education, many students are taught to rely on the five-paragraph essay structure (introduction which includes the claim;

three body paragraphs, each of which include evidence and reasoning; and a conclusion). Many teachers believe that this structure provides a necessary scaffold to support inexperienced writers. However, without more purposeful instruction about how to structure arguments, the five-paragraph essay structure can become a restrictive framework that forces students to include irrelevant ideas in order to have enough paragraphs or to leave out interesting and exciting information in order to avoid having extra paragraphs. Instead of teaching students a single structure, working with students to have a more elastic, expansive idea of how to structure their arguments also supports them to think about their audience and purpose more clearly.

A sophisticated writer with a strong grasp of a particular topic might mix and match their beginnings, middles, and endings depending on the audience and purpose he or she is writing to and for. For instance, imagine that a student wants to argue that the school day should start later and wants to publish their argument in a teen magazine read by readers who are likely to more or less agree with them. Then that writer might think about their purpose. Do they want readers to take action? Or do they simply want to give readers more evidence so that they can make better arguments themselves. Either way, this writer might not need to spend a lot of time on recognizing and refuting counterarguments, but each of these purposes might call for a different conclusion. On the other hand, if that writer is making the same arguments to harried parents who already have trouble getting to work on time, they might need to carefully consider how to frame the argument (maybe a bit of history for how we got here, would be helpful, or perhaps an acknowledgment of parents' worries right up front before explaining the problem of early start days for teenagers).

Having students think about the "kernel" (Bernabei & Hall, 2012) of their argument, practice it orally, and imagine the "parts" as "building blocks" that they can move around depending on their audience provides practice in thinking flexibly about argument structures and their relationships to audience and purpose. Figure 3.8 illustrates possible ways students might organize their arguments depending on what exactly they want to say and to whom the writing is addressed—not to mention what impact they hope their arguments will have.

How Can Our Instruction Help Students Prepare for College Success While Also Helping Them Be Successful Right Now?

Because most students need to develop better writing skills to succeed in college, writing often acts as a gatekeeper to postsecondary entry and

Claim: ____________________

ESTABLISH THE CLAIM AND CONTEXT			SUPPORT WITH EVIDENCE		CONFIRM CLAIM AND ACTION	
A bit of history commentary + 1+ evidence + commentary	**Nuanced claim** claim + discussion of stance	**Here's the problem** evidence set + commentary	**Evidence that supports my view** commentary + evidence set + commentary	**Other people think, but** countering and supporting evidence set + commentary	**Most significant issue evidence + commentary + revised or nuanced claim**	**Call for action commentary + revised or nuanced claim**
Select one, two, or all			**Include both or use multiple times**		**Select one or use both**	

Examples of Argument Combinations: Arguments could use four to six paragraphs. Paragraphs below illustrate possible combinations.

Other people think, but	**Here's the problem**	**Evidence that supports my view**	**The most significant issue**		
The most significant issue	**Other people think, but**	**A bit of history**	**Evidence that supports my view**	**Call for action**	
A bit of history	**Claim or nuanced claim**	**Evidence that supports my view**	**Other people think, but**	**Evidence that supports my view**	**Call for action**

FIGURE 3.8. Planning and experimenting with argument structures: There's more than one way to write an argument.

success, especially for students in rural, economically poor schools, for students of color, and students learning English as an additional language. Writing is also an essential skill for communication, learning, and success in college and beyond (ACT, 2016; National Commission on Writing, 2003). Internationally benchmarked standards recognize academic writing in general, and argument writing in particular, as a key college- and career-ready skill (National Governors Association, 2011). Yet nearly one-third of all first-year college students enroll in either English or mathematics remediation courses, which they must pass prior to entering credit-bearing courses (Bettinger et al., 2013). Such courses can ultimately keep young people from completing college; this is particularly true for low-income students. A recent study of college remediation practices argues that although students are more frequently placed in mathematics remedial courses, being well prepared for college-level English "may be even more critical to a student's academic success because reading and writing skills are fundamental to most other subjects" (Bettinger et al., p. 96). Further, most college students must pass a credit-bearing first-year college composition course, which emphasizes the ability to make arguments using evidence (ACT, 2016). In a survey, ACT found that 70% of college instructors felt their students were not well prepared to develop writing topics, and 75% believed that entering college students were not well prepared to logically organize their writing (ACT, 2016). These studies make clear that students need to develop better writing skills for success in college.

However, telling young people that they need to work hard in order to prepare for a far-off future that they may or may not want (and often cannot imagine) is often not motivating enough to help them work their way through developing complex writing skills. Just as student athletes need real, immediate opportunities to put their skills to the test, so too do student writers need real-life opportunities to utilize their burgeoning skills. C3WP helps teachers ground their teaching of argument writing in a framework that scaffolds the development of cognitive skills and strategies that students will need to succeed in college but with an understanding that they should have the opportunity to write about issues that affect them and their communities today. Students in C3WP classrooms come to understand that they *can* write arguments, that their arguments can make a difference in the world, and that because arguments are powerful, we all have to engage them with care and responsibility.

Part of the reason that C3WP argument writing program is so effective is that the instructional units are built around text sets about important topical issues in the world today. Student practice in argument writing is situated within an opportunity to say real things to real people about issues that are important to adolescent writers right now.

Much of the classroom practice in C3WP units includes oral rehearsals and other classroom talk so that students are writing arguments with their classmates and also challenging their classmates' arguments. But at its best, middle and high school students in the program also have opportunities to share their writing outside of the classroom. C3WP includes curricular units that help teachers support students' independent research. It also includes resources that support study of genres such as the op-ed. Many C3WP teachers end their year with an opportunity for students to produce public writing that they share in their community. As an example, two students in Columbus, Montana, created an op-ed arguing for a local referendum that would raise taxes to pay for Advanced Life Saving Services in their rural community. Their piece ran in the local newspaper and helped contribute to passing a referendum to support the ambulance service.

Students in C3WP classrooms are engaging in civic arguments in their local communities, opening conversations with community leaders, elected officials, and the newspaper-reading public. We would argue, then, that C3WP, in building students' confidence in reading comprehension and analytical skills, not only improves students' writing but also creates in students a sense of writerly identity. Students with skills *and* the opportunity to use them can see themselves as writers now and not only in some distant future.

Conclusion

Coaches rarely think of the people they coach as "students" but more as athletes. Coaches know that to get the most out of their athletes they need to isolate and develop particular skills, teach strategies, and also prepare their athletes to combine all these in a real game or match. On top of that, coaches must attend to students' sense of drive, purpose, and efficacy, their sense of themselves as athletes with the desire and ability to play the game.

What happens in writing classrooms when teachers treat young people as writers rather than students? In a previous study of NWP work, Whitney and Friedrich (2013) describe the difference between a "student," conforming to technical standards, and a "writer," creatively and agentively using tools and ideas to author an original work:

> Whereas a student completes assignments, a writer composes texts. Where a student fulfills expectations, a writer makes decisions. Where a student writes well or poorly, or gets a good or bad grade, a writer communicates effectively or doesn't, persuades or doesn't, delights readers or doesn't.

> Writers are different from students in that writers develop and pursue agendas while students work within agendas set by others—as in standards documents or a teacher's lesson plans. (pp. 83–84)

While it is true that instruction can improve students' performance on writing assignments, for writing instruction to *make writers* it must be embedded in opportunities for those writers to make choices and feel ownership over their writing.

Not only can teachers create classrooms and learning experiences that engage young people as writers, but teachers who have organized their classrooms to teach student writers this way also report an increased sense of efficacy. One teacher reported, "Previously I struggled with teaching writing to all students—specifically those who were extremely high or low . . . With these new tools, I am able to work one-on-one with each member of the class and offer suggestions that are tailored to their specific need." Teachers in C3WP may come to see their classrooms, and even their jobs, very differently. One C3WP teacher described the change in her work this way: "Everything is different. Before, I was the authority, and the students came to me for everything. As I have worked through the C3WP, I am the facilitator and my students and I create knowledge now. . . . We write every day, and it is more of a collaboration, a conversation about what we are reading." If this kind of classroom and these kinds of outcomes sound appealing to you, here's how you can get started teaching writers how to write arguments today.

ACTION STEPS

- While getting started with argument writing can seem overwhelming, teachers can develop routines over time. We recommend starting by developing classroom routines that support a writer's development across the year. Consider introducing writers' notebooks and routine argument writing, and try to build in opportunities for student writers to take stock of their progress, reflect, and set their own writing goals.
- Next, consider what you would most like students to learn about argument writing and how to explicitly teach that skill. Think not only about the paper that students will be writing next but about the student writer and how clear instruction, modeling, practice, and reflection might help her not only write a better paper but make writerly decisions in all her writing to come.
- Think about whether the way you organize your classroom and your writing instruction offers plenty of opportunities for students to

practice writing for real audiences, including their classmates. Do they get to share ideas, try something out orally, and get feedback from their peers, thereby creating situations in which they can write about things they care about for an audience of their peers?

- Finally, notice what your students worry about, think about, care about. What do they love about their school, their town, their country? What would they like to see change? What do they believe we or they could do better? These things are not distractions from writing, but opportunities to do so. How can you take advantage of your students' interests in order to engage them now in building transferable skills for their future?

REFERENCES

ACT. (2016). *ACT National Curriculum Survey 2016. www.act.org/research.*

Applebee, A. N., & Langer, J. A. (2011). "EJ" extra: A snapshot of writing instruction in middle schools and high schools. *The English Journal, 100*(6), 14–27.

Arshan, N. L., & Park, C. J. (2021). *Research brief: SRI finds positive effects of the College, Career, and Community Writer's Program on student achievement.* SRI International.

Bernabei, G., & Hall, D. (2012). *The story of my thinking: Expository writing activities for 13 situations.* Heinemann.

Bettinger, E. P., Boatman, A., & Long, B. T. (2013). Student supports: Developmental education and other academic programs. *The Future of Children, 23*(1), 93–115.

Ferretti, R. P., & Lewis, W. E. (2019). Argumentative writing. In S. Graham, C. A. MacArthur, & M. Hebert (Eds.), *Best practices in writing instruction* (3rd ed., pp. 135–161). Guilford Press.

Graham, S., Kim, Y.-S., Cao, Y., Lee, J. W., Tate, T., Collins, P., . . . Olson, C. B. (2023). A meta-analysis of writing treatments for students in grades 6–12. *Journal of Educational Psychology, 115*(7), 1004–1027.

Graham, S., McKeown, D., Kiuhara, S., & Harris, K. R. (2012). A meta-analysis of writing instruction for students in the elementary grades. *Journal of Educational Psychology, 104*(4), 879–896.

Graham, S., & Perin, D. (2007). *Writing next: Effective strategies to improve writing of adolescents in middle and high schools—A report to Carnegie Corporation of New York.* Alliance for Excellent Education.

Grant, A. (2021). *Think again: The power of knowing what you don't know.* Penguin Books.

Harris, J. (2006). *Rewriting: How to do things with texts.* Utah State University Press.

Hillocks, G. (2011). *Teaching Argument Writing, Grades 6–12: Supporting claims with relevant evidence and clear reasoning.* Heinemann.

Kane, T. J., Owens, A. M., Marinell, W. H., Thal, D. R., & Staiger, D. O. (2016). *Teaching Higher: Educators' perspectives on Common Core implementation. https://cepr.harvard.edu/teaching-higher*

Kuhn, M. R. (2005). A comparative study of small group fluency instruction. *Reading Psychology, 26*, 127–146.

National Center for Education Statistics. (2012). *The Nation's Report Card: Trends in academic progress.*

National Commission on Writing. (2003).*The neglected "R": The need for a writing revolution.* College Entrance Examination Board.

National Governors Association. (2011). *Common Core State Standards for English language arts & literacy history/social studies, science, and technical subjects.* Center for Best Practices & Council of Chief State School Officers.

Opfer, V. D., Kaufman, J. H., & Thompson, L. E. (2016). *Implementation of K–12 state standards for mathematics and English language arts and literacy.* RAND.

Powell, A., Jenkins, K., Gulledge, B., & Sun, W. (2021). Teaching social justice and engaging Gen Z students in digital classrooms during COVID-19. *Journal of the Scholarship of Teaching and Learning, 21*(4).

Whitney, A., McCracken, C., & Washell, D. (2019). *Teaching writers to reflect: Strategies for a more thoughtful writing workshop.* Heinemann.

Whitney, A., & Friedrich, L. (2013). Orientations for the teaching of writing: A legacy of the National Writing Project. *Teachers College Record, 115*, 1–37.

"Why Johnny Can't Write." (1975, December 8). *Newsweek.*

Chapter 4

Self-Regulated Strategy Development in Secondary Classrooms

Amber B. Ray and Steve Graham

Writing is a powerful communication tool facilitating the sharing of stories, opinions, ideas, and thoughts. It also functions as a device for processing and learning new material. Proficiency in writing significantly impacts success in academic, professional, and personal spheres (Troia et al., 2017). While writing may not be instinctive for many students, it is a skill that can be cultivated through instruction and practice. Strategy instruction is an effective approach for teaching writing to secondary students (Graham et al., 2023). It is an instructional approach that teaches students learning strategies through explicit description and discussion, teacher modeling, and scaffolded practice. Learning strategies are often a series of steps that assist students in completing an academic task (Reid et al., 2013).

GUIDING QUESTIONS

1. What is the power of strategy instruction?
2. What are the key components of self-regulated strategy development (SRSD) instruction?
3. How can teachers apply SRSD instruction to help middle and high school students write informative essays that incorporate information from credible sources?
4. What strategies can secondary teachers apply to teach writing across genres and the curriculum?
5. How can teachers integrate culturally sustaining pedagogy with SRSD?

What Is the Power of Strategy Instruction?

Strategy instruction is effective because students are able to acquire learning strategies that help them master content-specific skills and material through a systematic approach (Deshler & Schumaker, 1986; Reid et al., 2013). Strategy instruction for writing can teach students a learning strategy for the entire writing process or focus on a specific stage of the writing process (e.g., planning, writing, revising, editing). In a recent meta-analysis on writing instruction for secondary students (Graham et al., 2023), the most effective approach of writing strategy instruction is the self-regulated strategy development (SRSD) instructional model. In this chapter, we provide an overview of SRSD, an in-depth example of SRSD instruction for informative essay writing using source texts, a discussion of how SRSD aligns with culturally responsive teaching practices, and the use of SRSD across genres and content areas.

What Are the Key Components of SRSD Instruction?

SRSD is an instructional approach developed by Karen Harris in the early 1980s as an effective instructional approach to address complex learning across content areas. While early studies focused on instruction for students with learning disabilities and students in need of additional instructional support, by the early 1990s it was evident that SRSD was effective for all students within general education classrooms (Harris & Graham, 2018). By 1992, the instructional procedures had been refined, and the term *self-regulated strategy development* was coined. Within SRSD instruction, students are explicitly taught self-regulation and writing strategies through teacher modeling, collaborative practice, and independent application (Harris & Graham, 1996). Self-regulated learning is the process in which students employ strategies to manage their affect, behavior, and cognition that supports them in achieving their goals. Students learn to use self-regulation procedures such as goal setting and self-evaluation to effectively apply the writing strategies taught and navigate the intricacies of the writing process (Graham et al., 2017). The instruction also includes intentional support for generalizing the use of taught strategies within other content areas and settings. While SRSD is an effective approach for teaching students reading, writing, and arithmetic, this chapter focuses on using the SRSD instructional model for teaching genre-specific writing to students in middle and high school.

There are three essential components to SRSD, including (1) strategies for self-regulating the writing process, (2) strategies for writing, and (3) the six stages of instruction. The goal of SRSD is for students to become independent writers through the use of the taught self-regulation and writing strategies. These components are designed to support students' learning across genres and writing tasks.

Strategies for Self-Regulating the Writing Process

To assist students with the complex task of writing, self-regulation strategies are incorporated as part of SRSD instruction (Graham et al., 2017). These strategies include goal setting, self-monitoring, self-statements, and self-reinforcement. These self-regulation strategies are commonly used to help students monitor and manage their use of the taught writing strategies, the writing process, and writing behavior, as well as promote transfer of strategy use (Brown et al., 1983; Zimmerman & Labuhn, 2012). Within SRSD lessons, teachers and students set writing goals. Often, these are classwide goals that focus on using the operations incorporated in writing strategies taught, as well as individualized student goals that focus on specific areas of writing development based on students' prior writing performance. Then, within SRSD lessons, students receive peer and teacher feedback and self-monitor their progress through self-evaluation of their writing and graph or visually illustrate their progress. Such visible records provide students with a concrete visual representation of their current writing abilities and their writing progress thus far; students' efficacy as writers can also be gauged (Graham et al., 2024).

Further, during SRSD instruction, teachers model using self-statements to help them work through the writing process. Students then develop a personalized list of self-statements they can use to help them apply the targeted writing strategies and self-regulation procedures effectively (e.g., "I can use peer feedback to revise my essay and help me reach my writing goals"). Self-statements can help students define the task, focus their attention, remind them to use a strategy, assist with self-evaluation and error correction, provide support for coping and self-control, and self-reinforcement.

Self-regulation further incorporates student self-reinforcement (Graham et al., 2017), a process where students reward themselves when they meet a specific criterion. This can be done by having students determine writing goals, select a reinforcer, evaluate their own performance, and then self-award the reinforcer when the goal is met. As some writing tasks can occur over an extended period, it is important for students to celebrate both small and large successes along the way.

Strategies for Writing

SRSD teaches students to take a strategic approach to writing, just like proficient writers (Graham & Harris, 2009). SRSD instruction uses learning strategies, such as a mnemonic, to help students easily remember the essential cognitive operations they will apply when carrying out a specific writing task. Mnemonics are memory tools that help students acquire new knowledge and promote students' retention of information.

To illustrate, a common strategy that is taught with SRSD is POW, which reminds students to engage in the following operations: **P**ull apart the prompt, **O**rganize my notes, and **W**rite and say more. This strategy can be applied any time a student needs to complete a writing task. Students can also be taught to select a genre-specific strategy to help them with the "organize my notes" operation of POW. For example, when learning to construct an argument, students can be taught the PEA strategy, which is aligned with Toulmin's principles of basic argumentation and the language utilized by social studies teachers (Washburn et al., 2016). The PEA strategy stands for **P**oint (state your point), **E**vidence (back it up with evidence), and **A**nalysis (make a connection through compare-contrast, cause-effect, and/or context). Teaching genre-specific strategies helps students develop and organize a plan for writing, produce an essay that includes all essential genre elements, and evaluate and revise essays. Teaching students to utilize the POW strategy to identify the genre (or type of writing) they are assigned and then use a strategy that corresponds to that genre helps focus their attention on the steps needed to complete the writing task successfully.

Six Stages of Instruction

The SRSD instructional process takes place through six stages. The stages of instruction include (1) Develop and Activate Background Knowledge, (2) Discuss It, (3) Model It, (4) Memorize It, (5) Support It, and (6) Independent Performance (see Figure 4.1 for a description of each stage). The SRSD instructional process is scaffolded, with the responsibility for applying targeted writing strategies and self-regulation procedures slowly shifting from the teacher to students. These stages are discourse-rich, allowing teachers to engage students as collaborators in the writing process. During instruction, teachers also address students' current attitudes and beliefs about writing and how these factors may impact writing. Feedback about students' writing and use of the target writing strategies and self-regulation procedures is provided to students via teacher and peers. The instructional sequence is recursive, allowing teachers to adjust instruction to meet students' needs. Overall, the six

Stage	Description
Develop and Activate Background Knowledge	• Activation of students' current knowledge about the writing purpose • Building background knowledge needed for the writing purpose • Introduction to key vocabulary
Discuss It	• Introduction to the writing and self-regulation strategies • Develop understanding of the benefit of the strategies • Introduction of a graphic organizer • Analysis of exemplar piece of writing using the writing strategy(s) • Analysis of a poor piece of writing and revision using the writing strategy(s) • Student self-evaluation of a piece of their own writing that was completed for the same purpose using the writing strategy(s) • Student goal setting for writing
Model It	• Teacher think-aloud of the writing process, modeling analyzing the prompt, organizing notes using the writing strategy(s), and writing a complete piece • Teacher modeling the use of self-statements, self-evaluation, graphing progress towards a writing goal, and self-reinforcement • Analysis of teachers' think-aloud and discussion of changes • Student development of individualized self-statements
Memorize It	• Student memorization of the writing strategy(s), including what each letter in the mnemonic stands for, the purpose of each step, and how to implement the step • Teacher continues to confirm memorization in subsequent stages
Support It	• Guided practice completing the writing task utilizing the writing and self-regulation strategies • Gradual release of responsibility starting with whole class practice, then small group or partner practice, to independent practice • Teacher support and guidance are slowly faded
Independent Performance	• Student independent completion of the writing task while utilizing the writing and self-regulation strategies • Class discussion about generalization and maintenance of strategies

FIGURE 4.1. Overview of the SRSD stages of instruction.

stages of SRSD instruction are utilized to introduce and develop students' independent use of writing and self-regulation strategies to help them become stronger and more confident writers.

How Can Teachers Apply SRSD Instruction to Help Middle and High School Students Write Informative Essays That Incorporate Information from Credible Sources?

The following provides a description of SRSD instruction that supports secondary students in developing the ability to utilize ubiquitous technology tools to identify quality source texts, complete a close reading of each source text, and plan and write an informative essay that integrates and incorporates information across these source texts (Ray et al., 2025). These capabilities are essential to success in high school and make a substantial contribution in preparing students to be successful in college (Ray, Poch, et al., 2023; Ray et al., 2025). Prior to the start of instruction, students complete a preassessment where they write an informative essay using source texts in order to gain insight into their current levels of performance and to help them set goals for writing an informative essay from source texts.

Stage 1: Develop and Activate Background Knowledge

Instruction begins by introducing key vocabulary terms (e.g., informational text, citing, transitions, revise). Then students brainstorm a list about the qualities of credible source texts and look at examples of credible sources via the citation and source text content. When reviewing the content within a source, the class looks to see if the information is accurate, relevant to the topic, recent and up to date, and unbiased. The teacher also activates students' background knowledge about plagiarism and illustrates plagiarism by examining samples of students' writing for plagiarized, paraphrased, and correctly cited quotes and content. Finally, students' knowledge about the writing process is reviewed through a discussion about analyzing prompts, planning, writing, and revising. Students then read and discuss example informative essays to develop knowledge about the characteristics and qualities of strong informative writing and the goals of the instructional unit.

Stage 2: Discuss It

During this phase of instruction, students are introduced to strategies for writing. First, students learn a strategy for the general writing process represented by the earlier introduced POW mnemonic. Then, a strategy that reminds them to include all the essential components of a quality informative essay is introduced through the mnemonic HIT BOOKS^3 (see Figure 4.2).

Students learn about how HIT BOOKS^3 helps them organize an introduction for an informative essay, using (1) HIT to develop the introductory paragraph, (2) BOOK to create the body of the essay (with at least three paragraphs), and S^3 to create their concluding paragraph. Students and teacher discuss the meaning of each of the components in detail with an emphasis on the fact that most components need more than one sentence to inform the reader. The detailed components include (1) Hook—open with a hook that engages the reader; (2) Introduce topic—provide relevant background information and context about the topic that the reader needs to know; (3) Thesis—make a statement that presents the

HIT BOOKS^3

Hook
Introduce topic
Thesis

Begin with central ideas
Outline supporting details and facts
Offer cited examples
Key connections

S^3
- **S**upport your thesis
- **S**tate relationships
- **S**ignificance of the topic

FIGURE 4.2. HIT BOOKS^3 strategy for source-based informative essay writing.

main point of your essay, explaining what you are going to teach your reader about in the essay; (4) **B**egin with central ideas—develop the topic thoroughly by selecting the most significant ideas; (5) **O**utline supporting details and facts—write about the concrete supporting details and relevant facts; (6) **O**ffer cited examples—provide extended definitions, quotations, or other information and examples to extend the audience's knowledge of the topic; (7) **K**ey connections among ideas—link the major sections of text to create cohesion and clarify the relationships among the complex ideas and concepts presented; (8) **S**upport your thesis—provide support for the information presented within the essay; (9) **S**tate relationships—explain the relationships among the central ideas you wrote about; and (10) **S**ignificance of the topic—synthesize the essay by articulating implications or the importance of the topic.

Students are introduced to a graphic organizer for informative writing, which is used first as a tool to analyze both exemplary student essays and poorly written student essays (see Figure 4.3). The class works together to read the example student essays and then identify and label each part of HIT BOOKS^3 within the essay (see Figure 4.4). The teacher also models making short notes in the graphic organizer as each part is identified. The teacher further engages the class in a discussion about the qualities of good notes when constructing plans for writing essays.

The teacher explains that the goal for every informative essay is to include 18 or more genre elements, which are outlined as part of HIT BOOKS^3 and count the parts of HIT BOOKS^3 within the example essay (see Figure 4.4, an essay with 20 parts of HIT BOOKS^3). The teacher then has students write the class goal of "I can write an informative essay that includes at least the 18 informative genre elements of HIT BOOKS^3" on their graphing sheet (see Figure 4.5). Finally, students self-evaluate and graph their progress on their own preassessment essay. In this phase of SRSD, discourse between the teacher and students is critical in order to build students' understanding of their current writing abilities, the importance of effort when writing, and the benefits of strategy use.

Stage 3: Model It

The Model It stage encompasses interactive teacher modeling. The teacher does a think-aloud, verbalizing their thoughts to model completing all the operations applied in POW and HIT BOOKS^3. First, the teacher reads aloud the prompt and models how to determine the essay topic, the genre and expectations, and the target audience. Since the teacher developed students' background knowledge about the qualities of source texts during Stage 1 of SRSD instruction, the next step can be

H	Hook:
I	Introduce Topic:
T	Thesis:
B	Begin with central ideas:
O	Outline supporting details and facts:
O	Offer cited examples:
K	Key connections:
B	Begin with central ideas:
O	Outline supporting details and facts:
O	Offer cited examples:
K	Key connections:
B	Begin with central ideas:
O	Outline supporting details and facts:
O	Offer cited examples:
K	Key connections:
S³	Support your thesis:
	State relationships:
	Significance of the topic:

FIGURE 4.3. HIT BOOKS³ graphic organizer.

done collaboratively. The teacher and students collaboratively evaluate multiple source texts by examining the citation and source text content. The teacher decides which sources are credible and which ones are not. For instance, the teacher might think aloud: "Now that we have examined the citation and the content, we can make an informed decision about whether the source is credible. Source 2 is not credible because it is from an outdated blog that does not include any references or support from experts in the field. I will not read, annotate, or use information from Source 2 because it is not credible." Once the credible sources are identified, the teacher models reading the source texts by either reading aloud the sources or using a text-to-speech feature for the entire class to listen to.

Example Student Essay

H I T — Are you looking for a fun, inexpensive, and healthy hobby? Pick up running! Running is a form of exercise where an individual is moving forward quickly on the ground and there is a brief moment when both feet are off the ground in each step. Running requires no equipment, and people can see new sights while running. Running is a hobby teenagers may be interested in learning about because it improves health, is easy to learn, and is a social way to exercise.

- Commented [RA1]: Hook
- Commented [RA2]: Introduce topic
- Commented [RA3]: Thesis

B O O O K — To begin with, running has many health benefits. Running just five to ten minutes per day can add years to a person's life according to a study in the Journal of American College Cardiology. Dr. Aaron Baggish is a cardiologist and says, "There is no question that the fitter you are and the more exercise you do, the longer you live and the better quality of life" (Harvard Health Blog, 2014). Besides being good for the heart, running also helps bones and muscles. Another benefit is that running can make people feel good. It can boost a person's mood when they exercise daily (Harvard Health Blog, 2014). Besides helping you stay healthy, running can be a simple way to exercise.

- Commented [RA4]: Begin with central idea
- Commented [RA5]: Offer cited examples
- Commented [RA6]: Outline supporting details and facts
- Commented [RA7]: Offer cited examples
- Commented [RA8]: Key connection

B O O K — Furthermore, running is an easy sport to take up and learn. The only equipment needed are gym shoes. When learning to run, a person should first start with "brisk walking" for about thirty minutes (Better Health Channel, 2022). Then build up to a jog. The individual can then rotate between walking and jogging. Next, they can start to jog more and more minutes each time they train. Soon the individual will be able to run. This process may take from six weeks to a couple of months (Better Health Channel, 2022). Many people, including teenagers may find it helpful to ask someone to start running with them.

- Commented [RA9]: Begin with central ideas
- Commented [RA10]: Outline supporting details and facts
- Commented [RA11]: Offer cited examples
- Commented [RA12]: Key connection

B O O O K — Lastly, running can be a social activity. This hobby can be done with a friend or a family member. It is a great way to socialize (Better Health Channel, 2022). Also, according to Better Health Channel (2022), many people join and have fun in running clubs. Teenagers can join the cross country or track team at their high school. People in running clubs or teams can meet others that enjoy running, motivate each other, and then train for competitions together. Running clubs and teams can also lead people to explore new areas in the community.

- Commented [RA13]: Begin with central ideas
- Commented [RA14]: Outline supporting details and facts
- Commented [RA15]: Offer cited examples
- Commented [RA16]: Outline supporting details and facts
- Commented [RA17]: Key connections

S S S — All in all, running is a great exercise that can become a hobby. In addition to being good for a person's health, running is easy to take up, and can include social aspects. All of these advantages to running can extend beyond teenage years because running can be a lifelong hobby. Running has many benefits for overall well-being and most importantly, it can be fun!

- Commented [RA18]: Support your thesis
- Commented [RA19]: State relationships
- Commented [RA20]: Significance of the topic

FIGURE 4.4. Evaluation of exemplar informative essay using HIT BOOKS[3] strategy.

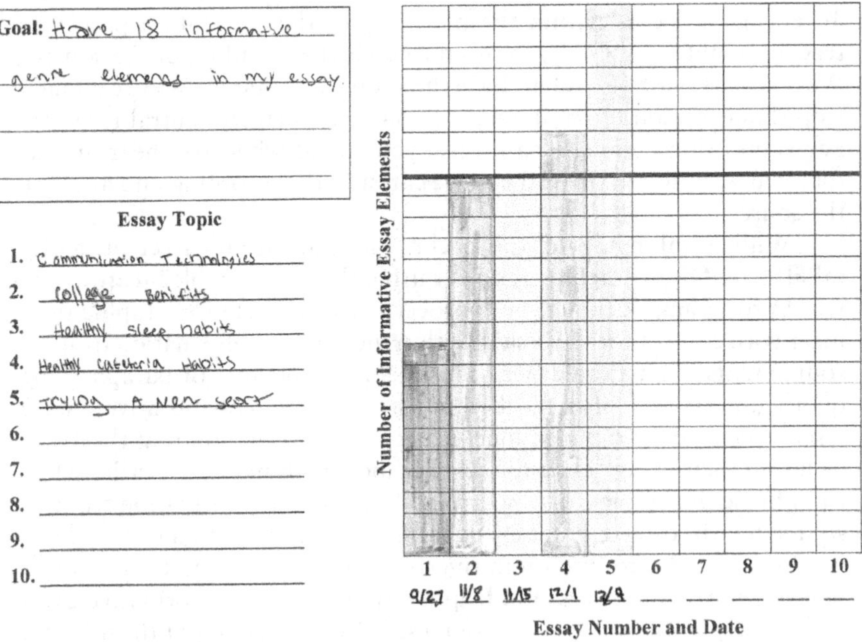

FIGURE 4.5. Example of a student's graphing sheet.

The source texts are then reread and annotated on the digital document. The teacher makes connections to previous uses of annotation and the annotation symbols used within other classes at the school. Some ways that the teacher might annotate the digital texts include using the "comments" feature to write brief comments about the content or to mark the text. Some possible annotation symbols and meanings are:

*– Important ideas that you might use as a central idea in your essay;
?– Confusing parts or anything you have a question about;
!– Parts that are interesting or surprising that you might use for an essay;
O– Offer cited examples.

Another way the teacher might annotate the digital text is by highlighting parts that they may want to use in their essay. For example, the teacher might highlight in green any parts that they could use to begin with central ideas in their essay and highlight in yellow any parts they could use to outline supporting details and facts or offer cited examples.

To engage students within the modeling of the annotation process, a teacher might say, "Okay, we need to do a close reading of the sources. We can use text-to-speech to have the source read aloud. We are going to stop the read-aloud to annotate the source to identify central ideas and key supporting details. Please raise your hand when you hear an idea that you want to annotate. Then we can stop the recording and annotate the source."

While thinking aloud, the teacher then models how to create a digital HIT BOOKS[3] graphic organizer using the "insert table" feature on a word processing document and proceeds to complete the graphic organizer with content for the essay. Within their notes, information from the source texts is integrated with the teacher's modeling of paraphrasing, quoting, and citing. The teacher and students can collaboratively select a sentence or two from the source text with information that they want to use in their essay. Then the teacher models thinking about how they can phrase this in their own words and adding the information from the source text into their graphic organizer. The teacher might say, "There is a lot of good information in the source texts. Using additional information from the sources will help me write a better informative essay. When using information from sources, I always need to put the information in my own words." The teacher emphasizes that notes do not have to be complete sentences and that information within the notes can be moved, changed, or edited at any point during the writing process.

Next, the teacher models using the notes in the graphic organizer to write the multiparagraph essay. To start, the teacher might say, "How shall I start my essay? I need to catch the reader's attention, tell the reader what my topic will be, and have a thesis." The teacher can then ask a student to read aloud what was written in the graphic organizer for the introduction. The teacher pauses to think about the introduction and then types or utilizes the speech-to-text feature to compose the full introduction paragraph. This process continues until the complete essay with five or more paragraphs has been composed. The teacher also models continuing to think about the reader while writing by adding or changing at least one idea or example while working on the essay, reminding students that the *W* in POW stands for "write and say more."

To begin modeling the revision process, the teacher first rereads the essay using a text-to-speech feature. The teacher then models revising the essay by looking at the content and organization by marking all the parts of HIT BOOKS[3] within the essay. This can be done by using the comments feature to type the letters of HIT BOOKS[3] in the margin next to where they are written, using different colors to highlight the different parts of HIT BOOKS[3] within the essay, a HIT BOOKS[3] checklist, or another marking system of choice. The teacher can engage students by having them take turns coming up to the board to label the parts of HIT

BOOKS[3] within the essay. The teacher might ask the class questions such as: Do all the genre elements in the essay make sense? Are there any ideas or examples that are saying the same thing and need to be revised? Revisions are made to the essay as needed, with the teacher modeling utilizing shortcut commands such as the cut, paste, and undo features within word processing.

Finally, the teacher models editing the essay with technology supports. This includes looking for any spelling, grammar, or punctuation mistakes that need to be fixed and scrutinizing word choice to improve the essay. The teacher discusses that on a word processor, blue lines under words indicate where potential grammatical errors may be, and red lines identify potential spelling errors. The teacher may ask the class: Did you see any blue or red lines where there may be a grammatical or spelling error that needed to be fixed? The teacher can have the students select the spelling and grammar suggestions to attend to and collaboratively decide whether changes should be made based on the suggestions. It is helpful to have a class discussion that not all suggestions are correct and that students need to think through the suggestions and then decide whether to accept or ignore the suggestion from the spelling and grammar check tool. The teacher then models making edits to the essay.

After modeling the entire writing process from start to finish, the teacher leads students in a discussion about all the operations that the teacher modeled. Students can discuss what the teacher did well, where the teacher encountered challenges, and how the teacher persevered. This leads to a conversation about the self-statements the teacher elicited to guide their behavior and complete the writing process. The class can then brainstorm self-statements they can use to get started (e.g., I can reread the credible sources for ideas to help me write a better essay), while they work (e.g., What order do I want to present my ideas in the body paragraphs? What makes the most sense for my reader?), and when they are finished (e.g., I can use text-to-speech to read aloud and check my writing). The students then write their own self-statements to help them with their writing (see Figure 4.6). These self-statements should be personalized and aligned to the specific needs of each student. To illustrate, a student who may feel overwhelmed by writing assignments could add the statement "It's okay to pause and take a deep breath" to their self-statements list. While another student may need a reminder to concentrate on the writing assignment and could write the statement "I need to stay focused on the writing task."

At the end of the Model It stage, the teacher reminds students that a good informative essay has at least 18 informative genre elements (i.e., the parts of HIT BOOKS[3]) and reminds students that 18 informative genre elements do not equal 18 sentences. Rather, most genre elements require more than one sentence in order to adequately inform the reader.

Self-Instructions

To think of good ideas:

"Don't overthink it; you can always come back to it."
"What do I already know about the topic?"
"What is the prompt asking?"
"I need to make a plan."
"Think of interesting ideas from the sources."
"How can I teach the reader about the topic?"
"I can reread credible sources for ideas to help me write."

While I work:

"I can always go back and revise my work."
"I can do it!"
"Close your eyes and take a deep breath."
"I need to take my time."
"What do I need to do next?"
"I need to put information in my own words."
"I need a clear thesis statement."
"I can look at my notes on my graphic organizer."
"I can do this. I know all steps of HIT BOOKS^3."

To check my work:

"I can have someone else read over my work."
"Have I cited my sources?"
"This is great—my reader will be informed!"
"I am getting better at this!"
"Do I have key connections?"
"Do I have all of HIT BOOKS^3?"

FIGURE 4.6. Example of a student's self-statements chart.

The teacher then models writing the class goal of "I can write an informative essay that includes at least the 18 informative genre elements of HIT BOOKS^3" on the graphing sheet (see Figure 4.5). Then the teacher models self-evaluating the essay that was written for the parts of HIT BOOKS^3 and models graphing the informative essay, with each square on the graph being colored in for each part of HIT BOOKS^3 that was written.

Stage 4: Memorize It

Memorization of the strategies POW + HIT BOOKS^3 begins in the earlier stages of instruction as the strategy is reviewed and practiced at the start of every lesson. However, once the Memorize It stage of instruction is reached, the teacher needs to ensure that students have the strategies memorized. Students need to know what each letter of the mnemonic stands for, how to implement that step, and why it is important. For instance, students need to know (1) that the H in HIT BOOKS[3] stands for hook, (2) that a hook is the first sentence of an essay, and (3) the hook is important because it engages the reader and helps the reader want to continue reading the essay. Students can engage in various practice activities to aid in the memorization of the strategies, such as creating flash cards, class choral response, quizzing a partner, or review games (e.g., Kahoot, Blooket, Memory Game, Jeopardy).

Stage 5: Support It

The "Support It" stage of instruction is the longest stage which starts the gradual release of responsibility from teacher to the student for the entire process of pulling apart the prompt, analyzing source texts, annotating text, organizing notes, writing an informative essay, revising and editing the informative essay, and self-evaluation and graphing of progress (Harris & Graham, 2018). This often starts with collaborative whole-class practice. The class works together to respond to the same writing prompt with the teacher guiding the process and students generating ideas for the class collaborative notes and essay.

The teacher continues to reduce the amount of support provided by moving on to small group or partner practice and then independent practice. Within each practice opportunity, students are writing about a new topic and using new source texts. The teacher also provides various levels of feedback along the way. The teacher may also decide to have different parts of the process completed with various levels of support based on students' needs. For example, the teacher may decide to have students work with a partner to analyze source texts for credibility and then independently read and annotate the credible sources. The teacher might facilitate a whole-class collaborative process for writing notes on the HIT BOOKS[3] graphic organizer, followed by having the majority of students work in partners and a small group of students who need additional support working with the teacher to write, revise, and edit the essay.

During this stage, the teacher slowly fades guidance on the writing and self-regulation strategies by gradually reducing the level of assistance they are providing to students and returns to earlier stages of instruction as necessary. For example, if a teacher notices that all the collaboratively written essays cite sources using long quotations, they may decide to do a mini-lesson that again models how to use paraphrasing when citing information from sources. The teacher can also work with students who have met the initial writing goal to establish more challenging goals, such as incorporating a fourth body paragraph or identifying additional credible sources. Additional individualized goals could include:

- I can utilize appropriate and varied transitions to link the major sections of my essay.
- I can write a strong thesis statement that presents the main point of my essay and explains what I am going to teach my reader about.
- I can integrate information from each credible source through paraphrasing.
- I can use precise vocabulary that is relevant to the topic.

Stage 6: Independent Performance

The Independent Performance stage of instruction occurs once students are able to use the targeted writing and self-regulation strategies independently. The teacher continues to monitor student performance and returns to earlier stages of instruction to support students as needed. During this stage, introducing a peer-review process can help support students' writing development. The teacher explains that during peer review, students exchange electronic copies of their essay with a partner. Both partners read each other's essay at the same time and use the peer-review form (see Figure 4.7) to mark the parts of HIT BOOKS[3] that were completed successfully, and they write one thing they learned from their peer's essay, one thing they liked about their peer's essay, and one way their peer could improve their essay. The students then take turns talking through their peer review with their partner. Partners can ask each other any clarifying questions. Establishing clear routines for peer review is essential to foster positive support for writing development (Graham, 2019).

This stage concludes with students completing a postassessment. See Figures 4.8 and 4.9 for a student's independently written graphic organizer and essay in response to the prompt "Write an informative essay explaining the ways communication technologies (such as blogs, websites, live video, social media, email, etc.) can be used to connect people with one another including the social implications of these technologies." The student was also provided with multiple credible sources from online newspapers. The students are then given access to a copy of their postassessment to self-evaluate and graph their process. Students are asked to reflect on their writing goals and consider what they are doing well and how they can continue to improve in their informative writing. Additionally, the teacher leads a discussion about generalizing the use of strategies to other content-area classes and future use of the strategies. Goals to do so can be set. Ideally, the teacher collaborates with another content-area teacher to provide students with authentic practice utilizing the strategies within another content-area class.

Peer Review for Informative Writing

Are all the parts of HIT BOOKS[3] included in the essay?

_____ Yes	_____ No	Hook
_____ Yes	_____ No	Introduce topic
_____ Yes	_____ No	Thesis
_____ Yes	_____ No	Begin with central idea #1
_____ Yes	_____ No	Outline supporting details and facts #1
_____ Yes	_____ No	Offer examples #1
_____ Yes	_____ No	Key connections #1
_____ Yes	_____ No	Begin with central idea #2
_____ Yes	_____ No	Outline supporting details and facts #2
_____ Yes	_____ No	Offer examples #2
_____ Yes	_____ No	Key connections #2
_____ Yes	_____ No	Begin with central idea #3
_____ Yes	_____ No	Outline supporting details and facts #3
_____ Yes	_____ No	Offer examples #3
_____ Yes	_____ No	Key connections #3
_____ Yes	_____ No	Support your thesis
_____ Yes	_____ No	State relationships
_____ Yes	_____ No	Significance of the topic

FIGURE 4.7. Peer review checklist.

How Can Teachers Integrate Culturally Sustaining Pedagogy with SRSD?

Students who are culturally and linguistically diverse and are taught writing using SRSD make meaningful gains in their writing abilities (Ray, Torres, et al., 2023; Torres & Black, 2018; Torres & Ray, 2022). SRSD instruction is aligned with research-based recommendations for teaching writing to English learners (see Torres & Ray, 2022). There are many ways teachers can implement SRSD writing instruction that is culturally responsive. First, teachers can ensure they dedicate ample

Planning Page	
H	From cave paintings to instant messaging, communication is always changing.
I	Evolving communication technology has linked more people to one another in various ways.
T	In the present day, new communication technology has impacted the world by connecting people easily, spreading a new culture, and establishing emojis as the global form of communication.
B	Technology has made communication easier.
O	Messages that once needed an operator or postage stamp are now as simple as tapping a name on your screen.
O	The new technology has also come with new rules. "Every generation and group of friends has its own slang and customs. Internet culture has given birth to a new set of these rules" (Ivory, *USA Today* 2019).
K	Perfectly natural for social manners to change as communication formats evolve.
B	Confusing situation by breaking the new rules for communicating
O	The guidelines of manners must evolve as well.
O	Do not want you to call them unless you've texted to make sure it's OK to call. "Don't text me and say, 'Hey, did you get my last text?' You know that I got it." Do not leave a message after the voicemail beep. Do not send too many texts in a row.
K	Another technological evolution is the world of emojis.
B	Emojis can be understood by everyone. Emojis are like tone of voice and body language all in one.
O	3.2 billion people who have regular internet access in the world; 9 out of 10 of those 3.2 billion people regularly send emojis.
O	Paralanguage, which is your tone of voice and how you are delivering the words Kinesics, and that has to do with body language Without emojis, it can be hard to express emotion when you text or send an email.
K	However, emojis are only one development of the vast expansion of communication technology.
S	In conclusion, communication technology has expanded, making it easier for people to connect, share a new culture, and speak the global language of emojis.
S	The ease of connection using new communication technology has quickened the spread of new culture, including emojis.
S	Billions of people today use communication technology to link to one another. It should be appreciated by all who use it. Without it, humans might still be painting on cave walls.

FIGURE 4.8. Sample student planning page.

Writing Assignment: Communication Technologies

From cave paintings to instant messaging, communication has changed over the course of time. Evolving communication technology has linked more people to one another in various ways. In the present day, new communication technology has impacted the world by connecting people easily, spreading a new culture, and establishing emojis as the global form of communication.

First, communication technology has made connecting easier. Many decades ago, messages that were predominantly in the form of letters required an operator and a postage stamp. It was considered inconvenient compared to today's technology. Nowadays, messages can be sent and received at one's fingertips. A few clicks on the screen or keyboard—and voilà! A message was sent in an instant. Additionally, the evolution of communication technology is attached to the evolution of culture. "Every generation and group of friends has its own slang and customs. Internet culture has given birth to a new set of these rules" (Ivory, *USA Today* 2019). The evolution of culture in communication is natural, however. "It's perfectly natural for social manners to change as communication formats evolve" (Swann, *USA Today* 2019). While current communication is easier to navigate than it's ever been, some may find that the current communication rules are more difficult to understand.

Evolving communication technology has brought about a new culture and manners. This may cause some to find the new rules difficult. For instance, people who break the new rules for communication may cause confusion, especially for folks of older generations. Some of these rules and manners may go unwritten but may have a large effect on the person on the receiving end of the communication. To illustrate, many people today accept rules such as not calling a person without texting to make sure it's OK to call, not leaving a message after the voicemail beep, not sending too many texts in a row, etc. "Don't text me and say, 'Hey, did you get my last text?' You know that I got it" (Bruce, *USA Today* 2019). While new culture is a symptom of the evolution of communication technology, the establishment of emojis as a global form of communication is another.

Emojis are recognized by the world because they are understood by everyone. From the 3.2 billion people who regularly use the internet, more than 90% often use emojis (*Chicago Tribune* 2017). The reason why emojis resonate with people globally is linked to the types of language it portrays. Not scripted language, but paralanguage and kinesics. Paralanguage refers to the tone of voice while delivering words, and kinesics refers to body language. Emojis incorporate both, which is why they are effective for everyone around the world. Without emojis, emotion would be hard to express. A person who views a message may misinterpret the message that the sender meant, causing confusion. That is why it is even considered beneficial to use emojis. Although emojis are great, they are only one development of the vast expansion of communication technology.

In conclusion, communication technology has expanded, making it easier for people to connect, share a new culture, and speak the global language of emojis. The ease of connection using new communication technology has quickened the spread of new culture. Even emojis are beneficial to use in the world of developing communication. Today, billions of people use communication technology to link to one another. It should be appreciated by all who use it. Without it, humans might still be painting on cave walls!

FIGURE 4.9. Sample 10th-grade student posttest essay.

time to modeling the writing process and utilization of self-regulation strategies. Moreover, they can offer scaffolded assistance as both modeling and instructional scaffolding constitute key elements of culturally responsive teaching (Aceves & Orosco, 2014). Furthermore, educators have the opportunity to choose writing prompts that resonate with students' personal lives beyond the classroom, align with their cultural backgrounds, and delve into subjects pertaining to social justice and equity. Such topics can be the focus of the types of writing students apply as they learn to use strategies with SRSD. Additionally, collaboration is an important part of culturally responsive teaching (Aceves & Orosco, 2014). Within SRSD instruction, whole-class collaborative writing and peer collaboration are a part of instruction. Finally, within SRSD instruction, teachers and peers provide frequent feedback regarding students' writing. Incorporating responsive feedback is integral to culturally responsive teaching (Aceves & Orosco, 2014). Students engaged in SRSD instruction benefit from individualized support and feedback, enabling teachers to consider and adapt to their students' diverse cultural and linguistic backgrounds.

What Strategies Can Secondary Teachers Apply to Teach Writing Across Genres and the Curriculum?

While this chapter provided an in-depth example of using SRSD instruction to teach informative essay writing using source texts, there are three main genres of focus for secondary students, including argumentative, informative, and narrative writing (National Governors Association and Council of Chief School Officers, 2010). Additionally, secondary students are frequently asked to produce a range of writing (National Governors Association and Council of Chief School Officers, 2010; Ray, Poch, et al., 2023), including complete written worksheets; short answer responses (e.g., quick writes; Mason et al., 2013), or multicomponent writing tasks (e.g., multiparagraph research reports; Ray et al., 2025). Using SRSD instruction, students can learn the versatility of writing strategies and can effectively employ them across genres, disciplines, and lengths of writing assignments (see Figure 4.10 for examples of writing prompts across the content areas).

Argumentative Writing

Within the argumentative genre, students are asked to evaluate multiple perspectives on a given issue, develop their own thoughts on the issue, and develop claims and counterclaims that are supported by valid reasoning and evidence. Quality argumentative essays have a beginning that catches the reader's attention, provide a thesis statement that states the author's claim, provide reasons to support the claim, present relevant evidence, address various perspectives and counterclaims, and conclude with a summary that supports the argument presented. Some examples of strategies taught using SRSD instruction for argumentative writing include HIT SONGS^3 (Ray & Graham, 2021; Ray et al., 2019) and STOP & DARE (Jacobson & Reid, 2010, 2012). The strategy HIT SONGS^3 helps students organize a five- (or more) paragraph essay in a way that includes all key argumentative genre components, with HIT the outline for the introduction paragraph, SONG the outline for the body paragraph (repeated three or more times), and S3 the outline for the conclusion paragraph. The mnemonic HIT SONGS^3 stands for "Hook," "Introduce topic," "Thesis," "State perspective," "Outlook on the perspective," "Need to discuss with examples," "Give your opinion," "Support your thesis," "State relationships," and "Summary." Another strategy for argumentative writing is STOP & DARE, which stands for "Suspend judgment," "Take a side," "Organize ideas," "Plan more as you write," "Develop topic sentence," "Add supporting ideas," "Reject other side," and "End with conclusion."

A strategy for writing short answer argumentative responses is TREE (Mason et al., 2013), which stands for "Topic sentence," "Reasons: three or more," "Explanations," and "Ending sentence." A way to integrate writing in any classroom can be through quick writes, a brief, informal writing activity. Quick writes are often 10-minute timed responses that can be used as a way for students to express their opinions or reactions. Using SRSD to teach a strategy such as TREE for quick writes can help students organize their thoughts about a particular topic in almost any content area.

Informative Writing

Informative writing is another way students are asked to demonstrate their knowledge about a topic. When writing informative texts, students must effectively convey information about complex ideas and topics. The information needs to be accurate and organized in a way that expands readers' knowledge about the topic through presenting significant facts, details, and examples. Further, students need to cite information within their writing from multiple sources. The informative strategy of HIT BOOKS^3 (Ray et al., 2025) taught using the SRSD was detailed earlier within this chapter and helps students organize an essay of five paragraphs or more. Another strategy for informative writing from source texts is TWA+PLANS (Parks-Ennis, 2016), which stands for "Think before reading," "While reading," "After reading," "Pick goals," "List ways to meet goals," "And make Notes," and "Sequence notes."

Quick writes can also be utilized to assess students' prior knowledge or current understanding of a topic through informative writing prompts. The strategy TIDE2 (Benedek-Wood et al., 2014), which stands for "Topic sentence," "Important Details," "Elaborations," and "Ending," can be taught using SRSD to help students organize their thoughts and convey their content knowledge. Once students reach independent performance (SRSD Stage 6) in applying the writing and self-regulation strategies for informative quick writing, generalization can be taught and implemented. A few ways teachers across the content areas can integrate informative quick writes are at the beginning of classes to review content from previous instructional days or assigned readings, at the end of a class period to have students reflect on the content or activities from that day, or to share key ideas learned across a unit of instruction (see Figure 4.10).

Narrative Writing

Writing narratives, whether based on real or imagined experiences, is the third main genre secondary students are expected to master. Narrative writing requires students to present a sequence of events that engages the reader through a plot line. Using SRSD instruction, students can learn to incorporate literary elements such as characters, setting, and conflict, along with narrative techniques such as dialogue, foreshadowing, and imagery, all to convey a vivid picture of the story they are telling. Narrative writing can be incorporated across the content areas (see Figure 4.10) and can be composed over an extended period of time or within a single sitting. Some strategies that can help assist students in crafting their narrative are STACS (Foxworth et al., 2017) ("Setting," "Tension," "Rising action," "Climax," and "Solution") and the strategy C-SPACE (Vander Hart & Power, 2022) ("Characters," "Setting," "Purpose," "Action," "Conclusion," and "Emotions."

Conclusion

Overall, SRSD is effective with a broad range of writers including general education students (Graham et al., 2023), struggling writers and

Genre	Content Area	Writing Prompt
Argumentative	Science—Chemistry	Which of the following two elements would have the most similar reactivities: lithium, oxygen, aluminum, or potassium? Justify your answer using what you know about the arrangement of elements on the periodic table.
	Social Studies—United States History	United States History: Overall, did the civil rights movement make progress during your assigned time period? Support your response with evidence from your assigned documents in your document-based question packet.
	Mathematics—Algebra	Describe which method of solving a system of equations would be easiest to solve the following system of equations: $3x + 2y = 10$ and $y - 4x = 8$. Provide reasons for why you believe this method is the easiest.
	Fine Arts—Music	Write a critical review of a song.
Informative	Science—Physics	Describe the motion of a drag racer from the very beginning of the race to the very end of the race. Be sure to include physics vocabulary learned in the kinematics unit (e.g., acceleration, velocity, etc.).
	Social Studies—World History	Describe environmental factors that played a role in the development of the Mesopotamian civilization.
	Physical Education or Health	Explain the ways participating in different types of sports can benefit teenagers, including how sports can contribute to a teenager's health and happiness.
	Fine Arts—Visual Arts	Identify and describe an art movement of the 20th century.

(continued)

FIGURE 4.10. Examples of writing prompts across the curriculum.

Genre	Content Area	Writing Prompt
Narrative	Science—Biology	Write a narrative that follows the life cycle of a particular animal. Explore aspects of birth, growth, development, reproduction, and death.
	Social Studies—Geography	Imagine you and your friends are going on a road trip across the United States. You begin at the Mississippi River and travel west to the Pacific Ocean. Write a story about your adventure and include the types of geographical features you encounter.
	Language Arts—World Literature	Write a narrative of an episode from the *Odyssey* from a crew member's point of view. Remember that Odysseus loses all his men for one reason or another.
	Foreign Language	Practice writing in the past tense. Write an email to a friend describing your weekend. Be sure to include several events from your weekend.

FIGURE 4.10. *(continued)*

secondary students with disabilities (Ray, 2023), and culturally and linguistically diverse student populations (Ray et al., 2023; Torres & Black, 2018; Torres & Ray, 2022). Teaching students using the SRSD instructional model gives them the tools needed to be successful independent writers. The various genre strategies can be implemented across content areas to enhance both students' writing skills and content-area knowledge.

Numerous resources are available for teachers to support the implementation of SRSD across all three genres (e.g., the books *Building Comprehension in Adolescents: Powerful Strategies for Improving Reading* by Mason et al. [2012] and *Writing in Content Areas and Strategy Instruction for Students with Learning Disabilities* by Harris et al. [2008]). Some online resources include Teaching in the Middle (*www.teachinginthemiddlepd.com*) and Dr. Amber Ray's research webpage (*https://education.illinois.edu/profile/amber-ray*). Further insights on how to lead school-based professional development on SRSD for secondary teachers can be found in Ray and FitzPatrick (2024). Additionally, online professional development is available through sources such as SRSD Online or thinkSRSD.

ACTION STEPS

- Identify the writing genre and corresponding strategy you want to teach.
- Create or access lesson plans from SRSD resources and adapt them to align with your instructional content and context.
- Create or access writing prompts to align with the writing genre and content.
- Implement SRSD instruction with your students to develop and support their writing skills.
- Integrate culturally sustaining pedagogy with your SRSD instruction.
- Reflect on your implementation of SRSD instruction. Consider what went well, areas for improvement, and revisions you would make when implementing the instruction in the future.

REFERENCES

Aceves, T. C., & Orosco, M. J. (2014). *Culturally responsive teaching* (Document No. IC-2). *http://ceedar.education.ufl.edu/tools/innovation-configurations.*

Benedek-Wood, E., Mason, L. H., Wood, P. H., Hoffman, K. E., & McGuire, A. (2014). An experimental examination of quick writing in the middle school science classroom. *Learning Disabilities: A Contemporary Journal, 12*(1), 69–92.

Brown, A. L., Bransford, J. D., Ferrara, R. A., & Campione, J. C. (1983). Learning, remembering, and understanding. In J. H. Flavel & E. M. Markman (Eds.), *Handbook of child psychology: Cognitive development, volume 3* (4th ed., pp. 77–166). Wiley.

Deshler, D. D., & Schumaker, J. B. (1986). Learning strategies: An instructional alternative for low-achieving adolescents. *Exceptional Children, 52*(6), 583–590.

Foxworth, L. L., Mason, L. H., & Hughes, C. A. (2017). Improving narrative writing skills of secondary students with disabilities using strategy instruction. *Exceptionality, 25*(4), 217–234.

Graham, S. (2019). Changing how writing is taught. *Review of Research in Education, 43*(1), 277–303.

Graham, S., & Harris, K. R. (2009). Almost 30 years of writing research: Making sense of it all with *The Wrath of Khan. Learning Disabilities Research & Practice, 24*(2), 58–68.

Graham, S., Harris, K. R., MacArthur, C., & Santangelo, T. (2017). Self-regulation and writing. In D. H. Schunk & J. A. Greene (Eds.), *Handbook of self-regulation of learning and performance* (2nd ed., pp. 138–152). Routledge.

Graham, S., Kim, Y-S., Cao, Y., Lee, W., Tate, T., Collins, P., Cho, M., Moon, Y., Chung, H. Q., & Olson, C. B. (2023). A meta-analysis of writing treatments for students in grades 6–12. *Journal of Educational Psychology, 115*(7), 1004–1027.

Graham, S., Ng, C., Santangelo, T., Aitken, A., Camping, A., & Nusrat, A. (2024). *Can teaching writing enhance students' writing self-efficacy?* [Manuscript submitted for publication].

Harris, K. R., & Graham, S. (1996). *Making the writing process work: Strategies for composition and self-regulation.* Brookline Books.

Harris, K. R., & Graham, S. (2018). Self-regulated strategy development: Theoretical bases, critical instructional elements, and future research. In M. Braaksma, K. R. Harris, & R. Fidalgo (Eds.), *Studies in writing; Vol. 34. Design principles for teaching effective writing: Theoretical and empirical grounded principles* (pp. 119–151). Brill Academic.

Harris, K. R., Graham, S., Mason, L. H., & Friedlander, B. (2008). *Powerful writing strategies for all students.* Brooks.

Jacobson, L. T., & Reid, R. (2010). Improving the persuasive essay writing of high school students with ADHD. *Exceptional Children, 76*(2), 157–174.

Jacobson, L. T., & Reid, R. (2012). Improving the writing performance of high school students with attention deficit/hyperactivity disorder and writing difficulties. *Exceptionality, 20*(4), 218–234.

Mason, L. H., Kubina, R., & Hoover, T. (2013). Effects of quick writing instruction for high school students with emotional disturbances. *Journal of Emotional and Behavioral Disorders, 21*(3), 163–175.

Mason, L. H., Reid, R., & Hagaman, J. L. (2012). *Building comprehension in adolescents: Powerful strategies for improving reading and writing in content areas.* Brooks.

National Governors Association and Council of Chief School Officers. (2010). *Common Core State Standards. www.corestandards.org*

Parks-Ennis, R. (2016). Using self-regulated strategy development to help high school students with EBD summarize informational text in social studies. *Education and Treatment of Children, 39*(4), 545–568.

Ray, A. B. (2023). Writing interventions using SRSD for secondary students with and at-risk for learning disabilities: A review of empirical research. In X. Liu, M. Hebert, & R. Alves (Eds.), *The hitchhiker's guide to writing research: A Festschrift for Steve Graham* (pp. 233–252). Springer.

Ray, A. B., Connor, K. E., Brenner, H., & Kim, C. (2025). Effect of an SRSD informative writing intervention for high schoolers with learning disabilities. *Learning Disabilities Quarterly, 48*(3).

Ray, A. B., & FitzPatrick, E. (2024). Practice-based professional development for self-regulated strategy development writing instruction with secondary teachers. *Teaching Exceptional Children, 56*(5), 356–368.

Ray, A. B., & Graham, S. (2021). A college entrance essay exam intervention for students with high-incidence disabilities and struggling writers. *Learning Disability Quarterly, 44*(4), 275–287.

Ray, A. B., Graham, S., & Liu, X. (2019). Effects of college entrance essay exam instruction for high school students with disabilities or at-risk for writing difficulties. *Reading and Writing: An Interdisciplinary Journal, 32*(6), 1507–1529.

Ray, A. B., Poch, A., & Datchuk, S. (2023). Secondary educators' writing practices for students with disabilities: Examining distance learning and in-person instruction. *Journal of Special Education Technology, 38*(4), 472–487.

Ray, A. B., Torres, C., & Cao, Y. (2023). Improving informative writing in inclusive and linguistically-diverse elementary classes through self-regulated strategy development. *Exceptionality, 31*(5), 319–343.

Reid, R., Lienemann, T. O., & Hagaman, J. L. (2013). *Strategy instruction for students with learning disabilities.* Guilford Press.

Torres, C., & Black, R. S. (2018). Culturally responsive self-regulated strategy development in writing for college students with disabilities. *Multiple Voices for Ethnically Diverse Exceptional Learners, 18*(1), 42–59.

Torres, C., & Ray, A. B. (2022). Supporting English learners with disabilities in writing through self-regulated strategy development. *International Journal of TESOL Studies, 4*(4), 79–105.

Troia, G. A., Graham, S., & Harris, K. R. (2017). Writing and students with language and learning disabilities. In J. M. Kauffman, D. P. Hallahan, & P. Cullen Pullen (Eds.), *Handbook of special education* (2nd ed., pp. 537–557). Routledge.

Vander Hart, N., & Power, M. (2022). Teaching writing strategies with tiered supports for middle school students with and without special needs: A case study. *Preventing School Failure: Alternative Education for Children and Youth, 66*(2), 167–174.

Washburn, E., Sielaff, C., & Golden, K. (2016). The use of a cognitive strategy to support argument-based writing in a ninth-grade social studies classroom. *Literacy Research and Instruction, 55*(4), 353–374.

Zimmerman, B. J., & Labuhn, A. S. (2012). Self-regulation of learning: Process approaches to personal development. In K. R. Harris, S. Graham, T. Urdan, C. B. McCormick, G. M. Sinatra, & J. Sweller (Eds.), *APA educational psychology handbook, Vol. 1. Theories, constructs, and critical issues* (pp. 399–425). American Psychological Association.

Chapter 5

Writing Like an Expert

GRAMMAR AS A RESOURCE FOR TEACHING WRITING IN THE DISCIPLINES

Debra Myhill

Without a doubt, the expectations of learning in middle and high school are that students become increasingly competent and confident in communicating their disciplinary understandings in the written forms typical of the discipline. Fundamentally, this requires a happy symbiosis of *disciplinary content learning*—the concepts, ideas, and facts at the heart of the discipline—and the *communication of that learning in written form*. As Carter et al. (2007) explain, "Students do not learn to write the discourses of the disciplines simply to master those discourses; rather, they write to learn, in addition to the subject matter of the discipline, the ways of knowing and doing that define the discipline" (p. 280). In other words, disciplinary writing involves both learning about the disciplinary content and learning about the way knowledge is expressed in that discipline.

Recognizing the importance of mastering writing in different disciplines is not new (Hyland, 2009; Bazerman et al., 2017), but research has tended to focus more heavily on writing expectations and learners' needs in higher education or university courses. Indeed, sometimes the writing in different disciplines is referred to as a "professional genre," reflecting a concern with how a lawyer might need to write professionally, compared with, for example, a scientist or a geologist. The locus of attention of this book and this chapter, however, is fundamentally concerned with the effective teaching of disciplinary writing in middle and high schools, and how best we can support *all* learners in understanding the thinking and writing integral to each discipline. Because research in this area uses a bewildering array of terms to describe this kind of writing—disciplinary discourses, academic genres, professional genres, writing in the disciplines, academic writing, to name but a few—I will refer principally to the idea of "writing like an expert" throughout this chapter, sometimes substituting "expert" with a specific discipline, such as "writing like a scientist." This choice is deliberate because it makes visible that students are being inducted into the particular approach that experts in that subject community use to express their disciplinary understanding. Moreover, the idea of "writing like an expert" is a reminder that students are gaining access to disciplinary communities of writers and establishing a relationship with readers who share understanding of that discipline.

However, we know from research that learning to write like an expert is challenging for many learners, especially making the transition from the broader and more generalized ways of writing experienced in elementary school to the different expectations of subject teachers in middle and high school. Martin (2013) observed the change in language practices as students progressed through school, with "subject-based teaching and learning involving highly specialised discourse of various kinds" (p. 23). The Education Endowment Foundation (EEF, 2021) maintains that the academic challenges that students face on transition are "underestimated," noting that students have to adjust "to being taught by a range of teachers' and to 'using a range of new types of texts, which are often dense and more technical than those encountered in primary school" (EEF, 2021, p. 6). More recently, a major corpus study by Deignan et al. (2023) has looked specifically at the linguistic transition students are expected to make as they progress through middle and high school education. They contrast the academic language students experience and are expected to use in school with the more everyday language they encounter at home and in social situations.

A critical point about this linguistic transition from everyday writing to writing like an expert is that students from different linguistic and cultural backgrounds are not equally positioned to bridge this linguistic transition because their experiences of using language at home are very different from the expectations of school. Schleppegrell (2001) noted that these discontinuities particularly affect multilingual and multidialectal students and argues that for these students "the linguistic demands of schooling pose challenges that are not being effectively addressed in many classrooms" (p. 455). In Australia, there has been an ongoing concern about how some students are disadvantaged by the expectations of school writing in middle and high school. Martin maintained that this is "an issue of social justice" (2009, p. 11), arguing that unless the language expectations of writing in different disciplinary subjects are made clear and visible, then "only students from the right background are positioned to learn by osmosis what has to be learned but is never made explicit" (2013, p. 34).

I would challenge Martin's use of the term "right" background because every student's home background is valuable and legitimate, but the key point that Martin makes is, nonetheless, crucially important: Unless we show students how to write like an expert, we risk excluding some learners from access to these disciplinary discourses. Deignan et al. (2023) conclude their corpus study of writing across the elementary–high school transition by noting that language challenges are greater for students from less educated, literate family backgrounds, with the consequence that they "are disproportionately disadvantaged by the ways that academic language is used in teaching" (p. 204). If we aim to adopt culturally inclusive pedagogies, then these researchers are making a powerful statement about the need to bridge the linguistic transition between everyday writing and writing like an expert for *all* students from *all* cultural, social, and linguistic backgrounds.

A further challenge for writing instruction in the disciplines is that students' reading experiences may not adequately prepare them for the kind of writing expected in each discipline. Students' earlier reading experiences of science, history, or geography, for example, tend to be in books written specifically for children and those in which authors do not use the relevant disciplinary discourse. In most cases, authors of nonfiction books for children prioritize the mediation of disciplinary content in ways that make it accessible to young readers: although subject-specific vocabulary is frequently used, the writing style does not align with the writing like an expert expected in middle and high school. Many science books for primary children have a high integration of verbal and visual material, nonlinear layouts, everyday language, and direct address to the readership. Consider, for example, the prizewinning nonfiction book, *Nano—The Spectacular Science of the Very (Very) Small*, written for primary school children by physicist Jess Wade (2022). The book begins:

> Something **light** or something **heavy**,
> Something **strong** or something **bendy**,
> Something **smooth** or something **rough** . . . each of
> These "somethings" is perfect for a different job.
> And scientists call them **materials.**

Here, the writing is in accessible language for young children and uses adjectives familiar to them from their everyday experiences. The repetition of "something" supports the sense of listing characteristics of materials, and the nonstandard or poetic use of the plural noun "somethings" introduces the reader to the idea of "things" before explaining that scientists use the term "materials" for these things. This is a very effective and crafted introduction to *materials*, a conceptual building block for understanding nanotechnology, which the rest of the book addresses. But it is not "writing like a scientist" that would be more likely to define *materials* at the start, avoid the vagueness of "something" (and its repetition), and sound less like a conversation with the reader. Similarly, you might consider the "America's Funny but True History" series by Elizabeth Levy, presenting historical information through humor and everyday language.

Many of these books about history, geography, science, or other subjects are superbly written and illustrated, and they play an important role in mediating complex concepts and ideas to young children. Their focus is on the disciplinary content, and the writing style is adapted to meet the needs of this young group of learners. But in contrast, the disciplinary writing in middle and high school draws on adult genres that may be unfamiliar from students' own reading and represent a specific community of writers. The implications for classroom practice of creating communities of writers who are increasingly accomplished at writing like an expert are well summarized by Bazerman et al. (2017). They maintain that teachers need "to be prepared to engage students in the genres of their disciplines, to assess the spectrum of their students' abilities, and to tailor instruction to meet their students' needs' and that doing so requires 'for specialized linguistic knowledge, as well as pedagogical knowledge, for apprenticing students into new discursive practices' " (p. 358). This linguistic knowledge draws on grammar, which is concerned with "how sentences and utterances are formed" (Carter & McCarthy, 2006, p. 2) at word, phrase, and clause level. However, grammar is not only about sentences but also about text—how text is sequenced and organized, and how ideas are connected through the text (Halliday & Matthiessen, 2004, p. 31).

In this chapter, I set out to shine a spotlight on how this grammatical understanding can support writing like an expert and to explore practical pedagogical strategies that enable student understanding of the writing demands of different subjects encountered in middle and high school. Underpinning this throughout is the recognition that this is an issue of social justice and central to a culturally inclusive writing classroom. The chapter will be informed by the following guiding questions:

GUIDING QUESTIONS

1. Why does grammar matter when teaching disciplinary writing?
2. How can attention to language choices be meaningfully addressed within your subject area?
3. What does it mean to think like an expert about vocabulary choices in disciplinary texts?
4. How does understanding of syntax and sentence shaping in disciplinary texts support writing like an expert?
5. What do teachers need to consider when using grammar as a resource for teaching disciplinary writing?

Why Grammar Matters When Teaching Disciplinary Writing

The linguistic implications of writing like an expert have frequently been expressed in terms of teaching students how to use "academic language," in contrast to the language they ordinarily use in everyday situations (see, e.g., research by Chamot & Malley, 1994; Deignan et al., 2023; Pilgreen, 2006; Snow & Uccelli, 2009—all of whom foreground the concept of academic language). But despite the widespread use of the term, there is relatively little agreement about what it means. Indeed, Snow and Uccelli (2009) point to the multiplicity of ways that academic language is defined: for example, as the language of education, the language of school, language of advanced literacy, scientific language, or academic English (p. 112). Approaching this issue of academic language specifically from the perspective of second or additional language learners, Cummins (1979, 2008) proposed a distinction between Basic Interpersonal Communicative Skills (BICS) and Cognitive Academic Language Proficiency (CALP). BICS refers to *conversational fluency* (Cummins, 2008, p. 71) using language in everyday, social interactions; and CALP refers to "students' ability to understand and express, in both oral and written modes, concepts and ideas that are relevant to success in school" (Cummins, 2008, p. 71). The recognition that there is a variety of language used in school that may be challenging to access—and that there is a distinction between conversational fluency and competence in school writing—is helpful in identifying the problem. Snow and Uccelli (2009), however, remind us that this is not simply a problem for second-language learners and argue that "academic language is intrinsically more difficult than other language registers and that thinking about the educational experiences that promote its development is a crucial task for educators of all students" (p. 114).

Nevertheless, the term "academic language" is not entirely helpful in the context of the classroom, partly because it is not always clear what it means, and partly because research shows learners can misunderstand what it means (Deignan et al., 2023; Meston et al., 2020). (I will discuss this in more detail later in this chapter when I look at vocabulary.) In terms of writing like an expert, considering academic language is fundamentally concerned with the grammar of disciplinary discourses.

For many teachers, grammar is principally corrective, addressing the grammatical errors and mistakes that students may make in their writing. This, of course, has a valid place in the teaching of writing: direct teaching of specific grammar points can meet the linguistic needs of underserved multilingual learners of English, and for all learners there are times when linguistic accuracy and terminology may be prioritized in some instructional contexts. However, restricting grammar to a matter of accuracy hugely underestimates the power of grammar to make visible how texts are constructed and how meanings are made: in other words, to be precise about the characteristics of academic language. This is a view of grammar that emphasizes the *language choices* writers make in different disciplinary communities. It draws heavily on the work of Halliday, who saw grammar as "a *system of meaning potential*" (1978, p. 39), and as "*a resource for making meaning*" (Halliday & Matthiessen, 2004, p. 3). As a systematic functional linguist, Halliday was centrally interested in the relationship between form and function and explored how grammatical choices and their meanings are shaped by the purposes and contexts of writing. The importance of such language choices can be seen clearly if we compare Jess Wade's writing for young children about nanotechnology (Wade, 2022) with a similar explanation of nanotechnology written for adults by the National Institute for Occupational Safety and Health (NIOSH, 2023; see Table 5.1).

Here you can see that Wade makes grammatical choices that are designed to ensure both accessibility and engagement of her young readership. She uses the informal contraction, *it's*, and informal expressions such as *it's taken years, it's just . . .* , and *it's been worth it* to establish a closer, more direct relationship with her readers. The use of an exclamation mark and capitalization of "AMAZING!" mirrors contemporary writing habits, particularly on social media. Her explanations are very much in a conversational style and use vocabulary that her readers are likely to understand (e.g., *tiny, small, amazing*), and the use of the verbs *have* and *be* is dominant. In contrast, the NIOSH description is more detailed and more precise: There are long noun phrases, concisely packaging explanatory detail (*the manipulation of matter on a near-atomic scale to produce new structures, materials, and devices; the heart of*

TABLE 5.1. Explanations of Nanotechnology Written for Children (Left) and Adults (Right)

Graphene is a NANOMATERIAL—and it's just one atom thick. "Nano" is the word scientists use for anything this tiny. Because atoms are so very small, scientists have to build new machines to study them and to move them around. And even so, it's taken years—and lots of failed experiments—to make materials like graphene. But it's been worth it because some nanomaterials are AMAZING! From *Nanotechnology* by Jess Wade (2022).	Nanotechnology is the manipulation of matter on a near-atomic scale to produce new structures, materials, and devices. The technology promises scientific advancement in many sectors such as medicine, consumer products, energy, materials, and manufacturing. Nanotechnology refers to engineered structures, devices, and systems. Nanomaterials have a length scale between 1 and 100 nanometers. At this size, materials begin to exhibit unique properties that affect physical, chemical, and biological behavior. Researching, developing, and utilizing these properties is at the heart of new technology. From *Nanotechnology* by the National Institute for Occupational Safety and Health (2023).

From Wade, J. (2022). *Nano—The spectacular science of the very (very) small.* Walker Books; National Institute for Occupational Safety and Health. (2023). *Nanotechnology. https://www.cdc.gov/niosh/nano/about/index.html*

new technology). Detail is also provided through listing (*engineered structures, devices, and systems; physical, chemical, and biological behavior*). There is precision regarding the size of nanomaterials, rather than Wade's *tiny* and *very small*, and Wade's comment that "*some nanomaterials are AMAZING*" is explained as exhibiting "*unique properties.*" The scientific concept is often foregrounded in subject position, and the verbs are more varied. Overall, the relationship with the reader is more detached than close.

This brief analysis of some of the grammatical choices in these two texts is not an evaluation of the quality of these two texts but intended to demonstrate how scientific content is communicated differently through grammatical choices. The two texts show the critical interrelationship between disciplinary content and how it is expressed. Jess Wade is not trying to write like a scientist; rather, she is a scientist writing for a younger audience. The NIOSH explanation is very much writing like a scientist, reflecting its more informed adult audience. It is worth noting, however, that Jess Wade is not a "deficient" writer because of her more conversational style: indeed, she is an expert writer who has successfully crafted her text to present some of the most abstract ideas in science to a young audience. Teaching students about the grammatical choices that support writing like an expert is crucially concerned with learning how to make choices that align with the expectations of the readership and that this is "not in order to impress or confuse others, but because it has to do different things" (Deignan et al., 2023, p. 30).

Grammar is important, therefore, in allowing teachers to be explicit about the ways in which writing in different disciplines is constructed and thus in enabling students "to be aware of the effects of different choices" (Lefstein, 2009, p. 382) in their own writing. This means that teaching needs to be strongly oriented toward developing understanding of the relationship between a particular grammatical choice and its intended effect in writing, so that students are learning *why* choices are made and not simply *what* choices are present. Making decisions and making language choices is part of understanding the craft of writing, and we need to help writers understand how the language choices they make are not arbitrary or about correctness and "putting things in" but central to how they communicate their ideas. Specifically, given the focus of this book, we need to develop students' understanding of the *different* language choices that characterize writing in different disciplines, and the reasons for those choices: just as we have looked at the different ways nanotechnology is communicated to two different audiences. This kind of thinking about language choice is *metalinguistic understanding,* the capacity to reflect on and think about language (Gombert, 1992, p. 13). The primary focus for developing metalinguistic understanding about writing is fostering understanding of how language works in written texts, not merely the naming and identification of grammar or other aspects of language. Our interest is in ***why*** a writer might choose, for example, to use the present tense in a science text, rather than simply identifying it as present tense. Creating opportunities for learners to talk about, investigate, and reflect on language use in the disciplinary texts they read and the choices they make in their own disciplinary writing builds metalinguistic understanding. This supports growing independence as a writer: making authorial decisions that are informed by an understanding of how to write like an expert. Our role as teachers is to "*teach the student how to think, as well as write*" (Kellogg, 1994, p. 213).

The LEAD Principles: Addressing Language Choices Meaningfully in Your Subject

For over 15 years, the writing research team at the University of Exeter has been investigating the teaching of writing, a major strand of which has been exploring the role of grammar in writing instruction. At the heart of our approach has been a reorientation of traditional ideas about grammar to more contemporary views that articulate more powerfully what grammatical (or metalinguistic) understanding can accomplish in how writing is taught. We have drawn on the theories of Halliday, who saw grammar as "a network of inter-related meaningful choices" (Halliday & Matthiessen, 2004, p. 49), shaped by purpose and context. We emphasize the concept of grammatical choice very deliberately to foreground the purpose of the text and the context in which it is written, not just the form of the text. This relationship between choice and meaning has long been recognized by modern linguists. Biber et al. noted that in both speech and writing "we are faced with a myriad of choices: not only choices in what we say but in how we say it" (1999, p. 4); Crystal (2004), too, argued that writing "is always a matter of choice" (p. 13); and Carter and McCarthy (2006) distinguished between grammar as a system and grammar as choice, emphasizing that "every choice carries a different meaning, and grammar is concerned with the implications of such choices" (p. 6). An important aspect of this idea of grammar as choice is that it is a potent reminder of authorship—there are writers behind the construction of texts, and these writers make decisions about their texts based on what they want to achieve. Our approach shifts attention from grammar as the study of parts of speech and sentences to what grammar can do. Our goal is to redirect pedagogical attention from grammatical form (*what* it is) to function (*how* it is working in the text), and to enable students to make informed decisions about the composition of their texts, leading to greater agency, autonomy, and authorial intentionality as they progress through middle and high school.

Historically, however, there has been little evidence that teaching grammar has any beneficial impact on student writing. Much of this research investigated traditional grammar teaching, involving the naming and identification of grammatical forms and an emphasis on grammatical accuracy, rather than making connections for learners between grammatical choice and its meaning-making purpose in a text. More recently, a meta-analysis by Graham et al. (2023) adopted a more rigorous approach and excluded studies where grammar was simply a measure in a control condition. This, combined with the inclusion of more recent studies, including our own, found an effect size of 0.47 for grammar instruction on writing quality. Our research has demonstrated that showing writers how the grammatical choices they make are central to how meaning is communicated can be effective in improving students' writing outcomes, including for students with low initial writing attainment (Myhill et al., 2012, 2018; Jones et al., 2013). It has also signaled the importance of teachers' grammatical subject knowledge (Myhill et al., 2013) and their management of metalinguistic discussion (Myhill &

Newman, 2016; Newman & Watson, 2020) in ensuring the effectiveness of this approach. We have worked collaboratively with teachers, drawing on our research findings to develop a set of teaching principles that support the practical implementation of this approach in the classroom. These principles have evolved and refined over the years; we now call them the LEAD principles, an acronym drawing on the initial letter of each principle, signaling that they are designed to *lead* professional practice. The LEAD principles are intended as a temporary scaffold for teachers to help become familiar with this way of teaching writing: they are not intended as a rigid framework or model. As with all new strategies or classroom practices, it takes both time to master and opportunities to practice and reflect.

Link

The first principle addresses the need to make a learning link between the grammar structure being introduced and how it works in the writing being taught. This establishes a meaningful reason for addressing grammar and connects grammar with meaning, purpose, and rhetorical effect. For example, in a science lesson, you might draw attention to the way the *present tense* is used to express universal truths about the science, whereas the *past tense* is used to report how an experiment was conducted.

Examples

The second principle foregrounds the importance of showing students examples of the grammatical structure, as well as naming it. This is, firstly, to avoid a subject lesson being deflected into a grammar identification lesson with lengthy grammatical explanations, which shifts the focus back to the naming of parts rather than grammar as choice. Secondly, it allows students to access the grammatical structure through seeing it, even if the grammatical concept itself is not fully understood. In classroom practice, showing student examples can be achieved using color, or font styles; card sorts which invite them to manipulate the target examples; or the use of software such as PowerPoint.

Authentic Text

The third principle emphasizes the use of authentic disciplinary texts as models for exploration and discussion. This reminds us that writing like an expert is about becoming part of a broader community of writers in that discipline: using texts that members of this community have written offers genuine models of disciplinary writing and purposeful opportunities for investigating the language choices made by published disciplinary experts. Another benefit of using authentic texts is that it makes visible the integration of reading and writing and supports reading comprehension of disciplinary texts as well as writing. All the examples used in this chapter are authentic disciplinary texts, and the sources have been acknowledged.

Discussion

The fourth principle signals the need to build dialogic metalinguistic discussion into any lesson about a grammatical structure and its effects in a disciplinary text. It is possible that this may be the most critical principle of all because it prioritizes the learner and their metalinguistic understanding of the learning point being addressed. As our research has developed, this principle has evolved from "Talk" to "Dialogic talk" to "Dialogic Metalinguistic talk" because classroom observation revealed that classroom talk could be very teacher centered, inviting limited answers and very little student thinking. In contrast, it was evident that where teachers opened up discussion and asked students to explain and justify their responses, student learning about grammatical choice was more effective. The aim of discussion is to promote deep metalinguistic learning about why a particular choice works and to develop independence as a writer. This involves asking initiating questions that open discussion, such as *Why do you think the writer chose to use present*

TABLE 5.2. LEAD Principles in Practice

Learning context	A grade 10 geography class is studying plate tectonics and has had an initial introductory lesson, investigating what existing understanding they have about the formation of mountain ranges, ocean trenches, earthquakes, and volcanoes. In the lesson described here, the focus is on introducing and developing understanding of tectonic plates. The teacher is using the *National Geographic* resources on plate tectonics, designed for grades 9–12.
Link	How *repetition* of a key word (*plate*), in a variety of noun phrases, can create cohesion and connectivity across an explanation and how the *substitution* of precise, subject-specific words for an everyday word (*layer*) increases the detail and specificity of an explanation.
Authentic text	*National Geographic* article "Plate Tectonics" (n.d.)

tense in the first sentence, but shifts to past tense in the second? But critically important are the follow-through questions that respond to what students have said and invite further thinking: for example, *Can you explain that a little more?* or *Can you be more specific about why this choice was made?*

Table 5.2 shows how the LEAD principles might be implemented in classroom practice.

- Having watched and discussed together the *National Geographic* video on plate tectonics, the class read the *National Geographic* (n.d.) article (five paragraphs). The teacher uses this to teach key concepts in plate tectonics (such as *tectonic plates, the mantle layers, subduction, seafloor spreading*).
- Reading only the first two paragraphs (which follow) and working in pairs, the students (1) underline in red all the noun phrases that include the word *plate/s* and (2) underline in green every occurrence of the word *layer* and any words that are more scientific or specific terms for *layer.*

> Plate tectonics is a scientific theory that explains how major landforms are created as a result of Earth's subterranean movements. The theory, which solidified in the 1960s, transformed the earth sciences by explaining many phenomena, including mountain building events, volcanoes, and earthquakes.
>
> In plate tectonics, Earth's outermost layer, or lithosphere—made up of the crust and upper mantle—is broken into large rocky plates. These plates lie on top of a partially molten layer of rock called the asthenosphere. Due to the convection of the asthenosphere and lithosphere, the plates move relative to each other at different rates, from two to 15 centimeters (one to six inches) per year. This interaction of tectonic plates is responsible for many different geological formations such as the Himalaya mountain range in Asia, the East African Rift, and the San Andreas Fault in California, United States.

- The teacher displays the text on a whiteboard [**Examples**] with the noun phrases including "plate" underlined in red, and the occurrence of "layer" and the semantic field of words that relate to the earth's layers in plate tectonics (*lithosphere, asthenosphere, crust, upper mantle, plates*) in green. The teacher then leads a dialogic metalinguistic **Discussion** exploring why the writer chose to repeat noun phrases with "plate," but to substitute the noun "layer" with other words for "layer" or "layers" in the earth's structure.

• In pairs, the students then reread paragraph 4 of the article and write collaboratively an explanation (no more than 150 words) of how tectonic plates form undersea mountain ranges and ocean trenches. This explanation can draw not only on the article but also on information from the video at the start of the lesson. As they write, they should discuss how the key concept of "plate tectonics" might be repeated in varied noun phrases to create cohesion in the explanation and whether any everyday words might be substituted by more precise words or phrases relating to plate tectonics.

• The lesson ends with two or three of the explanations being shared, and formative teacher questioning of the class about the formation of mountain ranges and ocean trenches to check their understanding. Finally, one or two students are asked to explain the language choices they made regarding repetition or substitution of nouns or noun phrases.

Thinking Like an Expert about Vocabulary Choices in Disciplinary Texts

In the past three decades, a significant emphasis on the importance of teaching vocabulary has emerged in many Anglophone countries, prompted by the oft-cited Hart and Risley (1992) study and their claim of a 30-million-word gap between children from low and high socioeconomic backgrounds. But this study has received serious critique, particularly with regard to its small sample size, data collection methods, and the generalized assumptions they draw from this data (see, e.g., Baugh, 2017; Johnson, 2015; Kuchirko, 2019; Sperry et al., 2018). Others have argued that the broader social disadvantages experienced by students from low socioeconomic backgrounds are far more significant than their vocabulary size (Darling-Hammond, 1995; Green, 2011), and Adair et al. (2017) have signaled the negative impact this could have on teachers' assumptions about the students they teach. And while Hart and Risley focused on the vocabulary difference between high and low socioeconomic groups, other researchers—notably Flores and Rosa (2015), Flores (2020), and Cushing (2022, 2024)—have pointed to the raciolinguistic ideologies that underpin the notion of a word gap. Cushing (2022) argues that "low-income and racialized speakers' language practices are perceived as deficient, incomplete, and indeed, full of gaps when compared against the language practices of the idealized white middle-classes" (p. 306). These are deficit discourses, which as Kuchirko (2019) points out, have "profound consequences for children's lived experiences" (p. 553).

So what does this academic debate mean for writing instruction? No one would argue that vocabulary is *not* important for both reading comprehension and writing, but it is not helpful to generalize about particular social groups. It is also worth noting that a student's vocabulary might be highly effective in one field and less successful in another. A friend's daughter, who is not an enthusiastic reader or writer (despite my best efforts!) was, as a 9-year-old, passionately interested in snakes and talked confidently to me about the difference between venomous and poisonous creatures; explained rear fangs, toxins, and toxic saliva; and taught me the word *brumation*. And she learned this vocabulary through watching YouTube videos made by a teenage reptile enthusiast. This variability in vocabulary appropriate for particular writing tasks is highly significant for writing in the disciplines because the content-based vocabulary required for a given writing task is often highly specific to the topic. So what is crucial is to be sharply attentive to the vocabulary needs of the students you teach for a specific writing task and to recognize that the vocabulary demand of a writing task is not simply about "words" but about the grammatical function of those words in the text.

Many teachers are already familiar with Beck et al. (2013) and three vocabulary tiers: Tier One (familiar everyday words), Tier Two (high-utility words useful in academic/school writing), and Tier Three (discipline-specific specialized words). In practice, teachers in different disciplines do tend to teach the Tier Three specialist words, not least because they are often the precise focus of content being taught. These are very often nouns, as the following example list indicates:

- Geography: *erosion, earthquakes, tundra, equator, latitude*
- History: *conflict, reign, revolution, monarchy, chronology*
- Science: *molecule, acid, mitochondria, cell, anatomy*
- Language arts: *metaphor, personification, rebuttal, haiku*

However, from a grammatical perspective, it is helpful to extend the emphasis from single-word nouns to noun phrases, which are frequently used to communicate ideas and concepts in the subject. These noun phrases are collocations, words that have a high frequency of usage together—such as *global warming, industrial revolution, terminal moraine, fractional distillation, economic migrant*, and *pathetic fallacy*—and represent typical language choices for disciplinary communication. You might glance back to the *National Geographic* explanation, used earlier, which uses several collocations relevant to the topic: *plate tectonics, earth sciences, geological formations, mountain building events*, and *mountain range*.

You can also support writing like an expert by giving explicit attention to verbs: if nouns represent the concepts and ideas of a topic, then verbs represent the processes, reporting, and thinking typical of the discipline. Some of these verbs are discipline-specific (*cultivate, overthrow, condense, interpret*), but many are more general verbs that may not be part of a student's linguistic repertoire but are crucial to disciplinary writing. These words would be Tier Two vocabulary in Beck et al.'s model and often receive less explicit attention in disciplinary teaching (Snow & Uccelli, 2009, p. 215). In the language arts, for example, when students are writing critical pieces about texts they have studied, they are often more confident about what they want to say about the text and its interpretation but less confident in how to say it. They may know the discipline-specific nouns of literary terms but need greater support in using verbs that help them communicate their thinking, as follows:

- Verbs for suggesting: *implies, infers, intimates, hints*
- Verbs for describing: *evokes, portrays, depicts, displays, foreshadows*
- Verbs for telling: *explains, presents, shows, reveals, illustrates, conveys*
- Verbs for argument: *argues, challenges, contests, rejects, rebuts, affirms, subverts*
- Verbs for structure: *begins, builds, establishes, develops, extends, concludes*

Another key element of vocabulary in disciplinary contexts is that words are often polysemous, where familiar, everyday words take on different, disciplinary meanings. As a novice secondary (high school) English teacher, I well remember setting a writing assignment following the study of *Macbeth*, where I asked students to consider who was responsible for Duncan's death and asked them to "*illustrate their answer with close reference to the text*." I was very surprised when at least half the class submitted assignments with multiple illustrations, until I realized that my disciplinary-specific use of the verb *illustrate* was not the same as their everyday understanding. Deignan et al. (2023) identified this as a major issue for middle and high school students tackling disciplinary writing because they naturally drew on their understanding of the everyday word. They emphasize that the meaning of a polysemous word is "*context-dependent*" (p. 202) with the implication that we need to be explicit in drawing students' attention to the disciplinary meaning. This

TABLE 5.3. LEAD in Support of Art Expert Vocabulary

Learning context	A grade 8 art class is studying the work of van Gogh. In previous lessons, they have learned a little about his biography and have looked at a range of his paintings. This included a detailed exploration of *Starry Night*, where the class discussed their responses to the painting and what they thought van Gogh was trying to depict. In this teaching episode, the teacher wants to build on this initial understanding of van Gogh's life and works by exploring his artistic technique and developing understanding of the vocabulary used to describe it.
Link	How art-specific noun phrases and verbs are needed to describe the style of van Gogh like an art expert.
Authentic text	The article "Vincent van Gogh Style and Technique" by Artble (2024)

is also a reminder of the importance of context for vocabulary learning: Word banks or word lists are rarely supportive of appropriate vocabulary learning because the subtleties of context are absent. McKeown (2019), discussing this issue of polysemy and learning in context, also points to the fact that the meaning of a word, or a collocation, is learned incrementally through multiple encounters with the word in context.

The teaching example in Table 5.3 outlines how the LEAD principles might be used to support learning of vocabulary for writing like an expert in art. Table 5.4 outlines some of the subject-specific vocabulary found in this chapter.

TABLE 5.4. An Example of Disciplinary Writing Vocabulary

Verbs describing art processes	expressed; copying; drawing; depicting; sketch; capture; experimenting; apply; imitate
Nouns/noun phrases referring to materials	pencil; black chalk; red chalk; blue chalk; reed pen; charcoal; medium; material
Nouns/noun phrases referring to art techniques	impasto; bold, dramatic brush strokes; drawing technique; depiction of figures, light, and landscape; broken brush strokes; pointillist technique; heavier brush strokes; perspective; form; movement
Nouns/noun phrases referring to color	bold palette; bold, vibrant colors; shades; dark and melancholy colors; a lighter palette of reds, yellows, oranges, greens, and blues; contrasting dots of pure color; dark outlines; thick color; complementary color contrasts

• The teacher asks the class to describe in their own words how van Gogh has painted *Starry Night*, and they share descriptions [**Discussion**]. The teacher explains that she or he wants the class to be able to write like art experts about this painting by using the words and phrases that art experts use.

• In groups of three, students are given a section of the "Vincent van Gogh Style and Technique" article (Artble, 2024) to read—Early Years, Middle Years, or Advanced Years—and the teacher explains that this is writing like an art expert. They are given a table to collate vocabulary in their section that relates to verbs describing art processes; nouns and noun phrases that refer to art materials; art techniques; and to color [**Examples**].

• As a class, on an interactive whiteboard, they collate the verbs and noun phrases from each group to create a master copy (see Table 5.4 for an example). The teacher points out the collocation, *brush strokes*, and checks understanding of *impasto* and *palette*, all key words for describing van Gogh's technique. The teacher draws attention to the verb *capture* in its context in the text (*He deliberately used colors to capture mood*) and invites students to explain what *capture* means in an art (rather than everyday) context.

• The class considers whether any of the vocabulary on the table might be helpful in describing van Gogh's technique in *Starry Night*. The teacher then asks the students whether any of the nouns or noun phrases referring to color are appropriate for *Starry Night* and encourages them to adapt or create noun phrases that express the use of color aptly (e.g., *contrasting dark blues and bright yellows* or *a vibrant palette of light and dark colors)* [**Discussion**].

• The teacher adds to the table some specific vocabulary that is particularly useful to describe the technique in *Starry Night*, perhaps *vertical lines, swirls, spirals*.

• Individually, each student writes one paragraph explaining van Gogh's technique in *Starry Night*, using the table and the discussion as support for writing like an art expert.

As noted earlier, at the heart of using grammar as a resource for teaching about disciplinary writing is developing metalinguistic understanding about language choices. However, research suggests that students do not always understand that vocabulary choices relate to effective communication in a discipline; instead, they attribute social value to vocabulary, seeing word choice as concerned with good, better, or posher words (Deignan et al., 2023; Meston et al., 2020; Galloway et al., 2015). Simply treating disciplinary vocabulary as words that need to be learned is not enough—students need experience of "manipulating ideas around words in order to extend and deepen knowledge of the word, its uses, and its connections to other words and situations" (McKeown, 2019, p. 471) to develop metalinguistic understanding. If you look back at the earlier van Gogh classroom example, students are given opportunities to manipulate words and phrases both in the table task and the later task of generating words and phrases to describe color in *Starry Night*, alongside metalinguistic discussion.

Understanding Syntax and Sentence Shaping in Disciplinary Texts

While vocabulary, especially specialized content vocabulary, is often given prominent attention in teaching in the disciplines, much less attention is given to sentence shaping and sentence structure. This may be because sentence structure requires more grammatical understanding, particularly understanding the syntactic chunks in a clause or sentence. Yet research into the characteristics of academic language and disciplinary writing consistently points to the importance of sentence structure, syntactical structure, clause-combining, clausal complexity, and logical/thematic links within and across sentences (Grey, 2021; Schleppegrell, 2001; Snow & Uccelli, 2009). Being able to talk about adverbials or the subject of a sentence, for example, can really open up thinking about where information is placed in a sentence. Consider this explanation, from *Encyclopedia Britannica* (Lambers & Basham, 2024), of the role of photosynthesis in the creation of fossil fuels:

> Energy produced by photosynthesis carried out by plants millions of years ago is responsible for the fossil fuels (i.e., coal, oil, and gas) that power industrial society. **In past ages,** green plants and small organisms that fed on plants increased faster than they were consumed, and their remains were deposited in Earth's crust by sedimentation and other geological processes. **There, protected from oxidation,** these organic remains were slowly converted to fossil fuels.

The paragraph begins with the subject at the start of the sentence, which allows the writer to progress naturally into the main argument of the sentence, that historical photosynthesis generated the energy for the fossil fuels we use today. You might also reflect on the information density of this noun phrase. The subsequent two sentences both begin with adverbials: "in past ages" connects back to "millions of years ago" in the previous sentence, and foregrounds that the information that follows is about the past. The next sentence begins with the adverbial "there," which points back to the remains deposited in the earth's crust. The second adverbial "protected from oxidation" informs or reminds the reader that sedimentation prevented oxidation, before making the clear statement about the conversion of remains to fossil fuels. The three sentences are carefully shaped to communicate the disciplinary content clearly, concisely, and logically.

However, sentence shaping is not only about syntactic structure but also about how information is packaged within a sentence and across sentences. One of the most common features of disciplinary texts is nominalization, the linguistic process by which a noun or noun phrase is created from a verb or an adjective: for example, the verb *depicts* becomes the noun *depiction*; the adjective *happy* becomes the noun *happiness*. Another common form of nominalization is the transformation of a clause to a noun phrase, as in the following example:

> The heart attack was triggered because the blood was flowing too slowly through the arteries.
>
> The heart attack was caused by poor circulation of blood.

What is important about nominalization, however, is what this change to a noun or noun phrase achieves in a text. The shift from verb or clause to a nominalization tends to shift the expression from more concrete communication to more abstract communication. In the two previous sentence examples, the first focuses on the *action* of blood flowing through arteries, whereas the second focuses on the *idea* of circulation. Derewianka and Jones (2023) explain that nominalization is "a text-level strategy for crafting the packaging and flow of information" (p. 310). Nominalization can also package information more concisely, build connections within or across sentences, and give the writer more choice about whether the noun phrase should be at the beginning or end of a sentence or clause (whereas verbs very often have to be midclause or midsentence). Research has shown that nominalization is a very prevalent feature of technical and disciplinary writing (Biber & Grey, 2013; Hyland, 2009), so it is helpful for students to recognize it as part of their linguistic repertoire.

Let's look at some examples of nominalization, all taken from the *Encyclopedia Britannica* explanation of chemical reactions (Treichel & Kotz, 2024).

> Therefore, equations depicting reactions must be balanced; that is, the same number of atoms of each kind must appear on opposite sides of the equation. The balanced equation for the iron-sulfur reaction shows that

> one iron atom can react with one sulfur atom to give one formula unit of iron sulfide.

In this example, the clause "equations depicting reactions must be balanced" in the first sentence becomes the noun phrase "the balanced equation" in the second. This creates cohesion across the two sentences, supported by the position of the nominalization at the start of the second sentence. It also packages the information about balanced equations more concisely, as the reader has had a full explanation in the first sentence.

Consider also this sentence, again from the *Encyclopedia Britannica* text:

> The formation of compounds from the constituent elements is almost always exothermic

This sentence uses the nominalization, "the formation of compounds from the constituent elements": in contrast, the following possible alternative sentence does not use a nominalization.

> When compounds form from constituent elements, the reaction is almost always exothermic.

You can see that the subordinate clause beginning with "when" in the second sentence is represented by the noun phrase in the first, and verb "form" is represented by the noun "formation." This allows the writer to foreground the process of formation and to focus on the idea of compound formation rather than the action of forming compounds.

When teaching about nominalization in disciplinary writing, metalinguistic discussion is particularly important because nominalization can be a very effective grammatical choice to communicate abstract ideas and concepts in a discipline and to express ideas concisely. But nominalization can also be overdone, leading to texts that are so densely packed with information in long noun phrases that they are very hard to read. Derewianka and Jones (2023) argue that using nominalization is "a strategic choice," which "used with discernment . . . can result in a coherent, compact text that is well-structured and logically organised" (p. 310). This kind of strategic decision-making is facilitated through metalinguistic talk that opens up discussion about the appropriacy of a nominalization in a particular text.

Table 5.5 offers an example of attention to sentence shaping using the LEAD principles; in this example, the focus is on sentence structure and patterning.

TABLE 5.5. LEAD Principles and Sentence Structure

Learning context	The students have been studying the American Civil War and are approaching the end of the unit of work. In this lesson, the teacher aims to consolidate their understanding of the significance of the war, drawing on a text by the American Battlefield Trust (2023).
Link	How sentence length and sentence structure can support the expression of a historical argument
Authentic text	"A Brief Overview of the American Civil War" by the American Battlefield Trust (2003)

- The teacher leads a whole-class discussion, drawing out the class's thinking about the significance of the American Civil War.
- Writing collaboratively in pairs, students write a single paragraph of about 100 words explaining the significance of the American Civil War.
- The teacher then uses the model text that follows to deconstruct and make explicit how careful structuring of sentences can support the explanation of significance.

> The Civil War is the *central event* in America's historical consciousness. While the Revolution of 1776–1783 created the United States, the Civil War of 1861–1865 determined what kind of nation it would be. The war resolved two fundamental questions left unresolved by the revolution: whether the United States was to be a dissolvable confederation of sovereign states or an indivisible nation with a sovereign national government; and whether this nation, born of a declaration that all men were created with an equal right to liberty, would continue to exist as the largest slaveholding country in the world.

- After reading the paragraph, the teacher uses PowerPoint or similar software to display the text as three separate sentences organized in a vertical list. She uses the software to highlight in sequence the key grammatical points outlined as follows:
    - The short single-clause opening sentence, which makes a summary statement about the Civil War's significance in America's historical consciousness. The brevity and the single clause make this point unambiguous and clear to the reader.
    - The balanced structure of the two clauses in the second sentence, with the counterpointing of the verbs *created* and *determined* and the first subordinate clause, completed by the second main clause. The significance of the Civil War is expressed in the main clause.

  - The parallel structure in the third sentence. The main clause (at the start of the sentence) communicates a key point of significance, the resolution of two fundamental questions. The colon leads into two multiply-claused parallel structures, both using the conjunction "whether" to elaborate on the "two fundamental questions" referred to in the main clause.
  - The pattern of sentence length in the paragraph, moving from a short initial sentence making an argument statement about the Civil War's significance, to a longer sentence, expanding that argument, to the final long sentence elaborating in detail the reason for the war's significance.

- She then asks the students why they think the writer chose to use present tense in the first sentence, and past tense in the rest of the paragraph. **[Discussion]**
- The students return to their own written paragraph and consider whether any of the sentence patterning the teacher has introduced would help them to write more like a historian with clarity and authority.
- The teacher selects one or two pairs to share their paragraph and explain any revisions they made and why, and other peers are invited to make alternative suggestions. **[Discussion]**
- The lesson closes by returning to the model text and discussing to what extent they agree with the author's view of the significance of the Civil War. Whose position does it represent—or silence?

What to Consider When Using Grammar as a Resource for Teaching Disciplinary Writing

The capacity to write like an expert and to understand the effect of the grammatical choices in a text enables students to make writerly decisions about their own compositional choices, and this should empower all students of any background to become increasingly agentic in their linguistic decision-making. However, I would like to raise some critical comments here about three interrelated ideas that, if carried through into the writing classroom, can serve to disempower student writers.

Firstly, we need to avoid suggesting that writing like an expert is about mastering greater complexity in writing. The word *complexity* is often interpreted as better than simplicity, or more sophisticated than the everyday. Linguistic complexity occurs in many language forms, spoken and written, formal and informal, everyday and academic, but the way that this complexity is realized differs according to purpose and context. Moreover, the term *grammatical complexity* does not valorize complexity over simplicity, it simply describes the different structures involved. The example early in this chapter of the two different ways that nanotechnology is explained for a young readership or for an adult audience is an apt reminder that effective writing can be achieved through different language choices that address different contexts, readers, and purposes. We have also seen how students misunderstand vocabulary choice as about learning how to be posh or having a more sophisticated vocabulary, as though words have an intrinsic hierarchical value; and we have seen how complexity, such as through nominalization, can be a useful strategy in disciplinary writing but also how it can impede effective communication. What is critical is to be explicit about the language choices that are appropriate for the purpose of communicating disciplinary content in the context of an expert community.

Secondly, there have been critiques of the idea that being explicit about the conventions of disciplinary genres in bilingual, marginalized, or socially disadvantaged contexts will enable academic success for these students. Such critiques rightly express concerns that the rich linguistic repertoires and backgrounds of these students are, at best, not acknowledged and, at worst, devalued. This connects with the idea of deficit and/or raciolinguistic discourses about language discussed in this chapter. Addressing these serious critiques, Schleppegrell (2024) argues that "by not acknowledging that schooling brings with it linguistic expectations that can be made explicit, these critiques in the end leave students without opportunities to participate and thrive in learning contexts that they very much want to succeed in" (p. 1). Similarly, Snow and Uccelli (2009) show how social disadvantage can be perpetuated without access to "academic language" (p. 113). Building on these arguments, this chapter emphasizes authorial choice and agency, and the need for metalinguistic discussion about those choices, and how they relate to the particular texts in particular contexts.

This leads directly to my final critical comment. The chapter advocates the importance of explicit teaching about the grammatical choices that typify writing in a disciplinary community. But this is not about normative prescriptivism: A close look at a selection of texts within any discipline shows variation in choices made, not conformity. And disciplinary texts evolve over time; in science writing, for example, the standard guidance not to use first person is frequently not observed and is a source of debate within the community. One risk of explicit teaching of disciplinary texts is that students are taught, in effect, schooled genres that do not always reflect the authentic writing in the disciplinary community. To counter this risk, this chapter emphasizes student understanding of *why* and *how* grammatical choices work in a text, rather than knowledge of *what* should go into text. The goal of the explicit teaching of grammatical choice is fostering metalinguistic understanding that supports students in understanding why certain choices might be made; the outcome is not normative compliance but principled understanding.

In summary, then, this chapter signals the symbiotic relationship between subject content and the grammatical choices that express it and makes the argument that grammar is a powerful resource for learning about writing and being a writer. Crucially, it emphasizes the facilitation of metalinguistic understanding about language choices through discussion, which opens up critical questions, challenges misconceptions about language hierarchies, and avoids normative or deficit discourses. In this way, student writers are empowered to make appropriate decisions about the language choices in disciplinary texts: an induction into the disciplinary community of writers.

ACTION STEPS

- Reflect on your own subject knowledge of and attitude to grammar.
- Select three or four published examples of writing in your subject area and annotate these with notes about how the grammar choices support effective disciplinary writing.
- Develop a 10- to 15-minute episode of teaching in your subject using the LEAD principles to explicitly address a relevant grammatical choice in a disciplinary text. Teach it, evaluate it, refine it!

REFERENCES

Adair, J. K., Colegrove, K. S., & McManus, M. E. (2017). How the word gap argument negatively impacts young children of Latinx immigrants' conceptualizations of learning. *Harvard Educational Review, 87*(3), 309–334.

American Battlefield Trust (2023). *A brief overview of the American Civil War. www.battlefields.org/learn/articles/brief-overview-american-civil-war*

Artble. (2024). *Vincent van Gogh style and technique. www.artble.com/artists/vincent_van_gogh*

Baugh, J. (2017). Meaning-less differences: Exposing fallacies and flaws in "the word gap" hypothesis that conceal a dangerous "language trap" for low-income American families and their children. *International Multilingual Research Journal, 11*(1), 39–51.

Bazerman, C., Graham, S., Applebee, A., Matsuda, P., Berninger, V., Murphy, S., Brandt, D., Rowe, D. W., & Schleppegrell, M. (2017). Taking the long view on writing development. *Research in the Teaching of English, 51*(3), 351–360.

Beck, I. L., McKeown, M. G., & Kucan, L. (2013). *Bringing words to life: Robust vocabulary instruction* (2nd ed.). Guilford Press.

Biber, D. & Gray, B. (2013). Discourse characteristics of writing and speaking task types on the TOEFL iBT Test: A lexico–grammatical analysis. *TOEFLiBT Research Report (TOEFL iBT-19).* Educational Testing Service.

Biber, D., Johansson, S., Leech, G., Conrad, S., & Finegan, E. (1999). *Longman grammar of spoken and written English.* Longman.

Carter, M., Ferzli, M., & Wiebe, E. N. (2007). Writing to learn by learning to write in the disciplines. *Journal of Business and Technical Communication, 21*(3), 278–302.

Carter, R., & McCarthy, M. (2006). *Cambridge grammar of English: A comprehensive guide.* Cambridge University Press.

Chamot, A. U., & O'Malley, J. M. (1994). *The CALLA handbook: Implementing the cognitive academic language learning approach.* Addison-Wesley.

Crystal, D. (2004). *Making sense of grammar.* Pearson.

Cummins, J. (1979). Cognitive/academic language proficiency, linguistic interdependence, the optimum age question and some other matters. *Working Papers on Bilingualism, 19*, 121–129.

Cummins, J. (2008). BICS and CALP: Empirical and theoretical status of the distinction. In B. Street & N. H. Hornberger (Eds.), *Encyclopedia of language and education. Volume 2: Literacy* (2nd ed., pp. 71–83). Springer Science + Business Media.

Cushing, I. (2022). Word rich or word poor? Deficit discourses, raciolinguistic ideologies and the resurgence of the "word gap" in England's education policy. *Critical Inquiry in Language Studies, 20*(4), 305–331.

Cushing, I. (2024). Tiered vocabulary and raciolinguistic discourses of deficit: From academic scholarship to education policy. *Language and Education, 38*(6), 969–987.

Darling-Hammond, L. (1995). The role of teacher expertise in students' opportunity to learn. In P. Brown (Ed.), *Strategies for linking school finance and students' opportunity to learn* (pp. 19–23). National Governors' Association.

Deignan, A., Candarli, D., & Oxley, F. (2023). *The linguistic challenge of the transition to secondary school: A corpus study of academic language.* Routledge.

Derewianka, B., & Jones, P. (2023). *Teaching language in context.* Oxford University Press.

Education Endowment Foundation (EEF). (2021). Improving literacy in secondary schools. Author. *https://educationendowmentfoundation.org.uk/education-evidence/guidance-reports/literacy-ks3-ks4*

Flores, N. (2020). From academic language to language architecture: Challenging raciolinguistic ideologies in research and practice. *Theory into Practice, 59*(1), 22–31.

Flores, N., & Rosa, J. (2015). Undoing appropriateness: Raciolinguistic ideologies and language diversity in education. *Harvard Educational Review, 85*, 149–171.

Galloway, E., Stude, J., & Uccelli, P. (2015). Adolescents' metalinguistic reflections on the academic register in speech and writing. *Linguistics and Education, 31*, 221–237.

Gombert, E. (1992). *Metalinguistic development.* Harvester Wheatsheaf.

Graham, S., Kim, Y-S. G., Cao, Y., Lee, J., Tate, T., Collins, P., . . . Olson, C. B. (2023). A meta-analysis of writing treatments for students in grades 6 to 12. *Journal of Educational Psychology*, 115(7), 1004–1027.

Green, L. J. (2011). *Language and the African American child.* Cambridge University Press.

Grey, B. (2021). *On the complexity of academic writing: Disciplinary variation and structural complexity.* Routledge.

Halliday, M. A. K. (1978). *Language as social semiotic: The social interpretation of language and meaning.* Edward Arnold.

Halliday, M. A. K., & Matthiessen, C. (2004). *Introduction to functional grammar.* Routledge.

Hart, B., & Risley, T. R. (1992). American parenting of language-learning children: Persisting differences in family–child interactions observed in natural home environments. *Developmental Psychology, 28*(6), 1096–1105.

Hyland, K. (2009). Writing in the disciplines: Research evidence for specificity. *Taiwan International ESP Journal, 1*(1), 5–22.

Johnson, E. (2015). Debunking the "language gap." *Journal for Multicultural Education, 9*(1), 42–50.

Jones, S. M., Myhill, D. A., & Bailey, T. C. (2013). Grammar for writing? An investigation into the effect of contextualised grammar teaching on student writing. *Reading and Writing, 26*(8), 1241–1263.

Kellogg, R. (1994). *The psychology of writing.* Oxford University Press.

Kuchirko, Y. (2019). On differences and deficits: A critique of the theoretical and methodological underpinnings of the word gap. *Journal of Early Childhood, 19*(4), 533–562.

Lambers, H., & Bassham, J. A. (2024). Photosynthesis. In *Encyclopedia Britannica. www.britannica.com/science/photosynthesis*

Lefstein, A. (2009). Rhetorical grammar and the grammar of schooling: Teaching "powerful verbs" in the English National Literacy Strategy. *Linguistics and Education, 20*(4), 378–400.

Martin, J. (2009). Genre and language learning: A social semiotic perspective. *Linguistics and Education, 20*(1), 10–21.

Martin, J. R. (2013). Embedded literacy: Knowledge as meaning. *Linguistics and Education*, 24, 23–37.

McKeown, M. G. (2019). Effective vocabulary instruction fosters knowing words, using words, and understanding how words work. *Language, Speech and Hearing Services in School, 50*(4), 466–476.

Meston, H. M., Phillips Galloway, E., & Brown McClain, J. (2020). "They're the ones who hold the answers": Exploring educators' and students' conceptions of academic conversation. *Journal of Adolescent and Adult Literacy, 64*(4), 409–491.

Myhill, D., Jones, S., & Lines, H. (2018). Supporting less-proficient writers through linguistically-aware teaching. *Language and Education, 32*(4), 333–349.

Myhill, D. A., Jones, S. M., Lines, H., & Watson, A. (2012). Re-thinking grammar: The impact of embedded grammar teaching on students' writing and students' metalinguistic understanding. *Research Papers in Education, 27*(2), 139–166.

Myhill, D. A., Jones, S., & Watson, A. (2013). Grammar matters: How teachers' grammatical subject knowledge impacts on the teaching of writing. *Teaching and Teacher Education, 36*, 77–91.

Myhill, D. A., & Newman, R. (2016). Metatalk: Enabling metalinguistic discussion about writing. *International Journal of Education Research, 80*, 177–187.

Nagy, W., & Townsend, D. (2012). Words as tools: Learning academic vocabulary as language acquisition. *Reading Research Quarterly, 47*(1), 91–108.

National Geographic. (n.d.). *Plate tectonics. https://education.nationalgeographic.org/resource/plate-tectonics*

National Institute for Occupational Safety and Health. (2023). *Nanotechnology. www.cdc.gov/niosh/topics/nanotech*

Newman, R., & Watson, A. (2020). Shaping spaces: Teachers' orchestration of metatalk about written text. *Linguistics and Education, 60*, 100860.

Pilgreen, J. (2006). Supporting English learners: Developing academic language in the content area classroom. In A. Terrel & N. L. Hadaway (Eds.), *Supporting the literacy development of English learners* (pp. 41–60). International Reading Association.

Schleppegrell, M. J. (2001). Linguistic features of the language of schooling. *Linguistics and Education, 12*(4), 431–459.

Schleppegrell, M. J. (2024). Value your students' bilingualism? Nurture them through development of school-based registers! *Language Teaching.* [Epub ahead of print] *https://doi.org/10.1017/S0261444823000459*

Snow, C. E., & Uccelli, P. (2009). The challenge of academic language. In D. R. Olson & N. Torrance (Eds.), *The Cambridge handbook of literacy* (pp. 112–133). Cambridge University Press.

Sperry, D., Sperry, L., & Miller, P. (2018). Reexamining the verbal environments of children from different socioeconomic backgrounds. *Childhood Development, 90*(4), 1303–1318.

Treichel, P. M., & Kotz, J. C. (2024). Chemical reaction. In *Encyclopedia Britannica. www.britannica.com/science/chemical-reaction*

Wade, J. (2022). *Nano—The spectacular science of the very (very) small.* Walker Books.

PART II
WRITING IN THE DISCIPLINES

Chapter 6

Telling the Stories of Our Lives in Prose and Poetry

Penny Kittle

In Doris Lessing's 2007 Nobel Prize in Literature speech, she said, "The storyteller is deep inside every one of us." Those stories cross time, experience, and country. English teachers are told to blow dust off the covers of well-worn copies of literature in the department book room and deliver them as sacred texts to teenagers hunched over phones. We are told to ignore disinterest and assign literary analysis papers, which are widely available on apps or websites in seconds, and to spend most of the school year summarizing what someone said someone said about something written before their grandparents were born.

What is in this chapter is what I know *is* sacred: We center the lives and experiences of the young people we teach through the study and composition of their stories, both imagined and lived.

GUIDING QUESTIONS

1. Why teach storytelling through prose and poetry?
2. How can composing life stories increase student investment in drafting, revising, editing, and sharing writing?
3. What are effective strategies for engaging students in narrative and poetry writing?
4. How can the study of story and poetry deepen students' understandings of form and genre?
5. Why is a teacher's model of thinking essential in teaching writing?
6. How can story bind students together as a community?

I define narrative and poetry as the Rosetta Stones of teaching writing. The Rosetta Stone is literally a stone, discovered in 1799, with a message carved in it three times: in hieroglyphs, in Demotic (a script), and in ancient Greek. Greek was known, so the Rosetta Stone provided a key to understanding hieroglyphs. And here's the leap I want you to make with me: Narrative and poetry operate as Rosetta Stones to unlock student interests, relationships, and belief systems about themselves and about writing. It is glue that binds not only a student to faith in the writing process but also a community of writers together in pursuit of something more than correctness or compliance. It allows students to see each other and to be seen. And the process of crafting stories in community (in prose and poetry) teaches essential elements of crafting in any genre.

Just as the original Rosetta Stone led to deep understandings of culture and history, reading students' narratives and poetry will lead you to an understanding of them that is unavailable otherwise. Let me make this point in a story from my teaching life last semester.

On Will and Wishes and Wonder

IN SOME WAYS my semester starts like all the others, the late summer light streaming a welcome through windows, narrow and impossibly tall across two walls. A mixture of sadness and joy ripples as I hoist them open: summer has ended, and college begins in Rounds Hall, room 107. We've all waited for this.

I'm early on this first day, taking time to dust books and arrange them into piles on desks. I fall in love, again, with one title after another, running fingers across *Dear Martin* (Stone, 2018) and *Just Mercy* (Stevenson, 2014) and the surprise of *Me (Moth)* (McBride, 2023). I see the faces of past students—the joy they found in each of these. Will my new students love them, too? Will anyone read them?

Soon my room is full of teenagers. They've arrived just three months past high school graduation, absent the bravado of seniors on the brink of everything. These kids have waved goodbye to parents and already miss their dogs and their rooms at home. They aren't sure they've chosen well, to swap siblings and comfort for this campus in the middle of the mountains. There is fear in widened eyes. They glance from me to the whiteboard to books in a pile nearby. They hold phones a little desperately, clinging to connection.

Will moves easily to an open desk near the back. He is lanky and athletic—hockey, I think. Maybe soccer or lacrosse. He doesn't carry a backpack. He holds a spiral notebook. He meets my eyes with a genuine smile. "Hi," I say, "I'm Mrs. Kittle."

"Hello, Professor," he says. I explain I'm not a professor: I stopped 12 credits short of my dissertation. Six years into teaching composition I realize students will ignore my correction, no matter how often I repeat it. When I continue to protest, most students will say, "You're Professor to me." That label seems to signify this place, instead of research, sacrifice, exams, or defense.

The first move in leading young writers, of course, is to know them. As I confer with students about reading and writing, I learn who they are. Will is here to play hockey. He seems at ease in the room and with these kids he doesn't know, although he's come farther than anyone: from a tiny town in Czechia, the Czech Republic. He loves fantasy, he tells me, and is a regular reader. I think of how alone he must feel, so far from home.

We move quickly into regular reading, writing in notebooks, and studying the elements of story. Will asks if this first writing assignment includes fiction. Of course, I assure him. As Virginia Woolf (1929) said in a favorite book of mine, "Fiction is like a spider's web, attached ever so lightly perhaps, but still attached to life at all four corners" (p. 42). We want student writing to vibrate with life, don't we? Some will only write the truths they know if they can be concealed in an imagined world. Why not free them to do so?

The central qualities of story are the same in personal narrative and fiction: voice, details, dialogue. Students have studied people throughout their lives: the subtleties of gesture, the way a person attempts to conceal an important truth. We are a curious species. Why not let them use that knowledge in writing about a place and characters they imagine? It is a safer space than memoir for some. I reject story as it is often used in school: a type of writing—safely contained within memoir to avoid fiction's feral wandering. Thomas Newkirk (2014) reminds us, "Narrative is not a type of writing. Or merely a type of writing. It has deeper roots than that. It is a property of mind, an innate and indispensable form of understanding as instinctive as our fear of falling, as our need for human company" (p. 34).

Will is one of only two students in his class to embrace fiction, but he launches his writing that day with a trio of starving characters in a small cabin set deep in the woods. By the next class he has written hundreds of words. I skim them to see how it is developing. I see both the brilliant lines and the hesitations. It is the potential and the challenge of the first draft.

And this is an essential piece of the pedagogy of teaching writing: the individual path. As much as we would like to believe that scripted programs and fidelity to whole-class instruction will move every child at the same pace, the approach denies the truth of our work. It leaves teachers frustrated and weary. Will brought a draft to class; many more students have not yet started. Will needs help developing his draft; the students on both sides of him need to narrow their subjects. As Adam Grant (2023) said in *Hidden Potential*, "To discover and develop the potential in each of their students . . . schools create cultures of opportunity by enabling students to build individualized relationships, *receive individualized support*, and develop individualized interests" (p. 161, italics mine). Grant names the key to hidden potential in every student as individualization and response, not programs and rubrics. In freedom, not in conformity. In the challenge of creation, not in the repetition of the same form of writing year after year.

Our students develop confidence when they study the craft of writing, both in the books they are reading and, in the stumbling, developing drafts of other students in the room.

So I ask Will, "Can we look at your story in class tomorrow?"

"You and me?" he asks. Cautious.

"Well, actually, I'd love to share it with the class and open up a discussion of the challenge of crafting stories like yours."

He raises an eyebrow and holds my gaze. I expect he's considering the risk. Judging my intentions.

"Why not?" he says. "Can I keep working on it tonight?"

I smile, "Of course. If you email it by 7 a.m., I will make copies."

"Deal."

To be continued . . .

Before we move on in this chapter, go back and consider the structure of the first half of my narrative essay. Kelly Gallagher and I (Kittle & Gallagher, 2022) wrote about the importance of teaching high school students to consider what we call "the drone view" of an essay. Consider the shifts between narrative and commentary. Can you find places where the story informs my thinking about teaching and the transitions that smooth those shifts for readers? We want students to be able to study writing and to learn from the moves other writers make; that begins with us.

I opened this chapter with a story to bring you with me as I teach. I hoped it might increase your respect for narrative, which deserves a prominent place in the curriculum at every grade level. We are, after all, teachers of literature. We believe in story and poetry. This means we believe in the hard work of writing well to communicate what is important in our lives and in the lives of others; we also believe the possibility story holds to disrupt divisions in our world. We don't just analyze good writing, we imitate it. Story invites a community of young writers to respect and support each other.

But let me add one more thing we seek in teaching: a habit of persistence. Thomas Newkirk (2021) reminds us, "Of course we want students to be able to persist in tasks. But in my experience, those who do persist do so because they find a way to love, or at least enjoy, what they are doing" (p. 140). This is true for Will and dozens of students I teach each year. Students persist in shaping stories that matter to them. Students delight in finding the right words to describe what they've experienced. Students commit to and even, yes, *love* writing when they see what is most important to them on the page. Those moments of persistence often live in both the study of both narrative and poetry.

How Do Our Own Beliefs About Writing Inform Our Teaching?

Teaching beliefs ground us. What we believe about writing is evident in what we prioritize in our daily plans. Consider your own plans as you read my beliefs about writing:

1. Writing well is not as much an accumulation of skill as an accumulation of practice across genres. Practice increases confidence in using the tools available to reach an audience. The writing process is a spiral curriculum (Bruner, 1977) where students learn and relearn through practice in negotiating writing's unpredictable twists and turns. We learn and relearn form and craft in writing, year after year.

2. Teaching with our values in mind brings freedom and wholeness to our work. It is this wholeness and joy in our efforts that we all seek. "Your pedagogy is your protest. Think about your teaching as an opportunity to be equitable," Dr. Christopher Emdin (2021) says. "Think about your practice in the classroom as a march, as a protest; think about the art of teaching and learning as a movement toward social justice" (p. 1).
   a. Most of us live in an ecosystem of performance, reward, and far too often shame: "not yet," "not enough," but somehow, "keep going." We find joy when we resist with practices that center writers—not assignments.
   b. Resist the schoolification of writing as a performance of traits and skills for next year's performance, a racetrack you'll never exit but will just continue to circle ring after ring. Kaitlin B. Curice (2023) says, "Resistance itself is a living, breathing being—when we enter into the flow of resistance, we enter into a sacred, embodied, connected way of being that brings freedom and wholeness" (pp. 12–13).

3. We shape stories every year of our lives—in ways that are new to us and ways that circle back to learning and relearning. Students are not simply collectors of genres or lessons. Instead, I see young people as conduits of their own life force through stories in poetry and prose. Their skills deepen in complexity as they age.

4. Recognize the intersections of genre. Think of form as packaging for the stories and experiences that drive us to compose. We aren't learning form as a series of arbitrary rules about paragraphs; we must recognize that cultures use form in different ways that deserve equal representation in our classrooms. Peter Elbow (1990) asks us to rethink what we mean by *form* or *structure*. As often presented to students, structure (the outline, for example) is static, a set of claims and supports. It is spatial, architectural, and silent about the motives for the reader. As Elbow (1990) describes form, it is "dynamic, seductive, active, and operating in time; it is a form of energy that the writing generates to sustain reading" (p. 14).

5. Writing stories and poetry is heart-and-soul work, sustaining our emotional health. Approach writing as a search—"tapping that

trap door that holds so many treasures," says Padraig Ó Tuama (2022, p. 314)—taking one experience out to examine it and learn from it.

6. Separate transcription (how we apply editing rules) and composition (creation) in your mind, in your learning, in your planning for class, and in your response to student writing. You must learn to welcome the ways people come to share their stories and vision.

7. Reframe fiction as a narrative form. It might be the safest way a student has to tell their own truths and stories. Quite frankly, Will would never have written this story as a memoir.

8. Understand that narrative and poetry are present in every genre. Hanif Abdurraqib (2023) says he was criticized as a music reviewer because his writing was too poetic. Consider how Clint Smith's poetry is woven into storytelling in *How the Word Is Passed* (2021). The detailed rendering of experience in writing is central to our learning across content areas. Narrative matters in all content areas. Siddhartha Mukherjee (2010) says, "Even scientific discourse, normally thought so distant from narrative, depends on establishing causal relationships or sequences, even stories . . . cancer is a story, with antecedents and consequences. To the extent these phenomena can be *told* as stories, readers will have a better chance of taking in the information" (p. 11).

Strategies for Narrative

A caution here: You might think of storytelling as easy to teach. "Just give kids time to write," my department chair told me decades ago, "it's the easiest throwaway unit of the year." Just giving kids time to write will result in summaries of important moments or a years-long connection to a sport, a cat, a grandmother, written with little of the passion that rumbles within that connection. In fact, it is not uncommon for students to recycle a story they wrote the year before. The teaching strategies I share next change this. I approach the unit with the same intellectual rigor I bring to literature study. I lift students' understanding of this genre with intentional lessons and practice with story craft.

Strategy 1: A Volume of Practice

• *Discover subjects together.* Daily writing binds a community together. We write together every day. I provide the provocation—which is always optional, since students who begin to live like writers see their own subjects as they walk across campus to class. This unformed, exploratory writing is our anchor. They know we will write together, and at first, they do not understand why. But every year of the four decades I have taught so far, students discover how much they love the practice. Writing practice has four central characteristics:

1. We write in notebooks by hand. We revise our first thinking by hand.
2. Notebooks are graded for completion only.
3. Notebook writing is shared only if the writer chooses to share it.
4. I write beside them.

One morning, we write one scene from all the scenes we've lived in as much detail as possible. My scene of this "boat moment" appears in my notebook (Figure 6.1). I have not rewritten it or used it in a longer piece. I simply record it here. I wonder about it. It fuels my belief that subjects that surprise me also invite me to write about them. But I don't have to. A writing notebook should be a rich resource that surprises the writer, holds thinking, and allows for daily practice in noticing and recording that leads to a commitment to longer works of art.

• *Invite fiction. Play in writing is welcome.* Pulitzer Prize–winning journalist Donald Murray (1984) said, "It is intoxicating to play around with language, to hear music of what we say, to see more clearly as we speak, to follow the unexpected paths where words take us" (p. 88).

• *Tom Newkirk's (2014) "favorite assignment"* . . . "I invite students to pick some inanimate object that is in some way precious to them—best if it's the kind of thing no one else values. Then, address that object and provide details justifying that attention" (p. 7; see Figure 6.2).[1]

• *Close-ups.* Choose a photograph from your phone. Study it. Write what you don't see at first. Long before we carried phones in our pockets, Don Murray taught me this at the University of New Hampshire Summer Institutes. Murray (1995) wrote, "Close-ups bring immediacy. We do not photograph the field of spring flowers but move in on one poppy" (p. 62).

• *Write a dream.* One of my first mentors, Dr. Tom Romano (2013), said that "dreams are delicious. Nowhere else in my life do I experience such vividness, mystery, anxiety, elation, and surreal madness. . . . Misfortune is a staple of dreams. Plans go awry. Chances are missed. People don't cooperate. Desires go unfulfilled. What happens is often bizarre.

---

[1]I wrote next to this prompt today in an airport. "Hello, necklace. I remember when Pat placed you in my open hand," and I wanted to keep writing.

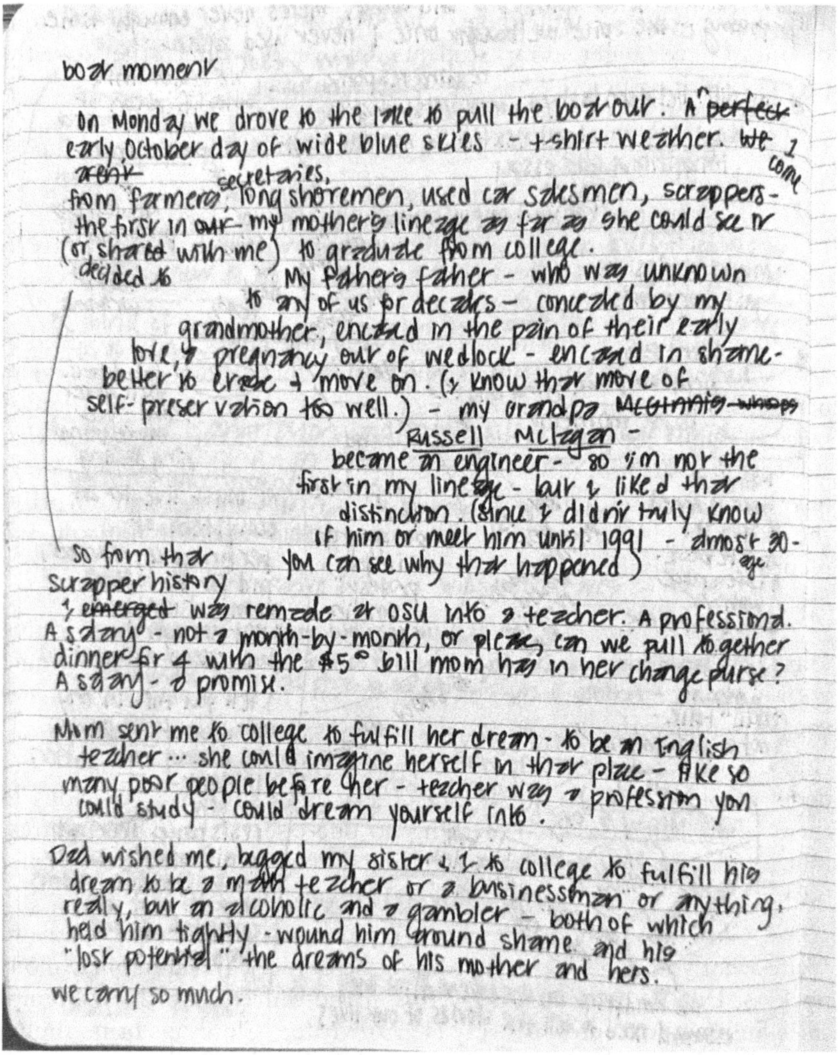

boat moment

On Monday we drove to the lake to pull the boat out. A ~~perfect~~ early October day of wide blue skies - t-shirt weather. ~~We~~ ~~went~~ I come from farmers, secretaries, longshoremen, used car salesmen, scrappers - the first in ~~our~~ my mother's lineage as far as she could see it (or shared with me) to graduate from college. My father's father - who was unknown to any of us for decades - concealed by my grandmother, encased in the pain of their early love, a pregnancy out of wedlock - encased in shame - decided to better to erase + move on. (I know that move of self-preservation too well.) - my grandpa ~~McGlynn~~ Russell McLagan - became an engineer - so I'm not the first in my lineage - but I liked that distinction. (Since I didn't truly know of him or meet him until 1991 - almost 30 - age you can see why that happened.)

So from that scrapper history I ~~emerged~~ was remade at OSU into a teacher. A professional. A salary - not a month-by-month, or please, can we pull together dinner for 4 with the $5 bill mom has in her change purse? A salary - a promise.

Mom sent me to college to fulfill her dream - to be an English teacher ... she could imagine herself in that place - like so many poor people before her - teacher was a profession you could study - could dream yourself into.

Dad wished me, begged my sister & I to college to fulfill his dream to be a math teacher or a businessman or anything, really, but an alcoholic and a gambler - both of which held him tightly - wound him around shame and his "lost potential" the dreams of his mother and hers.

We carry so much.

FIGURE 6.1. I intend to write a scene of details of my father but am quickly distracted by explaining how unlikely it is that I am driving a boat across a lake. How surprised my ancestors would be. Students watch and listen to me struggle to explain how my story fits with my ancestors. This is what writers do—following ideas that sometimes lead them astray.

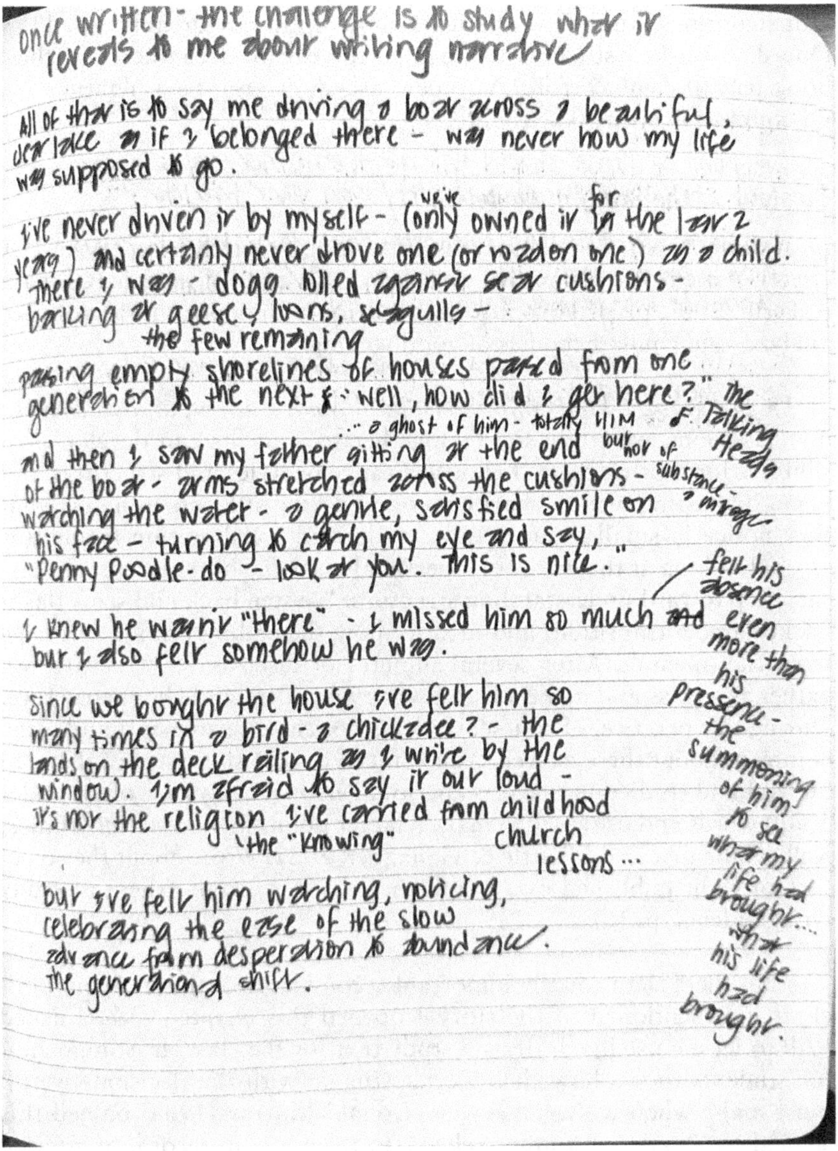

once written - the challenge is to study what it reveals to me about writing narrative

All of that is to say me driving a boat across a beautiful, clear lake as if I belonged there - was never how my life was supposed to go.

I've never driven it by myself - (only we've owned it for the last 2 years) and certainly never drove one (or rode on one) as a child. There I was - dogs lolled against seat cushions - barking at geese, loons, seagulls - passing empty shorelines of the few remaining houses passed from one generation to the next & - well, how did I get here?" the Talking Heads

... a ghost of him - totally HIM but not of substance - a mirage

and then I saw my father sitting at the end of the boat - arms stretched across the cushions - watching the water - a gentle, satisfied smile on his face - turning to catch my eye and say, "Penny Poodle-do - look at you. This is nice."

I knew he wasn't "there" - I missed him so much and but I also felt somehow he was.

felt his absence even more than his presence - the summoning of him to see what my life had brought... what his life had brought.

Since we bought the house I've felt him so many times in a bird - a chickadee? - that lands on the deck railing as I write by the window. I'm afraid to say it out loud - it's not the religion I've carried from childhood church lessons... the "knowing"

but I've felt him watching, noticing, celebrating the ease of the slow advance from desperation to abundance. the generational shift.

FIGURE 6.2. I add to my first page in the second class I teach—moving from details about the shore to those about my father. The addition of dialogue brings my father alive. This is what I share with students. Dialogue brings details to life.

Our hauntings, anxieties, and fears show up in our dreams" (p. 119). One day, I asked students to imagine the dream a character in their book had the night before. A student asked, "Can it be a nightmare?" Of course. Our pens take flight.

Strategy 2: The Study of Models

In *Writing Next*, a meta-analysis of writing research, one of the "11 effective strategies to improve writing" is the study of models (Graham & Perin, 2007, p. 5). This provides students with opportunities to read, analyze, and emulate models of good writing.

- *Study three kinds of models: published, student, and teacher.* In my classroom, we study stories together so students can develop possibilities for writing them. I choose a range of styles and structures and begin by pasting one on chart paper and asking students to name what they notice in small groups. Talk, study, and collaboration frame this work. Looking at the whole of a personal essay or short story is a necessary step toward understanding structure. We step back and see a flashback, name a transition, and identify how the ending echoes an image from the opening. After several minutes of discovering structure, we gather as a class and make a list of what we understand about structure. During this practice, of course, students notice voice and style and often comment about these as well. You want to choose short stories that can be read and studied in one class period. Personal essays are often under 1,500 words and use story to make a larger point. In *4 Essential Studies*, Kelly Gallagher and I (Kittle & Gallagher, 2022) wrote about the structure of eight published essays and the reason we chose them to study with students (p. 16).

But there is an equally important second layer of the study of models that I mentioned in the story I opened this chapter with. I asked Will to let me use his draft as a study text for the class. It is important for students to see how their peers struggle with the decisions we all must make when we write stories. Donald Murray (1984) named this struggle to "make meaning of chaos, to celebrate, to record, to attempt to understand the world in which we are living" (p. 84). I tell my students, consider this: your ideas, your lived experiences, and your passions are partially formed as stories and poems already. Lines appear in your mind—you see possibility, you hear the voice of your father and want to explore that memory. A friendship fractured in high school, but you never understood why. The loss of your dog held you in sorrow for months, but you haven't written about him. You are filled with so much to say. You may be unsure of what it requires to write as *an attempt to understand* your own life and not as a performance for a grade. Narrative *thinking* is what Peter Elbow (1990) defined as "thinking that renders experience, thinking that reveals rather than explains, thinking that shows more than it tells" (p. 191). We look for evidence of this thinking in models.

Your students hold so many possibilities inside of them—but the question we must answer is, how do I write this? When students study the work of someone in their class, they have an opportunity to question the author and examine the text while it is still being written. This increases their willingness to make their own first attempt.

And lastly, when we ask students to write what matters to them—we must show them how we do it ourselves. I have never seen this more effective than in writing stories.[2] Each semester, I not only participate in notebook practice in front of my students but I bring in a draft I'm working on in the genre they are studying. I ask students to comment on qualities of the writing in mini-lessons. (You can see a student referencing this model of my draft in a video of three conferences in my high school classroom from 2013 [Kittle, 2013].) I teach from my own thinking and writing because it is authentic and clear. I know what I'm trying to say and why, and I am able to model for students the questions I ask myself as I work.

It is impossible to orchestrate this commitment to writing, not as an assignment but as an exploration of identity and understanding—and in writing classrooms, that exploration must happen for both students and the teacher. When a writer owns a subject, the urge to make sense of it drives word, sentence, structure, and development work. As Don Murray (1984) advised, first we awaken hunger: "Until there is an evolving text, the teacher's materials are abstract, unrelated to the student's knowledge or experience . . . as the students run into the problems of using language to explore, understand, and communicate a subject, they become hungry for solutions—they need and want instruction from the writers around them" (p. 83). Hungry students. We need more of them.

Strategy 3: The Study of Craft Moves in Short Texts

I have students look at a passage from a book I recommend, introducing them to the author's voice and style but also to study the craft moves the

---

[2]I'm afraid you might discount this idea if you haven't written something meaningful to yourself. But how to teach what we do not know? You know: not very effectively.

writer is making. One morning, I shared this opening passage from Hala Alyan's brilliant novel *The Arsonists' City*:

> Tonight the man will die. In some ways, the city already seems resigned to it, the Beirut dusk uncharacteristically flat, cloudy, a peculiar staleness rippling through the trees like wind. It's easy to costume the earth for grief, and tonight the birds perched upon the tangled electricity wires look like mourners in their black and white feathers staring down at the concrete refugee camps without song. There are orange trees in the courtyard, planted by the children the previous year; the NGO workers had wanted something bright and encouraged the youngest children to tie cheap ribbons to the branches, but they'd forgotten about the mud season and now the ribbons flap limply, streaked in dirt. (2021, p. 1)

Students talked to partners about what they noticed about the passage. Students mentioned the clarity of plot in the opening line, the specific sensory details in the list that followed, and the confidence in the voice of the storyteller. We all try on this voice and structure in our notebooks. (No doubt you see I placed my imitation at the start of my essay about Will, on pp. 164–166).

These short lessons are models of excellent writing, and they complement the drone view of a whole piece. Over the course of our study of stories, I offer examples of dialogue, of details that illuminate settings, of shifts in voice due to word choice. There are many writing lessons in short passages. Ask how the text works: What can we learn well about writing well from this passage (Kittle, 2022)?

Strategy 4: Feedback to Increase Confidence

This weekend, I have 40 personal essays to read. I parcel them out into stacks of five and take breaks throughout my reading to walk my dogs. Feedback on student writing is important; writers grow when we, as instructors, highlight precision and clarity in their sentences. It is also challenging; I need breaks to regain focus. We persist because we know the power of feedback on student achievement. In the 2023 meta-analysis by Graham et al., feedback had a statistically significant positive effect on all measures of writing quality (see p. 43).

But we also know that adolescents crave peer acceptance and support. Students need a group, not just a teacher, to read their evolving work and to see the range of experiences that others write about. I make time for writing groups in my class to provide this essential layer of feedback. As these groups evolve over the semester or year, student confidence in their ideas, their beginning drafts, and their questions about revision grow.

• *Read your work aloud into a voice recorder.* Isabel Allende said, "I read everything that I write aloud. First, the paragraph. Then, the page. Then, the chapter. And finally, I read the whole book aloud. Because I want to hear my voice reading it, and I need it to sound natural" (quoted in Murray, 1995, p. 9). This has been a staple in my teaching for more than a decade. I ask students to record a few pages of the book they are reading "as the author intended this to be read." This practice prepares students to read their own work aloud as regular practice and to share it in writing groups in class. Finished drafts come to me with a voice recording.

• *Writing groups.* I wrote in front of my third graders what I assigned in my first year of teaching. It felt natural to show them how. But I truly grew as a writer—in so many important ways—when I responded to my colleague Eben Plese's invitation to join a teachers' writing group. I learned what Murray articulated: "The act of writing is not complete without a reader, and most writers need one or two or three readers, perhaps five, but rarely more, who will appreciate what is being said and how it is being said" (1984, p. 86). I learned possibility in listening to other teacher writers.

Writing groups bind students together as a community. They are the essential glue in the classroom and provide vision for what is possible. I put students in groups within the first month of the year, and they stay together. At first they might only share a notebook entry, but as the semester or year unfolds, they become serious about analyzing the writing of their classmates. They learn from each other. Sometimes they learn from word choice or the effectiveness of conventions; sometimes they learn from their classmates' subjects. When turning in a draft, Isaac asked me, "Can I start over? After listening to what these guys [motioning to his writing group] are writing about, I want to take this more seriously."

Strategy 5: A Healthier Relationship with Grading and Evaluation

No doubt teachers are in a bind: encouraged to grade everything and then input scores into programs that immediately calculate an average. Percentage points bounce up and down across a semester, and students too often measure their ability or value by those points. Not what any of us had in mind, I'm sure. And it gets worse . . .

Our human responses to writing are strangled by the traits and features of rubrics. Early in my career, I was handed a rubric to evaluate the writing of my 9-year-old students. My response echoed my mentor Thomas Newkirk (2021): "I refuse to have my reaction parceled out in traits or features. I will try to stay whole, to view writing as a human action that invites me to be attentive, curious, and generous—to be in a relationship—helpful, I hope, but not objective, because I am attending to a human gesture and not an object" (p. 128). I continue to resist rubrics for this reason.

As researchers Buckingham and Goodall explained, "Learning is less a function of adding something that isn't there than it is of recognizing, reinforcing, and refining what already is. Neurologically each brain grows where it is already strongest . . . getting attention to our strengths from others catalyzes learning whereas attention to our weaknesses smothers it" (2019, pp. 5–6). We want our feedback to be useful, not smothering.

There are many alternatives. Consider the student's engagement with a process of evaluating both what they do well and what they are struggling to do well. This can happen through portfolio evaluation (Kittle, 2008), student-centered goals and conversations over time (Zerwin, 2020), the history of the writing as central to understanding the process of the writer (Rief, 1992), and using end notes to help you understand a student's journey in writing each piece (Romano, 2009). May you find peace with this complicated element of schooling.

Form is a decision: A partnership between narrative and poetry

I struggle to separate narrative and poetry simply because form is a decision a writer makes during the process of bringing experiences to life. Genre units are an artificial separation of writing skills instituted by school, which elevates differences rather than similarities in forms of writing. And yet, you—my audience for this chapter—are teachers who live within the constraints of school.

I began teaching writing by encouraging students to choose which genres to work in. I was content for years as I moved through elementary and middle school classrooms, but once I moved to the high school, student conferences each day were increasingly difficult without a grounding in genre. I had to shift language about writing to the genre the student was attempting to write in, sometimes multiple times in a class period. This was a lot of information to juggle in my head, class after class. I felt genre units would create natural bridges between mini-lessons, whole-class text study, and the students in the room. And they did (Kittle, 2008).

But I ask myself today, at what cost? Do genre units shoehorn students into form?

Listen to Clint Smith on how he chooses form. In his collection, *Above Ground*, he describes the death of a young man in the electric chair. I interviewed him for the Book Love Foundation in 2023. Clint said, "When I'm creating the poem, I'm like 'okay, what—how do I want the words to look on the page in a way that is going to reflect, uh, that sort of heartbeat—that feeling of a heartbeat'?" The form came from the subject. Clint read an account of the first attempt to execute a young man. The young man described feeling his heartbeat. Clint said, "I thought it would be fascinating to have the form of the poem be in the shape of a chair to sort of further reinforce how cruel and barbaric what happened to this child was, to force the reader to see, to directly confront not only the content of the poem but in the image of the poem, the chair that has brought on this violence to this boy. You make different decisions for each poem" (2023).

Writers should know that genre is a decision. It comes as the writer considers the form that best matches his intent. Perhaps the answer is to study narrative as both prose and poetry. Or study prose then poetry, both as narrative forms. (But you have read poems that are arguments, so this idea is limiting as well.) The truth that I hang on to is that writing well is not dependent on form. Narrative and poetry are partners in expressive writing. We can resolve the conflict of where to place our attention by choosing both.

Strategies for Teaching Poetry

I became a serious student of poetry when we moved to New Hampshire. My love of poems came not from the rugged granite cliffs of our mountains or the legendary poets (Donald Hall, Robert Frost, Jane Kenyon) who wrote here, but from my friendship with Don Graves, who became my close friend and writing companion. Don gave me two collections of *Good Poems* (from 2002 and 2005) selected by Garrison Keillor for *The Writer's Almanac* (*www.garrisonkeillor.com*). Figure 6.3 is a note from Don in the first of these collections. Don and his wife, Betty, invited me to gatherings on their deck in the late afternoon where they read poems while snacking on graham crackers.

Don read poems aloud in the Manchester airport as we waited for our flight to Baltimore for the National Council of Teachers of English Annual Convention just months after the planes hit the Twin Towers in New York City. Don's voice settled the anxious travelers who surrounded us.

Poems are light in the darkness of living—like the spray of stars above me as I walked my dogs this morning at four, before I sat down to write.

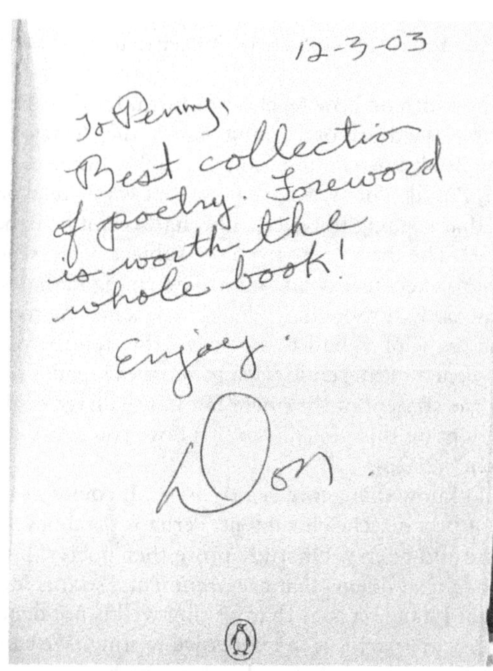

FIGURE 6.3. Don Graves's personal inscription in a book of poetry he gave me makes me smile. Handwriting is an intimate, personal mark.

Don's passion for poetry was a contagion. He invited me to read widely and find poems to read again. I loved those that brought me close to the anguish of a poet, like "A Letter to the Girl I Used to Be" by Ethan Smith (2014). Don read aloud. I listened. A poem is a small ask in the overcrowded schedules and hustle of school life. Tom Romano told me he starts every class with a poem, and I invite you to imagine that possibility. The strategy is to fill your unit with poems—a small glimpse of life rendered in beautiful words. We can leverage poems to deliver a simple, good thing to young people: to be seen and understood. To see and understand. To feel. The strategies here help me do just that.

Strategy 1: The Study of Spoken Word

The most reliable way to get my students writing poems is listening to the performance of poets and then writing their first thinking in notebooks. Each semester, my students begin class with two to three quick writes, almost always next to poems in a range of styles. They create a notebook of their responses that is fat with possibility.

One of the most effective collections is from Chicagoland High School (Karth, 2023). *Respect the Mic* contains 20 years of student poetry (Kahn, 2023a, 2023b). It invites students into writing poetry with essays by Hanif Abdurraqib, Franny Choi, former student Dan Sullivan, and the teacher and coach of this high school group, Peter Kahn. All poems are held in an online anthology where your students can listen to the poet perform the poem and then discuss how it was written.

This practice of listening and writing next to poems provides students access to personal subjects they haven't considered before. Poetry is a universe of thinking about experiences. Poems are built on repetition, literary devices, momentum, and clarity, familiar narrative tools, but spoken word holds particular power. Begin your study with Button Poetry (join millions of followers on TikTok, YouTube, Instagram) or follow the Poetry Slam competitions offered at high schools and many universities. I often play finalists in the National Poetry Slam competition.

We learn by studying spoken word that the "gateway line" is the poem's thesis (MasterClass, 2021). Support for this central idea is built in the poem like narrative with sensory images and precise language. An added bonus, the more students study spoken word, the more likely they hear their own phrases as they write them and imagine performing them.

Strategy 2: The Poetry Bracket

Students tune into an analysis of the form, content, and mechanics of individual poems when they compare them. I turned this into an annual poetry bracket (16 poems, 8 on each side in rounds like the annual March Madness college basketball tournament) after watching a colleague use this idea to teach Harlem Renaissance poetry (Kittle, 2003, p. 83). No matter the grade level, students respond with increased attention as we study and restudy the poems in the bracket. Often the declared winner in one class is different than the next, which ignites a lot of conversation in the halls: a definite win.

Many students nominate poems for study, increasing the collection of resources in our classroom. This is an effective strategy whether you create a bracket with page poems or stage poems, as my colleague Kelly Gallagher (Kittle & Gallagher, 2022) says.

Strategy 3: Copy Change

Ask students to read a poem and imitate its language, structure, or approach. Tom Romano calls this activity "a clear illustration of

Vygotsky's 'zone of proximal development.' The student apprentices herself to a more experienced, more accomplished other" (2013, p. 101). Romano continues, "Such imitation has a long, respected tradition among poets" (p. 101). Students imitate the approach of poets and find their own poems.

> "DAYS" by Billy Collins (1995)
>
> Each one *is* a gift, no doubt,
> mysteriously placed in your waking hand
> or set upon your forehead
> moments before you open your eyes.
>
> Today begins cold and bright,
> the ground heavy with snow
> and the thick masonry of ice,
> the sun glinting off the turrets of clouds.
>
> Through the calm eye of the window
> everything is in its place
> but so precariously
> this day might be resting somehow
>
> on the one before it,
> all the days of the past stacked high
> like the impossible tower of dishes
> entertainers used to build on stage.
>
> No wonder you find yourself
> perched on the top of a tall ladder
> hoping to add one more.
> Just another Wednesday
>
> you whisper,
> the holding your breath,
> place this cup on yesterday's saucer
> without the slightest clink.

We can all write about one day. Student pens fly.

Other student favorites are Webb's invitation to name how people should live, Crooker's vivid description of a first job, and Smith's reflection on one thing you should know about him: "How to Live" by Charles Parker Webb (2006), "Patty's Charcoal Drive-In" by Barbara Crooker (2015), and "Something You Should Know" by Clint Smith (2016).

Strategy 4: Understand Prose Poems and Transform Prose into Poetry

A prose poem might be paragraphs or an entire page. The text is not broken into lines but makes use of poetic devices. It is concentrated. It might be one or several poems in a collection where the author uses this fluid form to communicate the wholeness of the reflection on the subject. First my students read prose poems from Mary Oliver's (2013) collection of *Dog Songs*. We make a list of what we notice about prose poems.[3] Kaitlin B. Curtice (2023) calls a prose poem "a potent hybrid of writing that provides the comfort of prose with the compression of poetry . . . a sweetly slippery concept" (p. 108). Sweet and slippery, it is, because prose poems break rules of genre.

Understanding prose poems is great work for writing groups as this is a work of discovery, free of evaluation and easy answers. Students read prose poems together and consider how and where they might break the lines of a poet's work to prepare them to break their own.

I then ask students to reread their notebooks and look for entries that are particularly sensory and precise, as they make good playgrounds for transformation (see student notebook entry). Choose one, I say. Then take that burst of writing and reimagine it with line breaks. I tell them we are creating a poem from prose. After creating these, we look at the two drafts and discuss what form makes possible.

The most natural move in transforming a notebook entry into a poem is to create breaks in content. Leonard Cohen (1992) famously wrote this lyric, "There is a crack, a crack in everything—that's how the light gets in," and I use this to remind students that a line break might lead them to new understandings of their subject. The break or "crack" allows them to shed light on another idea—to extend their thinking.

Sometimes students leave space as they work—as if creating stanzas—when they feel these cracks of light, so that they can return to them in a second draft. Poet Danusha Laméris (2024) wrote, "The reader is like a carpenter bee, looking for a way into the siding of the poem. Where is the crack to get in? Where is an opening? There are many ways to offer an entrance by "breaking" our writing: the lines, the images, the syntax, the thinking, and more" (*danushlameris.com*). Likewise, as students read and reread, they understand the differences between prose

---

[3]Other excellent models include "How Prayer Works" by Kaveh Akbar and "When We Were 13, Jeff's Father Left the Needle Down on a Journey Record Before Leaving House One Morning and Never Coming Back" by Hanif Abdurraqib (2022, pp. 178, 260).

poems and poetry in stanzas, couplets, and so forth. Form determines *how* words and lines are read and understood.

I also have students play with transformation by choosing a character in the novel they are reading in book clubs and write an element of that character's story in verse (their own). They bring these experiments to their book club meetings and share them. Many students say it is challenging work that they wrote and rewrote, trying to get the character's voice and perspective to match what they know from the book.

Strategy 5: Study Novels in Verse

One way to expand an understanding of the power of poetry in storytelling is to read novels in verse. A novel in verse moves fast with few words on each page, but don't be fooled; those few words hold power. I've seen students read and reread pages as they come to understand the importance of a turning point in a novel. (I also recommend memoir and nonfiction in verse.)

Many students gain confidence when they read novels in verse. In an interview for *PBS News Hour*, Jason Reynolds (2017b) called the white space that surrounds one verse in a novel "breathing space" for a reader who is intimidated by the density of the text in most books. My students echo that observation: they believe they can stay with a book written in verse. They lose their fear and follow the story because they believe they can finish it. Short texts help them concentrate, they tell me, especially if they have not been reading in some time.

I introduce these books with a sample of the text—showing how a verse holds power in both language and line breaks. We collect observations in our notebooks of the beautiful language as well as the literary devices we recognize. Figure 6.4 is a sample from my own notebook where an eighth-grade class collected observations of craft with me while we read *Martin Rising: A Requiem for a King* by Andrea Davis Pinkney (2018). These two-page spreads of thinking (Kittle & Gallagher, 2022) have been remarkably successful in helping students pay close attention to the writing craft in reading. Teacher modeling (Guiding Question #5) helps students see and understand our expectations for collecting observations and writing about reading.

In middle and high school classrooms, I have created Novel in Verse Book Clubs to increase understanding of both prose and poetry. You might start with selections from this talented array of authors: Aida Salazar (*Land of the Cranes* [2020], *A Seed in the Sun* [2022]), Kwame Alexander (*Swing* [2018], *Solo* [2017], *The Door of No Return* [2022]), Diana Farid (*Wave* [2022]), Andrea Davis Pinkney (*The Red Pencil* [2014]), Jason Reynolds (*A Long Way Down* [2017a]), and Jacqueline

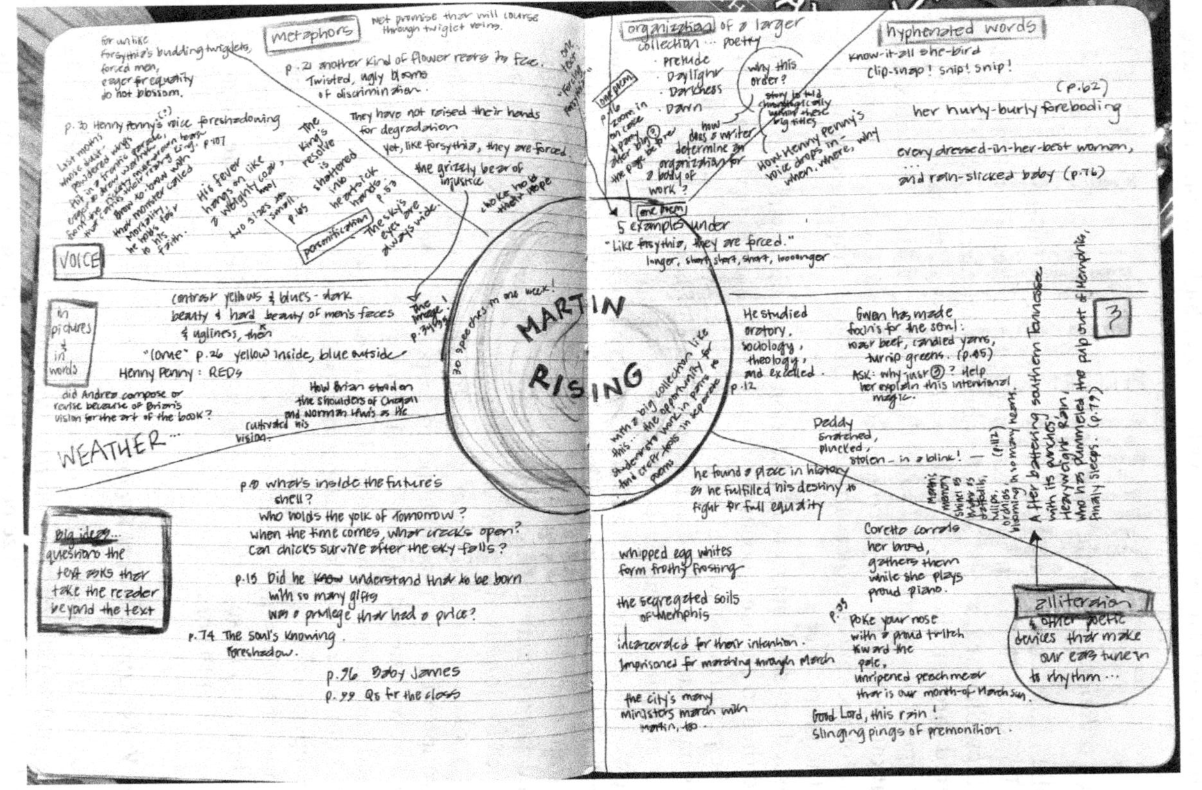

FIGURE 6.4. In *Martin Rising*, the teacher directed students to collect examples of alliteration, metaphors, and voice. The other five categories were created by me as I read and noticed patterns in the reading. We shared these collections as we discussed the book together as a class.

Woodson (*Brown Girl Dreaming* [2014]). All of these texts produce singular magic. All have been hits with middle, high school, and college students, often cited as their favorite books of the year.

Strategy 6: Reinterpret Published Poems

Last fall I used a collection of poems as my core text for the composition course I teach at Plymouth State University. The collection tells the story of Matthew Shepard, a college student brutally murdered in Wyoming in 1998, told through the voices of the deer, the moon, the fence, the ICU housekeeper, the frat boys, and so forth (Newman, 2012). The collection is remarkable, not just for its content and its implications for humanity but also for the myriad voices that illuminate what happened that night and in the years after.

I asked my students to read a section of 20 pages with a partner or two and then to choose a poem they would be willing to perform for the class. The performance would be in two or three voices. This means my students had to take a poem and imagine which lines should be read by one voice and which would be better read as a chorus. Their practice session allowed me to circulate and listen, offer encouragement, and marvel at their ability to interpret the author's meaning with their voices. They choose important lines to emphasize as a chorus. They whispered other lines and played with how to break lines between speakers—even to add silence for long beats between moments in the poem. No doubt our study of spoken word gave them vision for these performances. When three groups all chose the same poem to perform, our understanding increased as we listened to their differing interpretations line by line.

I used this same strategy with high school students as we neared the end of our poetry bracket competition (strategy 2). Students got into small groups to reimagine the poem with similar moves: silence, a chorus reading of lines, and an emphasis on words or ideas through many voices. They used these performances to argue for their favorite poem to move forward in the bracket.

Strategy 7: Assign Analytical Projects

I might have heard a sigh of relief from you, dear reader. Yes? *Finally*, you might have said, *we are getting to the good stuff.* Most secondary teachers I meet love to analyze poems. But ironically, few secondary students do. Here's how I've made poetry analysis successful in my room.

Each student identifies an analytical project. They will work on this project over a period of weeks during our poetry study. The project might be to analyze the works of one poet or a collection of poems on a subject. It might be to create a collection (as I was assigned long ago in ninth-grade English) of favorite poems, organizing them by themes, and reflecting on why and how these poems matter. (My project—which I still have in a box in my basement—was to collect 100 poems over the year.) Other project ideas include a songwriter's "10 Best Tracks" alongside "Cut Lists" of their less successful work and mash-ups of two poems merged into one—what to cut? What to keep? Why do they work together? Taylor Swift has made mash-ups a regular feature of her Eras concert tour (Mendez, 2024). Many recent students have been immersed in this idea.

Lastly—an idea for a project I have yet to suggest to students. In *Invisible Strings: 113 Poets Respond to the Songs of Taylor Swift* (Frederick-Daugherty, 2024), poets contribute an original poem that alludes to a Swift song without mentioning it. Consider it as a collection of little mysteries that readers are invited to decode. I can imagine students creating their own series of poems in this form—mystery poems based on other works of art, for example.

The key, of course, is delight. I want students fascinated by analysis. An analytical project is individualized by the student to increase their ability to closely read poems, to understand the power of literary devices, and to analyze an author's choices and their impact on readers. I encourage students to learn about the poet's process of writing. And most of all, I want to inspire students to apply their understandings in beginning to write their own poetry and novels in verse.

In closing, the rest of Will's story . . .

Will's second draft confirms my hunch. In the first few days of class, Will had shared lines from his notebook about missing his grandparents and younger sister in Czechia. His fiction tells of a mother and two children: an older brother and his sister. When Mom abandons them, the older brother must provide for the sister he adores. It is a dark story of loss and desperation but ends suddenly when the mom returns.

In fiction we can write the ending we long for.

He arrives early to class the next day, and I hold up copies of his draft.

He smiles, "What did you think of it?"

I applaud the courage it takes to tackle difficult things with a deep concern for characters. I read the lines I love out loud to him.

I pause. "I'm just not sure about the ending."

"Yeah, the ending feels wrong—a cliché, right?" and I nod, but before I can say more, he says, "It's more likely she never comes back." A pause. (The longest pause in the history of pauses.)

I don't know what to say. He continues, "And if she doesn't, how will it end?" Yikes. Can he sort that out here in writing?

"Hmmm," I nod. I acknowledge the challenge; I can't offer solutions.

You know, this is another reason teaching writing is so complicated. Will's draft is his first attempt to write this story. And I imagine him in his room typing fast and furiously. The sentences are rambling, often without ending punctuation, and there are few paragraphs. The easy teacher move is to correct his punctuation and hand it back. This doesn't help writers; I know you know that.[4]

Will needs help developing his ideas first. It's a more important move as his teacher, but it's thornier. Where do I focus? What do I ignore? I ask questions in the margin. I celebrate his beautiful lines.

I struggle to develop strengths in all my students. You've likely felt the impact of someone harping about your failings while missing your small moves towards better. Maybe it was an observation from a principal who wrote one thing after a classroom observation: *write your objective higher on the board.* (True story. And that sure didn't catalyze my daughter's learning.)

The goal of feedback on drafts is to send the writer back to work with renewed, focused energy. As Don Graves said, you must receive the piece—notice something about it—before you can nudge the writer to improve (Graves & Kittle, 2005). The best conferences are led by students. As Carl Anderson (2000) taught us to ask, "How can I help you?" and the student directs you to comment on what they need most to move forward.

All of this takes time. As does writing. Let's face it: one-and-done writing rarely reaches its potential. When we give students long stretches of time to write in class—in the company and under the influence of other writers—we see progress. Will needs time and emotional space to write the piece he is reaching for. Giving students time to revise and turn their work in again invites students to take their work much, much farther. The result is deeper learning for many.

In the last week of our course, Will handed me a revised draft. In it, the mother does not return. The brother and sister move on without her. I sighed as I read it; it's a tough story. But I could see his pride as he handed it to me . . . he got it *right*. Right for him.

Will was more satisfied, perhaps, because he had the courage to face one hard truth and imagine an ending of healing and joy. He told me he was grateful for my help throughout the semester—"with more than the writing," he said.

I gave him space and time to write, yes, and I saw him. I think of these lines from a lovely poem by U.S. Poet Laureate, Ada Limón, "A dream to be made whole by being not a witness but witnessed" (2022, p. 6).

And no, his punctuation was not perfect in that best draft. Nothing is in teaching writing.

---

[4]A student told me last semester, "You have to mark all of my errors; that's how I learn," and I replied, "If that were true—if you *learned* from someone marking your errors, then I think you would have learned by now. Aren't you just making the same ones still?" We know the answer.

Since the semester ended in the fall, I've had more time for my own reading and writing. For thinking about Will and all of my students—wishing next semester I will be a better teacher. We must cultivate a love of what we teach, Linda Rief (1992, 2016, 2018, 2022) has always reminded me. I've been savoring *The Book of (More) Delights* by Ross Gay (2023) for months. I have all of Gay's books; he is a clear and specific witness to the world, but he also sees joy and delight more than sorrow, and he helps me see it, too.

I stand next to Ross Gay and write my own delights as wishes for you, my readers, here in the dark of early morning.

A List of Wishes

May you walk hand in hand down a quiet cul-de-sac away from the blinking school bus belching out little people. On one side is your six-year-old granddaughter in a tasseled knit hat telling you about art class and recess while her sister, 3-year-old Lila races ahead, her tennis shoes pat-pat-patting across the wide street absent of cars.

May you stop when one girl says, "Grandma, look!" and see the leaf, the twig, the shadow, the smear of clouds that could be a wolf. Listen to why it matters. Know that "Hmmmm," is enough.

See chipped polish on tiny fingernails, a dot of glitter, and feel a firm grip on your arm. "Grandma, listen—" Lila holds a floppy bunny to your ear.

You say, "Oh, what is that?"

She whispers, "A tiny bunny heartbeat," and grins with possibility.

Wonder of wonders: these girls. I wish you this.

I have wishes for you, my colleagues. Will is one story of the dozens I lived last fall. I never made it to a hockey game, and I can't know how it will all work out for him—or any of the other students I worked beside for weeks.

We are caught in the wildness of a school year, and I wish you this:

May you find colleagues you love and admire. May they listen and console you when you act without thinking things through. May they bring you coffee. May they stay late to listen. May they help you figure out how to help a young writer. How to inspire a reader.

May you find leaders to believe in. May they see you. May they hear you. May they learn from you.

May you trust the process of teaching. May you forgive yourself when your plans seemed smart, but you say the wrong thing, and it all falls apart. When you wish you could start the day over. May you understand that we are always *becoming* teachers.

May you stay curious about student behavior. Listen and learn. Likewise, be curious about your colleagues who seem hardened into positions of power and control, even of curriculum. Wonder is more powerful than certainty. Consider: what am I missing here?

May you be open to all you don't know, no matter how many years you've done this. May you learn beside the young, brilliant minds who sit before you.

May you find joy and delight in teaching. It has gifts for a lifetime.

If we are to live in this work of teaching English with joy, we must cultivate our own love of reading, writing, revising, and sharing. It will sustain us through student disinterest and challenge. It will motivate us in the storm of curriculum adoptions we don't believe in. It will remind us that we have stories to tell that no one can tell but us, and whether we write them in prose or poetry, they are gifts to those who come after us. Evidence that we were here. We witnessed the brilliance of young people, and we want to tell about it.

ACTION STEPS

- Buy a notebook. Begin short daily writing next to poetry, images, ideas, and your own bright and lively mind. Every few days, go back and reread what you've written and work with the language. Make the writing better. Watch for patterns that emerge in your work as a writer.
- Collect poetry, art images, passages from books, and other things that will provoke a response in writing from students. Check out this Padlet of ideas: *https://padlet.com/pennykittle/notebooks-so-many-inspirations-for-writing-xytvgqza1hif5lf8*
- Read with a writer's eye. Collect your own stack of vibrant mentor texts across genres.
- Learn from poets and other authors who discuss their process as thinkers, writers, and teachers. Start your own collection of favorite poems.
- Begin collecting beautiful sentences from the books you read that you can study as craft with your students.
- Follow the advice of prolific author Gary Paulson, as retold by Bruce Coffey Jr. (2023): "Read like a wolf eats." Read everything. Continue to fill yourself up with prose and poetry and the thinking it ignites in you.

REFERENCES

Abdurraqib, H. (2022). *Poetry unbound.* Norton.

Abdurraqib, H. (2023). *On writing* [Respect the Mic session]. NCTE Annual Convention, Columbus, OH.

Akbar, K. (2021). How prayer works. On Being podcast. *https://onbeing.org/poetry/how-prayer-works*

Alyan, H. (2021). *The arsonists' city.* HarperCollins.

Alexander, K. (2022). *The door of no return.* Hachette Book Group.
Alexander, K., & Hess, M. R. (2017). *Solo.* HarperCollins.
Alexander, K., & Hess, M. R. (2018). *Swing.* HarperCollins.
Anderson, C. (2000). *How's it going? A practical guide to conferring with student writers.* Heinemann.
Bruner, J. (1977). *The process of education* (2nd ed.). Harvard University Press.
Buckingham, M., & Goodall, A. (2019). The feedback fallacy. *Harvard Business Review, 97*(2), 92–101.
Coffey, B. (2023, January 27). Read like a wolf eats: An appreciation of Gary Paulson. *Read to Them Blog. https://readtothem.org/read-like-a-wolf-eats-an-appreciation-of-gary-paulsen*
Cohen, L. (1992). "Anthem" [Song]. *The future.* Columbia Records.
Collins, B. (1995). Days. In *The art of drowning.* Pittsburgh University Press.
Crooker, B. (2015). Patty's charcoal drive-in. In *Selected poems.* Future Cycle Press.
Curtice, K. B. (2023). *Living resistance: An indigenous vision for seeking wholeness every day.* Brazos Press.
Elbow, P. (1990). *What is English?* National Council of Teachers of English.
Emdin, C. (2021, May 5). Thinking of pedagogy as protest with Dr. Chris Emdin. *Houghton-Mifflin-Harcourt Literacy Blog. www.hmhco.com/blog/pedagogy-as-protest-chris-emdin*
Farid, D. (2022). *Wave.* Amulet Books.
Frederick-Daugherty, K. (2024). *Invisible strings: 113 poets respond to the songs of Taylor Swift.* Ballentine.
Gay, R. (2023). *The book of (MORE) delights.* Algonquin Books.
Graham, S., Kim, Y. S., Cao, Y., Lee, W., Tate, T., Collins, P., Cho, M., Moon, Y., Chung, H. Q., & Olson, C. B. (2023). A meta-analysis of writing treatments for students in grades 6 to 12. *Journal of Educational Psychology, 115*(7), 1004–1027.
Graham, S., & Perin, D. (2007). *Writing next: Effective strategies to improve writing of adolescents in middle and high schools.* Carnegie Corporation.
Grant, A. (2023). *Hidden potential: The science of achieving greater things.* Viking.
Graves, D., & Kittle, P. (2005). *Inside writing: How to teach the details of craft.* Heinemann.
Kahn, P., Abdurraqib, H., Sullivan, D., & Choi, F. (2023a). *Respect the mic.* Penguin Random House.
Kahn, P., Abdurraqib, H., Sullivan, D., & Choi, F. (2023b). *Respect the mic. https://spokenword.oprfhs.org/respect-the-mic-anthology*
Karth, P. (Ed.). (2023). *Respect the mic: Celebrating 20 years of poetry from Chicagoland High School.* Penguin.
Kittle, P. (2003). *Public teaching.* Heinemann.
Kittle, P. (2008). *Write beside them: Risk, voice and clarity in high school writing.* Heinemann.
Kittle, P. (2013). *NCTE 2013 three conferences* [Video]. YouTube. *www.youtube.com/watch?v=YpY0h0dAk3w&t=292s*
Kittle, P. (2022). *Micro mentor texts.* Scholastic.

Kittle, P., & Gallagher, K. (2022). *4 essential studies: Beliefs and practices to reclaim student agency*. Heinemann.

Laméris, D. (2024). *Writing the broken poem* [Video]. YouTube. *www.youtube.com/watch?v=FM1STMbOt4w*

Lessing, D. (2007). *"Doris Lessing: On not winning the Nobel Prize," Nobel Prize Lecture, Dec. 7, 2007. www.nobelprize.org/uploads/2018/06/lessing-lecture_en-1.pdf*

Limón, A. (2022). Sanctuary. In *The hurting kind*. Milkweed Editions.

MasterClass. (2021, August). *How to write spoken word poetry. www.masterclass.com/articles/how-to-write-spoken-word-poetry*

McBride, A. (2023). *Me (moth)*. Square Fish.

Mendez II, M. (2024). All the song mashups Taylor Swift has played during the Eras Tour. *Time. https://time.com/6957475/taylor-swift-eras-tour-song-mashups*

Mukherjee, S. (2010). *The emperor of all maladies: A biography of cancer*. Scribner.

Murray, D. M. (1984). *A writer teaches writing* (2nd ed.). Heinle.

Murray, D. M. (1995). *The craft of revision* (2nd ed.). Harcourt Brace.

Newkirk, T. (2014). *Minds made for stories: How we really write informational and persuasive texts*. Heinemann.

Newkirk, T. (2021). *Writing unbound*. Heinemann.

Newman, L. (2012). *October mourning: A song for Matthew Shepard*. Candlewick Press.

Oliver, M. (2013). *Dog songs: Poems*. Penguin.

Ó Tuama, P. (2022). *Poetry unbound*. Norton.

Pinkney, A. D. (2014). *The red pencil*. Hachette Book Group.

Pinkney, A. D. (2018). *Martin rising: A requiem for a king*. Scholastic.

Reynolds, J. (2017a). *A long way down*. Atheneum.

Reynolds, J. (2017b). *How poetry can help kids turn a fear of literature into love* [Video]. PBS News Hour. *www.pbs.org/video/how-poetry-can-help-kids-turn-a-fear-of-literature-into-love-1513386092.*

Rief, L. (1992). *Seeking diversity*. Heinemann.

Rief, L. (2016). *Read write teach*. Heinemann.

Rief, L. (2018). *The quickwrite handbook*. Heinemann.

Rief, L. (2022). *Whispering in the wind*. Heinemann.

Romano, T. (2009). "How to write . . . with Endnotes." *Ohio Journal of English Language Arts*, 2(49).

Romano, T. (2013). *Fearless writing*. Heinemann.

Salazaar, A. (2020). *Land of the cranes*. Scholastic.

Salazaar, A. (2022). *A seed in the sun*. Penguin Random House.

Smith, C. (2016). Something you should know. In *Counting descent*. Write Bloody.

Smith, C. (2021). *How the word is passed*. Little, Brown.

Smith, C. (2023). *Personal interview* [Video]. YouTube. *www.youtube.com/watch?v=R_5iyjDbwXA*.

Smith, E. (2014, May 16). A letter to the girl I used to be. Button Poetry. *www.youtube.com/watch?v=Lkn06Y8prDU*

Stevenson, B. (2014). *Just mercy.* One World.
Stone, N. (2018). *Dear Martin.* Simon & Schuster Children's Books.
Webb, C. H. (2006). How to live. In *Amplified dog.* Red Hen Press.
Woodson, J. (2014). *Brown girl dreaming.* Penguin.
Woolf, V. (1929). *A room of one's own.* Hogarth Press.
Zerwin, S. (2020). *Point-less: An English teacher's guide to more meaningful grading.* Heinemann.

Chapter 7

Teaching Argument Writing in the English Language Arts Classroom

DIVERSITY AS RESOURCE

Carol D. Lee

As George Hillocks (2011) points out, argumentative writing is the core of critical thinking. In his words, "Argument is not simply a dispute, as when people disagree with one another or yell at each other. Argument is about making the case in support of a claim in everyday affairs—in science policy making in courtrooms and so forth" (p. 1). In this chapter, I seek to address the implications of this conception of argumentative writing for pedagogical practices. I will address the holistic needs of students as learners and recruit the breadth of cultural repertoires they bring from their everyday experiences as resources for robust learning. As such, the chapter will address the following questions:

GUIDING QUESTIONS

1. What does argument writing in the English language arts (ELA) classroom entail?
2. What is the role of literary reasoning and argumentation?
3. How do we design learning environments that foster motivation, engagement, and persistence in the argumentation process?
4. How can Cultural Modeling using cultural data sets support oral and written argumentation?

Teaching argument writing in the ELA classroom includes reasoning, epistemology (e.g., what counts as knowledge, viewing knowledge as simple or complex), oral language, and the conventions of composition. The focus of argumentation in ELA classrooms, of course, includes responding to literature but not limited to literary analyses. Topics subject to argumentation can range from responding to texts across disciplines but also to topics that require research on the part of students around issues within the school, as well as the broader society and indeed world. If we conceptualize creating robust opportunities for students to compose arguments in the ELA classroom, we also need to start from broad conceptualizations of the range of registers (formal and informal ways of using language with different audiences), rhetorical structures, and breadth of warrants and backings on which students may draw in addressing an array of audiences. In argumentation, backings include the relationship between claims and evidence provided to support claims. Warrants include the evidence that supports the warrant. This chapter will focus on this problem space with regard to teaching argument writing in middle grades through high school ELA classrooms and will include particular attention to what is made possible when we recruit the everyday knowledge, language, and epistemological repertoires that students bring from their participation in routine cultural practices outside of the classroom.

Often the focus of teaching argument writing in middle and high schools is primarily on grammar and composition (e.g., structure of paragraphs). However, not only does argumentation writing entail more than grammar and composition skills, in many respects, these technical skills are the most straightforward to teach and do not require the deep reasoning many teachers are after. Figure 7.1 captures the breadth of what is entailed in argumentation.

Reasoning in Argumentation

Reasoning in argumentation entails claims, evidence, warrants, and backing (Toulmin et al., 1984), with warrants and backing articulating why an audience should believe the evidence offered to support claims. In this model articulated by Toulmin, complex arguments also include structures of superordinate claims and subclaims as well as anticipation of and response to counterarguments. Despite the fact that there are critiques of the Toulmin model, this chapter argues that it is the understanding of the diversity of warrants and backings that captures the diversity of the kinds of arguments that are possible, which contributes to equity. When we disagree, to the extent that we do not understand the underlying reasoning and values that inform the positions we hold, we are less likely to find common ground. In the context of the democratic system of governance in the United States, there are many questions in the civic domain over which we have deep divisions that can either restrict or expand equity in terms of life course opportunities. For example, our divisions over questions of abortion are more informed by beliefs about when life begins and about relationships between the rights of women and the rights of fetuses. Even differences in terminology like *fetus* versus *unborn child* reflect the warrants and backings that drive different and hotly contested divisions. If we believe that life begins at conception, we are likely to draw on very different evidence than if we believe that viability is the warrant to support particular claims. It is because of the ways that evidence, warrants, and backings are essential to rational argumentation as a tool of civic reasoning and discourse that this conceptualization of argumentation is an essential goal of public schooling in the United States.

And it is precisely the lack of explicit articulation of warrants and backing that makes it difficult to respond to arguments that one disagrees with, a problem particularly salient in today's deeply contested political environment, both in the United States and abroad. Warrants and backings in the context of schooling are very much rooted in

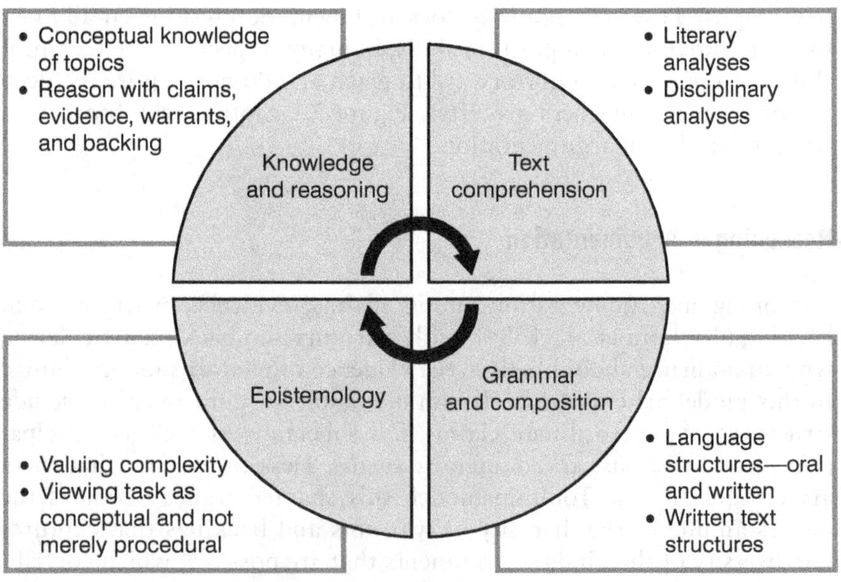

FIGURE 7.1. Argumentation in ELA.

traditions of academic disciplines, but it is also important to recognize as we teach that there are contestations over such warrants and backings. For example, in the field of literary reasoning or literary criticism, there are long-standing differences in what counts as support for claims, and these differences also reflect differences in cultural traditions and particular issues that arise within and across cultural-historical time (e.g., Black Aesthetic, feminist, LGBTQ traditions). Some traditions of literary criticism and theory privilege strict adherence to what is presumed to be the author's point of view and privilege language and structural choices solely within the confines of the text itself. On the other hand, there are traditions that privilege the points of view of the reader, the experiences that communities of readers bring to interpreting characters, plot, and themes. These traditions identify what counts as evidence for claims. At the same time, literary interpretations as arguments are often—especially in the contexts of schooling—aimed at others. And so, anticipation of the warrants that will be valued by particular audiences is important in trying to convince others.

Epistemological orientations are essential to argumentation in terms of whether students conceptualize writing, for example, as procedures to follow versus viewing writing and reasoning as nuanced. To the extent that argumentation in ELA classrooms involves interpreting literary texts, for example, epistemological orientations toward reading literature matter (Lee, Goldman, Levine, & Magliano, 2016). Yukhymenko-Lescroart and colleagues (2016) developed an instrument to measure readers' epistemological orientations toward literature. The instrument captured what readers valued about reading literature, whether they valued multiple readings, and the social functions of personal meaning making through literature. The instrument is published and available for use in classrooms. I have used the instrument in several studies and found positive relationships between students' epistemological orientations to reading literature and their skills in literary reasoning and argumentation captured in essay writing (Lee, 2016). I will further explore the conditions of teaching that are required as pedagogical practices and classroom culture to enhance opportunities for students to engage and internalize such knowledge and dispositions.

Hillocks (2011) asserts the importance of teaching argumentation as reasoning and not simply as rhetorical structures. He has created exemplars across multiple publications to illustrate scenarios that invite students to interrogate the available data and articulate and discuss among themselves the warrants and backings that inform their claims. This focus on reasoning, however, does not preclude the need to teach students rhetoric for communicating ideas.

Literary Reasoning in Argumentation

As this chapter focuses on argumentation in ELA classrooms in middle and high school, I address the role of literary reasoning in argumentation. Most of the units we teach in ELA classes focus on literature but can and should include reading informational texts, often as sources of background information for literary texts. These may include informational texts addressing the historical background in which the plot of literary texts takes place, or may include informational texts that can help explain the psychological states and life experiences of characters in literary texts. Robust literary reasoning requires deep and detailed understandings of literary texts. In what follows, I offer research that helps us actually teach students how to interrogate literary texts, with the understanding that such interrogation is a prerequisite to arguing about interpretations of texts, whether such arguments focus on author intent or the reader's connections with the themes and problems that the texts address.

Hillocks (Hillocks & Ludlow, 1984) has articulated a taxonomy of question types for narrative texts. The taxonomy includes seven levels of difficulty, ranging from what he calls key details and basic stated information, to two levels of inferencing (simple implied inferences to complex implied relationships), to the two most challenging comprehension tasks. Table 7.1 lists and defines each question type.

TABLE 7.1. Hillocks's Taxonomy of Skills in Reading and Interpreting Narrative

1. Basic stated information—Details about conditions without which the story would not be possible
2. Key detail—Key details take place at important points in the narrative and embody causal relations within the plot.
3. Stated relationship—Stated relationships are explicit and entail at least two points of information that may include events, characters.
4. Simple implied inference—Simple implied inferences require the reader to draw from information across the text.
5. Complex implied inferences—Complex implied inferences require the reader to draw from across details in the text to infer meanings.
6. Author generalizations—Author generalizations entail constructing themes about what the reader infers about the world beyond the text itself. Such generalizations require inferring from across the breadth of the text what the author seeks to convey about the human condition.
7. Structural generalizations—Structural generalizations require the reader to attend to the choices the author makes about rhetoric and structure to convey meaning but also to attend to how the parts of the text work together to create particular effects.

The value of the taxonomy is that it provides windows into the depth of understanding students have of narrative texts. Students who cannot answer questions of basic stated information initially and then the different levels of inferencing are not likely prepared to construct literary arguments that address the most robust goals of literary interpretation.

Author generalizations are essentially about themes, what the text says about the world beyond the text itself, what it says about life, and what it says about the conundrums of the human condition. Structural generalizations focus on the significance of the choices that authors make with regard to structure and language. Both of these tasks of interpretation represent the most rigorous goals of reading literature, regardless of the literary theory of criticism the reader invokes or on which instruction focuses. Appleman (2000) has argued for and demonstrated how high school ELA classes can teach students to engage in different literary theories and models of literary criticism.

In the case of author generalizations, students need to be able to develop criteria for detecting and evaluating themes. Themes can be thought of as generalizations about conundrums of the human condition, very much represented by what are called archetypal themes: good versus evil, courageous action in the face of adversity. Hillocks (2011) offers examples of scenarios used in middle and high school classrooms to prepare students to extrapolate criteria for judging themes and character types (e.g., mythic hero, trickster). Smagorinsky and colleagues (1987) also offer an additional array of scenarios, cases, and surveys used in real classrooms that support students in articulating criteria for judging themes and character types. Such criteria essentially capture the warrants and backings for claims, in this case, claims about what themes are being explored and/or about broader extrapolations about characters represented in narrative texts.

Rabinowitz (1987) argues that as readers, we bring a toolkit of reading strategies before we open the literary text. These strategies include the following:

- Rules of notice—details authors use to draw our attention
  - Repetitions
  - Ruptures
  - Privileged positions—for example, titles, endings, first and last lines
- Rules of signification—the significance we attribute to outer and inner attributes of characters, the attribution of moral significance to actions and inner states, point of view or who is talking, and associations we make with details we notice

- Rules of configuration—as we are reading, what patterns we notice that we continue to test as we read, expectations of stasis or disruption; a process of predicting as we read how this is going to turn out
- Rules of coherence—a sense, post hoc, of how all the pieces of the work fit together or not.

Rules of notice and rules of signification are essential building blocks for wrestling with the questions that Hillocks has identified as author generalizations and especially structural generalizations. Rules of notice include details that authors use to attract the reader's attention. Rules of signification include the sources of information on which we draw to impose meaning on that which we notice. Such noticing and signification go beyond simply identifying elements of the plot. These literary practices invite readers into a wonderful and engaging dialogue with the text, the author, oneself, and others with whom one interacts around the text. It is unfortunate that few assessments of literature available to schools either ask students to engage in such interpretive work, and if they do, provide no tools for understanding why students can or cannot engage in such theorizing. But it is my position that without developing these skills, particularly of noticing and signification, students will not learn to love literature and thus be inspired and motivated to engage in deep literary argumentation.

What Rabinowitz calls rules of configuration and coherence represent important epistemological practices (e.g., attitudes about what is important to note in reading literature or other kinds of texts), not only in the reading of literature but informational texts as well. I have often argued that reading comprehension is akin to what we do in putting together complex jigsaw puzzles. We don't know what the whole will look like when we start, even if we have a picture of the finished product on the jigsaw box. We look at pieces of the puzzle and look for patterns. And as we put together pieces of the puzzle in what we hypothesize will be meaningful patterns, we are in a hypothetical state of mind, testing hypotheses against evidence as we read. This is the same process we engage in close reading, moving from sentence to sentence, from detail to detail, from paragraph to paragraph, from chapter or stanza to chapter or stanza, trying to figure out what it all means. We must be metacognitive in monitoring how and if our emerging hypotheses continue to be supported. This is the process that Rabinowitz calls *configuration*. Coherence is the process of generating a broader takeaway of the whole after we have completed reading. Both processes are metacognitive reading processes but also the meaning-making foundation for proposing claims, evidence, warrants, and backing. Metacognition is the act of monitoring while we read, paying attention to what we understand, what we don't understand, and what we think is important. A basic tenet of routine teaching of reading comprehension, such as annotations, is to support students in being metacognitive as they read. We need to be able to engage these processes both in oral language and dialogue and then to be able to translate that reasoning into written composition.

It is important to note that these broad categories of strategies outlined by Rabinowitz do not mean that readers will come to the same conclusions about the meanings they attribute to the text. Rather, these strategies are heuristics (e.g., routine ways of solving problems) that can guide readers in their problem solving, but particularly with regard to signification, configuration, and coherence. Readers who are deeply involved and engage in their meaning making will quite likely draw on different warrants and backings and even evidence for their claims. Thus, I argue that this focus on how to read is essential for preparing students to construct arguments, particularly in ELA classrooms.

Contributors to Motivation, Engagement, and Persistence

At its best, argumentation—oral and written—should be a process in which the learner is deeply engaged. Robust argumentation is complex, entails probabilistic reasoning, and demands the invocation of multiple sources of knowledge and dispositions. Argumentation, in the civic domain and as it should be practiced in schools, should also be respectful and embody ethical commitments for good; anticipating counterarguments to one's position should entail empathy for others (Lee et al., 2023). Because argumentation is complex, the design of learning environments intended to prepare students for civic life should be informed by deep understandings of human learning and development.

Current syntheses of research across various fields of psychology, human development, the learning sciences, and the neurosciences document how thinking, perceptions of the self, tasks, settings, relationships with others, and the emotional salience we attribute to experience work in tandem (Cantor et al., 2021; Immordino-Yang et al., 2019; Lee et al., 2020; Nasir et al., 2020; Osher et al., 2018). This means that designing robust learning environments, in this case preparation for argumentation in the contexts of schooling, should not be viewed purely through the lens of cognitive demands. What I have outlined so far captures the multiple cognitive dimensions of argumentation. While these multiple cognitive dimensions of argumentation are necessary in their fullness, they are not sufficient for instructional design. Classrooms must be organized such that students feel emotionally and physically safe, efficacious, and see the relevance of investing energy in the tasks. While there is current attention in schooling to social and emotional learning (SEL; Jagers et al., 2019), it is typically addressed as a set of experiences that often take place outside of academic classes and is not viewed as connected and indeed essential to the cognitive work of schooling.

Efficacy (Schunk & Pajares, 2002; Zimmerman et al., 1992) is supported as we make the processes of reasoning visible and provide feedback as learners are engaged in acts of problem solving. As argumentation in ELA classes most often includes analyzing texts, teachers need to provide supports in helping students create external representations of their reasoning processes. Outside of graphic organizers and some ways of annotating, in reading comprehension, there are few forms of external representations of reasoning, in comparison, for example, to mathematical reasoning (Lee, 2023).

Designing a Classroom Climate to Support a Sense of Safety and Connection

A classroom climate in which students learn to listen to one another, to respect one another's points of view, and to collaborate with each other supports a sense of safety and connection. The question of designing instruction that supports students' sense of the relevance of tasks is complex. Addressing the question of relevance requires that we both interrogate common assumptions about cultural membership (Gutierrez & Rogoff, 2003) and assumptions about the foundations and history of knowledge in the disciplines we teach. For example, often our literature curricula typically assume that only texts that have evolved out of the Eurocentric traditions count as classic. Schools typically act on two assumptions about cultural membership. First, it is presumed that there should not be distinctions in what and how students are taught. Second, students are presumed to belong to single, homogenous cultural communities. Both assumptions are flawed. We know from everyday experiences that one size rarely fits all. Parents with more than one child recognize that while children will share family practices, they are also individually different. In the classroom, individual variation is always challenging because of how many students teachers need to accommodate.

With regard to cultural membership, students belong to and participate in multiple cultural communities of practice. These include the family, intergenerational, and often cross-national practices often associated with ethnicity, cultural-historical cohorts (e.g., children of the Great Depression), religious communities, age cohorts (teenagers), as well as communities of shared interests (e.g., basketball, anime, hip-hop, etc.). One way of navigating between individual variation and group memberships is to analyze potential relationships between the range of repertoires that students bring from their routine experiences outside of schooling (and within schooling outside of the disciplinary classroom)—such as Nasir's (Nasir, 2000; Nasir & Hand, 2008) work connecting the statistical knowledge around basketball of students on the school's basketball team and how they are taught and experience their math classes, or Brown's (Brown & Kloser, 2009) work examining the knowledge of the school's baseball team around the physics of pitching and the formal physics class. In the case of argumentation in ELA classes, this includes trying to understand relationships among how students engage in narrative reasoning outside of school (e.g., reading graphic novels, interpreting song lyrics, interpreting movies and TV programs that are narratives) (Champion, 1998, 2003; Heath, 1983, 2001) and the demands of literary and other texts students are reading.

This work of connecting also requires that we reexamine our assumptions about the history and scope of knowledge construction in the disciplines we teach. In fields like mathematics, this has included attention to areas like ethnomathematics (e.g., mathematical practices in different cultural communities across the world, typically outside of formal schooling) (Ascher, 1991); in science to Indigenous knowledge systems around the natural world (Bang & Marin, 2015; Bang & Medin, 2010; Marin & Bang, 2018; Medin & Bang, 2014); in history to examining the full range of historical actions across time and space; in literature to both understanding the full diversity of literary forms across time and space (e.g., magical realism from Toni Morrison and William Faulkner to Gabriel Marquez to Franz Kafka to Amos Tutuola) and narrative and poetic forms in the popular market (e.g., film, TV, music) to narration and figuration in everyday language genres (e.g., signifying in African American English). Making these conceptual connections is challenging because there are virtually no commercial curricula available that make such connections.

Because the goal here is both oral argumentation as well as written argumentation, recruiting everyday language registers, including recruiting languages other than English, is another resource in the intellective toolkit required to address the challenge of making instruction relevant. There is a significant body of research demonstrating how in classroom talk everyday language repertoires are recruited, illustrating deep engagement with complex reasoning tasks (Ball & Farr, 2003; Gutiérrez & Orellana, 2006; Jensen et al., 2021; Johnson et al., 2017; Lee, 1997, 2005; M. Orellana & Eksner, 2006; M. F. Orellana & Reynolds, 2008). Such everyday registers (e.g., ways of using language for different audiences) include use of African American English or languages other than English, of genres of talk such as signifying in African American English (a form of ritual insult), as well as using everyday words for academic language.

I will now illustrate how this conception of argumentation in literary reasoning—the multiple dimensions of such reasoning, recruiting everyday knowledge, language repertoires, and epistemological orientations that students bring to instruction, and addressing the conceptual dimensions of task relevance—has been used over three decades of instructional design in my work in Cultural Modeling.

Cultural Modeling: Exemplar in Practice

Cultural Modeling is a framework for the design of instruction that supports deep reasoning, disciplinary reasoning, and classroom discourse, which in turn support oral and written argumentation (Lee, 1993, 1995a, 1995b, 2001, 2007; Lee et al., 2003). Cultural Modeling seeks to address the instructional challenges of motivating engagement, perceptions of relevance, and self-efficacy by recruiting everyday cultural repertoires (knowledge, epistemology, language registers and genres, narrative sense-making) to support reasoning (in this case, literary reasoning). For close to three decades, this research and instruction have taken place in schools serving African American students in middle and high school low-income communities.

Design Principles

Cultural Modeling is a framework for designing instruction that supports students in conceptual understanding by recruiting repertoires that students develop from their participation in routine cultural practices outside of schooling. Our work in Cultural Modeling has focused on literary interpretation by recruiting cultural repertoires from African American students, particularly those who are speakers of African American English. The framework requires examining relationships between the demands of literary texts and specific analytic tasks. These relationships may be conceptual and/or epistemological (Lee et al., 2016). The design of instruction aims to make problem solving public and explicit, to create routine practices where students share their analyses with other students in service of creating oral and written arguments and a classroom culture that helps students develop a sense of self-efficacy, positive social relationships, and a sense of relevance.

Designing Instructional Units

The design of instructional units requires articulating one or more essential questions that address any or some combination of the following: theme, problems of figuration (e.g., symbolism, irony, satire, unreliable narration), character type (e.g., mythic hero, the trickster), or genre (e.g., magic realism, fable, haiku, mystery, science fiction). Drawing heavily on the work of George Hillocks, it should be noted that the conception of literary genres is different from how genre is typically categorized in commercial anthologies typically used in schools (Hillocks, 1989, 2016; Smith & Hillocks, 1988). Typically, genres are identified as short stories, novels, poems, and plays. The problem is that these distinctions do not provide insights around structural properties that can guide comprehension. The distinctions Hillocks makes around genres, on the other hand, guide expectations. For example, when reading a fable, a haiku poem, or a work of magical realism, the expert reader comes to the text with expectations that can reliably guide comprehension—unless, of course, the author is satirizing or critiquing the specialized genre.

Text sets are organized to provide students with multiple opportunities over time to wrestle with the same interpretive problem, including examining the problem by constructing oral and written arguments. To recruit students' relevant prior knowledge and epistemological dispositions, the design entails identifying what are called "cultural data sets," which are texts—broadly defined—with which students would interact in their routine practices outside of school. These texts entail problems similar to the ones students will meet in the texts in the instructional unit. These everyday texts might include music lyrics, movies or movie clips, TV programs, cartoons, or visual images. After being taught Rabinowitz's rules of notice and rules of signification, students initially analyze the cultural data sets on their own (since they already do this outside of school) and then make their own problem-solving strategies public and connect them with Rabinowitz's rules of notice and signification. The purpose of this element of the framework is to support students' sense of self-efficacy: in other words, support the idea that they already know how to do this work. Another purpose is to support the relevance of this kind of problem solving and to recruit their existing epistemological orientations to value the complexity of this work.

The instructional units focus on one or more of the following: theme, problem of figuration (e.g., symbolism, irony, satire, unreliable narration), character type, or genre (as previously defined). With one or more of these foci, we develop key questions that are explored across the texts. To the extent that we can identify points of convergence and/

or divergence across the texts, the topics about which students develop arguments will accumulate analyses across texts in order to argue about points of similarity and/or difference and why these similarities or differences matter.

Because Cultural Modeling in literature engages students in identity wrestling and development, the texts are selected not only for the technical interpretive opportunities they offer but for how the texts invite students to think about challenges and difficult questions with which they are engaged by virtue of their age, the cultural communities they routinely participate in, the social relationships that are important to them, and how they imagine their future selves. I view canonical literature (children's, adolescent, adult) as dispersed across time and space and canonical authors (including contemporary authors who produce extraordinary works) as persons with the gift of second sight, who have meaningful insights into the human experience. So Cultural Modeling seeks to include texts that provide meaningful opportunities for holistic development of students—and not merely engaging students in technical exercises.

From their analyses of cultural data sets, students then move on to apply the same strategies and epistemological dispositions to the formal texts in the instructional unit. In our work with African American students who are speakers of African American English, we have recruited the epistemological disposition to value figuration, particularly in a speech genre called "signifying." Signifying (Smitherman, 1977, 2000) is a form of playful ritual insult, often involving satire: "Yo mama so skinny she could do the hoola hoop in a cheerio." Such language play, passed on across generations, values figuration over the literal, reading between the lines, making inferences. It is not only the skills being developed but also the value placed on engaging in such meaning making.

This design process requires the designers themselves to engage in close analyses of the sources of text complexity in the texts assigned for students to read. This is another instructional challenge that requires teacher professional learning communities—ideally within schools and/or departments within schools—because there are few resources available for teachers to draw on to analyze such sources of text complexity (Goldman & Lee, 2014; Lee, 2023). Teachers often use Lexile measures (White & Clement, 2001) and resources on the Lexile site to identify, minimally, a grade-level measure. However, Lexile measures sentence length and vocabulary. But there are other sources of text complexity that are really important to comprehension that are not addressed in Lexile scores. For example, the short story *Flowers* by Alice Walker

(1973) is less than a page in length, has a Lexile score of fifth grade, but is deeply complex. Some of those sources of text complexity have to do with the demands of the theme. In the case of *Flowers*, the loss-of-innocence theme would be a challenge for a fifth grader even if they were an excellent reader with regard to phonics, fluency, and decoding. Other sources of text complexity invite invocation of Rabinowitz's rules of notice (e.g., title, character name, repetitions, and disruptions) and signification (e.g., invoking knowledge of the historical period of Jim Crow, lynching, the psychological impacts of racism, and the lost-innocence theme).

Understanding sources of text complexity is essential to the selection of text sets and the identification of cultural data sets, as students will need to be supported in navigating the range of sources of text complexity they will meet in the instructional unit. This attention to supporting close reading comprehension is an essential component of preparation for argumentation. Students can argue opinions outside of schooling, but schooling should prepare them for navigating a knowledge-rich society in which texts serve as both reliable and unreliable resources for making judgments (Hess, 2009; Wineburg & McGrew, 2016). And in our diverse democracy, currently and historically embroiled in deep differences, literature can serve as a consequential resource for entering worlds different from our own and developing empathy for others.

Recruiting Language Repertoires

In Cultural Modeling and other robust instructional designs, discussion is essential for learning and provides a medium through which argumentation should take place before students commit to positions in writing (Haroutunian-Gordon, 2009; Michaels & O'Connor, 2015). Of course, students can write arguments first and then discuss and debate, but it is likely and ideal that through dialogue, they have opportunities both to rethink their positions and anticipate possible counterarguments that may be made to their positions.

In the work we've done in Cultural Modeling, we have worked with African American students who are speakers of African American English; classrooms are organized such that students feel free to bring their linguistic resources as they engage in learning. In terms of speakers of African American English, this means loud talking and involves overlapping exchange, body movement, and what Boykin (1979, 1994) calls "verve." In some classrooms, especially ones that are driven by formal lecture, this kind of speech would be viewed as disruptive. In Cultural Modeling classes, this loud, overlapping, rhythmic, and embodied talk is the norm, resulting in high levels of engagement by all students. This level of engaging oral discussion recruits more propositions on the table, more interrogation of claims and evidence (Lee, 2001).

Supporting Argumentation

One more recent development in Cultural Modeling has been the digital tool Sense-Making in the Disciplines (SMD; Lee et al., 2016). SMD is a digital authoring tool in which teachers can place their own texts and tasks (*www.sensemaking.northwestern.edu*). The underlying design of the tasks in the tool supports close reading in literature and social studies/history texts. Texts are divided into short segments with the expectation that students will work closely to construct meaning before moving on, akin to Rabinowitz's rules of configuration. To support metacognitive reasoning, students annotate the text chunks. However, one important difference in this task is that teachers create tags. As students highlight text they are paying special attention to, they explain what they notice and also identify a tag teachers create in the system that provides a window into what concept informed their decision (e.g., attention to character, plot, symbolism).

In sum, students highlight text that draws their attention, provide an explanation of what they are thinking in relation to that highlighted text, and then select a tag created by the teacher that identifies, from a metacognitive perspective, why this stretch of text drew their attention. In addition to annotation tasks, the teacher creates close reading questions that address essential information students should derive from reading that chunk. However, the most unique aspect is problem-solving organizers. These organizers include questions that students should ask themselves in order to focus their attention and seek to impose meaning on particular categories of details. For example, there are organizers for rules of notice and for detecting symbolism, irony, or unreliable narration, and there are criteria for detecting particular themes. As students move from one chunk of text to another, the problem-solving organizers continue such that students accrue a body of evidence that can serve as their individual databases for constructing arguments about themes, character types, or problems of figuration.

This tool supports argumentation in that individual students are expected to put in the effort to identify significant details organized to support their ability to recruit data to support claims. It is expected that after a series of lessons on sequential chunks and/or at the end of reading, students can download their accumulated organizers in order to engage in small and whole group discussion and debate, leading to written arguments that include claims, evidence, warrants, and backings, as well as anticipation of counterarguments.

Illustration

Among the many instantiations of Cultural Modeling, I will share data from one longitudinal study as part of an Institute of Education Sciences-funded research, Project READi (Lee, 2016). READi was part of a larger initiative by the Institute of Education Sciences, Reading for Understanding. I will focus on one unit in the third year of the project with a group of high school seniors who were African American and speakers of African American English, living in low-income urban communities and attending an African-centered charter school. The primary text in the literature unit was *Beloved* by Toni Morrison (1987). We examined symbolism, what life was like under the African Holocaust of Enslavement, and what contributed to resilience in the face of this challenge.

To prepare students to understand how symbolism contributes to understanding possible themes, students reviewed *Sax Cantor Riff*, an episode on a TV program called *Subway Stories* (available on YouTube). This episode runs around 6 minutes and was written and directed by Julie Dash, the director and producer of the film *Daughters of the Dust*.

Sax Cantor Riff served as the primary cultural data set for the unit. It was chosen because it was on a popular TV program, which suggested that it would be easily accessible, aimed at being interpretable by a broad audience. The details embody Rabinowitz's rules of notice: repetitions, disruptions, significance of beginning and ending, title, and parallelisms. Students were deeply engaged in interpreting what was symbolic and why and what they thought Julie Dash might be trying to convey. They drew on their own life experiences, many of which were rooted in intergenerational practices in the African American community, to attribute significance to details. This helped generate warrants and backings for why their claims were accurate. In small groups, they engaged in performance (singing, moving their bodies, and speaking with rhythm and musical tone), built upon one another's claims by jointly constructing evidence, backing, and warrants; they connected what they saw in the film to parallels in African American history, even though there was no explicit reference to this in the film.

Their small-group discussions were essentially dialogic argumentation in which claims, evidence, warrants, and backings were made and elaborated in collaboration and debated. This analysis of a cultural data set prepared students to deploy similar strategies and ways of interacting with one another as they engaged the complexities of Toni Morrison's *Beloved*. It should be noted that these were not students with high reading comprehension scores on the assessments mandated by the district. Yet, with the preparation of recruiting knowledge and strategies and dispositions that they had already developed (largely from their participation in routine cultural practices outside of school), they approached this demanding novel with interest and rigor.

We also used problem-solving organizers similar to those that would eventually be incorporated into the SMD tool. Students had to do the hard work of analysis (initially individually) and then bring their analyses to small-group discussions where they debated interpretations and moved to write arguments supporting their analyses of symbolism, character, and theme in the novel.

One interesting debate revolved around how they evaluated Sethe's decision to take the life of her baby. I was able to videotape discussions of both *Sax Cantor Riff* and *Beloved*. In one small group, student opinions differed over whether Sethe was justified in taking the life of her baby. In the video, one young man argues that anticipation of life under slavery was not enough to morally justify Sethe's actions. To make his case, he takes out the Afro pick he uses to comb his Afro hairstyle and walks across the room to another student, holding the pick over her head as if he was about to kill her, saying "Ima gonna kill Marsha cuz she gonna through some pain tonight at work. It's wrong ta kill."

Through extensive videorecording, we captured interactions of students as they engaged in literary analyses and argumentation. We assessed their skills in literary analyses with pre- and posttests where they read two short stories and were asked to write an argument analyzing sources of similarity and difference across the two stories regarding symbolism and character development. We approached this work with the goal of not only developing their skills in literary analyses and argumentation but also supporting self-efficacy, a growth mindset that effort mattered, and an epistemological disposition to value literature as a source of personal meaning making and valuing the importance of multiple readings. We also sought to examine how their sense of racial identity contributed to their outcomes in terms of literary argumentation. Therefore, we deployed measures of these constructs as possible predictors of how well students improved in the technical skills of literary reasoning and argumentation. We analyzed students' pre- and post-essays using rubrics that documented the rigor of their thinking as well as the written structure of their essays. This distinction is important to my overarching argument because the model I have offered for argumentation, in this case, literary analysis and argumentation, includes both reasoning and composition. My hope here is to argue that robust teaching of written argumentation must include more than just grammar and the structure of essays (e.g., paragraphs, transitions).

Overall, we found growth in literary reasoning and argumentation. Importantly, we also found that a positive sense of racial identity, a belief in effort, a positive sense of self-efficacy, and an epistemological orientation regarding the role of literature in personal meaning making and valuing multiple readings were all positively correlated with growth in literary reasoning and argumentation. See Lee (2016) for a more detailed report on the findings from this work.

Conclusions

I have offered a conception of what students must learn in order to be able to construct robust arguments—oral and written—when examining literature in ELA classrooms. This conception goes beyond learning procedures for essay writing and the technical skills of reading comprehension.

There are challenges and opportunities to bringing this vision to scale. Among the challenges is shifting the focus of accountability beyond limited technocratic conceptions of learning as solely cognitive. The research literature across disciplines clearly documents that thinking, feelings as the emotional salience we attribute to experience, perceptions of self along multiple dimensions, tasks, and settings are all dynamically interacting as we engage in learning. At the same time, even the cognitive dimensions of learning formal argumentation in schooling are underconceptualized in commercial curricula and assessments. Neither commercial curricula nor assessments address how indicators of argumentation are connected to the multiple demands of comprehending texts on which students draw in constructing written arguments. These demands include epistemological orientations to interrogating texts (written, visual, digital, multimodal) as well as sources of text complexity. In teaching reading comprehension—both generic and disciplinary—we are constrained by insufficient tools to analyze sources of text complexity beyond Lexiles. As a result, we teach generic skills that may or may not be specific to particular texts students are expected to comprehend, and our practices, curricula, and assessments typically focus on outcomes of comprehension, shedding little light on understanding the reasoning processes that inform what students do and do not comprehend.

As reading and argumentation are intricately linked, the current public debates around restrictive conceptions of what reading comprehension requires and the current attention to what is being called the "science of reading" pose huge challenges. And finally, we are also challenged by lack of sufficient understanding and appreciation of the wide range of knowledge, skills, and dispositions that students across diverse backgrounds develop in their routine cultural practices outside of schooling as generative resources for formal learning in and across disciplines within the school environment.

ACTION STEPS

Addressing these challenges at scale will require substantive shifts in policies that shape the work of schooling. This would include policies at the federal, state, and district levels. Bringing these questions to organizations such as the Council of Great City Schools and the National Education Association represents a reasonable starting point. Sufficiently addressing policy at scale is beyond the purview of this chapter. We also, of course, need to address how teacher education programs can prepare practitioners and school leadership to engage in lifelong professional learning. I include attention to policymakers because they, in large part, create the conditions under which teachers work. Such policies need to focus on the holistic needs of students and to support the recruitment of the diverse array of cultural repertoires that students develop outside schooling (e.g., knowledge, dispositions, everyday literacy practices, and ways of using language).

However, it is possible at smaller scales to create professional learning communities of teachers who are committed to studying their practices. On an international scale, the practice of "lesson study" (Lewis et al., 2006) is a powerful exemplar. Within the United States, literacy exemplars such as the National Writing Project and Breadloaf offer inspiration about the power of teacher professional learning communities, initiated by teachers themselves. Within individual schools, teachers can create professional learning communities. School-based learning communities, however, require support from school leadership and require that districts not impose restrictions that impede such teacher organizing. In this political moment, the deeply politicized contestations over topics that can be addressed and books that can be read pose consequential challenges. These contestations are particularly difficult regarding the idea of argumentation. The national literacy associations—the National Council of Teachers of English, the International Literacy Association, and the Literacy Research Association—at this moment are playing important roles in raising the importance of teaching as a professional intellectual practice requiring ongoing professional inquiry. In these efforts and venues, such professional learning communities must address the following at least minimally:

- current research in the science of human learning and development to examine the role of
  - the multiple dimensions of identity
  - child and adolescent development
  - the role of emotions in learning
  - the role of perceptions of self, tasks, settings; of relationships as these intersect to influence motivation, engagement, and persistence
  - the significance of what students know and value from their diverse experiences outside of formal schooling
- the full range of what is entailed in reading comprehension, both generic and discipline specific
- the limitations of current assessments of both reading comprehension and writing and resources available to address these limitations
- structures, resources, and supports that are needed for teachers to study their practices in environments that are safe and professionally affirming

At the school and district levels, teachers need time to read through the relevant literature around learning and development, around the complexities of reading comprehension and argumentation, and to bring findings from these areas of study to critically examine the curriculum they use and both the assessments they choose and the ones they are required to use. An important feature of teaching as a professional practice is that resources made available to them—commercially or by the school or district—are resources and not recipes. Teachers need to be empowered to critically examine such resources to determine what is relevant for their students, what supports the holistic and multiple dimensions of learning to engage in argumentation and to reject that which does not address such needs. They need to be empowered to create their own practices but to always critically examine what and how they teach in terms of impacts on students' development and learning. This should involve both videotaping instruction with analyses of how the multiple demands of reading comprehension and argumentation are addressed in tandem with student work. This should also involve gathering data on students' perceptions of their learning experiences. Creating such cases of professional learning and student learning allows them to become resources for sustainability—sustainability of the practices for current and future teachers within the school community. The

National Writing Project remains an exemplar of such practices led by teachers themselves.

In this work, it is important to understand how participation works in routine cultural practices within and across spaces. Recruiting cultural repertoires that students bring from their experiences in the world beyond the walls of schooling is essential for the simple reason that prior knowledge matters and that knowledge in the academic disciplines is rooted in the real world, an environment students experience in a variety of ways. Creating environments in which the diversity of experiences and of points of view do matter as we seek to prepare our students to engage in this democratic experiment that requires both the ability and the disposition to think critically, to weigh evidence, and to empathize with others. These dispositions are central features of the kind of argumentation needed for civic reasoning, discourse, and engagement. Education can and should play a central role in preparing our students as civic agents.

As a field, we need to identify such efforts, uplift them, and share them. We need to learn from our international colleagues where professional learning communities are the norm.

REFERENCES

Appleman, D. (2000). *Critical encounters in high school English: Teaching literary theory to adolescents.* Teachers College Press.

Ascher, M. (1991). *Ethnomathematics: A multicultural view of mathematical ideas.* Brooks/Cole.

Ball, A., & Farr, M. (2003). Language varieties, culture and teaching the English language arts. In J. Flood, D. Lapp, J. Squire, & J. Jensen (Eds.), *Handbook of research on teaching the English language arts* (2nd ed., pp. 435–445). Erlbaum.

Bang, M., & Marin, A. (2015). Nature–culture constructs in science learning: Human/non-human agency and intentionality. *Journal of Research in Science Teaching, 52*(4), 530–544.

Bang, M., & Medin, D. (2010). Cultural processes in science education: Supporting the navigation of multiple epistemologies. *Science Education, 94*(6), 1008–1026.

Boykin, A. W. (1979). Psychological/behavioral verve: Some theoretical explorations and empirical manifestations. In A. W. Boykin, A. Franklin, & J. Yates (Eds.), *Research directions of Black psychologists* (pp. 351–367). Russell Sage.

Boykin, A. W. (1994). Afrocultural expression and its implications for schooling. In E. Hollins (Ed.), *Teaching diverse populations: Formulating a knowledge base* (pp. 50–51). State University of New York Press.

Brown, B. A., & Kloser, M. (2009). Conceptual continuity and the science of baseball: Using informal science literacy to promote students' science learning. *Cultural Studies of Science Education, 4*(4), 875–897.

Cantor, P., Lerner, R. M., Pittman, K. J., Chase, P. A., & Gomperts, N. (2021). *Whole-child development, learning, and thriving: A dynamic systems approach.* Cambridge University Press.

Champion, T. (1998). "Tell me somethin' good": A description of narrative structures among African-American children. *Linguistics and Education, 9*(3), 251–286.

Champion, T. (2003). *Understanding storytelling among African American children: A journey from Africa to America.* Erlbaum.

Goldman, S. R., & Lee, C. D. (2014). Text complexity: State of the art and the conundrums it raises. *Elementary School Journal, 115*(2), 290–300.

Gutierrez, K., & Rogoff, B. (2003). Cultural ways of learning: Individual traits or repertoires of practice. *Educational Researcher, 32*(5), 19–25.

Gutiérrez, K. D., & Orellana, M. F. (2006). At last: The "problem" of English learners: Constructing genres of difference. *Research in the Teaching of English, 40*(4), 502–507.

Haroutunian-Gordon, S. (2009). *Learning to teach through discussion: The art of turning the soul.* Yale University Press.

Heath, S. B. (1983). *Ways with words: Language, life and work in communities and classrooms.* Cambridge University Press.

Heath, S. B. (2001). What no bedtime story means: Narrative skills at home and school. In A. Duranti (Ed.), *Linguistic anthropology* (pp. 318–342). Blackwell.

Hess, D. E. (2009). *Controversy in the classroom: The democratic power of discussion.* Routledge.

Hillocks, G. (1989). Literary texts in classrooms. In P. W. Jackson & S. Haroutunian-Gordon (Eds.), *From Socrates to software: The teacher as text and the text as teacher* (pp. 135–158). National Society for the Study of Education.

Hillocks, G. (2011). *Teaching argument writing, grades 6–12.* Heinemann.

Hillocks, G. (2016). The territory of literature. *English Education, 48*(22), 109–126.

Hillocks, G., & Ludlow, L. (1984). A taxonomy of skills in reading and interpreting fiction. *American Educational Research Journal, 21*, 7–24.

Immordino-Yang, M. H., Darling-Hammond, L., & Krone, C. R. (2019). Nurturing nature: How brain development is inherently social and emotional, and what this means for education. *Educational Psychologist, 54*(3), 185–204.

Jagers, R. J., Rivas-Drake, D., & Williams, B. (2019). Transformative social and emotional learning (SEL): Toward SEL in service of educational equity and excellence. *Educational Psychologist, 54*(3), 162–184.

Jensen, B., Valdés, G., & Gallimore, R. (2021). Teachers learning to implement equitable classroom talk. *Educational Researcher, 50*(8), 546–556.

Johnson, L., Terry, N. P., Connor, C. M., & Thomas-Tate, S. (2017). The effects of dialect awareness instruction on nonmainstream American English speakers. *Reading and Writing, 30*, 2009–2038.

Lee, C. D. (1993). *Signifying as a scaffold for literary interpretation: The pedagogical implications of an African American discourse genre.* National Council of Teachers of English.

Lee, C. D. (1995a). A culturally based cognitive apprenticeship: Teaching African American high school students' skills in literary interpretation. *Reading Research Quarterly, 30*(4), 608–631.

Lee, C. D. (1995b). Signifying as a scaffold for literary interpretation. *Journal of Black Psychology, 21*(4), 357–381.

Lee, C. D. (1997). Bridging home and school literacies: A model of culturally responsive teaching. In J. Flood, S. B. Heath, & D. Lapp (Eds.), *A handbook for literacy educators: Research on teaching the communicative and visual arts* (pp. 330–341). Macmillan.

Lee, C. D. (2001). Is October Brown Chinese: A Cultural Modeling activity system for underachieving students. *American Educational Research Journal, 38*(1), 97–142.

Lee, C. D. (2005). Culture and language: Bi-dialectical issues in literacy. In P. L. Anders & J. Flood (Eds.), *Culture and language: Bi-dialectical issues in literacy* (pp. 241–274). International Reading Association.

Lee, C. D. (2007). *Culture, literacy and learning: Taking bloom in the midst of the whirlwind.* Teachers College Press.

Lee, C. D. (2016). *A longitudinal study of disciplinary literacy development in literature and history as a resource for identity development and psychosocial well being.* Project READi.

Lee, C. D. (2023). We ask students what they understand, not how they understand: Making reasoning comprehension processes visible and explicit. *The Reading Teacher, 77*(3), 371–382.

Lee, C. D., Goldman, S. R., Levine, S., Brown, M., & Loh, B. (2016). *Sense-making in the disciplines: A digital tool to support content area* (READI Technical Report #12). *www.projectreadi.org/wp-content/uploads/2017/04/READI-Tech-Report-12_Sense-Making-in-the-Disciplines-Digital-Tool.pdf*

Lee, C. D., Goldman, S. R., Levine, S., & Magliano, J. (2016). Epistemic cognition in literary reasoning. In J. Greene, W. Sandoval, & I. Braten (Eds.), *Handbook of epistemic cognition* (pp. 165–183). Routledge.

Lee, C. D., Meltzoff, A., & Kuhl, P. (2020). The braid of human learning and development: Neuro-physiological processes and participation in cultural practices. In N. I. Nasir, C. D. Lee, R. D. Pea, & M. McKinney de Royston (Eds.), *Handbook of cultural foundations of learning.* Routledge.

Lee, C. D., Nasir, N. I. S., & Immordino-Yang, M. H. (2023). What the sciences of human learning and development tell us about civic reasoning and discourse. *The Annals of the American Academy of Political and Social Science, 705*(1), 54–72.

Lee, C. D., Rosenfeld, E., Mendenhall, R., Rivers, A., & Tynes, B. (2003). Cultural Modeling as a framework for narrative analysis. In C. L. Dauite (Ed.), *Narrative analysis: Studying the development of individuals in society* (pp. 38–62). Sage.

Lewis, C., Perry, R., & Murata, A. (2006). How should research contribute to instructional improvement? A case of lesson study. *Educational Researcher, 35*(3), 3–14.

Marin, A., & Bang, M. (2018). "Look it, this is how you know": Family forest walks as a context for knowledge-building about the natural world. *Cognition and Instruction, 36*(2), 89–118.

Medin, D. L., & Bang, M. (2014). *Who's asking? Native science, Western science, and science education.* MIT Press.

Michaels, S., & O'Connor, C. (2015). Conceptualizing talk moves as tools: Professional development approaches for academically productive discussion. In L. Resnick, C. Asterhan, & S. Clarke (Eds.), *Socializing intelligence through academic talk and dialogue* (pp. 347–362). American Educational Research Association.

Morrison, T. (1987). *Beloved.* Knopf.

Nasir, N. (2000). "Points ain't everything": Emergent goals and average and percent understandings in the play of basketball among African American students. *Anthropology and Education, 31*(1), 283–305.

Nasir, N., & Hand, V. (2008). From the court to the classroom: Opportunities for engagement, learning, and identity in basketball and classroom mathematics. *The Journal of the Learning Sciences, 17*(2), 143–179.

Nasir, N. I., Lee, C. D., Pea, R. D., & McKinney de Royston, M. (Eds.). (2020). *Handbook of cultural foundations of learning.* Routledge.

Orellana, M., & Eksner, H. (2006). Power in Cultural Modeling: Building on the bilingual language practices of immigrant youth in Germany and the United States. *National Reading Conference Yearbook, 55*, 224–234.

Orellana, M. F., & Reynolds, J. F. (2008). Cultural Modeling: Leveraging bilingual skills for school paraphrasing tasks. *Reading Research Quarterly, 43*(1), 48–65.

Osher, D., Cantor, P., Berg, J., Steyer, L., & Rose, T. (2018). Drivers of human development: How relationships and context shape learning and development. *Applied Developmental Science*, 1–31.

Rabinowitz, P. (1987). *Before reading: Narrative conventions and the politics of interpretation.* Cornell University Press.

Schunk, D. H., & Pajares, F. (2002). The development of academic self-efficacy. In A. Wigfield & J. S. Eccles (Eds.), *Development of achievement motivation* (pp. 15–31). Academic Press.

Smagorinsky, P., McCann, T., & Kern, S. (1987). *Explorations: Introductory activities for literature and composition, 7–12.* National Council of Teachers of English.

Smith, M., & Hillocks, G. (1988, October). Sensible sequencing: Developing knowledge about literature text by text. *English Journal*, 44–49.

Smitherman, G. (1977). *Talkin and testifyin: The language of Black America.* Houghton Mifflin.

Smitherman, G. (2000). *Talk that talk: Language, culture and education in African America.* Routledge.

Toulmin, S., Rieke, R., & Janik, A. (1984). *An introduction to reasoning.* Macmillan.

Walker, A. (1973). Flowers. In *In love & trouble: Stories of Black women.* Harcourt.

White, S., & Clement, J. (2001). *Assessing the Lexile framework: Results of a panel meeting* (Working Paper No. 2001-08). U.S. Department of Education, Office of Educational Research and Improvement.

Wineburg, S., & McGrew, S. (2016). Why students can't google their way to the truth. *Education Week, 36*(11), 22–28.

Yukhymenko-Lescroart, M. A., Briner, S. W., Magliano, J. P., Lawless, K., Burkett, C., McCarthy, K. S., . . . Goldman, S. R. (2016). Development and initial validation of the Literature Epistemic Cognition Scale (LECS). *Learning and Individual Differences, 51*, 242–248.

Zimmerman, B. J., Bandura, A., & Martinez-Pons, M. (1992). Self-motivation for academic attainment: The role of self-efficacy beliefs and personal goal setting. *American Educational Research Journal, 29*(3), 663–676.

Chapter 8

Multilingual Learners

WRITING WITH SOURCES THROUGHOUT SOCIAL STUDIES INQUIRY

Chauncey Monte-Sano and Mary J. Schleppegrell

In this chapter, we share what we've learned through our experiences as elementary and high school teachers, curriculum designers, teacher educators, professional development facilitators, and researchers who work closely with students and teachers in classrooms. We ask the following guiding questions:

GUIDING QUESTIONS

1. What does social studies have to do with writing?
2. What is the role of writing in the context of social studies inquiry?
3. How can teachers build on the resources that multilingual learners with emerging English proficiency bring to social studies writing?
4. How can teachers engage all of their students as thinkers and writers during social studies inquiry?

We draw on our experiences with a summer program for middle school students who are recent immigrants to the United States to illustrate the points we make about writing with sources in the context of social studies inquiry.

Writing for Inquiry: Disciplinary Practices and Expectations

For students to be successful in writing social studies arguments, they must see that this school subject is open to interpretation. In addition, they must have a chance not only to work with the raw materials of social studies—complex questions and artifacts or sources with different perspectives—but also be supported and apprenticed into reading, analysis, synthesis, and communicating evidence-based argument through writing. With disciplinary and literacy-rich resources and structured opportunities to engage with texts and construct evidence-based arguments, writing in social studies can help students develop disciplinary thinking, understanding of the content, and written communication skills (see Monte-Sano, 2016).

What Does Social Studies Have to Do with Writing?

Deliberating and writing in response to complex questions and sources with varying perspectives is the core of social studies inquiry. This approach to social studies is supported by the C3 Framework and Common Core State Standards, which highlight disciplinary literacy expectations for reasoning and discourse. Social studies inquiries are guided by questions without clear right or wrong answers. Instead, students consider their own knowledge and make sense of and evaluate artifacts or sources that share multiple perspectives. On the basis of and in response to that evidence, students construct plausible arguments. Interaction with questions, texts, and each other establishes the foundation for students' argument writing. Social studies inquiry frames writing as collective thinking and foregrounds puzzling over different possible arguments and the evidence used to support those arguments.

An inquiry approach also foregrounds the interpretive nature of social studies by highlighting the disciplinary practice of revising arguments to reflect the available evidence and by using an audience and purpose to frame writing as dialogic and deliberative. Students aren't only writing to complete an assignment, they are in conversation with others about the meaning and significance of what they read and the unsettled issues they're investigating. As students discuss complex questions and sources, they refine their understandings, make sense of historical and social issues, and see the importance of communicating their ideas to others.

What Is the Role of Writing in the Context of Social Studies Inquiry?

Writing in social studies inquiry is not something that happens at the end of a unit of instruction; instead, it is an integral part of every phase of inquiry. Throughout this chapter, we refer to an investigation into child labor from the freely available *Read.Inquire.Write.* (*RIW*) curriculum that we developed with middle school teachers and students as an example of resources that support social studies–specific inquiry, discussion, and argument writing (see *http://readinquirewrite.umich.edu*). In the following sections, we introduce tools and structures embedded within all of the *RIW* investigations and describe how students interact with one another, the sources, and the compelling question to develop their understanding of a social issue and come to an evidence-based conclusion.

We first offer a brief overview of the initial phases of inquiry, where the foundations for argument writing with sources are established, and then elaborate on the composing and drafting phases. Throughout, we share specific disciplinary literacy tools from the *RIW* curriculum that create structure and scaffolding to engage and support students as speakers, thinkers, and writers, along with examples of how each tool was used during the summer program to foster ongoing collaboration and discussion as preparation for composing written arguments.

The central question of this investigation asks, "Why does hazardous child labor continue to exist in Nepal?" and focuses on the brick kiln industry there. The inquiry offers sources with perspectives from Nepali children working in the brick kilns (first-person accounts and a table with numeric data that tabulates 424 children's interview responses), and from a factory supervisor, a nongovernment organization, and an international news organization. In this and other investigations, social studies argument writing in the context of inquiry is a process that begins with and iteratively returns to the sources.

How Can Teachers Build on the Resources That Multilingual Learners with Emerging English Proficiency Bring to Social Studies Writing?

In our research, we have found that making sense of sources, deliberating about their meaning, drawing conclusions from them, and communicating their arguments to others is possible for all students, regardless of reading and/or language(s) proficiency (Monte-Sano et al., 2019). We have shown that students at all language and reading levels are able to engage in the challenging disciplinary practices of inquiry when supported by the kinds of scaffolding we describe here (Monte-Sano et al., 2021).

Our work has been developed in school districts where multilingual learners are a significant presence, so supporting them has been an important goal. *RIW* provides investigations accommodated for Spanish and Arabic speakers. We further adapted the Arabic version of the child labor investigation to support the more intensive summer program context focused on newcomers (see Figure 8.1). *RIW* offers further

Why does hazardous child labor continue to exist in Nepal?

Kumar, 12 years old كومار، ١٢ عاما

Headnote: *Kumar works in a brick kiln. He makes bricks, cooks, and gets water. His parents work for $5 per month. Kumar does not go to school. He has worked several jobs including selling tea. Researchers from IREWOC an organization from the Netherlands, visited brick kilns in Nepal and asked children about their experiences to write this report. IREWOC wants to learn why children work in bad conditions. IREWOC wants to find ways to help these children.*	**Circle and draw arrows to:** -Author -Publisher -Date -Type of Source	ضع دائرة حول و ارسم سهم بجانب: -المؤلف -الناشر -التاريخ -نوع المصدر	الترويسة: كومار يَعمل في فرن الطوب. يَصنع الطوب ويَطبُخ ويَحصُل على الماء. يعمل والديّه مُقابل ٥ دولارات شهريًا. كومار لا يَذهب إلى المَدرسة. عَمِل في العَديد من الوظائف بما في ذلك بَيع الشاي. زار باحثون من IREWOC - وهي مُنظمة هولندية- أفران الطوب في نيبال وسألوا الأطفال عن تَجاربهم لكتابة هذا التقرير. المؤسسة تُريد مَعرفة سبب عَمل الأطفال في ظُروف سيئة، وتُريد إيجاد طُرق لمُساعدة هؤلاء الأطفال.
We make the clay, so we can make bricks. When we finish making the bricks, we have to start to make the clay again, and so it never ends. I don't enjoy doing this work, but I am from a poor family, so I have to. But next year I do not want to come back.	**Underline and draw arrows to what Kumar:** -Thinks -Wants -Experiences	ضع خط تحت و ارسم سهم على ما : فكر به كومار يريده كومار جربه كومار	نَصنع الطين ، حتى نَتَمكّن مِن صُنع الطُوب. علينا أنْ نَبدأ في صُنع الطِين مَرة أخرى عِندما نَنتَهي مِن صُنع الطُوب ، وبِالتالي لا يَنتَهي هذا العمل أبدًا. أنا لا أستَمتع بِهذا العَمل ، لَكِنّي مِن عائلة فَقيرة ، لذا لا بد لي من ذلك. لَكِنّي لا أريد العَودَة العام القادم.
Attribution: Said by 12-year-old Kumar from Sindhuli in a 2010 report, "*Child Labour in Kathmandu, Nepal,*" by IREWOC, the foundation for International Research on Working Children, p. 20.	**Circle and draw arrows to:** -Author -Publisher -Date -Type of Source	ضع دائرة حول و ارسم سهم بجانب: -المؤلف -الناشر -التاريخ -نوع المصدر	الإسناد: قالها كومار البالغ من العمر ١٢ عامًا من السندولي في تقرير عام ٢٠١٠ ، "عمالة الأطفال في كاتماندو ، نيبال" من قبل IREWOC ، مؤسسة البحث الدولي عن الأطفال العاملين ، ص. ٢٠.

Factory Supervisor مُشرف المصنَع

Headnote: *Factory owners and supervisors do not always follow Nepal's laws to stop child labor. Four brick kiln supervisors talked about their experiences with child labor for this report. Some brick kiln supervisors did not want to talk. They thought talking about child labor is bad for their businesses. Supervisors do not follow the laws because they don't want to lose the money they make from child labor. Some brick kiln owners say that children do not have to work. They say that children want to help in their free time before and after school. Researchers from IREWOC visited brick kilns in Nepal and asked people about their experiences to write this report.*	**Circle and draw arrows to:** -Author -Publisher -Date -Type of Source	ضع دائرة حول و ارسم سهم بجانب: -المؤلف -الناشر -التاريخ -نوع المصدر	الترويسة: لا يَتبع أصحاب المَصانع والمُشرفون دائمًا قوانين نيبال لوقف عَمالة الأطفال. تحدّث أربعة من مُشرفي قمائن الطوب عن تَجاربهم مع عَمالة الأطفال مِن أجل هذا التقرير. لم يَرغب بَعض المشرفين على قمائن الطوب في التَحدُّث لقد اعتقدوا أنّ الحديث عن عَمالة الأطفال يَضُر بأعمالهم. لا يَتبع المشرفون القوانين لأنهم لا يُريدون خَسارة الأموال التي يَكسَبونها من عَمالة الأطفال. يقول بَعض أصحاب قمائن الطُوب أن الأطفال ليسوا مُضطرين للعمل. يَقولون أنّ الأطفال يُريدون المُساعدة في أوقات فراغهم قبل المدرسة وبَعدها. زار باحثون من IREWOC أفران الطُوب في نيبال وسألوا الناس عن تجاربهم لكتابة هذا التقرير.
It is not good that children work in a brick factory, but we do not have a law to stop child labor. Sometimes we tell parents that they should not let the children work, but send them to school. But these parents are not educated, and they think children waste time if they play. Parents think it is good when the child helps with work because they get more money to feed their family. Parents are happy when the child can work.	**Underline and draw arrows to what Factory Supervisor:** -Thinks -Wants -Experiences	ضع خط تحت و ارسم سهم على ما : فكر به المُشرف يريده المُشرف جربه المُشرف	عَمل الأطفال في مَصنع الطُوب لَيس جيدًا، لكن ليس لدينا قانون لوقف عَمالة الأطفال. أحيانًا نخبر أولياء الأمور أنه لا ينبغي السماح للأطفال بالعمل ، ولكن يَنبغي إرسالهم إلى المدرسة. لكن هؤلاء الآباء غير متعلمين ، ويعتقدون أنّ الأطفال يُضيعون الوقت إذا لعبوا. يَعتقد الآباء أنه من الجَيد أن يُساعد الطِفل في العَمل لأنهم يَحصلون على المَزيد من المال لإطعام أسرهم. يَسعد الآباء عندما يستطيع الطِفل أن يعمل.
Attribution: From a supervisor at a brick kiln in a 2010 research report, "Child Labour in Kathmandu, Nepal," by IREWOC, the foundation for International Research on Working Children, p. 29.	**Circle and draw arrows to:** -Author -Publisher -Date -Type of Source	ضع دائرة حول و ارسم سهم بجانب: -المؤلف -الناشر -التاريخ -نوع المصدر	الإسناد: من مُشرف في قمائن الطوب في تقرير بحثي عام ٢٠١٠ ، "عمالة الأطفال في كاتماندو ، نيبال" من قبل IREWOC ، مؤسسة البحث الدولي حول الأطفال العاملين ، ص. ٢٩.

FIGURE 8.1. Investigating child labor with sources accommodated for newcomers and emergent bilingual students.

recommendations for engaging emergent bilingual students and fostering an asset-based classroom that invites students to draw on all of their knowledge, languages, and meaning-making resources as they share their experiences and thinking (see *https://readinquirewrite.umich.edu/bi-multilingual-learners*; Schleppegrell et al., 2025). Throughout this chapter, we'll point out differences in the ways we further accommodated the child labor investigation in order to introduce inquiry and argument writing to newcomers in this particular summer school setting.

The intensive summer program was embedded in a summer school serving recent immigrants where students also attended classes in English language arts and mathematics. We worked with teachers in two classrooms, introducing inquiry in social studies to two student cohorts that were mixed groups from different grade levels (i.e., rising seventh, eighth, or ninth graders), all of whom had arrived in the United States during the previous school year. Across 4 days, the students' English language arts and social studies blocks were devoted to the child labor investigation. Figure 8.2 presents the goals for student learning across the 4 days, along with the relevant *RIW* resources used in each session. We explain those resources and lessons in the following sections of this chapter.

All students in the summer school program had been identified through WIDA assessments as level 1 ("Entering") English proficiency learners (in actuality, students' proficiency varied somewhat, but all spoke Arabic fluently). Each classroom also had a bilingual paraprofessional hired by the district to support the emergent bilingual students. In this context of classrooms where learners had low proficiency in English, we engaged in robust *translanguaging* (García et al., 2017), presenting content and inviting students to participate throughout in English and Arabic. Translanguaging supports students to draw on their experiences and knowledge by using all of their meaning-making resources, including Arabic. Translanguaging enabled students to participate in grade-level learning—the priority—as they learned English *and* continued to develop the language and knowledge they brought to their new linguistic and cultural context (Hernandez Garcia et al., 2023).

Writing Instruction as Collective Thinking Time: How Can Teachers Engage All of Their Students as Thinkers and Writers during Social Studies Inquiry?

An inquiry approach to social studies sets up students and teachers for ongoing conversation about their evolving interpretations of the social and historical issues under investigation. Such writing is not "quiet

	Day 1, Monday	Day 2, Tuesday	Day 3, Wednesday	Day 4, Thursday
Morning Session	**Orient to Content** Goal: Students share their experiences and future hopes related to work/working, make *personal connections* to the inquiry. Materials: Whiteboard or butcher paper for students to draw/share	**Analyze Source 1** Goal: Students analyze and make sense of the perspective of Kumar, a 12-year-old child working in a brick kiln in Nepal. Concepts to introduce: *inquiry, evidence.* Materials: Interview with Kumar, Bookmark tool	**Analyze Source 2, Compare Sources** Goal: Students analyze and make sense of a factory supervisor's perspective on children working in brick kilns in Nepal. Concepts to reinforce: *inquiry, evidence.* Materials: Factory Supervisor, Bookmark tool	**Develop and Evaluate Arguments** Goal: Students work together to plan arguments that present claims and evidence. Concepts to introduce: *corroboration, argument.* Materials: Planning Graphic Organizer, Useful Language tools
Afternoon Session	Goal: Students learn about child labor in Nepal. Concepts to introduce: *compelling question as a guide for inquiry, multiple perspectives.* Materials: Photos, map, video	Goal: Students evaluate the perspective of Kumar and revisit the compelling question. Concepts to introduce: *claim, reasoning, reliability.* Materials: Interview with Kumar, Bookmark tool	Goal: Students evaluate the factory supervisor's perspective and revisit the compelling question. Concepts to reinforce: *claim, reasoning, reliability.* Materials: Factory Supervisor, Bookmark tool	Goal: Students share the arguments they have developed together and respond to others' arguments. Concepts to reinforce: *corroboration, argument.* Materials: Planning Graphic Organizer, Useful Language, Reflection tools

FIGURE 8.2. Learning goals during the child labor investigation for newcomer bilingual students.

time" oriented around individual work. Instead, infusing talk throughout inquiry positions writing as collective thinking and rethinking about useful evidence, compelling perspectives, and plausible arguments, all while developing new language resources to communicate these ideas. Knowledge becomes public and thus shared.

The focus ideally shifts to collaboratively considering the merits and weaknesses of possible arguments, with a common goal of identifying strong evidence-based arguments rather than classifying individual responses as answers that are right or wrong. By talking about compelling questions and potential sources of evidence throughout an inquiry, students think together with their teachers and peers about possible interpretations or arguments about historical and social issues. Every student is recognized as authentically participating in meaning-making about the central question. Because student thinking is visible, teachers also have opportunities to take up students' ideas or provide ongoing feedback in ways that support their developing argumentation practices.

Finally, when students compose their written arguments, this work does not stand alone at the end of an inquiry but is instead a natural capstone of the thinking they've been developing throughout. In other words, since inquiries tend to go into depth about a topic and unfold over several days, students build content knowledge and understanding over time and can draw on this shared context as they formally express their ideas in writing toward the end of an investigation.

In a survey of students we conducted, many said that inquiry helps them talk with small groups, hear what other people have to say, and allows them to know that they're not always right. Small-group discussion is especially important for bilingual and multilingual learners. Teachers have noticed that if students are not socially or linguistically ready to participate in a whole-group discussion, they have the option to "gently join" or "gently not join," instead of having to make a bold choice to raise or not raise their hand in whole group. Small-group talk is most effective when preceded by individual thinking and followed by whole-group discussions. Brief and frequent small-group moments have many advantages for inquiry. They help break down complex disciplinary skills into smaller components with which all students can engage at a nuanced level. In small groups, students get the chance to try out their ideas and refine their understandings in a safe environment, and benefit from their peers' input (e.g., Estrada Rebull et al., 2022). We drew on this approach to fostering student talk during the summer school program, framing the writing process as collaborative and offering time to process ideas by talking throughout each phase of inquiry.

Early Phases of Inquiry Initiate Writing: Working with Personal Experiences, Content, and Sources

In the early phases of inquiry, students make personal connections and consider their own perspectives using *RIW*'s Orient to the Content tool (see upper right, Figure 8.3). In the child labor investigation, students reflected on their knowledge and experiences as they considered the work they or their family members do and the work they hope to do in the future. They each wrote and/or drew individually and then shared their knowledge in small groups and through a gallery walk of posters the groups created. Teachers learned that students came to the topic with many resources and ideas that could be drawn on to support the inquiry. During discussion of a video and mini-lectures, students also learned about Nepal and the particular perspectives of people who experience or know about child labor there (e.g., families, children, laws/government, factory supervisors, NGO leaders), taking notes in Arabic and/or English. A combination of centering students' prior knowledge and extending their existing knowledge values their cultural resources and offers new perspectives.

After drawing on their own knowledge as a resource, students made sense of and analyzed two sources that shared different perspectives: one from Kumar, a child working in the brick kilns, and another from a factory supervisor (as seen in Figure 8.1). Understanding sources is key to developing evidence-based arguments in social studies. We used *RIW*'s Bookmark tool to support students in making sense of each source, analyzing and evaluating them, and annotating each one with their thoughts (see middle right, Figure 8.3). The Bookmark tool helps students to read with purpose, guiding them to notice features of the source and its language and draw inferences and conclusions about the source in relation to the compelling question steering the inquiry. In this inquiry phase, students write annotations to capture their thinking about the content and reliability of the source, making notes that they will use later, as they compare sources and plan and compose their arguments. The robust ideas they generate about the sources and central question in this phase support them in bringing evidence and reasoning to their arguments.

After making sense of individual sources, students compared the perspectives in the different sources in small-group and whole-class discussions, guided by the Weigh the Evidence tool (see lower right, Figure 8.3). Corroborating sources bridges reading and writing and helps students develop evidence-based claims. Weigh the Evidence discussions help students think through and gain a deeper understanding of what they've read, identifying connections between sources and plausible arguments as they figure out what to write. Students draw on sources in

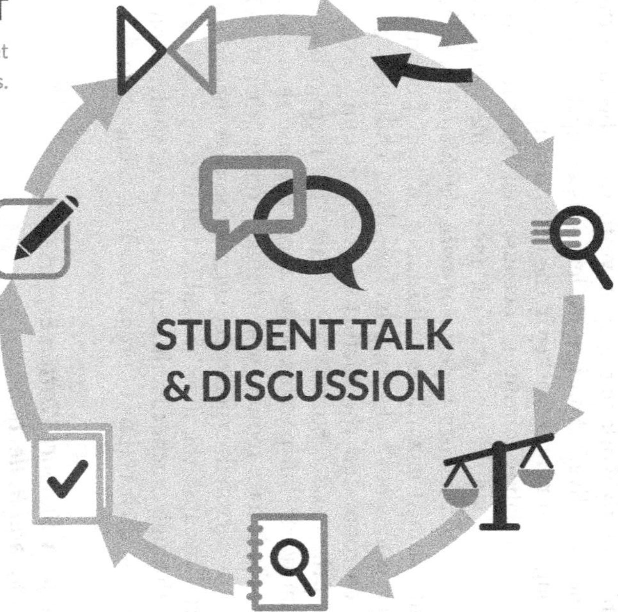

FIGURE 8.3. Disciplinary literacy tools set up routines that support talk and writing throughout inquiry.

different ways as they talk through possible claims that the evidence supports and reason about how the evidence supports the claims. This talk is the basis for developing a strong argument, as students corroborate evidence and further develop their thinking together through discussion.

In this case, after considering the perspectives of one child laborer and a factory supervisor via analysis of written texts, and those of a range of actors through discussion of a video news report, students in the summer program generated possible claims they thought the sources could support. One student drew on the perspectives of a child laborer (source 1) and a family (news report) to argue in Arabic that "the families don't want the kids to work but they have to work because they need to make money and live." Another student was compelled by the perspective of a nongovernmental worker in the news report and argued in Arabic that this child labor continues "because they want to recover from the earthquakes to rebuild the city." Yet another student corroborated the interview with a factory supervisor with the Nepali law they learned about and claimed hazardous child labor in Nepal continued "because the supervisor is not following the law about children's age." Another student corroborated the factory supervisor source with a family interview in the news report to argue that "the factory owners refuse that children work, but parents allow them because their needs are plenty but they don't have money or anything." Yet another student appeared to draw on personal experience, suggesting that the children are forced to work "Because the men are subjected to gangs." Sharing their perspectives through teacher-facilitated discussion, students build on, expand, and refine their claims in preparation for composing.

Later Phases of Inquiry Support Written Expression: Drafting, Composing, and Reflection

Here, we elaborate on the drafting, composing, and reflection phases of inquiry and share examples of how teachers used the Planning Graphic Organizer, Mentor Text, Useful Language, and Reflection tools from the *RIW* curriculum during the summer program for bilingual newcomers (see bottom, middle, and upper left side of Figure 8.3). Instead of treating writing as quiet time for individual work, we share how these tools can be used to integrate modeling with interactive activities that engage students in thinking and talking throughout the writing process.

Using the Mentor Text

Mentor texts (see Figure 8.4 for the Arabic and English versions of the mentor texts used in the summer program) offer students examples of

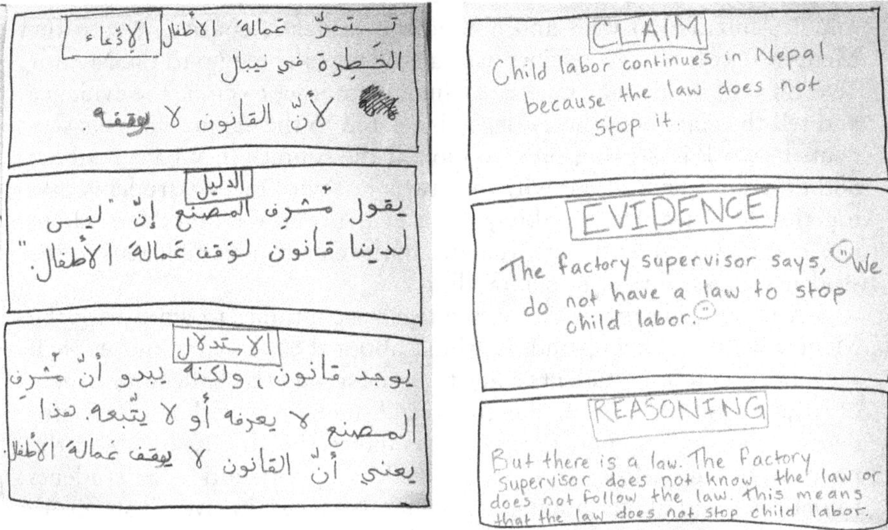

FIGURE 8.4. Accommodated Mentor Text for the child labor investigation.

disciplinary argument writing. *RIW*'s Mentor Text tool supports teachers to prompt students' interaction with mentor texts by identifying the features of argument writing and discussing how those features function or contribute to the quality of the argument.

In this summer program, students were engaging in their first investigation in preparation for their first social studies argument. In Figure 8.5, we present the teacher's explanation of the three argument moves exemplified in the Mentor Text as she thinks aloud about the ways the text presents the claim, evidence, and reasoning (an Arabic-speaking teacher interpreted this teacher's talk after each segment).

As we see here, the teacher stresses that the students are looking at "an example" of what they will write, not something they will copy. She highlights the key argument moves (Claim–Evidence–Reasoning [C-E-R]) modeled in the Mentor Text in both Arabic and English. She focuses on the relationship between these argument moves and the work students have already done in reading and annotating sources, pointing out that the evidence comes from a source they have read and supports the claim being made. She also points to the quotation marks on the model to initiate students into the important practice of indicating words that are taken from another text ("these are not my words").

After introducing the thinking behind the C-E-R structure of argumentation and the ways these argument moves are related, the teacher initiates interaction with and among the students, consistent with the Mentor Text tool. The teacher asks a student to come up to the Mentor Text on the board and circle the claim and another to circle the evidence and tell the class how the evidence is related to the claim. She asks students to work in small groups to look at the sources they have read for additional evidence about why the law is not working. As students talk together to share their thinking about evidence in relation to the claim (see Figure 8.6), the teacher circulates in the classroom and listens to the students to assess their understanding.

After considering evidence, the teacher continues to work with the Mentor Text by having students think about the reasoning move; we'll see more about how students come to understand this challenging aspect of argumentation later in the chapter. A mentor text thus offers students a concrete example that supports interactive discussion about the purpose of the C-E-R structure as well as opportunities for students to reason aloud about language. This modeling of the overall structure and expression of argument prepares them to move to the final phase of inquiry where they draft and share their own arguments.

Our accommodation of the Mentor Text for the investigation described here, in a context where students were newcomers with low

Teacher: This is an example of an argument. It is not the argument that you're going to write.

The claim here [pointing to the claim] is that hazardous child labor continues in Nepal because the law does not stop it.

[Pointing to evidence] Here we have the evidence to support this claim. Right here the factory supervisor says we do not have a law to stop child labor. This is what we read in our source. He said that there are no laws that prevent this.

[Holding the source up for students to see] I'm going to show it to you. It's from the source titled "Factory Supervisor." These words that I have here [pointing to the Mentor Text in Figure 8.4] for the evidence, I got from the text. And whenever we take information from the text, we always put quotation marks here at the beginning of the word of the quote and at the end of the quote, because these are not my words, these are the words from the text. Okay?

There's one more part to back up our claims. We have an answer to the question and a specific piece of evidence. Now we have to explain our reasoning. Our definition for reasoning is: *how do you know if the evidence you chose is reliable, helpful, or trustworthy?* Or *how does the evidence help you develop or support the claim?*

FIGURE 8.5. Using a Mentor Text to explain claim, evidence, and reasoning.

S1: مس يقول بعض أصحاب العمل ان الاطفال مش مطرين يعملوا

[Some of the factory owners say that children don't have to work.]

S2: هنا يقول ان الاطفال يريدون مساعدة في أوقات الفراغ قبل الدراسة وبعدها

[Here they say that the kids want to help during free time before school and after.]

FIGURE 8.6. Students share other possible evidence for the claim in the Mentor Text in small-group discussion.

proficiency in English engaging in an investigation for the first time, offers greater scaffolding than the nonaccommodated versions of the investigations available on the *RIW* website. Those Mentor Texts give students an opportunity to review and consider the overall structure of argumentation that is expected, but with a focus that would not draw on the same evidence or predispose students toward any particular claim in their own writing (see Figure 8.7 for the nonaccommodated website version of the child labor investigation Mentor Text). Figure 8.7 also displays an example of the more authentic contexts for writing in the nonaccommodated writing assignments: something that our brief intensive opportunity to work with these newcomer students did not allow. It's important to adapt the tools of inquiry to the particular students you work with and apprentice them in this challenging thinking and writing in ways that provide solid support and genuine accomplishment.

Introducing the Planning Graphic Organizer

At this point in the inquiry process, students are ready to decide what they will argue, making active choices among all of the ideas the class has discussed. The Planning Graphic Organizer (PGO) tool supports students as they make this move from talking about their ideas to organizing their thinking, making choices, and beginning to compose their arguments. It reminds students about the thinking they need to do in order to present and communicate their ideas through prompting questions that help students plan their Claims, Evidence, and Reasoning.

In this case, students started the class session by writing their individual responses to the central question of the investigation on note cards and sharing them with others. Recall the range of possible claims that students from the summer school class shared in response to the

Dear Child Labor Coalition,

Child labor in the clothing industry in Bangladesh is terrible. **Hazardous child labor exists in Bangladesh because they can pay the workers very little money and then sell the clothes for a lot more.** -C

For example, an article from World Vision says "thousands of child workers in Bangladesh [piece] together designer clothing [they'll] never be able to afford." It also says the workers make 480 pairs of pants a day and only earn $1. -E This tells me that the clothing industry is using children in Bangladesh to make the clothing for cheap. This source is reliable because World Vision is a humanitarian organization that works to fight against poverty and injustice. They know where the hazardous child labor is happening in the world. -R

Help us fight against the clothing industry in Bangladesh! Pay attention to where your clothing is made!

Sincerely,
Diana Prince

Your Assignment

Background: The Child Labor Coalition works to end hazardous child labor around the world. On their website, they publish reports from guest authors. You will write to the Coalition with your argument about *why hazardous child labor continues to exist in Nepal.* Explaining why hazardous child labor is happening is a part of understanding how to end it.

FIGURE 8.7. Nonaccommodated child labor investigation Mentor Text and writing assignment.

central question. The class had briefly discussed one another's claims and the kind of evidence that would be needed to support them, a modified weighing of evidence suited to this accommodated investigation with two sources. Figure 8.8 shows how the teacher asks students to decide on the claims they will make after introducing them to the PGO (see Figure 8.10 for an example of one student's PGO).

The way the teacher introduces the PGO continues to highlight the dialogic nature of argumentation: Students' claims are evolving; they can change them in light of what they have heard in other people's decisions about their claims. In this case, most students continued to argue for the claim they had written earlier. However, some were convinced to change theirs.

Note that the teacher kept the class moving through this drafting process and used a minimal amount of time (2 minutes) as she saw that most students had completed writing their claims. At that point she moved on to ask students to find evidence for their claims, at the same time allowing students who had not finished to continue working. Managing joint writing time and keeping the writing process moving along can be challenging. Allowing some students to fall behind the pace can keep the momentum going for the majority; not every student has to complete earlier steps before instruction can move on to the next steps. Having a paraprofessional or other assistance during writing sessions can allow teachers to support the class as a whole to move forward smoothly while offering additional support to some students who benefit from more time and scaffolding.

Teacher: First you're going to write your claim. At the beginning of the hour, you wrote a claim that answered our question, *Why does hazardous child labor continue to exist*? Okay. But you heard your classmates' ideas also. So you now can change your claim or you can use the same claim that you already have. Talk to others at your table about your claim, and when you're ready, you're going to write your claim right here in the red box [points to projected copy of the blank PGO in students' packets].

[Students discuss their claims in small groups.] After about 2 minutes:

Teacher: I know that you're still writing, but can we pause? It's okay if you're not done; just pause. Because for those people who are ready to move on, I want to make sure we know what to do next. Okay. Now that we have written a claim, we have to go find, in one of our sources, our piece of evidence from a source that helps us understand why you think your claim is true.

FIGURE 8.8. Prompting students to determine their claims and identify relevant evidence.

Ahmed and Hamza (all proper names are pseudonyms) had been working with a claim that asserted that child labor continues to exist because factory supervisors do not check the children's age, despite the law against it. As they worked together, the teacher joined them and interacted with them about the claim they both decided to make using both English and Arabic (see Figure 8.9).

The teacher supports Ahmed and Hamza by pointing out that they will need evidence for their claim that hazardous child labor continues to exist because the factory supervisor doesn't check the children's ages (children under 16 are not allowed to engage in hazardous labor in Nepal; Kumar, the child laborer who is interviewed in the source the

Teacher: So what do you have as your claim?

Ahmed

: مس انا حكيت ان ما بيجوا ما بشيكو على [inaudible] , ما بشيكو

[I said that they don't check on their age. They don't check on them]

Teacher:

فيك تلاقي شي دليل يثبت هذه؟

[Can you find evidence that proves this?] That's gonna be a tough one to find evidence for, about not checking their age.

مش عم يسأل عن العمر. في شي دليل عن هذا الذي قرأته، يسأل عن العمر للولد؟ ما عم بشوف اذا معه license او شي ورقة.

[He's not asking about the age. Is there any evidence about this that you read, that asks about the kids' age? He's not seeing their license or some paperwork.]
Can you find it here? If you can't find it

اذا ما فيك تلاقيها، لازم تغير ال claim

[If you can't find it, you have to change the claim]

Students spend some time looking at the sources.

Hamza: عندي فكرة بس مش عارف كيف بدي احكيها. هو بحكيلك ان اذا نحن وقفنا شغل الاولا، رح نبطل نطلع مصاري. و خلص اذا واحد منهم بده يشتغل، نقول خلص اشتغل.

[I have an idea but I don't know how to say it. He says that if we stopped child labor, we won't be able to make money. And that's it, if one of them wants to work, they should just work.]

: ... يتحدث ان تخفيف عمالة الاطفال يضر عماله. ان يعني اذا وقفوا هذا الموضوع يضر في علمه.

[He talks about reducing child labor and how it harms his work. So that means that if they stopped this stuff it will harm his business.]

Teacher: Oh it's bad for their business ...

FIGURE 8.9. Supporting group work and talk to develop thinking about aligning claims with evidence.

students have read is 12 years old). The students look at the sources for evidence but don't find any. While Hamza makes a good point about the benefits the factory business gains from the children's labor, and the teacher acknowledges this, this point does not offer the evidence needed to support a claim that the factory supervisors don't check the children's ages. In the end, both Hamza and Ahmed changed their claims (see Figure 8.10 for Ahmed's PGO).

In the nonaccommodated investigations, the PGO serves as a support when students move ahead to write their full drafts and should be treated as a place to take brief notes rather than write rough drafts or complete sentences. In working with bilingual learners with low English

Claim الإدعاء

Why does hazardous child labor continue to exist in Nepal? لماذا تستمر عمالة الأطفال الخطرة في نيبال؟

Hazardous child labor continues to exist in Nepal because... تستمر عمالة الأطفال الخطرة في نيبال بسبب ...

They are from a poor family and Thex have to work

Evidence #1 الدليل الأول

What information from the source(s) supports your claim?

ما هي المعلومات من المصدر (المصادر) التي تدعم ادعائك/مُطالبتك؟

(Source name) says that "...." (اسم المصدر) يقول أن"....."

"Kiomar says: "I don't enjoy this work but He's from a Poor family and He have to do it"

Reasoning #1 الاستدلال الأول

Explain how the evidence supports your claim. Also, why is your evidence reliable?

اشرح كيف يدعم الدليل ادعائك/مُطالبتك؟ ولماذا دليلك موثوق؟

This means that ..... هذا يعني أن .....

kumars family told him to do this but he don't enjoy that work.

The Poor family told There kids to work for Monay

This is reliabilitx because kumars was there and He said That

FIGURE 8.10. Ahmed's accommodated Planning Graphic Organizer.

proficiency, we did not expect them to write full essay drafts in this first investigation that they participated in. Instead, we accommodated the PGO to make it serve as the final product for displaying students' arguments. This involved embedding sentence starters into the PGO so the C-E-R structure would be coherently presented. In the nonaccommodated versions, instead of sentence starters, the Useful Language tool offers choices that support students in getting started with each phase of the argument.

Presenting the Useful Language Tool

Moving from planning arguments (using the PGO) to drafting arguments can be challenging. Students may know what they want to say but not be able to find the language to say it. Part of apprenticing students into the kind of thinking needed to argue with sources is supporting their understanding and use of language. As students begin to draft their arguments, using the notes they have made on the PGO, the Useful Language tool helps them get started with each of the different moves (Claim, Evidence, Reasoning). Instead of just providing a sentence starter, the Useful Language tool offers language choices, helping students understand that there is more than one way to make a claim and present evidence and reasoning in support of it. The Useful Language tool reminds students about and supports them in presenting the important thinking moves that make an argument strong. Figure 8.11 shows the version of the tool that supports the nonaccommodated version of the investigation on the *RIW* website.

When introducing the Useful Language tool, ask students to think with a partner about how the prompts for each argumentation move differ from each other. They may comment that all the prompts mean the same thing. You can help students understand that the prompts are alternatives; they have similar meanings. Students can use one of the prompts or start their sentences with other words that do the same work of introducing an argument move. For example, in Figure 8.11, starting the claim with "Hazardous child labor continues to exist in Nepal because . . ." is the simplest option; it is the one we have chosen for the accommodated PGO. It takes wording from the central question and indicates that the claim needs to have a reason ("because") that is then supported with evidence and reasoning; writing their own reason completes the claim. The second option, "We should all be aware that hazardous child labor continues to exist in Nepal because . . ." shows students that they can bring their own voices to the claim. Students who feel strongly about their claims often want to adopt a voice that shows they think other people need to know about the issue and perhaps do

Useful Language

MAKING A CLAIM:
Hazardous child labor continues to exist in Nepal because ...
We should all be aware that hazardous child labor continues to exist in Nepal because ...
I think hazardous child labor continues in Nepal because ...

PROVIDING EVIDENCE:
For example, in X (Source#), the headnote says that "..."
X (Source #) says that "..."
X (Source #) reports that "..."
Another example is that (Source name) says "..."

REASONING:
This evidence shows that ... / This means that ...
This makes me think that ...
This shows that ...
This source is reliable because ...

FIGURE 8.11. Nonaccommodated Useful Language tool that offers choices.

something about it. The third option, "I think that hazardous child labor continues to exist in Nepal because . . ." makes it clear that this is the student's own perspective. (Some teachers tell students not to use this option, suggesting that it diminishes the claim by casting it as an opinion. While we have found that many students who are being initiated into argument writing like to use this option to underscore that they have developed the argument themselves, you can follow your own classroom norms on this language choice.)

Using the Reflection Tool

Students can run out of steam and lose focus as they write. Using the Reflection tool periodically during and after the composing process guides students to remember their purpose in writing and to actively set goals for their next steps. Figure 8.12 presents one student's responses to the Reflection tool prompts as they considered their draft argument. The Reflection tool helps students monitor their progress and refocus their work, and it coaches students on key aspects of argument writing. In addition, it supports them in identifying ways to improve their writing—whether in completing their first draft, revising their initial

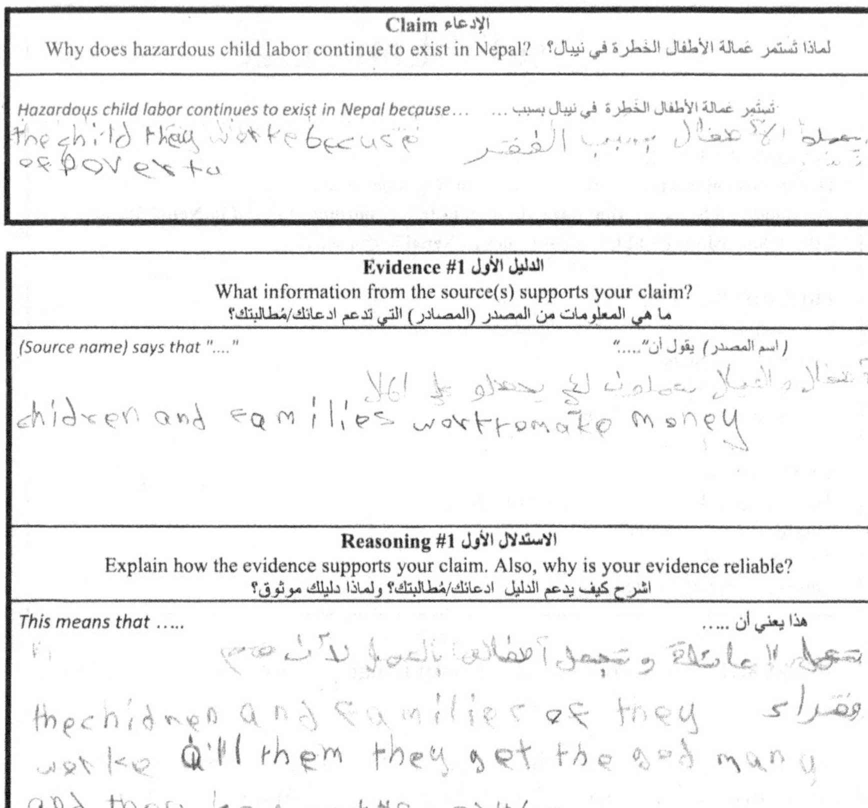

Claim الإدعاء
Why does hazardous child labor continue to exist in Nepal? لماذا تستمر عمالة الأطفال الخطرة في نيبال؟

Hazardous child labor continues to exist in Nepal because… تستمر عمالة الأطفال الخطرة في نيبال بسبب …
the child they worke becuse of poverta
يعمل الأطفال بسبب الفقر

Evidence #1 الدليل الأول
What information from the source(s) supports your claim?
ما هي المعلومات من المصدر (المصادر) التي تدعم ادعائك/مُطالبتك؟

(Source name) says that "…." (اسم المصدر) يقول أن"…."
الأطفال والعمال يعملون لكي يحصلوا على المال
chidren and familes wortromake money

Reasoning #1 الاستدلال الأول
Explain how the evidence supports your claim. Also, why is your evidence reliable?
اشرح كيف يدعم الدليل ادعائك/مُطالبتك؟ ولماذا دليلك موثوق؟

This means that ….. هذا يعني أن …..
تعمل العائلة وتجعل أطفالها بالعمل لأنهم فقراء
thechidren and familier of they worke all them they get the god many and they kan get $50 or $60

FIGURE 8.12. Amina's accommodated Planning Graphic Organizer (above) and Reflection tools (on the following page).

draft, making suggestions to a peer, or setting goals for what they might improve the next time they write an argument.

Working with students with low English proficiency during the summer program, the teacher oriented students to the Reflection tool after introducing the three argument moves and giving students time to work on their PGOs. She introduced the tool as one that "helps us look at our writing and make sure that our argument is a strong argument." Figure 8.13 shows how she modeled its use by using the prompts to think aloud about and evaluate the ways these moves are realized in the Mentor Text.

In this introduction to the Reflection tool, where students are encountering it for the first time, the teacher read each prompt and thought aloud about how to evaluate the model text in relation to each

Reflection Tool أداة للتفكير فيما سبق دراسته

Claim Does our claim state why hazardous child labor exists in Nepal?	☒ yes نعم ☐ no لا	الإدعاء هل يوضح الادعاء سبب وجود عمالة الأطفال الخطرة في نيبال؟
Does our claim connect with our evidence and reasoning?	☒ yes نعم ☐ no لا	هل يرتبط الادعاء بدليلنا واستدلالنا؟
Evidence Does our argument include evidence from the headnotes, attributions, or source(s) to support the claim?	☒ yes نعم ☐ no لا	الدليل هل تحتوي حجتنا على أدلة من الترويسة أو الإسناد أو المصدر (المصادر) لدعم الإدعاء؟
Does our argument quote from the source(s) to support the claim?	☒ yes نعم ☐ no لا	هل يتم اقتباس حجتنا من المصدر (المصادر) لدعم الإدعاء؟
Reasoning Does our reasoning explain how or why the evidence supports the claim?	☐ yes نعم ☒ no لا	الاستدلال هل يفسر استدلالنا كيف أو لماذا يدعم الدليل الادعاء؟
Does our reasoning explain the reliability of the source(s) as evidence to support the claim?	☐ yes نعم ☒ no لا	هل يفسر استدلالنا موثوقية المصدر (المصادر) كدليل لدعم الادعاء؟

FIGURE 8.12. *(continued)*

question. For the prompts about evidence, she considered the source of her evidence and the presentation of material from the source as a quotation. She interacted briefly with the class as a whole as they validated her thinking, and they saw her modeling what to do by checking the "yes" box on the Reflection tool. The teacher then asked students to work together, taking turns evaluating their own and then their partner's arguments using the Reflection tool (see Figure 8.14 for one example) with specific attention to whether their claims responded to the central question, if there was evidence to support their claim, and if they connected their evidence to their claim.

Amina has written her PGO in both English and Arabic (refer back to Figure 8.12) and begins the interaction with Aisha (see Figure 8.14) by reading her evidence in Arabic. Aisha asks her to read in English instead, but as Amina starts to explain her reasoning, she soon returns to Arabic, and the two girls continue to discuss the reasoning in Arabic. Amina has calculated how much money the family can make by having their children work, based on what she has read in the source about one person making $5 per month. Aisha is not convinced that Amina has done enough to explain the relationship between the claim and evidence, but we can't tell from the transcript what the girls were referring to when they point to "this thing." However, as we see in Figure 8.12, Amina evaluates her reasoning as insufficient on her Reflection tool.

The Reflection tool prompts students to think about two aspects of reasoning. The first is to explain how the evidence connects with the claim, the prompt Amina and Aisha have discussed. The second prompt about reasoning asks students to evaluate the reliability of the source for answering the central question. While students spent time discussing the reliability of both sources in the previous days, on this final day of the investigation, the reliability of evidence had not yet been in focus. In fact, the Mentor Text that the teacher used to model reasoning did not include this move. This had escaped the teacher's attention, but as she circulated around the class to review how students were using the

[The teacher has talked about the claim, and next models reflecting on evidence.]

Teacher: Let's go to the next point and look at our evidence. My reflection tool has two questions about evidence. First, does our argument include evidence from the headnotes, attribution or sources to support the claim? So I am going to look at my evidence. [Looking at the posted MT]: *The factory supervisor says, we do not have a law to stop child labor.* And I am thinking, I know I read that in a source. Where did I see it? Oh, that's right, I saw it in our factory supervisor text. So does my evidence fit that? Yes, it does. So I can say, okay, I'm good there.

Okay, so the next thing I'm going to look at, does our argument quote from the source or sources to support the claim? Did I write exactly what it says in the source? And I'm looking at the source right here. Yes, it does say *we do not have a law to stop child labor.* And did I use quotation marks? Yeah. So is this a yes or a no?

Students: Yes.

[Teacher continues to explain "Reasoning" and then wraps up with the following:]

Teacher: So now it's going to be your turn. We just went through how to use the checklist and we practiced with our claim and our evidence, but you guys wrote your own, so now you're going to use your checklist and write on it. You may think "Well, I wrote it, it must be really good." You've got to be a little bit more critical than that. We're going to challenge you to fix or change or make better at least one thing.

FIGURE 8.13. Modeling with the Reflection tool.

Amina: مكتوب ان الاطفال يعملون عشان يجيبوا المال. آخر وحدة .كمان في دليل ان في...

[It's written that the children work to make money. There's also evidence that …]

Aisha: اقرأي بالانجليزي.

[read in English]

Amina: Okay, the children and the families, they work, only they get the money and they can get 15 or 16 in the month.

انا كتبت هذا الشيء لأن هنا مكتوب ان الشخص الواحد فقت يجيب ٥ دولار بالشهر

[I wrote this thing because here it is written that one person only makes $5 a month.]

Aisha: بس انت لازم تقولي بآخر سؤال ليش why ان هذا الreasoning يدعم الدليل

[but you have to say on the last question why, why this reasoning supports the evidence.]

Amina: نفس الحين اكتب ان في...

[at the same time I wrote that there is …]

Aisha: لازم تكتبي why ليش انت كتبتي هذا الشيء و ليش يدعم هذا الدليل

[you have to write why you wrote that, why this supports the evidence.]

Amina: انا اقولها، عشان يحصل اذا الشخص اشتغل 5 dollars in the month فإذا اشتغلوا العائلة كلها يعني الشخص يطلع ٥ دولار، و حسب العائلة.

[I said it, because if a person worked they make 5 dollars in the month. So if the entire family works then each person makes 5 dollars depending on the family.]

نفس الشيء هم يشتغلوا عشان يأخذوا فلوس و يقدروا يأخذوا اكثر من هذا على حسب حجم العائلة المشتركة.

[the same thing, they work to make money and they can make more depending on how big the family is together.]

Aisha: هلق انت مثل هنا... كتبتي هذا الشيء، يشرح الذي انت كتبتيه. نفس الشيء لازم تعمليه هنا.

[now, like here … you wrote this thing it explains what you have written. You have to do the same thing here.]

Amina: بس حرفيا... لقيت صعوبة الاقي هذا الشيء.

[but literally … I had difficulty to find this thing.]

FIGURE 8.14. Amina and Aisha interact while using the Reflection tool.

Reflection tool, she realized that this was an issue she needed to discuss. She had seen that most students were checking "yes" on their Reflection tools without actually evaluating the reliability of their evidence.

At this point, the teacher went to the Mentor Text displayed on the board, drew students' attention to the missing reasoning move, and said she would add it now. She did so, writing the following: "This source, the factory supervisor, is reliable because . . ." and saying, "Then we would have a sentence at the end where we say why he was reliable." She then modeled this with one group of students, asking, "Why is Kumar reliable? What about Kumar—why would Kumar know about child labor in Nepal?" With the support of several follow-up questions, students responded by explaining that because Kumar worked in brick kilns in Nepal, he had firsthand experience on the topic and is therefore a reliable source.

After reviewing and revising their arguments, students moved to different groups and shared their final products by reading and discussing the arguments they had developed with a new group of their classmates. Arabic and English continued to be used throughout the week, with ongoing interpretation and translation. Students moved back and forth between the two languages in dynamic ways, enacting their bilingual identities as they developed the academic language relevant to the inquiry in both English and Arabic.

The Reflection tool thus models the kind of thinking students need to engage in as they give each other feedback and revise their arguments. We have found it useful to ask students to find one point for revision as they use the tool and to make the revisions on their PGOs or on the draft of their full argument (whichever is the expected final product).

Key Ideas

At the end of the investigation, every student in the two cohorts we worked with had developed a thoughtful argument about why hazardous child labor continues to exist in Nepal. The arguments were presented as detailed plans (not fully developed essays), but they nonetheless showed the kind of thinking students had learned to do. Talk and writing were the means through which that thinking developed. At the same time, teachers got to know their students better as they shared their experiences and perspectives. We noted earlier in this chapter that we see writing time as collective thinking time. Taking this perspective, we encourage you to focus on the thinking students are doing as they engage in writing tasks across the inquiry phases.

We have illustrated here how teaching writing for social studies inquiry can be heavily scaffolded to support students who may not be familiar with the argumentation practices that enable them to develop and express their perspectives on social and historical questions. Interaction through talk in different participation structures, supported by models and disciplinary literacy tools, gives students opportunities to share their experiences, build background knowledge, analyze sources of evidence, hear and consider different possible claims, and draft arguments that they discuss with their peers and revise with support.

Through this work, they learn that the questions they explore in social studies inquiry do not have fixed answers, that their own experiences are sources of knowledge, and that the perspectives they bring and develop can be resources for others. They also learn that they can change their ideas and claims as they learn more about the issues they are engaged with and consider multiple perspectives. In that sense, teaching writing is teaching students to think analytically about social studies.

We recognize that the agenda for social studies is full, and that having students write may seem to require time you don't have. You may also be concerned about responding to students' linguistic errors. We have not focused here on grammar, spelling, or other conventions that you might associate with teaching writing. In our experience, it is not necessary to spend time on language conventions in the routine activities of social studies teaching, including in teaching inquiry (see Truscott [1996] for a review of research on why grammar correction is not recommended). Students need opportunities to use language at school without having their errors pointed out, where the meaning they present is emphasized, not the forms they use. Students do not need to create final drafts of their arguments in every investigation you teach. Writing is hard work, and modeling for students that they can write without constant attention to the niceties of language supports them to develop fluency and confidence. Over time, their language will also improve.

Instead of responding to students' writing by marking problems with grammar and spelling, we have shown that the work of teaching writing during social studies involves ongoing support for and interaction with students' thinking. Teachers model what is to be written and move students through varied participation structures, sometimes asking them to think individually and write notes, other times having them interact with a peer or small group, and at other times facilitating discussion in the whole class. In facilitating discussion, they listen carefully to what students are saying and prompt them to say more, to elaborate on their points, or to respond to other students. When students are writing, teachers circulate in the classroom to monitor students' products and intervene with further modeling or discussion when needed.

When students are drafting essays, the teacher continues to monitor students' work, noticing when students are stuck and and pausing instruction to, for example, strategically invite a willing student to share their writing and collectively work through a challenge they're experiencing. Our research has found that modeling in this way is facilitative for diverse learners. Strong scaffolding of writing does not suppress students' voices; in fact, even emergent bilingual students will bring their own perspectives to what they write when offered models of what is expected (Schleppegrell et al., 2023).

Teaching newcomers calls for resources and collaborative structures that support their participation as they learn English and social studies simultaneously. In our case, we were able to position them to share their knowledge and experience from their home and community cultures by inviting them to interact with others by drawing on all the meaning-making resources they brought to the classroom, including their home language(s). In this context, translanguaging made it possible for all students to engage, enact their bilingual identities, and draw on all their meaning-making resources to participate in authentic ways (Hernandez Garcia & Schleppegrell, 2021). Translanguaging contributes to creating an assets-based classroom that recognizes the strengths learners bring as developing bilinguals and as people who share additional cultural insights—it is thus a move toward equity and social justice. But even in contexts where translanguaging may not be possible, we have shown the important role of talk and writing in enabling students to share and develop understanding. The disciplinary literacy tools in the *RIW* investigations are designed to support all learners through modeling, scaffolding, and interactive participation structures and can be adapted to other inquiry contexts.

ACTION STEPS

The *RIW* investigations present a progression in the thinking skills students develop over 3 years of middle school (Monte-Sano & Hughes, 2024). Try teaching a few *RIW* investigations with the embedded disciplinary literacy tools or use the tools to teach an investigation of your own. Keep in mind that learning to think analytically about texts and write arguments is complex work. Students will improve if they have opportunities to practice the disciplinary work highlighted by the literacy tools four to five times throughout the year.

We do not expect students to demonstrate proficiency after one investigation, but the exposure and practice they get with each investigation are key. Therefore, do not spend so long on any one investigation that your students become disengaged and unmotivated. Instead, build their stamina and confidence over time and treat each investigation as an opportunity to practice complex ways of thinking, reading, and writing. Teachers often remark on seeing changes and settling into classroom routines around the third investigation of the year. If your department can take a school-wide approach, students can build inquiry and argumentation practices over many years. By the end of each year spent on these goals, students' disciplinary thinking and argumentation, content knowledge, and civic skills will have improved.

REFERENCES

Estrada Rebull, M., Monte-Sano, C., Jennings, A., & Kabat, J. (2022). Embedding discussion throughout inquiry. In J. Lo (Ed.), *Making classroom discussions work: Methods for quality dialogue in the social studies* (pp. 124–141). Teachers College Press.

García, O., Johnson, S. I., & Seltzer, K. (2017). *The translanguaging classroom: Leveraging student bilingualism for learning.* Brookes.

Hernandez Garcia, M., & Schleppegrell, M. J. (2021). Culturally sustaining disciplinary literacy for bilingual and multilingual learners: Creating a translanguaging social studies classroom. *Journal of Adolescent and Adult Literacy, 64*(4), 449–454.

Hernandez Garcia, M., Schleppegrell, M., Sobh, H., & Monte-Sano, C. (2023). The translanguaging school: Engaging bilingual students and communities in new ways. *Phi Delta Kappan, 105*(2). *https://kappanonline.org/the-translanguaging-school-garcia/*

Monte-Sano, C. (2016). Argumentation in history classrooms: A key path to understanding the discipline and preparing citizens. *Theory into Practice, 55*(4), 311–319.

Monte-Sano, C., & Hughes, R. E. (2024). *Read.Inquire.Write.*: A scaffolded progression to support diverse learners' social studies argument writing in middle school. *Social Education, 88*(4), 234–240.

Monte-Sano, C., Hughes, R., & Thomson, S. (2019). From form to function: Learning with practitioners to support diverse middle school students' disciplinary reasoning and writing. In B. C. Rubin, E. B. Freedman, & J. Kim (Eds.), *Design research in social studies education* (pp. 31–57). Routledge.

Monte-Sano, C., Schleppegrell, M., Sun, S., Wu, J., & Kabat, J. (2021). Discussion in diverse middle school social studies classrooms: Promoting all students' participation in the disciplinary work of inquiry. *Teachers College Record, 123*(10), 142–184.

Schleppegrell, M. J., Hernandez Garcia, M., Al-Banna, S., & Monte-Sano, C. (2025). Agency and register in translanguaging: Middle school bilingual learners engaging in social studies inquiry. *TESOL Quarterly, 59*(2), 818–845.

Schleppegrell, M. J., Sun, S., & Monte-Sano, C. (2023). The value of models to support students' voice in middle school social studies argument writing. *Journal of Second Language Writing, 61*(3), Article 101043.

Truscott, J. (1996). The case against grammar correction in L2 writing classes. *Language Learning, 46*(2), 327–369.

Chapter 9

Teaching Counterarguments for Improved Historical Reasoning and Civic Discourse

Tanya Baker, Jacob Steiss, Carol Booth Olson,
Nicole Gilbertson, and Huy Q. Chung

In a living democracy, it is important for citizens to be able to read, watch, and listen to multiple, sometimes competing, sources of information. Further, democratic citizens need to be able to synthesize information from multiple sources, recognize where information agrees and disagrees, revise their thinking in light of new evidence, and draw conclusions to make decisions. Reaching consensus about important social and civic questions requires discussion of competing claims; therefore, all students need opportunities to engage in dialogic argumentation, a collaborative process where students with opposing views engage in a dialogue to justify their positions and challenge each other's positions. The term *dialogic* refers to communication that takes the form of a dialogue to explore the meaning of something (Monte-Sano & Allen, 2019).

Despite its importance in school and in civic life, most students find academic argumentation challenging (Olson et al., 2023; Salahu-Din et al., 2008). For example, in the 2011 administration of the National Assessment of Educational Progress (NAEP) for writing, only 25% of students' argumentative essays provided strong reasoning and supporting examples, but even those often failed to consider alternative perspectives (National Center for Education Statistics, 2012). Other researchers report that students are challenged by (1) developing warrants that explain why or how their evidence supports their claims, (2) adapting writing to various purposes and audiences, and (3) acknowledging and refuting potential criticisms of their positions (Ferretti & Lewis, 2018; Kuhn, 1991, 2005). It is clear from such research that students need direct instruction and practice in acknowledging, taking up, and sometimes countering perspectives other than their own. Teaching counterarguments directly offers the opportunity for students to isolate and practice these difficult skills.

Fortunately, the discipline of history, which prioritizes making meaning through evidence-based interpretation of multiple sources, provides a perfect context in which young people can practice and develop counterarguments as part of historical reasoning (Goldman et al., 2016). History standards, indeed, emphasize comparing interpretations and distinguishing claims (National Council for the Social Studies, 2013). This is because history itself is a discipline based on asking questions and interpreting evidence in order to answer those questions. Wineburg (2001) notes that while most research on reading focuses on what students know and what interpretations they can make of a single text, history requires readers to synthesize information across texts. He offers a metaphor for this kind of intertextual reading: "Instead of a single 'executive' directing a top-down process, mature readers of history may create inside their own heads an 'executive board' where members clamor, shout and wrangle over controversial points" (p. 72).

One way of making the need for such wrestling and wrangling clear to students is to help them imagine that there are potential readers of their interpretations who may draw different conclusions from the body of evidence. This can happen in real dialogic contexts or inside the students' minds, as Wineburg (2001) illustrates with the metaphor of clamoring board members. Imagining or reading other interpretations and wrestling with them can help students deepen their own thinking as they compare their interpretations with new and different ideas, considering which are best supported by the evidence and developing clear counterarguments against flawed interpretations.

This iterative thinking is supported by a belief that knowledge in history is tentative, that what we know about the past today could be revised tomorrow (Wiley et al., 2020). A belief that knowledge is tentative makes the continual revision of one's thinking a central disciplinary practice of history that allows us to get closer to the most accurate interpretation of the past (Monte-Sano & Allen, 2019; Nokes, 2017). While helping students advance arguments is important, disciplinary norms emphasize that engaging students in counterargumentation is at least equally important.

When addressing and responding to counterarguments, students practice the skills of listening, considering alternative viewpoints, weighing competing evidence, and drawing conclusions. Thus, centering counterarguments in instruction offers opportunities for teachers to position students as authentic disciplinary participants in a community that values diverse perspectives. When students craft evidence-based arguments independently and in conversation with their peers, they develop an understanding that their interpretation is part of a larger discussion of how we make meaning in history and that knowledge production requires conversation and consensus as we collectively strive to make meaning of our world. Further, these intertextual skills and the ability to develop an argument while considering and refuting the counterarguments are useful beyond the history classroom. They reflect the rigorous methods and dispositions guiding the decision-making we expect citizens to engage in as they participate in and lead our democratic society.

In this chapter, we share examples of how we have helped students deal with competing interpretations of historical text sets by imagining and thinking about and with counterarguments. The chapter provides examples of activities and classroom practices that teachers can enact in their own history classrooms. Readers may want to consider the following guiding questions as they make their way through the chapter:

GUIDING QUESTIONS

1. How do we get started teaching counterarguments?
2. How can teaching counterargument help students shift from adversarial to consensus thinking?
3. Why do dialogic teaching and opportunities for counterargumentation matter in history for democracy?
4. How do we encourage students to accept the tentative nature of historical knowledge through reflection, exploration, and hedging?

How Do We Get Started Teaching Counterarguments?

In order to help students meet the challenging demands of anticipating and addressing counterarguments, it is important to scaffold instruction to lessen the cognitive, linguistic, communicative, contextual, and textual constraints on student writers (Frederiksen & Dominic, 1981). Instructional scaffolding is the "tutorial assistance" provided by an adult or senior member of a learning community to help less experienced learners accomplish a task (Bruner, 1978). Scaffolding can include "reducing the size of the task, concentrating the learner's attention on something manageable, providing models of what is expected, and extending the opportunities to practice" (p. 254).

Langer and Applebee (1986) build on the theories of Jerome Bruner and Lev Vygotsky, who also holds that children can exceed their actual mental age and work at their "zone of proximal development" when they are provided with structure and guidance to engage in literate tasks they cannot yet perform independently (Vygotsky, 1986, p. 187). Langer and Applebee identified five components of instructional scaffolding. First, effective instructional scaffolding gives students *ownership* by providing "the room to say something of their own in their writing or in the interpretations they draw in their reading" (p. 185). Students must see a point to their task beyond simply responding to instructions posed by the teacher. Second, effective instructional scaffolding is characterized by *appropriateness*. It builds on the reading, thinking, and writing abilities students already have and stretches learners intellectually—prompting them to work in their zone of proximal development. Third, it is essential to make the *structure* of the task clear and to guide students through the specific task at hand in a way that enables them to apply the strategies in new contexts. Fourth, effective instructional scaffolding promotes *collaboration* among students and between students and the teacher so that knowledge can be constructed and shared interactively. Finally, the goal of the scaffolding approach is *internalization*, that is, the transfer of control from teacher to student as the students gain competence as readers, writers, and critical thinkers (p. 187).

Two scaffolded activities that teachers can use to help students meet the challenging demands of acknowledging and refuting counterarguments, think like historians, and gain confidence as writers are the *Weighing the Evidence* and *Four Corners* activities.

Weighing the Evidence

In this activity, students carefully consider evidence piece by piece, generating a new potential claim after reading each source, as opposed to approaching the task by generating a claim before reading a number of sources and adopting a claim based on an overall impression. Students are also prompted to consider counterarguments to their claims as they discover new evidence and hear other students' claims. This activity lightens the cognitive load of making claims and considering counterclaims by clarifying the structure of the task of reading across texts in order to make a claim; this approach also guides students to consider how each new piece of evidence interacts with a previous one. The gradual release of new information along with the opportunities to stop, think, talk, write, and change one's mind concentrates the learner's mind on something manageable and extends several iterative opportunities to practice. It also reduces the size of the task—imagining various interpretations or claims as possible responses to an inquiry question—into smaller pieces; concentrates the learners' attention on something manageable (focusing on a single piece of evidence at a time); and offers students opportunities for collaboration.

First, teachers curate two to six pieces of evidence from a text set organized around an inquiry question. These various pieces of evidence should support multiple potential claims in response to the inquiry question. The evidence, or sources, can be primary or secondary sources that are directly related to the inquiry question. For example, in answering the inquiry question *What led to the Battle at Lexington Green*, one piece of evidence may be a firsthand account indicating the British soldiers instigated the violence, whereas another piece of evidence may be a second source indicating the colonists played a major role in escalating the conflict. Second, the various pieces of evidence are distributed to individual students who read, interpret, and generate a *tentative* claim based on the single piece of evidence they have been given. Students are likely to generate different claims as they are writing them based on different pieces of evidence. Next, students collaborate with a peer who is working with a different piece of evidence. Each student shares the evidence they were given and the claim they wrote; then, together, they generate a new *tentative* claim based on the two pieces of evidence they are considering. The process can be repeated at this point, with two pairs of students joining together to write a third claim, with four pieces of evidence.

Figure 9.1 is a handout used for the activity. In addition to this handout, each student would be given one of several pieces of evidence. For instance, in an inquiry about the relative importance of historical figures' contributions to the women's suffrage movement, each student started with a single piece of evidence, such as an action or a statement by a particular historical figure. Figure 9.2 is an example of an evidence card given to a student in this activity.

Language Scaffolds to Support English Learners

While Weighing the Evidence offers lots of opportunities for differentiation (e.g., matching pieces of evidence to learners' first language, interests, or reading abilities), teachers of English learners might also choose to provide additional linguistic support through sentence stems. This can help students who are still acquiring proficiency in academic language. The following sentence stems provide models of language used in making claims, and also in anticipating and responding to counterclaims.

Part 1: Weighing Evidence and Generating Claims				
Students will consider and analyze multiple sources of evidence to generate potential claims to respond to a historical inquiry question 1. Give each person at your table a number, beginning with #1. 2. Examine the excerpt that corresponds with *your number.* 3. Complete Round 1. Given your excerpt, what is the best evidence, and what would be a good potential claim in response to the question: *How did the Women's Suffrage Movement succeed in passing the 19th Amendment?* 4. Wait to begin Round 2.				
Evidence				
1	**2**	**3**	**4**	**5**

Round 1:

My evidence	My claim

Round 2:

New evidence (paraphrase)	Revised claim

Round 3:

New evidence (paraphrase)	Revised claim

Part 2: Evaluating Potential Claims
Reflect: What criteria should we use to determine which claim is best?
Evaluate: Which claim do you think is best?
Anticipate: How would someone *counter* or attempt to argue against your claim?

FIGURE 9.1. Weighing evidence and generating claims organizer.

Evidence 2. Susan B. Anthony's Speaking Tour Address

Headnote: *Susan B. Anthony voted in the 1872 presidential election. Because women did not have the right to vote, she was arrested, put on trial, convicted, and fined $100. The following is an excerpt from a speech she delivered in numerous locations in 1873 to gather support for women's suffrage.*

The preamble of the Constitution says: "We, the people of the United States, in order to form a more perfect union . . ."

It was we, the people; not we, the white male citizens; nor yet we, the male citizens; but we, the whole people, who formed the union. And we formed it, not to give the blessings of liberty, but to secure them to the whole people—women as well as men. And it is downright mockery to talk to women of their enjoyment of the blessings of liberty while they are denied the use of the only means of securing them provided by this democratic-republican government—the voting ballot.

The only question left to be settled, now, is, Are women persons?

Source note: Modified from "Is It a Crime for a Citizen of the United States to Vote?" published in the *History of Women's Suffrage Volume 2* by Elizabeth Cady Stanton, Susan B. Anthony, and Matilda Joslyn Gage in 1881. Stanton, Anthony, and others published many volumes of *History of Women's Suffrage* before the 19th Amendment was passed.

FIGURE 9.2. Examples of evidence.

- ___________ was the most significant reason that ___________ succeeded because . . .
- Of the causes leading to ___________, ___________ was the most significant because . . .
- ___________ was the most important cause of ___________. This is the most important cause because a, b, and c.
- Although ___________ partially led to the success of ___________, ___________ was the most significant cause because . . .
- Many people think ___________ was the most significant reason that ___________. However, ___________ was the most significant reason because . . .

Four Corners Activity

Teachers can also scaffold students' skills in presenting and addressing counterarguments through the Four Corners Activity. In this activity, groups of students choose a claim, organize evidence to support it, and then take turns imagining possible counterarguments to one another's claims. This activity lowers the cognitive, linguistic, and communicative loads for students by providing extended opportunities for oral practice before making written arguments. This activity is appropriate in that it builds on students' oral capacity for argument making and promotes ownership of ideas and internalization of language for making claims and counterarguments. Through collaboration, it makes visible a variety of audiences for a piece of argument writing and counterarguments that students might not be able to conjure in their own minds.

The activity begins after students have read a variety of sources providing multiple perspectives on an essential inquiry question, such as *How did the women's suffrage movement succeed in passing the 19th Amendment?* and a more elaborated writing prompt framed around this question. Students are then presented with four different claims that could be made in response to the inquiry question, posted on chart paper in four corners of the classroom. These claims could be generated by students in the Weighing the Evidence activity mentioned previously, or the teacher may want to provide them. For an example of four possible claims in response to this question, see the example in Figure 9.3.

Based on their reading and understanding of the issue, students are asked to select which claim they think is the most convincing and can be best supported with evidence, providing them with ownership of the task. Then they proceed to the corner with the claim they have selected and collaborate with others to create a bulleted list of reasons and evidence on chart paper to support their claim. Often, by the time students

Claim 1	The protests and demonstrations in the 1910s put increased pressure on national political figures and most directly led to the passage of a constitutional amendment. Therefore, the tactics of the NWP were the most significant reason for the passage of the 19th Amendment.
Claim 2	Although the actions and tactics of the NWP were important, there would have been no political action in the 1910s without the advocacy of early suffragists like Susan B. Anthony.
Claim 3	The state-level efforts of NAWSA slowly changed opinions across the country, eventually leading to the passage of the 19th Amendment. Without these state-level victories, not enough states would have ratified the amendment in 1920.
Claim 4	President Wilson's timely appeal to Congress was the reason that led to the passage of the 19th Amendment.

FIGURE 9.3. Example of potential claims.

have done this kind of work, they have so much ownership of their own claims that they fail to anticipate alternative viewpoints (Ferretti & Lewis, 2013; Kuhn, 1991).

Therefore, in the next step of this activity, each group moves counterclockwise around the room so that they are now at a poster with a different claim from their own, supported by an outline of evidence and reasoning. The group's task now is to consider what "holes" might exist in the Claim–Evidence–Reasoning chain presented on the chart in front of them and leave notes for this group to help them see where their argument might be "leaky" or flawed. These notes can be in the form of warnings—"Look out, somebody's going to call you on that"—or questions, such as "Have you considered that some people might think . . . ?" One might explain to students, "You are like a friendly ghost, peering over this writer's shoulder, helping them see what they might have missed in their excitement about their own claim."

Sometimes it is still difficult for students to generate counterclaims or to organize their thinking or language to test someone else's claim. To help students engage in reasoning and dialogue to refute their classmates' claims, they can be guided to think about different aspects of historical reasoning. The following questions, adapted from Seixas and Morton's (2012) *The Big Six: Historical Thinking Concepts*, can serve as scaffolds that help students organize evidence into categories, evaluate the quality of both their own claim and their colleagues' counterclaims, and demonstrate the complexity of each argument:

- Compare contributions: Why is one person/event **more important** than another?
- Think about the order of events: Were **early** moments/ideas more important than things that occurred **later** or closer to the moment of change?
- Think about the pace of historical change: What were the **most influential** turning points or important historical moments for understanding a historical period?

Finally, this activity ends when groups of students return to their own posters and consider the questions and challenges their claims have received. They have to decide as a group how to address the questions and challenges: Will they modify their claim, add evidence or reasoning to bolster their argument for their claim, or address counters head-on? Or will they use a combination of these revision strategies to bolster their argument? Importantly, these questions and challenges encourage writers to further justify their positions with evidence and reasoning, which is essential in historical argumentation.

Again, teachers of English learners may also want to include language scaffolds focused on a manageable piece of the academic writing task students have been assigned, in this case, acknowledging and refuting counterclaims. After considering how to present their own claim, students can use one or more of the following sentence frames as they take turns acknowledging and refuting one another's claims with their own counterclaims and logical reasons to support them.

Acknowledging and Refuting a Counterargument Sentence Stems

- Some people may argue that ___________. However, ___________.
- Despite the argument that ___________, their evidence is not as convincing as ___________ because___________.
- Although ___________ is significant, the most compelling reason for ___________ is ___________ because ___________.
- Admittedly, ___________ was one reason ___________ succeeded/failed. Nevertheless, ___________ is a more convincing reason because ___________.

This oral practice helps students internalize the language structures they need to use when acknowledging counterarguments to their claims in writing. Additionally, engaging in the Four Corners activity helps them anticipate possible objections to their own argument that they can acknowledge and refute when they compose their essays.

How Does Teaching Counterargument Help Students Shift from Adversarial to Consensus Thinking?

Despite what we—and our students—might sometimes see (or practice) in face-to-face life and social media, addressing counterarguments is not inherently combative. Rather, as we have already seen, it can be productive and dialogic, it can make visible and accessible the reasoning and evidence supporting various claims, and it can generate effortful reasoning. Reaching consensus about important social and civic questions requires discussion of competing claims, depth in our understanding of contemporary and past issues, comfort with complexity, and willingness to move beyond binary thinking. Because we seek to support students in navigating an increasingly dense informational world so they can become informed citizens who are prepared to participate in and ultimately strengthen a healthy and vibrant democracy, it is helpful to be explicit in teaching students how to let go of binary thinking and wrestle with ideas in more complex and nuanced ways. We can do that by focusing on two big ideas.

First, in any argument worth making, students are joining a complex conversation already taking place. Second, in entering into that conversation, they should, to the best of their abilities, respect the other speakers in the conversation and use those speakers' words honestly and respectfully (Harris, 2006). How, then, can our instruction support students to enter into arguments in ways that help them to see multiple perspectives that go beyond pros and cons and are based on multiple pieces of evidence? One way is to clearly frame argument as participation in a conversation, rather than a debate. In this section of the chapter, we will share examples of scaffolded activities that support students to move from an adversarial stance toward consensus thinking by recognizing that they are part of an ongoing conversation and that they can use the language of others thoughtfully and respectfully, even when disagreeing.

Entering the Conversation via the Atwoodian Table

In this activity (see Figure 9.4), students are asked to imagine authors and/or speakers of their sources as sitting around a table and talking about the topic at hand. As they read each source, they imagine the author taking a seat at the table and summarize each author's stance, perspective, and key points or evidence. Finally, they are invited to "pull

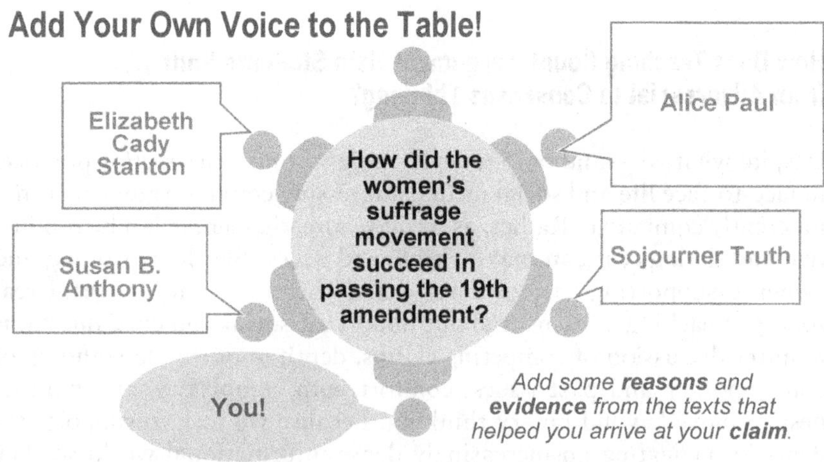

FIGURE 9.4. Entering the conversation.

up a chair themselves" and add their own tentative claim about the issue as participants in a *conversation*. This activity also scaffolds thinking by lowering the cognitive, communicative, contextual, and textual loads for students through creating a visual representation of the sources and their relationships to one another and helping students to imagine the sources they are reading as the words of actual human beings in conversation with one another. The Atwoodian table, then, first serves as metaphor for argument as a civil conversation; second, as a springboard for incorporating source material into written arguments; third, as a useful note-taking tool for students as they read texts, summarize claims and evidence found in the sources, and ultimately offer their own claim and evidence about the topic.

To use the Atwoodian table scaffolded activity is to ask students, literally, to draw a round table in their notebook and add a chair for the author of each source they are reading. As they read each source, they imagine the author taking a seat at the table and summarize each author's stance, perspective, and key points or evidence. To further help represent the idea that, as writers, we are putting these sources in conversation with one another, we may ask students to represent each author/source/chair on a sticky note so that they can be moved around the table. We can ask questions like "Who would sit next to each other?" or "Who seems like they might not know each other at all?" Finally, having considered the main ideas and key evidence of each piece they have read, as well as how the ideas relate to one another, students are invited to "pull up a chair themselves" and add their own claim in answer to the question on the table.

When they have completed this activity, students have summarized source material from multiple sources in their notebooks and created a "chair" for themselves. Looking at the summaries they've made for each source, they have decided where they stand (or sit) on the question. We've found that this activity serves a number of cognitive, metacognitive, and social purposes. First, it helps students with the cognitive strategy of summarizing. Second, it helps them to see the sources as coming from human beings who are trying to say something on a topic that is important to them. Third, it helps them see themselves as valued members of the community who have something important to say on the topic. Seeing themselves as informed participants in a conversation helps move the act of writing beyond a schoolish activity into a social one. By taking on the perspectives of historical figures and listening to their peers describe alternative points of view, students are invited to listen and empathize with a variety of diverse viewpoints on the topic, creating the opportunity to be more focused on developing understanding than on being right or "winning" an argument.

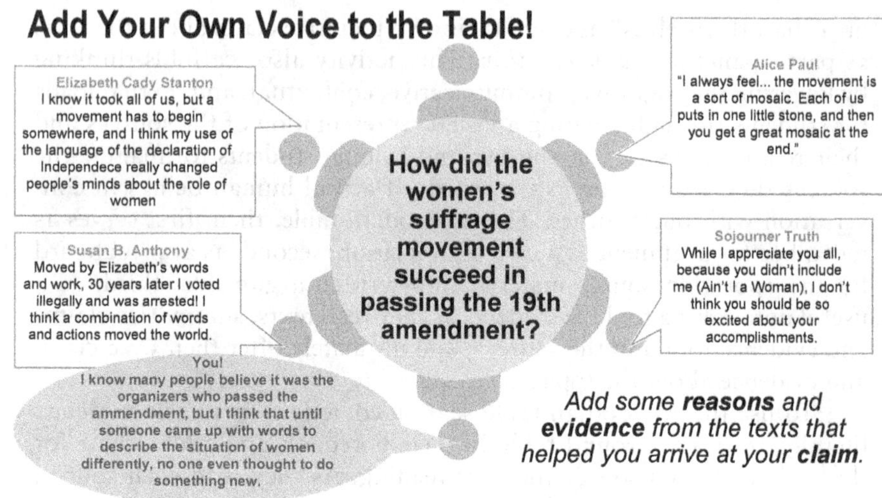

FIGURE 9.5. Student Atwoodian table.

Figure 9.5 is an example of 11th-grade students using the Atwoodian table to understand various perspectives and forces leading to the passage of the 19th Amendment.

The Historians' Table

Like most of the strategies discussed so far in this chapter, the Atwoodian table is a particularly *elastic* strategy; it can be used with all kinds of learners and in all kinds of disciplines to help students conceptualize all kinds of arguments. We know, though, that history teachers might want to think about what happens when a group of historians gather around a table and work together to make historical arguments. In the field of history, interpretations take place in a larger historical discussion and lead to a deeper understanding of the past. Knowledge construction in history is driven by curiosity and questions about what happened in the past and the consequences of these events for the people involved. Rarely is one historian the only individual engaging in a study of this moment in history; rather, they are participating in a conversation about a historical moment with other historians who have asked questions, engaged in archival research, studied a variety of sources—often with divergent perspectives—and developed interpretations that build upon our understanding of the past.

However, unlike in the classroom, historians often work independently to engage in research and writing. Nokes and Kesler-Lund (2019), interested in the social literacies of historians, constructed a cooperative experience and examined the ways historians collectively engaged in an interpretation of sources to answer a defined question. By creating a classroom-like setting and watching historians work, Nokes and Kesler-Lund found that historians engaged in several practices that highlight the civic nature of their work. One such practice was *affirming* one another, thereby demonstrating an open-mindedness to others' ideas. As they moved toward interpretation, historians engaged in *challenging*, a positive practice that created space for criticality and the shared value of the tentative nature of ideas. Finally, historians engaged in *chatting* to build community and connect their ideas to contemporary culture and concerns.

Nokes and Kesler-Lund (2019) also found that historians synthesized sources in conversation with one another and that the "collaborative nature of this activity facilitated corroboration" (p. 381) that led to identifying omissions, highlighting similarities, and developing judgments. The opportunity to be in conversation with one another made visible the skills and dispositions that historians engaged in as they discussed evidence and formulated interpretations about their findings and the importance of this for understanding our past. Nokes and Kesler-Lund believe these skills can be taught to students while they engage in historical inquiry that fosters skills essential for fact-based and consensus-driven civic engagement (p. 401) through classroom practices that create opportunities for students to engage in the historical thinking methods of historians—sourcing, corroboration, and contextualization (p. 380)—with their peers as they analyze sources to reach an interpretation.

For instance, by adding a historical dimension to the Atwoodian table, students have the opportunity to engage in conversations that center historical thinking. Students were asked, in conversation, in a classroom drama (in which each student in a group takes on the persona of one of the people at the Atwoodian table) or in a writing exercise, to use the historical framing questions mentioned earlier (Whose contribution is most important? What is the order of the contributions? In what context or under what circumstances was each contribution made?) and to *chat* about these questions. It was important to *affirm* ideas that they (or their chosen historical character) agree with and to *challenge* ideas they disagree with. We have also modified the Atwoodian table activity as a panel discussion. After summarizing each author or speaker's work and seating them at a table, students collaboratively decide what questions a historian might ask each speaker, how each speaker might answer, and which speakers would agree or disagree with one another. This activity could also be done in their notebooks or dramatized in the classroom with different students taking turns playing different roles in the scene.

Reflective activities can help students move beyond participation in an activity to creating knowledge from it. Adding a reflective dimension to any of the scaffolded activities we have discussed in this chapter can focus a student's attention on the reasons for the activity. In group activities, one might assign a student to act as a process recorder, noting which students participate in the conversation, what was said, and to whom, as a way to focus students on what they are learning about *how* to learn and participate in history. Groups can collaboratively review and code those notes for evidence of affirming, challenging, and chatting.

All of these activities are created to help students see the person behind the academic texts, to remember that reasonable people might well draw different conclusions from the same set of documents or other resources, and to treat these areas of disagreement with curiosity and respect, so that we might all deepen our understanding and even find our way to new ideas.

How Do We Encourage Students to Accept the Tentative Nature of Historical Knowledge through Reflection, Exploration, and Hedging?

As we have said throughout this chapter, historians undertake research by starting with questions: Why did this event occur, who was involved and who was excluded, and what and how did things change or remain the same over time? Then, they begin with a study of what other historians have asserted; they start to build their contextual knowledge of the period under study and consider the types of evidence and interpretations other historians have created. In this way, they enter into a discipline-specific dialogue with others as they discuss secondary sources and make evidence-based assertions within a community of inquiry. They have to understand each other's arguments and, if challenging them, do so with evidence and open-mindedness.

In the history classroom, teachers can create the context for students to engage in the work of historians. Historians work together to consider the complexity of the past and create interpretations that best reflect the evidence available to them, all while considering the ways that others may interpret the evidence and counter those claims. To participate fully and productively, then, students need to view history as an evidence-based, tentative, and evolving interpretation of the past instead of as a static collection of facts that is sometimes communicated through textbook-based instruction (Bain, 2006). They also need opportunities to engage in dialogue with peers and teachers to generate, debate, and contextualize knowledge claims. Classrooms rich in dialogue build skills and dispositions toward truth seeking that are essential for sound historical reasoning and democratic participation (Barzilai & Chinn, 2020).

Dialogic teaching, which allows students frequent opportunities to discuss and debate knowledge claims with peers, encourages students to take up the appropriate stance in future historical debates and (hopefully) important civic questions. To illustrate, Maggioni and colleagues (2009) identified different categories of student thinking in relation to studying history. First, some students take a *copier stance*, regarding claims about the past as accurate or inaccurate "copies" of the past. Students adopting the *subjectivist stance* recognize that experts can disagree but are unable to explain the disciplinary criteria used to judge historical interpretations. Finally, some students adopt a *criterialist stance*. These students understand the constructed nature of history and can evaluate historical interpretations by applying criteria to make judgments of the available evidence and interpretations. These students are more successful in constructing their own historical interpretations through classroom discussion and individual argumentative writing and engage in the vital skill of knowledge production.

When thinking about these stances in light of the complexity of the contemporary world, it is important to support students in taking criterialist stances. When they leave the classroom, our students will have to engage in interpretations of current events and construct interpretations of events and media to make decisions as citizens. Educators, researchers, and policymakers are increasingly concerned that citizens lack the requisite norms, dispositions, and skills to find the truth about important social and civic issues. In Barzilai and Chinn's (2020) description of a "post-truth" world, they emphasize the need to simultaneously build citizens' reasoning skills and knowledge for argumentation, establish shared norms for discussion and debate, and develop individuals' commitment to truth seeking, which means a willingness to revise understanding and to be intellectually humble.

Similarly, Seixas and Morton (2013) suggest that historical thinking fosters students' preparation for engagement as a critical citizenry: "As part of a community of inquiry, they know when their colleagues violate norms of evidence, when claims of significance are inadequately argued, and when causal explanations omit relevant conditions or events" (p. 2). As history teachers develop students' skills for inquiry, establish norms for argumentation—namely, a preference for evidence-based reasoning and openness to alternative perspectives—and help students practice revising understanding to reach consensus, they prepare them to uphold democracy. Activities like weighing evidence, considering relevant claims and competing interpretations, and revising their ideas through dialogue with peers are developed with inquiry-focused and dialogic instruction in history classrooms. Creating opportunities for students to develop evidence-based arguments, listen, and engage with alternative perspectives while responding with counterarguments creates a classroom context that centers reflection and exploration.

Teachers can remind students that they are creating arguments based on available evidence; students may want to consider how they might continue to explore other perspectives and sources and use language that reflects the tentative nature of their arguments given the available evidence. Positioning students as curious truth seekers, rather than in a competition for the "right answer," fosters open-mindedness and furthers dialogic reasoning. As students develop these competencies to find the truth in the past, they can also use them in the present to engage in productive civic discourse. In connection with this idea, we offer several activities that encourage a preference for "truth, accuracy, fair-mindedness, and open-mindedness [that] have become harder to pursue and achieve" (Barzilai & Chinn, 2020, p. 109). All these activities support a shift toward open-minded and evidence-based reasoning emblematic of a dialogic classroom.

Reflection for Learning

To foster students' engagement with the complexity of history and their ability to develop arguments that respond to multiple perspectives, teachers can include Reflections for Learning with activities previously discussed. These activities implicitly require students to adopt *criterialist stances*, engaging as "historical investigators who can ask questions that sources of evidence were not specifically designed to answer" (Maggioni et al., 2009, p. 195). In each activity, students have the opportunity to engage with multiple pieces of evidence to construct and refine their claims. Such activities position students as agentic knowledge creators who consider and corroborate evidence in consultation with their peers. To make this more apparent and *explicit*, we suggest that at the conclusion of each activity, teachers offer students opportunities to reflect on the types of thinking they used to reach conclusions. Chinn and colleagues (2020) describe these as "explorations into knowing" and argue that they promote a collective understanding of adaptive ways to pursue the truth with others. These reflections facilitate students' metacognitive understanding of historical reasoning. Consider asking students one of the questions in Figure 9.6.

- What do you know (about the past, the historical topic) now that you did not when you started the activity?
- How did your thinking change after listening to your fellow classmates' ideas?
- How did listening to your classmates affirm, expand, or contest your own interpretation of the past?
- What was the most compelling statement that you heard? How did this impact your thinking about the topic?
- In what ways do you have a more complicated understanding of the past after engaging in the activity?

FIGURE 9.6. Reflective prompts.

After individual or group reflections, teachers can lead their class to generate a list of norms for inquiry and debate, emphasizing the role of evidence to substantiate claims and the need to be open to revising one's thinking and being intellectually humble. If such discussions lead to disagreements about how we should learn, these disagreements can be addressed head-on by supporting students to create a set of community standards outlining what they see as valuable for debate (Duncan et al., 2018).

Explorations into Knowing

Conducting a more intentional "exploration into knowing" is a useful way to clarify norms for inquiry. Such an activity might also be the first time students explicitly name and articulate such norms and skills for coming to know what is true in the world, whether that be in the present or the past. Stanford History Education Group, now Digital Inquiry Group, has one such activity titled "Lunchroom Fight," in which students must discuss and establish how they come to know what really happened after a fight breaks out in the lunchroom as described in the teaching materials.

In our work with secondary teachers, we used a similar activity called the Livia problem. The activity was adapted from an article published by Barzialai and Chinn (2020). Zavala and Kuhn (2017) and Iordanou (2016) also feature the problem. The activity begins with teachers or students reading two accounts of the fictional "Fifth Livian War." The two accounts of the causes and resolution of the war, written by historians from warring North and South Livia, explicitly disagree on key points. Individuals then respond to the questions in Figure 9.7 and discuss their responses in groups:

1. Can you summarize what the Fifth Livian War was about and what happened?
2. Are the two historians' accounts of the war different in any important ways? In what ways are they different?
3. Could both of the historians' accounts of the Fifth Livian War be right? If no—why not? If yes, how can that be?
4. Could anyone be certain of what happened in the Fifth Livian War? If yes—how? If no, why not?

FIGURE 9.7. Questions to prompt discussions about stance.

Student responses are likely to include answers that come from the copiers stance (e.g., "The account is correct because he said it"), the subjectivist stance (e.g., "You can't know what happened; each historian has his own view"), or the criterialist stance (e.g., "We can try to find artifacts that will give us clues of what happened"). Teachers can help students understand that these are different stances, and they can teach students what learners adopting the criterialist stance do, that is, look for more evidence and try different analytical tools such as sourcing, corroboration, and contextualization. Using the questions, teachers can guide students to discuss what aspects of each historian's account use evidence, argue which evidence claims are most relevant, and co-create a counterargument to each of the historians' accounts. Like the "Lunchroom Fight," the "Fifth Livian War" can create an opportunity for students to develop an understanding of the role of counterargument in developing opportunities for dialogue and revision.

Hedging

Another effective disposition for civic participation that we gain from engaging in historical argumentation is intellectual humility, or a belief in the tentative nature of knowledge (Nokes, 2013). Studying a past event from the perspective of the present requires us to acknowledge the tentative nature of our knowledge of the past and the need to sometimes revise our understandings. Consequently, historians often use "hedging" language, softening claims and using words such as *appear, may,* or *probable.* Students need explicit instruction to understand that framing an argument with this type of language does not diminish the strength of the argument but rather acknowledges the complexity of knowing and the analytical tools (sourcing, corroboration, contextualization) that the historian has already employed to develop her argument.

Teachers might provide language support as students practice softening their assertions by creating a word wall or other scaffold to remind students of a range of language choices to indicate hedging (see examples in Figure 9.8). This sort of language scaffold can be helpful to all students and particularly so for students who are still acquiring proficiency in academic and disciplinary language.

Students may work as partners to share the ways they have included hedging in their writing and provide one another with feedback. As students discuss the rationale for using hedging language, they can also discuss ways they can strengthen their arguments or the types of evidence that could provide an alternative perspective or interpretation. By listening and responding, students can engage in affirming and further normalize hedging language as part of developing historical arguments.

The ways historians approach creating historical arguments—questioning, engaging in dialogue, acknowledging what they know and do not know yet—reflect the empathetic intellectual stance of the truth seeker. The activities described in this chapter all create opportunities for students to engage in these intellectual pursuits, where they are positioned to engage in collaborative truth seeking and grapple with multiple perspectives to identify the most plausible account of the past. This contrasts classroom activities that position students as passively digesting historical facts or engaging in confrontational debate. We argue it is vitally important to student learning and civic discourse that history teachers create classroom communities that value dialogue, are centered on evidence, provide multiple opportunities for discussion, and see diverse perspectives as valuable.

Hedging: Softening claims in academic writing with the use of:

- Verbs like *appear, seem, tend*
- Modal auxiliary verbs: *can, could, may, might*
- Adjectives: *likely, unlikely, probable, possible, plausible*
- Quantity expressions: *some, many, much*
- Adverbs: *perhaps, presumably, relatively, probably*
- Frequency words: *occasionally, generally, usually, often*

We use hedging language because this is what we know so far; the author is creating an interpretation based on what the author knows; additional evidence could become available.

FIGURE 9.8. Hedging language.

Conclusion

Students can find writing academic arguments difficult and especially struggle to consider alternative perspectives and acknowledge or refute potential criticisms of their own positions. Therefore, teachers may want to teach, scaffold, or offer opportunities for students to practice developing these important skills. The discipline of history offers a particularly rich context for the development of these skills because of the complexity of the past, the centrality of interpretation to the discipline, and the tentative and evolving nature of knowledge within the discipline. History teachers who wish to move their practice away from content coverage and toward interpretation might start with the following action steps.

ACTION STEPS

Identify areas in your instruction where there will be multiple perspectives/answers to guided inquiry questions.

- Plan where students should anticipate and hear alternative perspectives.
- Select activities with scaffolding in students' zones of proximal development.
- Guide students to reflect on their thinking.
- Reflect on your own developing practice by asking yourself these questions:
  - Are my students reasoning more with evidence?
  - As they make various claims, are they still open-minded?
  - Are they able to ask their own questions about their work and that of their peers?

REFERENCES

Bain, R. B. (2006). Rounding up unusual suspects: Facing the authority hidden in the history classroom. *Teachers College Record, 108*(10), 2080–2114.

Barzilai, S., & Chinn, C. A. (2020). A review of educational responses to the "post-truth" condition: Four lenses on "post-truth" problems. *Educational Psychologist, 55*(3), 107–119.

Bruner, J. S. (1978). The role of dialogue in language acquisition. In A. Sinclair, R. Jarvella, & W. J. M. Levelt (Eds.), *The child's conception of language* (pp. 241–256). Springer-Verlag.

Chinn, C. A., Barzilai, S., & Duncan, R. G. (2020). Disagreeing about how to know: The instructional value of explorations into knowing. *Educational Psychologist, 55*(3), 167–180.

Duncan, R. G., Chinn, C. A., & Barzilai, S. (2018). Grasp of evidence: Problematizing and expanding the next generation science standards' conceptualization of evidence. *Journal of Research in Science Teaching, 55*(7), 907–937.

Ferretti, R. P., & Lewis, W. E. (2018). Argumentative writing. In S. Graham, C. A. MacArthur, & M. Hebert (Eds.), *Best practices in writing instruction* (3rd ed., pp. 135–162). Guilford Press.

Frederiksen, C. H., & Dominic, J. F. (1981). *Writing: The nature, development, and teaching of written communication: Vol. 2. Writing: Process, Development and Communication.* Erlbaum.

Goldman, S. R., Britt, M. A., Brown, W., Cribb, G., George, M., Greenleaf, C., . . . Project READi. (2016). Disciplinary literacies and learning to read for understanding: A conceptual framework for disciplinary literacy. *Educational Psychologist, 51*(2), 219–246.

Harris, J. (2006). *Rewriting: How to do things with text.* Utah State University Press.

Iordanou, K. (2016). Developing epistemological understanding in scientific and social domains through argumentation. *Zeitschrift für Pädagogische Psychologie, 30*, 109–119.

Kuhn, D. (1991). *The skills of argument.* Cambridge University Press.

Kuhn, M. R. (2005). A comparative study of small group fluency instruction. *Reading Psychology, 26*, 127–146.

Langer, J. A., & Applebee, A. N. (1986). Reading and writing instruction: Toward a theory of teaching and learning. *Review of Research in Education, 13*(1), 171–194.

Maggioni, L., VanSledright, B., & Alexander, P. (2009). Walking on the borders: A measure of epistemic cognition in history. *The Journal of Experimental Education, 77*(3), 187–213.

Monte-Sano, C., & Allen, A. (2019). Historical argument writing: The role of interpretive work, argument type, and classroom instruction. *Reading and Writing, 32*, 1383–1410.

National Center for Education Statistics. (2012). *The Nation's Report Card: Trends in academic progress 2012* (NCES 2013-456). U.S. Department of Education, Institute of Education Sciences. *https://nces.ed.gov/nationsreportcard/pubs/main2012/2013456.aspx*

National Council for the Social Studies. (2013). *Social studies for the next generation: Purposes, practices, and implications of the College, Career, and Civic Life (C3) Framework for Social Studies State Standards.*

Nokes, J. D. (2013). *Building students' historical literacies: Learning to read and reason with historical texts and evidence.* Routledge.

Nokes, J. D. (2017). Exploring patterns of historical thinking through eighth-grade students' argumentative writing. *Journal of Writing Research, 8*(3), 437–467.

Nokes, J. D., & Kesler-Lund, A. (2019). Historians' social literacies. *The History Teacher, 52*(3), 369–410.

Olson, C. B., Maamuujav, U., Steiss, J., & Chung, H. (2023). Examining the impact of a cognitive strategies approach on the argument writing of mainstreamed English learners in secondary school. *Written Communication, 40*(2), 373–416.

Salahu-Din, D., Persky, H., & Miller, J. (2008). *The Nation's Report Card: Writing 2007* (NCES 2008-468). National Center for Education Statistics, U.S. Department of Education. *https://nces.ed.gov/nationsreportcard/pubs/main2007/2008468.asp*

Seixas, P., & Morton, T. (2013). *The big six: Historical thinking concepts.* Nelson Education.

Vygotsky, L. S. (1986). *Thought and language* (A. Kozulin, Ed.). MIT Press. (Original work published 1934)

Wiley, J., Griffin, T. D., Steffens, B., & Britt, M. A. (2020). Epistemic beliefs about the value of integrating information across multiple documents in history. *Learning and Instruction, 65*, Article 101266.

Wineburg, S. (Ed.). (2001). *Historical thinking and other unnatural acts: Charting the future of teaching the past.* Temple University Press.

Zavala, J., & Kuhn, D. (2017). Solitary discourse is a productive activity. *Psychological Science, 28*(5), 578–586.

Chapter 10

Constructing and Using Propositional Concept Maps for Writing and Learning in Science

Nancy Romance

Writing has always been a part of teaching science as classroom instruction usually includes note taking, journaling, short answer essays, written paragraphs with two or three sentences, and laboratory reports. And while all writing in science requires both skill and ability, along with grounding in the subject matter being taught at that time, most writing assignments are short and do not require in-depth conceptual explanations. For most students, the only science writing they are exposed to is what appears in textbooks. Here, the pages are characterized by lots of facts and technical information (e.g., diagrams, tables, illustrations) and with little deviation in style from one textbook to the next. As educators, science textbooks are valuable assets for instruction because the authors are well grounded in their disciplinary knowledge, proficient in offering detailed explanations of often very complex subject matter, and able to link concepts across topics to promote conceptual understanding. The basic attributes of such conceptually focused writing are desirable outcomes when thinking about instructing students in science writing.

However, for most middle and high school students, reading and learning from science textbooks as well as writing in science are challenging activities made even more so because generally there is little to no accompanying instruction in reading/language arts in science classrooms. What *is* commonplace is having students accumulate facts and information (e.g., memorizing vocabulary) and reproduce the same in question-and-answer activities. Yet, science teachers do engage students in investigations and hands-on activities that are related to what they are learning and/or reading. If, for example, during these active learning experiences, teachers strategically anchored both reading (e.g., focused on the concept[s] being learned) and writing (e.g., explanations that link concepts to the phenomena observed) into the instructional plan, there is the potential for deeper science learning, better comprehension, and new skills useful for expository writing. In this regard, subject-matter integration as envisioned here would link student experiences about real-world phenomena within a conceptual framework that deepens current learning, supports new learning, increases comprehension, and provides a logical structure for writing in science.

Generally speaking, however, literacy practices (e.g., oral or written communication) in science are geared toward serving very specific purposes and are not designed to build language proficiency, per se. Without direct attention to and instruction in how to develop disciplinary literacies (i.e., writing instruction for students that makes rhetorical forms of communication explicit and is integrated within a conceptual framework), students are not likely to achieve the desired learning outcomes necessary to become quality writers, a skill needed in college, in job applications, in industry or government work, or to address a variety of audiences (e.g., Hirsch, 1996, 2003; Romance & Vitale, 1999, 2006, 2017). In a recent government study (Goldman et al., 2019), which was part of the U.S. Department of Education "Reading for Understanding" initiative, the researchers noted that although students engaged in high-level scientific investigations, they were unsuccessful in the manner in which they were able to link concepts and conceptual relationships in written essay tasks to the investigations that they carried out during the project. Goldman and colleagues attributed this to the fact that students did not have the mastery of the rhetorical forms and language structures needed to express explanatory models in written text and noted that the study treatment did not include opportunities for students in groups or individually to learn how to write conceptually coherent passages related to their investigations.

I offer one final thought about linking science, writing, and reading. Current research suggests that when engaging in cross-disciplinary teaching, the learning outcomes in any one area have the potential to impact the other areas as long as that learning is grounded in a meaningful conceptual framework (e.g., Bereiter & Scardamalia, 1987; Bransford et al., 2000; Dansereau, 1995). The implications for instruction are clear. The integration of writing may be the critical "link" between science learning and reading comprehension, leading to the development of student proficiency in writing in science.

Addressing the Problem

In addressing the lack of quality writing instruction in science, you might be surprised to learn that a tool, *concept maps*, which has been around for quite some time, can, with some minor modifications in its design and use, actually improve student writing and learning in science and be applicable for use across K–12 classrooms and beyond.

Thus, the remaining parts of this chapter provide an overview of research evidence that underscores how and why the use of these modified concept maps, or Propositional Concept Maps (PCMs), leads to meaningful learning of domain-specific core science concepts (e.g., chemistry, biology, artificial intelligence) and improves expository writing. For teaching purposes, the chapter will also provide you with examples of PCMs, demonstrate how they serve as blueprints for expository writing, and provide explicit guidelines to assist you in creating PCMs and in using them with students in classroom settings. The chapter will also offer you a challenge. Can you pair up with colleagues to try to construct a group PCM on a soon-to-be taught topic in science?

What Is a PCM?

The modified concept map you learn about here, allowing you to construct, use, and apply in classroom instruction, is called a *Propositional Concept Map* (PCM). When used in the classroom, students are actively engaged in reading, writing, discussing, and organizing science ideas. In effect, student creation of a PCM is a multidisciplinary approach to active learning that guides students' thinking about how science concepts are related, how to graphically represent concept connections, and how use of the resulting PCM serves as a blueprint for well-crafted science expository writing.

PCMs can be described as graphic organizers that present concepts (i.e., represented by words and word phrases) and concept relationships (i.e., represented by verbs and verb phrases) organized in a hierarchical fashion that represents the conceptual structure of the knowledge to be learned. You can think of it as an instructional/learning tool where the big ideas are situated at the top of the map and conceptually relatable subconcepts flow from that point. The major difference between ordinary concept maps and PCMs is that they have connecting verb phrases that form complete ideas (i.e., complete sentences/propositions), thus serving as viable blueprints for expository writing.

Here's the clincher: What you will find most interesting is that the process of constructing a PCM is actually where most of the in-depth learning takes place, and when you collaboratively create a PCM, you will invariably see why. Also, your teacher-created PCM can then be repurposed as a blueprint for instruction and assessment of student learning outcomes.

The following questions guide the content of the chapter:

GUIDING QUESTIONS

1. What strategies support creation of a PCM and its use as a blueprint for expository writing? How versatile are these strategies?
2. How can supporting student creation and use of a PCM lead to development of academic language skills necessary for writing in science?
3. How does construction and use of a PCM benefit teachers and students?
4. What tools are available to guide teachers in constructing a PCM?

What Strategies Support Creation of a PCM and Its Use as a Blueprint for Expository Writing?

Teacher Construction of a PCM: First Steps

To facilitate teacher construction of a PCM, I first highlight features of a PCM followed by a discussion of several PCM exemplars and the associated writing samples illustrating how PCMs serve as a blueprint for conceptually coherent science writing. This is followed by step-by-step strategies for teachers working in small groups to create and use their own PCM for classroom instruction.

Figure 10.1 illustrates how a PCM is structured, including what it represents, what it highlights, and what it uses to explain concept relationships. Overall, a PCM is a representation of the organization of concepts focused on a specific topic in science. The main concepts or big ideas (core concepts) are at the top of the map, and lesser ideas (subordinate concepts) flow from the big ideas in a hierarchical fashion. PCMs use verbs and verb phrases to show concept relationships, thus providing a semantic map of concepts. As illustrated, the ideas (concepts) are in boxes, and the relationships among concepts are represented using verbs and verb phrases that are located on the connecting lines. The box–line–box configuration forms a complete idea (or sentence or proposition).

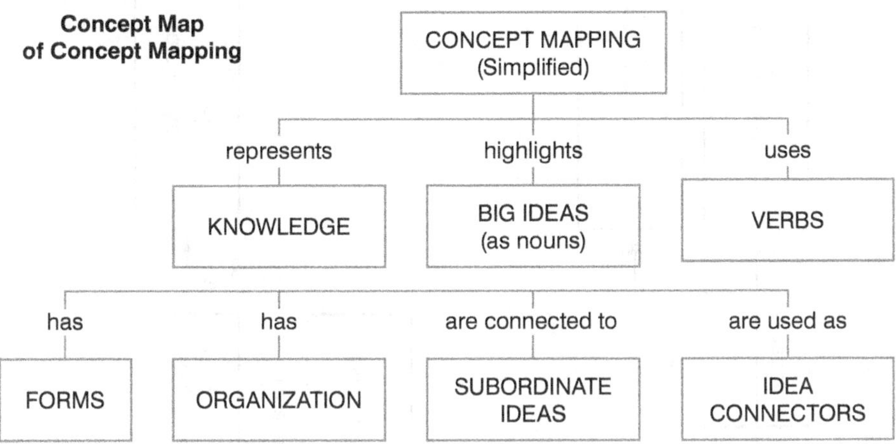

FIGURE 10.1. Concept map as a graphic organizer.

It is this feature of PCMs that differentiates them from other forms of graphic organizers.

Learning More about PCMs: Middle School Unit on Heat Energy

Figure 10.2 is a PCM on heat energy. Note that it has all the basic constituents of a good map. It has nouns and noun phrases in boxes and verbs and verb phrases on lines. Each connection forms a complete proposition (idea). Here you see that there are three major ideas guiding the organization of the map. One major concept would be "Heat Energy impacts both living and non-living things." The second big idea describes heat energy as an internal energy that has causes and that can be found in matter. The third big idea identifies the mechanisms by which heat energy is transferred. In examining the PCM, you'll notice these features: (1) the biggest idea is positioned at the top of the map while all the supporting concepts flow from that big idea; (2) the subordinate concepts explain the characteristics or relationships between and among concepts, that is, they present ideas that describe the main idea in more detail; (3) some of the concepts are arranged along the same plane (or line of vision) such as conduction, convection, and radiation because these three processes are the major factors in the transmission of heat energy; and, (4) along the bottom, you see smaller detail (i.e., subconcepts) about each heat transfer mechanism. Actual examples could form another layer in the following sections.

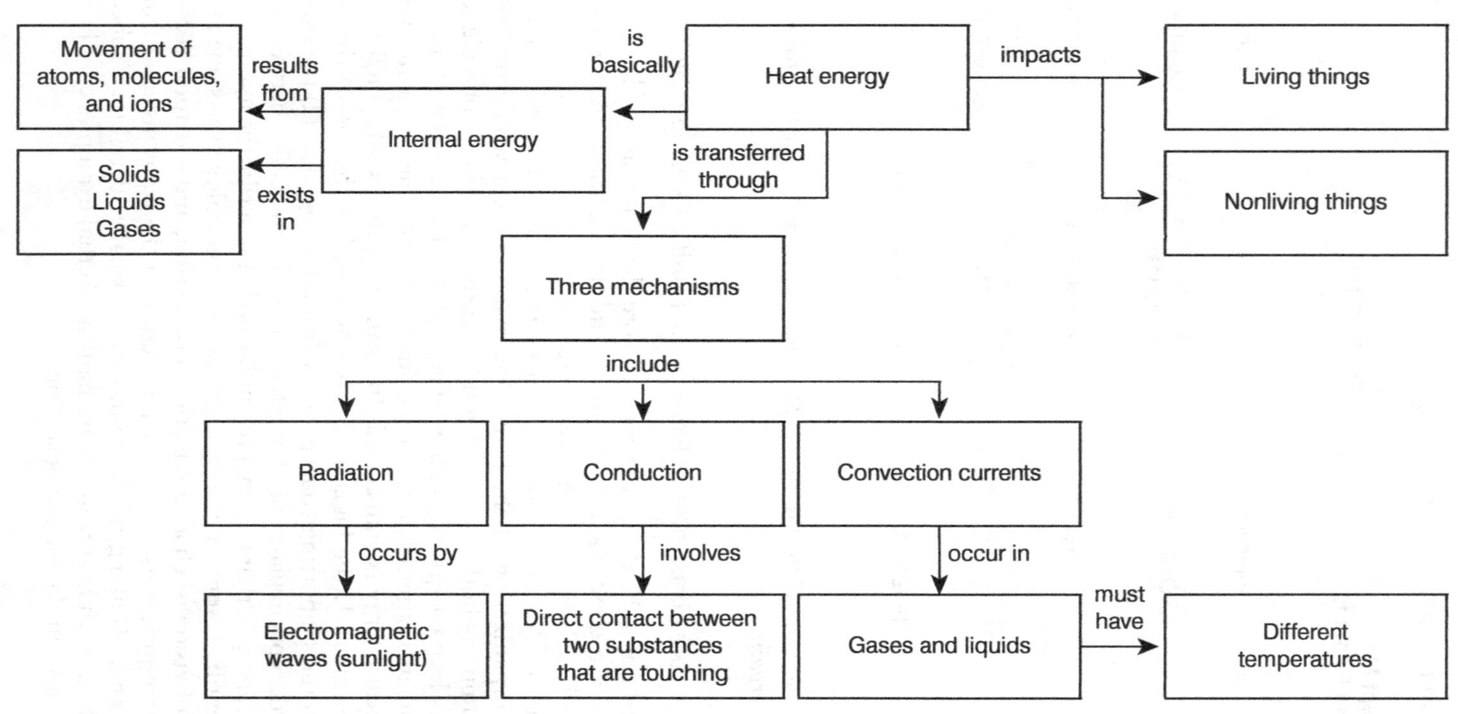

FIGURE 10.2. PCM on heat energy—grades 6–8.

Thinking about Creating a PCM to Outline a Unit of Study for Students

As teachers, imagine that you just completed a teaching unit on heat energy that included lots of experiments illustrating conduction, convection, and radiation. To teach this unit, you and your grade level colleagues had laid out the unit beforehand by creating a map similar to Figure 10.2. In subsequent sections of this chapter, you will learn about how to use a PCM as a blueprint (i.e., graphic organizer) to guide student expository writing. You will also learn why it is valuable to create your own group PCM first before working with students.

Using Figure 10.2 to Strategize How to Construct an Essay on Heat Energy

When examining the map, you can see that the main concept and the concepts directly linked to it provide the basis for a robust opening paragraph (i.e., the basic elements of heat energy, how it is transferred, and its impact). Then, when planning the second paragraph, you can write about the core mechanisms responsible for the transfer of heat energy. Ideas for paragraphs 3–5 would discuss the three different mechanisms of heat energy transfer in more detail. Finally, you could add a summary paragraph highlighting everyday examples (e.g., temperature of an object in direct sunlight versus the shade).

Figure 10.2 represents a typical PCM that could be created, with teacher guidance, by middle school students (e.g., grades 6–8). To see additional PCMs, visit *www.scienceideas.org/TeacherResources/BinderEnergy/Tab3/ConceptMaps.pdf*

Considering Versatility in the Construction of PCMs

Figure 10.3 is another PCM, on phase change in matter—process of evaporation. This map was created by a team of ninth-grade teachers planning a mini-unit of study lasting 1–5 days. Notice that the map is also organized in a hierarchical fashion, with big idea(s) located at the top, the subconcepts flowing from them, and the connecting verbs and verb phrases forming complete propositions. But this map is a little different because the teachers decided to emphasize *three different sets of ideas*: evaporation as a concept, everyday examples of evaporation, and factors associated with speeding up or slowing down the process of evaporation. In effect, teachers added factors associated with student investigations and observations of evaporation onto the map.

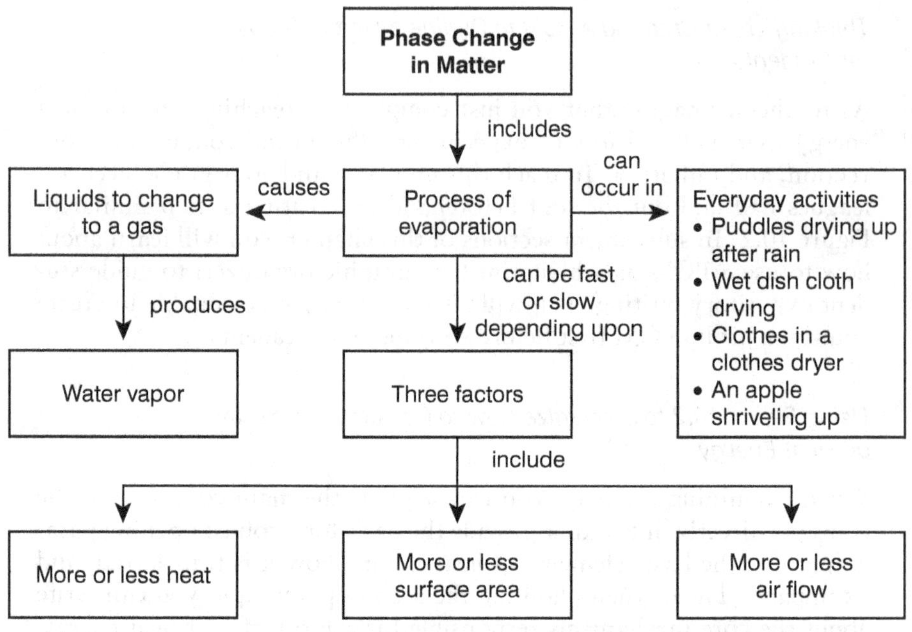

FIGURE 10.3. PCM on phase change in matter—grades 6–8.

Using the PCM as an Organizational Blueprint for Writing

Table 10.1 is a five-paragraph essay created using the PCM in Figure 10.3. As evident by looking at Table 10.1, the PCM served as a blueprint for construction of the five-paragraph essay. This process can be used by students while learning science and other subjects (e.g., social studies).

Another interesting benefit of a PCM involves modifications (e.g., additions of ovals superimposed on the map; see Figure 10.4) that transform the PCM into a blueprint for instructional planning. The following sections describe this process.

Using the PCM as a Blueprint for Instructional Planning

In this scenario (Figure 10.4), ovals served as an instructional teaching sequence for teachers.

1. First, teachers accessed students' prior knowledge about phase change in matter (Activity 1).
2. Next, teachers planned class time for students to observe (Activity 2) everyday examples of evaporation.

3. Then, teachers set up lab experiments (Activity 3) so students could investigate and write about the three major factors impacting the rate of evaporation.
4. Next, the students read their science text (Activity 4) and two trade books on evaporation and heat energy transfer.
5. Finally, the teachers used the PCM to guide student writing (Activity 5).

The PCM can be coupled with hands-on activities to easily enhance student writing abilities in a manner that has a lasting impact. *Keep in mind that these are very simple examples. PCMs can be much more*

TABLE 10.1. Essay on Phase Change in Matter—Water Evaporation

Using a PCM for writing in science	
Opening paragraph	Water evaporation is a comprehensive process that involves water changing phase. There are many everyday examples of evaporation that we can experience, like a puddle drying up once exposed to the sun. We also know that we can speed up or slow down the process due to the combined effect of three things (e.g., surface area, air flow, temperature). These factors are described next.
Second paragraph	Water evaporation is one of the steps in Earth's water cycle. During the process, water, a liquid, turns into a gas we call "water vapor." This is an invisible gas. The process involves a phase change in matter where liquids, plus the addition of heat energy, turn into invisible gas called water vapor!
Third paragraph	Every day, we can see examples of water evaporation, such as puddles drying, clothes drying in the dryer, a wet dishcloth drying up, and even an apple shriveling up after having been left in the refrigerator for too many weeks. There are many other everyday examples of evaporation. We know that under ordinary everyday conditions, water will eventually disappear or evaporate.
Fourth paragraph	In our science lab, we experimented to see if we could speed up or slow down the process of evaporation. The activities we did included adding heat, increasing air flow over a wet surface, or spreading out an object so that moving air covers as much surface area as possible. With each of these experiments, we were able to either speed up or slow down the process of evaporation. While we can do this with experiments in the classroom, in nature, there are very few ways that we could actually impact the process of evaporation.
Closing paragraph	Evaporation is an amazing process that is happening all around us every day. There are lots of benefits to us and to the Earth when evaporation takes place. The water vapor that goes into the air does eventually return to Earth in the form of precipitation, which is good for all living things and for the whole cycle to continue.

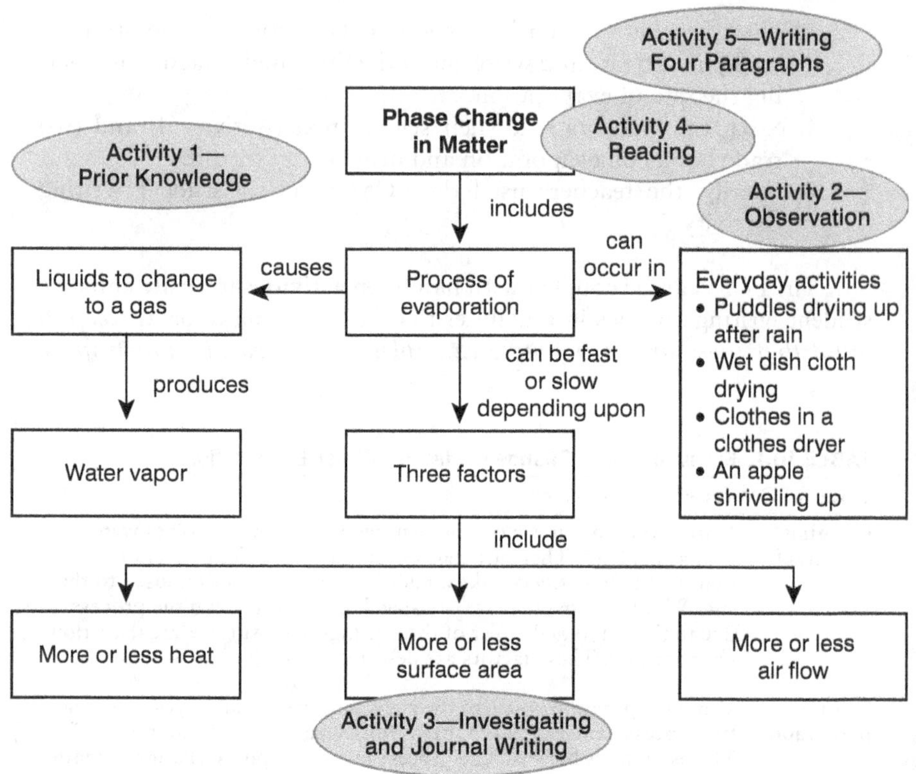

FIGURE 10.4. PCM on phase change in matter, with modifications.

complex, and the writing from these maps can be very comprehensive, that is, offering a complex depiction of highly interrelated conceptual relationships. (Note: At the end of the chapter, there are two more advanced PCMs—Climate, Figure 10.5, and Measurement, Figure 10.6—which, if used as blueprints, would support an increased level of complexity in the writing process.)

Teacher Strategies for Group Construction of a PCM

Generally, the same teacher strategies for constructing a PCM can also be used with students. It is recommended that you work with colleagues first and create a group PCM. Doing so really prepares you for doing this with students. (See "Student Notes" for some additional suggestions when working with students.)

Teachers Working in Groups. Across the many years of collaboration with classroom teachers, I have noted how very valuable and how much fun it was for teachers to work in teams to create a PCM representing a unit of study. I observed how different teachers might have similar or different ideas about the meaning of some concepts, as well as thinking about which concepts were more important. This made for lively discussion. Upon completion, the teachers reflected on the process and what they learned. Indeed, they agreed: the *power is in the process.* Imagine in-depth conversations about science concepts, what fun! By doing this, you have a much better idea about what students should be learning, what you will assess, and how to guide students in creating their group PCM and the writing activity that follows.

Student Notes. Basically, guiding students working in groups is very similar to teachers working in groups. Obviously, teachers provide oversight and guidance to students as they work in groups/teams.

Getting Ready to Construct a PCM.[1] Teachers assemble resources (e.g., science books, teacher editions, reference books, subject-specific books at a higher grade level, school district curriculum materials, state standards, Internet resources) and supplies (e.g., large chart tablet, sticky notes, markers). Next, teachers select a workspace where they can spread their materials out. Then, they begin to discuss and identify the concepts that should be taught, ensuring that all key concepts have been identified. Next, they place one concept (or concept phrase) on each sticky note (e.g., Evaporation, Phases of Matter), followed by arranging all the sticky notes in one corner of the chart tablet. (Caution: Try not to arrange the sticky notes while you are still brainstorming, as the process becomes quite cumbersome very fast.) Finally, teachers organize the sticky notes on the chart tablet according to how they perceive the relationships among the concepts.

Constructing the Group PCM. Now your team is ready to move the pile of sticky notes front and center so that everyone in the group can see them. Then, you will discuss, debate, and decide which concept is the biggest idea and will be the focus of the PCM. Place that sticky note on the top of your chart tablet. Continue to select the next biggest concepts that will link to the main concept. Continue this process until you have placed all the sticky notes (i.e., concepts) where you think they belong. Let the map sit for a day or two. Perhaps team members can look at the district curriculum to make sure all the key concepts are covered. Using

[1]These same strategies can be used with students.

other sources for a review is also a good move. You may, after doing this, decide on a few changes to your map. This is perfectly okay!

Adding Verb Phrases to Your PCM. Now you are ready to add verb phrases on lines between and among the concepts. Here's what you do. First, you can begin to draw lines between and among concepts. (Hint: Rulers are helpful.) Use a *pencil* for connecting lines and words, as you may move sticky notes around later if you change your mind. (Note: You may rearrange the concepts as many times as you like.) Second, place verbs and/or verb phrases on the lines, making a complete proposition or sentence. (Note: This can sometimes be a challenge because the verb phrases you select actually represent your understanding of the conceptual relationships.) Table 10.3 at the end of the chapter provides suggested verb phrases.

Student Notes. First, take time to review with students the essential elements of a complete sentence. Grammar is important, and many students need fundamental help with this. Show an example of how a PCM consists of verbs and verb phrases to convey complete sentences. Here's one other important rule related to linking concepts. There are certain words you cannot use (e.g., because, when, or any other conjunction) on the lines because when you do, you no longer have a complete sentence. Instead, you have a dependent clause. Now you're ready for a final look at your PCM. Bring all the teachers together and discuss whether changes need to be made or if additional detail is needed.

Constructing an Expository Paragraph from the PCM. The final phase involves creating your expository writing sample (e.g., informational paragraph or essay). Work as a group in doing this. Your PCM is organized into sections, each of which ideally can become a paragraph. The written essay is constructed around clusters of related concepts, creating viable and coherent paragraphs. For students, instead of memorizing concepts, they begin to organize concepts for new learning. Thus, the PCM is an ideal instructional tool to guide student expository writing. Each experience in doing this improves students' writing abilities. One way to think about PCMs is to consider them as visual and symbolic representations of science vocabulary that help learners understand and remember the meanings of the new words. One other valuable strategy is for students to read the PCM out loud, where they can emphasize the key concept relationships. A few final hints include maintaining focus on the relatedness among concepts, recognizing that one concept map may not be able to represent all the concepts you'd like to teach/learn, so you may need to build a family of concept maps in this case. One other final technique is the addition of arrows at the end of the lines to show the flow or direction one should follow while reading the map to ensure maximum coherence. (Note: Tables 10.2 and 10.3 at the end of the chapter provide, respectively, "quick starters for building PCMs," along with sample verbs and verb phrases.)

Other Instructional Benefits from Creating and Using Your PCM. After you have completed the teacher PCM, it can be used as a classroom display. Place the map strategically in front of the class (e.g., on a whiteboard) and use it as a blueprint for the multiple lessons you will teach until you complete the unit. Also, emphasize to students how they can follow along with the unit by using the map as their blueprint. They can tell which concepts they have learned and which ones they haven't, and they can see how they all fit together. PCMs serve as a roadmap for teaching and learning. This is valuable for all students because it adds conceptual coherence to instruction. It is surprising how many students are actually lost in the classroom, that is, they have no idea where a lesson is going. With the PCMs to guide them, they will not be lost anymore. Finally, teachers used the PCMs to guide whole-class construction of a three- to four-paragraph essay, using the entire map as the blueprint. In thinking ahead, teachers also let students know that they would be working in groups to create their own group PCM.

How Can Supporting Student Creation and Use of PCMs Lead to Development of Academic Language Skills Necessary for Writing in Science?

Propositional Concept Maps: A Useful Tool for Student Expository Writing

Constructing a PCM is a very useful graphic organizer and tool for building students' content-area knowledge and for introducing students to and guiding their expository writing and academic language development. Reflect for a moment on the five-paragraph essay on evaporation. Content-area writing requires learners to push the limits of their conceptual understanding when addressing complex topics (e.g., photosynthesis, plate tectonics, stoichiometry, climate, measurement) in science as well as challenging their linguistic abilities when both reading expository text and writing in science (e.g., technical vocabulary, multimorphemic words, ordinary words used in nonordinary ways, and problematic grammatical words such as prepositions, pronouns, and conjunctions) (Fang, 2006). The following sections will guide your thinking about academic language development in science classrooms.

Developing Student Academic Language: Where Do PCMs Factor in This Development?

Our work with students (and teachers) revealed that continued use of increasingly sophisticated PCMs helped develop students' complexity of thought, their high-order thinking, and their ability to grapple with and address abstract thinking and writing (Romance & Vitale, 2011). In reflecting on the PCMs in this chapter (see two additional maps at the end of the chapter), teachers can appreciate how their continued use can build students' academic language fluency. That is, PCMs require students to describe the complexity of concepts and concept relationships, engage in higher-order thinking, and connect the hierarchical structure of the science domain being addressed to their scientific investigations.

Developing Student Ability to Use Academic Conventions in Writing

Along with learning in science, constructing and writing prose from PCMs benefits students in the development of their academic language as they now learn to write following new conventions such as (1) being able to use explicit language (domain-specific and accompanying words) so that others can understand what is being written, (2) avoiding the use of opinions and feelings when writing (note: given that much student writing experience falls within the domain of narrative writing, it may be difficult for some to avoid the use of personal pronouns), (3) using terms and expressions for specific purposes (e.g., if . . . then clauses to express cause-and-effect relationships), and (4) learning how to use clauses in expressing multiple related concepts (Vitale & Romance, 2007).

Examining Specific Syntactical Features Used in Authentic Scientific Writing

Middle, high school, and college students all experience difficulty when trying to read science text for understanding, even though this is the main purpose of such reading. The same is true when they engage in expository writing. Students are not familiar with commonly used language conventions because, for many students, there is little to no instruction in higher-order writing skills embedded directly into their academic subject instruction in middle or high school or in college.

Here are some examples. Science texts are characterized by long sentences with embedded clauses and inferred cause-and-effect relationships. These are extremely challenging. For a great article on the demands of science reading and writing, see Fang (2006).

Further evidence reported by the national assessments in science as well as in reading/language arts (see National Center for Educational Statistics, 2009, 2011, 2019, 2022) indicates that students lack proficiency in higher levels of understanding in both subjects. Given the lack of relevant prior knowledge, it's no surprise that both comprehension and writing in science have suffered. Having students construct and use PCMs can address these two issues simultaneously. That is, PCMs foster the building of concept relationships and writing in an organized fashion to express these relationships. In effect, students' use of PCMs leads to improvement in reading and writing (see Romance & Vitale, 1999).

Another factor is the use of nominalizations (i.e., changing verbs or adjectives into noun phrases), which is key in reducing the length of many science texts but absolutely confusing for reading with comprehension and almost nonexistent in student writing. When reading a string of sentences, more and more information has been condensed and is referenced in complex grammatical ways, making the reader/writer responsible for knowing all the connections being implied. The cognitive load for doing this, whether as a writer or a reader, is fairly overwhelming when students have no training in these conventions. Notable, however, is the fact that publishers are offering custom solutions (i.e., institution-specific "designer" text, entitled *Chemistry and Chemical Reactivity: FAU CHM 1 – CHM 2045*, published by Cengage Learning) to accommodate the learning needs of their students (Kotz et al., 2015).

Using the Structure of PCMs Can Increase Student Writing Abilities

In reflecting on the maps on Evaporation and Heat Energy, it is clear that the organizational structure provides the blueprint for expository writing. The resultant writing is conceptually organized, concepts are meaningfully sequenced, and the essay can incorporate related materials and ideas (e.g., experiments and their results, everyday phenomena that illustrate a concept). All of these strategies increase students' meaningful learning and writing in science (Romance & Vitale, 1999).

Practicing the Essentials of Good Writing

Writing researchers also suggest that quality writing requires mastery of the processes associated with good writing. These include having skill in creating an organizational schema to guide the development of ideas to be included in the writing, being able to identify and garner the necessary resources to support the writing, and being able to draw upon needed control mechanisms that foster quality writing (Graham et al., 2016, 2020; Graham & Perin, 2017). The creation of PCMs gives students the practice they need to become better writers. Think about how the PCM serves as an organizational schema, along with related resources for writing and creating multiple iterations of a writing assignment, that supports students in becoming much better writers.

Modeling, Engagement, and Iterative Practice to Refine Writing in Science

Demonstrating for students and engaging them in the construction and revisions of multiple PCMs provides the modeling, engagement, and iterative practice needed to improve writing. It's clear that all three processes are necessary if enhancement of students' expository writing is to be meaningful and lasting across grade levels and subjects, as well as career pathways.

Classroom Discourse and Negotiating Meaning

By having groups of students work together on a PCM and production of a written essay, they can further develop their language skills by asking more open-ended questions, constructing responses, becoming better listeners, rethinking their ideas, leading small or large group discussions, comparing and contrasting ideas, and then rewriting their PCM-focused expository passage.

Reflecting on Related Research from Cognitive Science and Cognitive Psychology

PCMs were first researched and created by Joseph Novak (e.g., Novak, 2010; Novak & Canas, 2006; Novak & Gowin, 1984). PCMs are widely used across the world and at all levels of instruction (*www.ihmc.us*). Novak's team developed a "free" concept-mapping tool (e.g., C Map Tools; *https://cmap.ihmc.us/products*), which allows for synchronous development of PCMs (Institute of Human and Machine Cognition, 2007). Other researchers have been studying the use of computer-based tools for PCMs (e.g., Chang et al., 2001; Cheung, 2006; DeSimone et al., 2001).

In using PCMs, our research team was able to demonstrate positive outcomes in students' reading comprehension and science achievement across grades 3–5 with transfer effects to grades 6–8 (Romance & Vitale, 2011, 2012, 2017). Fang's (2006) research clearly showed the complexities of middle school science textbooks, and we suggest that the use of PCMs can address many of the challenges. What's particularly valuable is the iterative practice associated with their creation (Ericsson, 2006) and how engendering well-organized knowledge and scientific understanding for students improves comprehension and writing (Hirsch, 2003, 2006; Kintsch, 1988; McNamara & Magliano, 2009).

Summary of the Literacy Features Associated with Creating and Applying PCMs

PCMs, as a form of expository writing, are also useful when students engage in argumentation requiring a conceptual basis to combine ideas with evidence. PCMs are useful when students need to (1) draw conclusions following scientific investigations, (2) write answers to short essay questions, (3) use one set of concepts to explain other related concepts, and (4) write using facts and information to engage in disciplinary reasoning. PCMs fill a void in students' literacy instruction because they emphasize organizing ideas and details and visually depict how information can be organized into paragraphs. In effect, they develop a better representation of what a paragraph actually is. And PCMs can be combined with other literacy tools such as Review/Revise and Reflect (Graham & Harris, 2017; Graham et al., 2023), and the Substitute, Takeout, Add, or Revise (STAR) Method (Gallagher, 2006).

Best News for Teachers

For teachers, learning how to create and use PCMs for instruction is a powerful strategy and easy to implement with just a little practice. Once proficient, teaching students how to create these PCMs enhances their learning and writing in science. Cumulatively, over time, students become proficient in organizing concepts in science with the potential for carryover effects to other subjects as well (e.g., social studies). Understanding how an organizational structure, frame, or blueprint facilitates the writing process is a lasting skill for students throughout grades 6–12 and well beyond.

How Does Construction and Use of PCMs Benefit Teachers and Students?

Note that the teacher strategies for constructing PCMs that appeared in the previous section can also be applied to students constructing PCMs. What follows here is a slight elaboration of those ideas.

Student Strategies for Creating PCMs

General Considerations: Strategies for Constructing the First PCM with Students

When beginning with students, select a topic that you have just finished teaching. This way, students can build on their prior knowledge and the accompanying lab activities they completed.

Abbreviated Steps for Guiding Student Construction of a PCM

First, assemble resources such as charts, tablets, sticky notes, science textbook, science notebook, and other science materials. Next, brainstorm with students, having them list all the concepts they just learned and referencing their notebook or science textbook as needed. Place each concept on an individual sticky note and gather them in one location on their chart paper. Next, model using key statements that will help the class construct their PCM. Here are some key statements: (1) Identify the biggest or most inclusive idea (or concept) and place it on the top of the paper, (2) ask each other questions about each concept and arrange the sticky notes in a top-down (i.e., hierarchical) order, (3) think about guiding verbs to connect the concepts, and (4) edit and revise as needed.

The next two steps involve guiding students as they create a unified, whole-class version of the PCM and then use it for writing a class essay. Teachers can (1) use a Q & A format and ask students to make suggestions as they create a whole-class PCM, and (2) discuss how the class PCM deepened their understanding as they negotiated meaning in creating their group or class PCM.

Teachers are encouraged to repeat the process for a second time, wherein small groups of students first construct their group PCM and then reassemble to construct an agreed-upon whole-class PCM without much teacher intervention. Students can then use their maps for writing expository paragraphs, for negotiating meaning, and as a study tool for classroom assessment in science.

Constructing and Using PCMs Offers Global Benefits to Teachers and Students and for Learning in General

Benefits of Cross-Curricular Writing Activities

Cross-curricular instructional models have been the focus of cognitive psychologists for quite some time. Specifically, the cognitive psychologists address how cross-curricular innovations deepen students' scientific thinking, increase the versatility of their ideas, enhance their writing abilities, and improve comprehension (Graham et al., 2020; McNamara & Kintsch, 1996; McNamara & Magliano, 2009; Romance & Vitale, 2006, 2011, 2012).

Benefits of Using PCMs as Organizers for Handwriting in Science

Writing from PCM is a major activity associated with their use. Researchers have reported that the very act of "handwriting" improves learning outcomes. Brain scans using high-density EEG studies comparing cursive handwriting over typing have shown that the physical process of handwriting enhances brain connectivity, increases cognitive engagement, improves memory and retention, and improves writing quality, all of which are essential for learning. Using a digital pen on a touchscreen showed synchronized activity in the brain in areas related to memory formation, encoding new information, both optimal for learning. Typical handwriting activities (e.g., note taking, journal writing, visualizing, manually working through problems in math and science) were found to have a positive impact on learning, memory formation, and cognitive engagement (Askvik et al., 2020; Kein, 2013; López Lloreda, 2024; Mueller & Oppenheimer, 2014; Van Der Weel & Van Der Mer, 2024).

Benefits of Science-Specific Handwriting Activities

Findings associated with science-specific handwriting activities have been exciting and warrant new consideration. For example, handwritten notes improved memory and retention in science. Having students write out the definitions of scientific terms, or formulas, and engage in other science processes, can aide in comprehension, increase focus during instruction, promote critical thinking when notes must be summarized or synthesized, and help students visualize problems such as in chemistry when there's a need to visualize steps leading to solutions (BouJaiude & May, 2006; Schmidt & Telaro, 1990). The cognitive basis for constructing PCMs and using them as blueprints for writing conceptually sound passages is aligned with this emphasis on handwriting in science. Both the creation of PCMs and writing from PCMs are potentially viable instructional activities to promote long-term learner outcomes.

Linking PCMs to Theories about How People Learn

Early work (Ausubel, 1963, 1968; Ausubel et al., 1978; Novak & Gowin, 1984) along with Bransford et al.'s (1999) work *How People Learn*, provide evidence suggesting that as new knowledge is added to existing knowledge, what one knows deepens, becomes more refined, and can serve in an ongoing fashion for learning even more within and across domains. Specifically, Bransford's work indicated that how people learn requires mastery of discipline-specific core concepts and concept relationships that can then be applied to and support new learning (Bransford et al., 1999). First, all learning depends on having adequate prior knowledge to support the new knowledge that is being learned. Second, all knowledge must be organized around the core concepts that make up the discipline or body of knowledge (e.g., understanding heat energy transfer to explain global warming). And third, metacognitive skills help us to organize and reorganize the knowledge we are learning and to apply that knowledge across similar and different contexts. Does this sound familiar? It is, in fact, the basis for the creation and use of PCM.

Linking PCMs to Current Research on How People Learn: Volume II

The second volume of *How People Learn* offered additional insights. Namely, the development of expertise in a domain (1) affects what experts notice, how they organize, represent, and interpret information and how they reason, remember and solve problems, and (2) affects how and when they need to apply their knowledge, thus building new knowledge and being able to apply knowledge in new contexts. When learners have opportunities (and practice) to apply what they are learning across similar and novel contexts, they begin to develop deep and transferable knowledge (e.g., Dong et al., 2020; Ericsson, 2006; Romance & Vitale, 1999; Romance et al., 2000; Sowa, 2000). The iterative process of constructing PCMs is highly relatable to these findings.

Related Benefits Associated with Constructing and Using PCMs in Science

- *Fosters generating explanations and questions versus rote memorization.* The creation of PCMs helps learners visualize core concepts (big ideas) and concept relationships and understand how the knowledge being learned can be conceptually organized, thus being able to generate explanations and questions and avoid rote memorization.

- *Supports development of an organizational framework for writing in science.* Creating PCMs enables students to organize concepts in a hierarchical fashion and use that structure for content-area writing and reading comprehension.

- *Increases critical thinking.* The process of identifying and connecting concepts to create the PCMs promotes higher-order thinking and understanding complex scientific ideas (Freeman & Jessup, 2004; Shavelson et al., 1994).
- *Supports memory and retention.* Visualization resulting from creating and using PCMs increases memory and the recall of information.
- *Encourages synthesis.* Concept maps often require students to synthesize information from various sources (e.g., textbooks, lab reports, research articles), which is a critical skill in writing in science.

What Tools Are Available to Guide Teacher and Student Construction of PCMs?

The CmapTools (Canas et al., 2001) software was developed by Dr. Joseph Novak and the team at the Institute for Human and Machine Cognition, originally affiliated with the Florida Department of Education. CmapTools (*https://cmap.ihmc.us*) are free, can be used by learners at almost any age, and, when used, can link to various resources (e.g., photos, images, graphics, videos, charts, tables, texts, webpages).

Constructing and Using PCMs Is Valuable for All Users

Construction of PCMs can reverse students' reliance on rote memorization and use of mnemonics in learning complex concepts in any domain and can enhance their overall writing quality.

I have provided two other examples of PCM, one on climate (Figure 10.5) and one on measurement (Figure 10.6). These two topics were selected because they are both complex and quite different.

Figure 10.5 presents a comprehensive overview of the core ideas that, when combined, provide an understanding of the causes of Earth's climate, its variation due to geography, and how the combined impact of these causative factors is what accounts for the Earth having three major climatic zones. This PCM, coupled with students gathering climate change data, can significantly enhance students' ability to explain their findings and/or argue for a specific claim through verbal and written discourse.

Figure 10.6 offers additional perspectives about the benefits of PCM. At first glance, the map looks complicated, but on closer analysis, it is clear that all the concepts represented on the map have been taught to all of us at some point in our education.

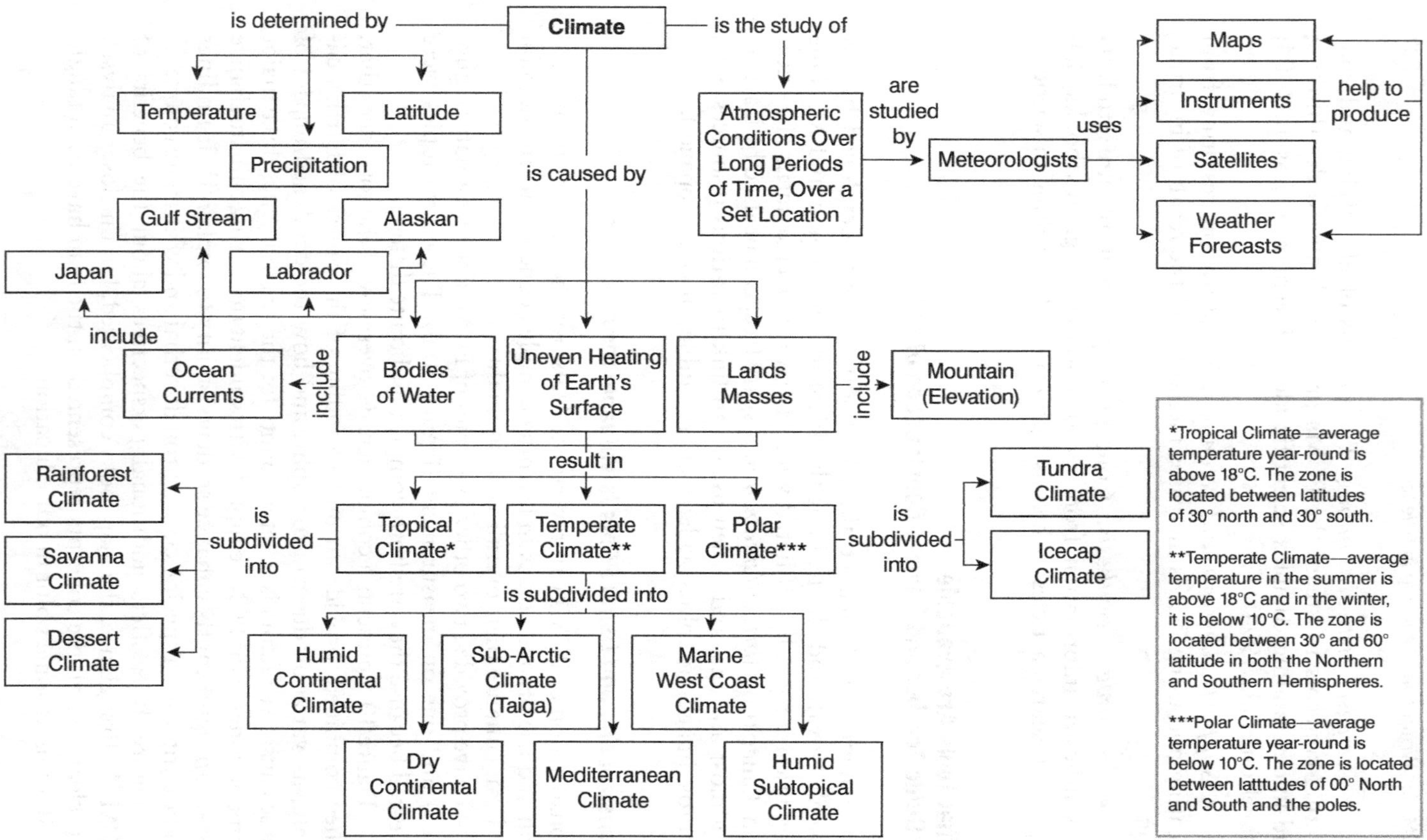

Climate
is determined by
Temperature
Precipitation
Latitude
is the study of
Atmospheric Conditions Over Long Periods of Time, Over a Set Location
are studied by
Meteorologists
uses
Maps
Instruments
Satellites
Weather Forecasts
help to produce
is caused by
Bodies of Water
Uneven Heating of Earth's Surface
Lands Masses
include
Ocean Currents
include
Japan
Gulf Stream
Labrador
Alaskan
include
Mountain (Elevation)
result in
Tropical Climate*
Temperate Climate**
Polar Climate***
is subdivided into
Rainforest Climate
Savanna Climate
Dessert Climate
is subdivided into
Humid Continental Climate
Dry Continental Climate
Sub-Arctic Climate (Taiga)
Mediterranean Climate
Marine West Coast Climate
Humid Subtopical Climate
is subdivided into
Tundra Climate
Icecap Climate

*Tropical Climate—average temperature year-round is above 18°C. The zone is located between latitudes of 30° north and 30° south.

**Temperate Climate—average temperature in the summer is above 18°C and in the winter, it is below 10°C. The zone is located between 30° and 60° latitude in both the Northern and Southern Hemispheres.

***Polar Climate—average temperature year-round is below 10°C. The zone is located between latttudes of 00° North and South and the poles.

FIGURE 10.5. PCM on climate.

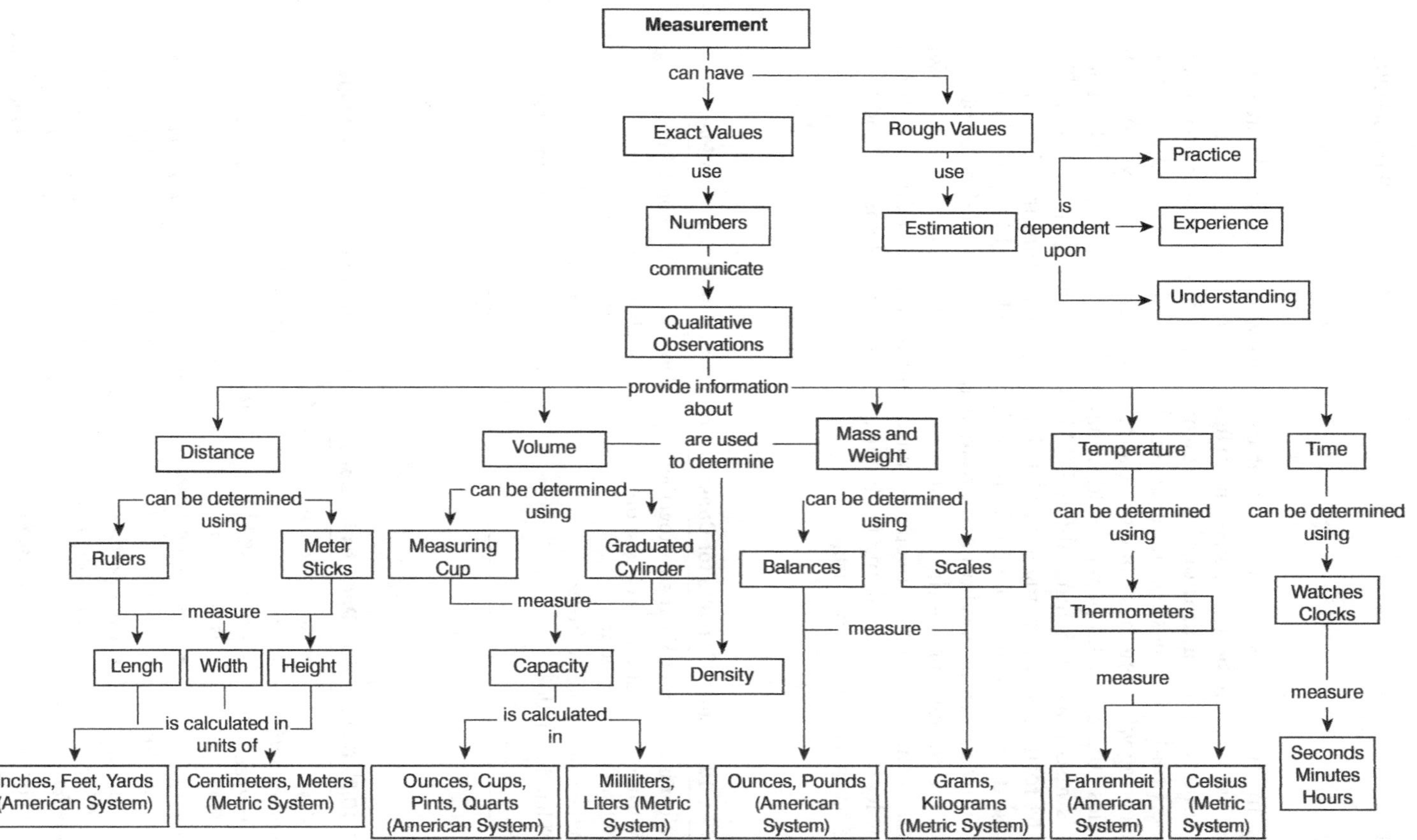

FIGURE 10.6. PCM on measurement.

ACTION STEPS

For many students, the process of expository writing has been unorganized and, at best, a constant struggle. Good writing requires, at a minimum, an organizational framework to guide the process to ensure conceptual soundness, coherence in the flow of ideas, and a way of reviewing what one has done to be sure it meets the necessary standards. Tables 10.2 and 10.3 provide additional tools for building PCMs. These tools also make teaching about PCMs to students a little easier. The PCM format will become a way of thinking, important in information-dense disciplines like science. This work on PCMs builds upon the work of many researchers who have broadened our understanding about the role and importance of the organization and structure of domain knowledge as the basis for (1) deep and meaningful understanding, (2) for all new learning, (3) for solving problems, (4) for comprehension, and (5) as the basis for quality writing.

TABLE 10.2. Quick Starters for Constructing Propositional Concepts Maps

• What is the same? What goes together?	• Does it produce something?
• What is it? What does it consist of? What does it contain?	• Does it have forms, types, or properties?
• Where does it come from?	• How can it be classified?
• What does it do?	• What are the important details?
• How does it do it?	• What are examples?

TABLE 10.3. Guiding Verb Phrases for Constructing Propositional Concept Maps

• *are either*	• *can represent*	• *Causes*	• *are composed of*
• *combines with*	• *can be categorized by*	• *is a combination of*	• *are identified as*
• *are grouped by*	• *is based on*	• *is connected to*	• *includes*
• *are obtained from*	• *can also be called*	• *contains*	• *is considered*
• *are represented by*	• *can be*	• *created by*	• *is determined by*
• *is transferred*	• *can be either*	• *depends on*	• *is influenced by*
• *are under*	• *can be expressed as*	• *describes*	• *is measured by*
• *are found only in*	• *can be used in*	• *is divided into*	• *refers to*
• *are organized by*	• *can be labeled as*		• *results from the combined effects of*

REFERENCES

Askvik, E. O., Van der Wee, F. R., & Van der Weel, A. H. L. (2020). The importance of cursive handwriting over typewriting for learning in the classroom. *Frontiers of Psychology, 11*, 1810.

Ausubel, O. R. (1963). *The psychology of meaningful verbal learning.* Grune & Stratton.

Ausubel, O. R. (1968). *Educational psychology: A cognitive view.* Holt, Rinehart & Winston.

Ausubel, D. P., Noak, J. D., & Hanesian, H., (1978). *Educational psychology: A cognitive view* (2nd ed.). Holt, Rinehart & Winston.

Bereiter, C., & Scardamalia, M. (1987). Knowledge telling and knowledge transforming in written composition. *Advances in Applied Psycholinguistics, 2*, 142–175.

BouJaiude, S., & May, A. (2003). The effect of using concept maps as study tools on achievement in chemistry. *Eurasia Journal of Mathematics, Science and Technology Education, 4*(3), 233–246.

Bransford, J. D., Brown, A. L., & Cocking, R. R. (Eds.). (2000). *How people learn.* National Academies Press.

Canas, A. J., Ford, K. M., Novak, J. D., Hayes, P., Reichherzer, T., & Suri, N. (2001). Online concept maps: Enhancing collaborative learning by using technology with concept maps. *The Science Teacher, 68*(4), 49–51.

Chang, K. E., Sung, Y. T., Chen, S. F. (2001). Learning through computer-based concept mapping with scaffolding aid. *Journal of Computer Assisted Learning, 17*(1), 21–33.

Cheung, L. S. (2006). A constructivist approach to designing computer supported concept-mapping environment. *International Journal of Instructional Media*, 33(2), 153–164.

Dansereau, D. F. (1995). Derived structural schemas and the transfer of knowledge. In A. McKeough, J. Lupart, & A. Marini (Eds.), *Teaching for transfer: Fostering generalization in learning* (pp. 93–121). Erlbaum.

DeSimone, C., Schmid, R. F., & McEwen, L. A. (2001). Supporting the learning process with collaborative concept mapping using computer-based communication tools and processes. *Educational Research and Evaluation,* 7(2–3), 263–283.

Dong, A., Jong, M. S-Y., & King, R. (2020). How does prior knowledge influence learning engagement? The mediating roles of cognitive load and help-seeking. *Frontiers in Psychology, 11.*

Ericsson, K. A. (2006). The influence of experience and deliberate practice in the development of superior expert performance. In K. A. Ericsson, N. Charness, P. J. Feltovich, & R. Hoffman (Eds.), *Cambridge handbook of expertise and expert performance* (pp. 683–704). Cambridge University Press.

Fang, Z. (2006). The language demands of science reading in middle school. *International Journal of Science Education, 28*(5), 491–520.

Freeman, L. A., & Jessup, L. M. (2004). The power and benefits of concept mapping: Measuring use, usefulness, ease of use, and satisfaction. *International Journal of Science Education, 26*(2), 151–169.

Gallagher, K. (2006). *Teaching adolescent writers.* Stenhouse.

Goldman, S. R., Greenleaf, C., Yukhymenko-Lescroart, M., Brown, W., Ko, M.-L. M., Emig, J. M., George, M., Wallace, P., Blaum, D., & Britt, M. A. (2019). Explanatory modeling in science through text-based investigation: Testing the efficacy of the Project READI Intervention Approach. *American Educational Research Journal, 56*(4), 1148–1216.

Graham, S., Bruch, J., Fitzgerald, J., Friedrich, L. D., Furgeson, J., Greene, K., . . . Smither Wulsin, C. (2016). *Teaching secondary students to write effectively. Educator's practice guide* (NCEE 2017-4002). What Works Clearinghouse.

Graham, S., & Harris, K. R. (2017). Reading and writing connections: How writing can make build better readers (and vice versa). In C. Ng (Ed.), *Improving reading engagement and achievement in the 21st-century: International research and innovations* (pp. 333–350). Springer.

Graham, S., Kim, Y. S., Cao, Y., Lee, W., Tate, T., Collins, P., Cho, M., Moon, Y., Chung, H. Q., & Olson, C. B. (2023). A meta-analysis of writing treatments for students in grades 6 to 12. *Journal of Educational Psychology, 115*(7), 1004–1027.

Graham, S., Kiuhara, S. A., & MacKay, M. (2020). The effects of writing on learning in science, social studies, and mathematics: A meta-analysis. *Review of Educational Research, 90*, 179–226.

Graham, S., & Perin, D. (2007). A meta-analysis of writing instruction for adolescent students. *Journal of Educational Psychology, 99*, 445–476.

Hirsch, E. D. (1996). *Schools we need. And why we don't have them.* Doubleday.

Hirsch, E. D. (2006). *The knowledge deficit gap.* Houghton Mifflin.

Hirsch, E. D. (2003). Reading comprehension requires knowledge of words and the world: Scientific insights into the fourth-grade slump and stagnant reading comprehension. *American Educator, 27*, 10–29.

Institute of Human and Machine Cognition. (2007). *Cmap tools: Knowledge modeling kit. http://cmap.ihmc.us*

Kein, J. (2013). The science of handwriting. *Scientific American Newsletter. www.scientificamerican.com/article/the-science-of-handwriting*

Kintsch, W. (1988). The role of knowledge in discourse comprehension: A construction- integration model. *Psychological Review, 95*(2), 163–182.

Kotz, J. C., Treichel, P. M., Townsend, J. R. & Treichel, D. (2015). *Chemistry and chemical reactivity: FAU CHM 1 – CHM 2045.* Cengage Learning.

López Lloreda, C. (2024, January 26). Handwriting may boost brain connections more than typing does. *Science News. www.sciencenews.org/article/handwriting-brain-connections-learning.*

McNamara, D. S., & Kintsch, W. (1996). Learning from texts: Effects of prior knowledge and text coherence. *Discourse Processes, 22*(3), 247–288.

McNamara, D. S., & Magliano, J. (2009). Toward a comprehensive model of comprehension. In B. H. Ross (Ed.), *The psychology of learning and motivation* (pp. 297–384). Elsevier Academic Press.

Mueller, P. A., & Oppenheimer, D. M. (2014). The pen is mightier than the keyboard: Advantages of longhand over laptop note taking. *Psychological Science, 25*, 1159–1168.

National Center for Educational Statistics. (2009). *The nation's report card: 2009 reading assessment.* U.S. Department of Education, Institute of Education Sciences. *https://nces.ed.gov/nationasreportcard/reading*

National Center for Educational Statistics. (2011). *The nation's report card: 2011 writing assessment.* U.S. Department of Education, Institute of Education Sciences. *https://nces.ed.gov/nationasreportcard/writing*

National Center for Education Statistics. (2019). *The nation's report card: 2019 Science assessment.* U.S. Department of Education, Institute of Education Sciences. *https://nces.ed.gov/nationsreportcard/science*

National Center for Education Statistics. (2022). *The nation's report card: 2022 reading assessment.* U.S. Department of Education, Institute of Education Sciences. *https://nces.ed.gov/nationasreportcard/reading*

Novak, J. D. (2010). *Learning, creating, and using knowledge: Concept maps as facilitative tools in schools and corporations.* Routledge.

Novak, J. D., & Canas, A. J. (2006). *The theory underlying concept maps and how to construct them.* Florida Institute for Human and Machine Cognition, University of West Florida.

Novak, J. D., & Gowin, D. B. (1984). *Learning how to learn.* Cambridge University Press.

Romance, N. R., & Vitale, M. R. (1999). Broadening the framework for student-centered instruction: Using concept mapping as a tool for knowledge-based learning. *College Teaching, 47*, 74–79. *www.jstor.org/stable/27558942*

Romance, N. R., & Vitale, M. R. (2006). *Concept mapping as a means for binding knowledge to effective content area instruction* [Paper presentation]. Proceedings of the Second International Conference on Concept Mapping, San Jose, Costa Rica. *www.scienceideas.org/RefDocs/004%20 Vitale_Romance_Costa_Rica_2006_FINAL.pdf*

Romance, N. R., & Vitale, M. R. (2011). A research-based instructional model for integrating meaningful learning in elementary science and reading comprehension: Implications for policy and practice. In N. L. Stein & S. W. Raudenbush (Eds.), *Developmental cognitive science goes to school* (pp. 127–142). Routledge.

Romance, N. R., & Vitale, M. R. (2012). Applying interdisciplinary instructional perspectives within a core concept framework to engender student conceptual understanding in science across grades K–5. In B. Fraser, K. Tobin, & R. McCampbell. (Eds.), *Second international handbook of science education* (pp. 1351–1374). Springer.

Romance, N. R., & Vitale, M. R. (2017). Implications of a cognitive science model integrating literacy in science on achievement in science and reading in grades 3–5 with transfer effects to grades 6–7. *International Journal of Science and Mathematics Education, 15*, 979–995.

Romance, N. R., Vitale, M. R., & Haky, J. (2000). Concept mapping as a knowledge-based strategy for enhancing student understanding. *The NSF Workshop Project Newsletter, 2*, 5–8.

Romance, N. R., Vitale, M. R., Widergren, P., & Hameister, J. (2002). Building content-area reading and literacy through an integrative curriculum strategy using reading, writing, and concept mapping strategies. In G. Shiel & U. Ní Dhálaigh (Eds.), *Proceedings of the 12th European Conference on Reading* (pp. 215–218). Reading Association of Ireland.

Schmidt, R. F., & Telaro, G. (1990). Concept mapping as an instructional strategy for high school biology. *Journal of Educational Research, 84*(2), 78–85.

Shavelson, R. J., Lang, H., & Lewin, B. (1994). *On concept maps as potential authentic assessments in science* (CSE Technical Report 388). CRESST University of Santa Barbara.

Sowa, J. F. (2000). *Knowledge representation: Logical, philosophical, and computational foundations*. Brooks Cole.

Van Der Weel, F. R., & Van Der Mer, A. L. (2024). Handwriting but not typing leads to connectivity: A high-density EEG study with implications for the classroom. *Frontiers in Psychology, 14*, Article 1219945.

Vitale, M. R., & Romance, N. R. (2007). A knowledge-based framework for unifying content-area reading comprehension and reading comprehension strategies. In D. McNamara (Ed.), *Reading comprehension strategies: Theory, interventions, and technologies* (pp. 75–103). Erlbaum.

Chapter 11

Writing-to-Learn in the Secondary Science Classroom

EXPLORING POSSIBILITIES FOR EQUITY

Catherine Lammert, Alison F. Warren, and Brian Hand

The purpose of this chapter is to describe evidence-based practices for using writing as a tool for learning within secondary-level science education. We engage with this topic through the lens that all students, including those from groups historically underrepresented in the sciences, are capable of problem solving and reasoning when provided with an equitable learning environment (Biesta, 2017). Given the magnitude of global crises such as climate change, it is crucial that every young person become scientifically literate and build their capacity to use their voice through writing to promote action. As such, maximizing the use of writing in the science classroom promotes teaching practices that are culturally responsive since they enable all students to view themselves as valuable members of the writing community (Graham et al., 2018). To enable readers to construct equitable learning environments in their own science teaching, this chapter provides clear models of teaching practices aligned to the findings of the recent meta-analyses that have guided this book as a whole (i.e., Graham et al., 2018, 2023).

We begin by describing some of our assumptions about literacy, language, and science learning as we outline the principles undergirding our work. First, following Norris and Phillips (2003), we argue that literacy is fundamental to learning science. By literacy in a "fundamental" sense, their explanation is as follows: "We first argue that nothing resembling what we know as western science would be possible without text; second, that because of the dependence of western science upon text, a person who cannot read and write is severely limited in the depth of scientific knowledge, learning, and education he or she can acquire" (Norris & Phillips, 2003, p. 224). In this view, it is impossible to communicate explanations for natural phenomena, a central goal of the sciences, without a means through which to communicate (Snow, 2010). For humans, this communication mechanism is language. Much of what is known about how the natural world functions was recorded by scientists through writing, and these texts serve to communicate disciplinary ideas. To demonstrate the fundamental sense of literacy in science, in our work we have often given teachers the following challenge: Imagine teaching a science lesson without using any language. How would you do it? They often suggest that they might use gestures, pointing, and body language or rely on pictures, figures, and drawings to evade the necessity of language. However, those multimodal elements, such as pictures, figures, and drawings, are included in what we mean by language and semiotics (Hand et al., 2013) as they are part of the sign systems of communication humans have developed. Thus, the first focus of this chapter is on the importance of multimodality within writing in science.

In the context of learning science, language plays a fundamental role in facilitating understanding and knowledge acquisition. Science, as a discipline, relies heavily on the precise use of sophisticated vocabulary to convey complex concepts and theories (Latour, 1987). Through language, scientists are able to articulate their findings and share them with the wider scientific community. This enables collaboration, peer review, and the advancement of scientific knowledge. It also allows for new ideas to be evaluated, reviewed, and explored in previously unexamined ways (Graham et al., 2018). In science, complex ideas are codified through scientific vocabulary and terminology. By encapsulating complex topics such as "photosynthesis" or "hibernation" in a single term, scientists can efficiently construct arguments about scientific phenomena (Snow, 2010); without these terms, the complexity of the explanations they provide would be limited by lengthy and circuitous wording (Schleppegrell, 2004). Thus, a second focus of this chapter is on the importance of vocabulary within writing in science.

Last, language enables engagement in scientific inquiry and critical thinking. By using language effectively, students can ask questions, make observations, and analyze data to formulate conclusions. Through language, students can engage in dialogue with their peers and with their teachers as they negotiate new meaning. To understand these occurrences, we ground our work in Biesta's (2017) notion of equity of intelligence. That is, although everyone has different knowledge (i.e., from one student to another, from students to the teacher, and from the teacher to scientific experts), we are all capable of problem solving.

As we have described elsewhere, the perspective of equity of intelligence suggests that "students have intellectual abilities commensurate with their teacher—the ability to think through and engage with ideas" (Hand & Cavagnetto, 2023, p. 11). A recognition of this within teaching science means that teachers must design generative learning environments in which students use writing to construct meaning and build new ideas. Accordingly, the third focus of this chapter is on the relationship between writing, revising, and publishing writing as a means of deepening one's own knowledge, which we term "writing-to-learn." In the sections that follow, we will demonstrate the ways writing-to-learn can take shape in the secondary science classroom.

The three topics previously mentioned, multimodality, vocabulary, and writing-to-learn, are outlined in the chapter that follows. We do so by describing what is known about these three topics through research (Graham et al., 2018, 2023), by emphasizing their relationship to equitable teaching, and by demonstrating how these elements work in practice. At each turn, we draw from the positions that literacy is fundamental (Norris & Phillips, 2003) and of equity of intelligence (Biesta, 2017). Then, we discuss ways to assess students' writing in secondary science and provide an example of a rubric that can be used for this practice. We encourage readers to consider the following guiding questions in mind.

GUIDING QUESTIONS

1. What additional science learning is made possible when multimodality is not just permitted but invited?
2. How can students' everyday language and everyday experiences be used in science classrooms aimed at building students' vocabulary knowledge?
3. How can writing be a space for students to clarify and negotiate their claims in science rather than just functioning as a mode for communicating their existing knowledge?

Inviting Multimodality

Defining Multimodality and Synthesizing the Supporting Literature

Multimodality involves how an individual "combines, interconnects, and integrates verbal text with mathematical expressions, quantitative graphs, information tables, abstract diagrams, maps, drawings, photographs, and a host of unique specialized visual genres seen nowhere else" (Lemke, 1998, p. 89). In a classroom context, multimodality is invited when students translate and interpret ideas across different modes and construct meaning through the translation process (Axelsson & Davidsson, 2012; Prain & Hand, 2016). Multimodal representations act as resources by which students make sense of their ideas and allow students to compare their different representations to negotiate shared understanding (see also Chapter 15).

Providing students opportunities to generate multimodal representations to express their understanding actively engages them in constructing, interpreting, and refining their own ideas (Waldrip et al., 2010). Research in this area emphasizes the importance of the different representations being student-generated, not just using different modes as a method of teaching (Kenny & Cirkony, 2018; Prain & Tytler, 2012; Tang et al., 2014). This perspective on the use of multimodality takes an epistemic approach where the focus is on what students come to know through the process of translating their understandings into different modes. This perspective runs in contrast to views that learners must be explicitly taught the underlying grammar of different modes of representation prior to their use- a view held by some scholars today (Unsworth et al., 2022).

In arguing that learners can and should develop knowledge of various modes through constructing, reading, and discussing texts with various modes, we point to research demonstrating that students may create meaning from producing a singular representation but also by embedding multiple modes in a greater task, such as a writing task (Jewitt et al., 2014; McDermott & Hand, 2013). As students learn to integrate multiple modes of representation, this increases their cognitive activity and overall conceptual understanding (McDermott & Hand, 2010). Specifically in science classrooms, having students engage with multimodal practices emulates how real scientists collaborate and communicate with each other and their audiences. Gaining the ability to construct and interpret such representations, texts or otherwise, will then further develop the student's science literacy (Kenny & Cirkony, 2018).

Using Multimodality to Provide Equitable Experiences to Underrepresented Students

Multimodality in the science classroom can be particularly helpful for English learners (ELs), as it maximizes the use of the meaning-making resources and schema that these students bring into the classroom (Grapin, 2018). Providing an equitable experience for students with different language backgrounds is key because it gives ELs opportunities to be active participants in the classroom environment. When teachers embrace multimodality and take the perspective that language is inclusive of images, diagrams, and even gestures, it leads to a more asset-based view of EL students. While these students' linguistic resources may differ from those of their peers who know more English, they are no less valuable. Allowing students to express their understanding through multimodal practices can in fact demonstrate their capabilities in subject-matter discipline more accurately (Yi & Choi, 2015). Studies in multilingual middle school classrooms have supported this idea and further suggest that encouraging multimodality can challenge students to take on new perspectives of phenomena, compare and consider affordances of using different modes, and lead students to ask and investigate new questions that arose during their construction process (Pierson et al., 2021).

Multimodality in the Classroom

Multimodal practices can be integrated at large and small levels. On the smaller side, encouraging multimodality can begin with bringing awareness by encouraging students to include different modes, such as visuals and graphs, in their written work. Teachers might also engage students in dialogue about how some modes are more beneficial for specific tasks, which can challenge students to think more critically about relationships between the modes and construct more sound explanations (Jewitt et al., 2001). Through an equity of intelligence perspective (Biesta, 2017), it is crucial that varying representations come from the students themselves. When students control the authorship of the representations, they may be more likely to embed multiple modes in their work and form more complex understandings.

An example of student work in Figure 11.1 portrays a student's response when asked to reflect, using whatever modes they preferred, on what they had learned in a given lesson. As this example shows, when students create their own representation of scientific concepts, the role of teacher can be to critique "and point out problems or inconsistencies with some student knowledge claims, and also model what students should do with their classes' knowledge claims" (Waldrip et al., 2010, p. 71). Other ways to more formally integrate multimodal practices into the classroom are through writing-to-learn tasks. Setting up a task where students are asked to explain a concept using text along with visuals, graphs, or other symbol systems, such as a children's book or a comic strip, can increase the student's understanding of not only the science content but also how to use different modes to communicate an idea (Hand et al., 2016). To assess student work with multimodal elements, Anderson and Kachorsky (2019) suggest developing clear expectations and criteria with the students prior to the writing task. This can be done through creating a collaborative rubric for the assignment, and

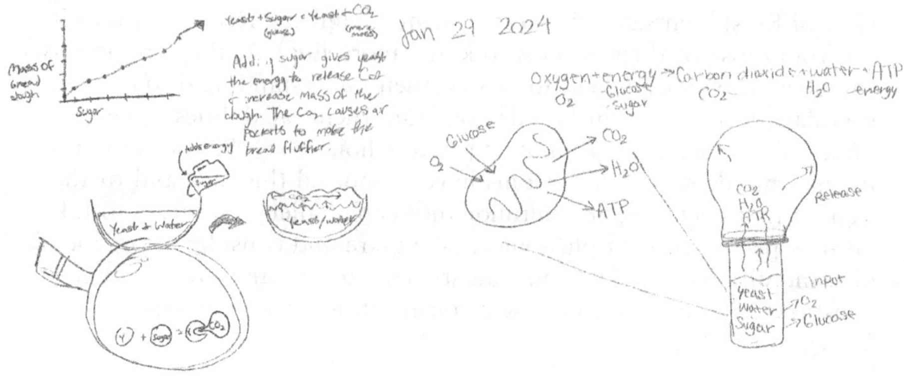

FIGURE 11.1. Examples of student work showcasing embedded multimodal representations.

if relevant, making it clear who the intended audience is. This helps guide student conceptualization and understanding of what modes will be the most beneficial and accurate.

Building Vocabulary Knowledge

Defining Vocabulary and Synthesizing the Supporting Literature

On the simplest level, vocabulary learning relates to knowledge of words and their meaning (Anderson & Freebody, 1981). While it may seem basic, especially to adults who are fluent in a particular language, understanding the underlying mechanism that drives word learning has fascinated linguists, education scholars, and psychologists for decades (Cummins, 1979; Quine, 1960). One reason is the relatively arbitrary relationship between the phonemes (i.e., sounds) that make up words and their morphology (i.e., meaning; Le Corre et al., 2016). Since these relationships may seem unpredictable, especially in an orthographically complex system like English, vocabulary learning is of central importance to writing in secondary science.

To date, most studies focused on how teachers support vocabulary development have occurred within literacy, reading, and language arts instruction (i.e., Carlisle et al., 2013; Nelson et al., 2015). Vocabulary development is crucial for readers because of its strong link to text comprehension (Duke et al., 2011). However, we argue that vocabulary plays an equally important role in writing instruction for middle and high school students in science. One reason is time. The English language contains a massive number of words; Webster's Third New International Dictionary (Merriam-Webster, 1961) contains 470,000 entries. Given the vastness of the language, it is logical that words might be taught inside content-area instruction rather than relegating all vocabulary learning to the English classroom.

A second reason to teach vocabulary in secondary science is domain-specificity. As researchers have documented (Anderson et al., 2023; Snow, 2010; Ucelli & Phillips Galloway, 2016; Wright & Gotwals, 2017), many words have a particular meaning in science that differs from the way that word is used in everyday conversation. This means that even if there were time to learn every vocabulary term inside literacy instruction, the specialized meanings of terms such as *observe* in biology or *plane* in physics would still be obscured for students. Despite the necessity of embedding vocabulary learning in science, social studies, and other content areas (Boykin et al., 2019) many secondary science teachers have a resistance to doing so, often stemming from the idea that it is the English teacher's job (Shanahan & Shanahan, 2008).

Using Vocabulary to Provide Equitable Experiences to Underrepresented Students

Using vocabulary to drive learning in the science classroom is of utmost importance for all learners, but especially for those from historically marginalized communities. It is established that students from lower socioeconomic status families (Carlisle et al., 2013; Heath, 1983; Norton-Meier, 2005) use language in ways that are less aligned with the linguistic norms of schooling than their more affluent white English-speaking peers. For example, Heath (1983) uncovered that the linguistic practice of adults asking children questions that the adult already knows the answer to, a practice common in schools, is rare outside of schools in some communities; thus, some children may be unaccustomed to being quizzed by the teacher in this fashion and less able to show their knowledge. Other research has drawn similar conclusions about students who speak languages in addition to English (Valdés, 2010) and those from communities of color (Delpit, 1988). Since the gap between some students' home/community language and the language used in science classrooms is so vast, some scholars have questioned the necessity of learning science vocabulary in the first place (Jensen & Thompson, 2020). In these scholars' view, academic vocabulary has become an unnecessary obstacle to learning and achievement for students. An alternative view, and the one we hold, is that "academic registers are not just pretentious ways of using language . . . the kinds of meanings that are created in academic contexts often cannot be expressed in the language of ordinary interaction" (Schleppegrell, 2004, p. 137). Since scientific vocabulary knowledge is functionally required for learning and communicating in secondary science, effectively teaching students to utilize scientific vocabulary supports rather than hinders equitable learning outcomes (Cetin et al., 2018). Furthermore, scientific content learning is better supported when vocabulary knowledge is assessed equitably by permitting students to use their full linguistic and cultural repertoires when constructing scientific explanations (Lammert et al., 2023).

When this teaching comes through immersion in language-rich science disciplinary learning environments—with curricula that draw on students' experiences and background knowledge—closing achievement gaps between monolingual white students and linguistically diverse students of color becomes easier (Moje, 2007). Through a lens of equity of intelligence (Biesta, 2017), all students are capable of learning scientific vocabulary when provided with meaningful immersive experiences in science practices (Weiss et al., 2022).

Vocabulary in the Classroom

In secondary science, the best place to build students' vocabulary knowledge is in environments where they must use that vocabulary to investigate a phenomenon. Within these environments, the role of the teacher is to be a dialogic partner and negotiator. Anderson and colleagues (2023) proposed a series of vocabulary "talk moves" that they have observed in science instruction. These vocabulary talk moves are grouped into the following major categories: those focused on building students' knowledge and understanding, those designed to support affective factors, and those designed to encourage metalinguistic and metacognitive awareness. These moves can serve an invaluable purpose inside secondary science writing as tools to support students' movement from everyday language to academic scientific language. Table 11.1 shows the relationship between several key vocabulary talk moves, as adapted from Anderson and colleagues (2023) and the Next Generation Science Standards (NGSS; NGSS Lead States, 2013) for high school: Earth's Place in the Universe. This standard states that students in grades 9–12 will "communicate scientific ideas about the way stars, over their life cycle, produce elements" and they will do so "in multiple formats (including orally, graphically, textually, and mathematically" (2013, n.p.). The goal of this comparison is to highlight the utility of vocabulary talk moves in supporting student writing in secondary science classrooms.

These vocabulary talk moves serve the purpose of extending students' thinking about language as they engage in the process of using scientific language in their writing. When mastering vocabulary, students

TABLE 11.1. Vocabulary Talk Moves to Support NGSS-Aligned Science Writing

Vocabulary move	Category	Example in secondary science instruction	NGSS alignment
Elicit ideas through examples and nonexamples	Knowledge and Understanding	Teacher asks the student to share one synonym or example of the word and one antonym or nonexample of the word, emphasizing the contrast between the two.	Teacher asks students to compare the terms protons and neutrons, giving examples and nonexamples of each to use in their writing.
Elicit student questions about a target vocabulary word	Knowledge and Understanding	The teacher introduces a scientific term, such as *hibernation*, and asks students what questions they have about the meaning, usage, or history of the word.	Teacher asks students what questions they have about the "Big Bang."
Provide visual support	Knowledge and Understanding	The teacher uses something in the physical teaching environment to visually demonstrate or provide an example of the word.	The teacher holds up various objects to demonstrate concepts such as light spectra and brightness and encourages students to use these terms when writing.
Acknowledge student ownership	Affective	The teacher encourages students to use words on their own in their writing and speech at later times, indicating that the students now "own" that vocabulary.	The teacher encourages students to share their written arguments about the compositional elements of stars with their families.
Highlight words across domains	Metalinguistic and Metacognitive Awareness	The teacher draws attention to the way the meaning of the word differs from one content area or discipline to another.	The teacher differentiates the term *energy* in other settings (e.g., physical education class) from electromagnetic energy.

need many opportunities to hear and read words used in different contexts, and practice using them in their own speech and writing, to gain a sense of ownership of their new language.

Writing-to-Learn

Defining Writing-to-Learn and Synthesizing the Supporting Literature

Using writing-to-learn about subject matter in different disciplines is an idea that has existed and been studied since at least the early 1970s. However, the problem of practice faced by many teachers is to implement writing into different disciplines so that it produces a benefit for students. Writing in different disciplines is often seen as a knowledge-telling practice, where students retrieve content knowledge from memory and translate it into text directly. We argue that if designed purposefully and given adequate classroom time, writing can be used as a tool to allow students to generate new knowledge as they think about and modify their understanding of the topic as they write about it (Galbraith, 2013; Hand et al., 2004). Here lies the key difference between what we establish as learning-to-write versus the alternative, writing-to-learn.

Writing-to-learn in this context refers to the utilization of writing as a way of creating new science knowledge for the individual. This differs from how writing is traditionally considered, which is as a form of representation or a product; here, writing is also a process. Writing in the fundamental sense (Norris & Phillips, 2003) provides learners with opportunities to express their current and possibly incomplete understandings and further explore, manipulate, and question their content knowledge (Lammert & Riordan, 2019; Wallace, 2004). Formal or informal writing-to-learn tasks emphasize student authorship, where their own ideas and understandings can be put forth to their intended audience. This is opposed to more traditional learning-to-write tasks, or derived writing tasks (Norris & Phillips, 2003), where students are only expected to recall existing or factual knowledge without generating novel, individual understanding.

Writing-to-learn leads students to engage with both cognitive and metacognitive strategies, such as making connections between content and their own lives or identifying what they do not fully understand, which in turn increases their learning (Klein et al., 2019). As Langer (1986) pointed out in her groundbreaking work on writing-to-learn, when students step back from their writing, they can "reconceptualize the content in ways that cut across ideas, focusing on larger issues or topics" (p. 406). In science, writing-to-learn tasks are constructive processes where students are using their existing science knowledge or experiences to form new interpretations, allowing them to better understand interconnecting ideas and complex science concepts (Glynn & Muth, 1994; Klein & Yu, 2013). In classrooms, such writing-to-learn tasks can take the form of informal daily writing probes or more extensive summative writing assignments.

In secondary science classrooms, using writing-to-learn can positively impact students' science literacy, or how they interpret, understand, and respond to scientific ideas (Norris & Phillips, 2003; Wright et al., 2018). Increasing students' scientific literacy is critical for strengthening abilities such as communicating concepts to others and making meaning of new scientific information. Both skills are necessary for student success in a secondary science classroom. In one study with six middle and high school teachers in a variety of science disciplines, teachers led their students in Argument-Driven Inquiry (ADI), followed by a written investigation report that was blindly peer reviewed by other students and then revised. ADI is a process where students design and collect data in an inquiry investigation and then construct individual or group scientific arguments to be evaluated and negotiated by their peers. The reflection and revision process for the following written work allows students to strengthen their reasoning and improve metacognitive strategies as they think about feedback they received and what they are doing as they write. It was concluded that content understanding not only increased, but student writing abilities, such as argument and complexity, also improved (Sampson et al., 2013). The need for structured support on these writing tasks is even higher for EL students and those from marginalized cultural backgrounds (Boykin et al., 2019).

Using Writing-to-Learn to Provide Equitable Experiences to Underrepresented Students

Writing-to-learn benefits all students in their science learning endeavors. In a mixed-methods study by Akkus and colleagues (2007), students participated in the Science Writing Heuristic (SWH) where they engaged in teacher-designed activities involving prewriting and journaling through their investigations and also student-led reflective writing. In this reflective writing, students wrote about their own questions, observations, and reflections on how their ideas changed over time. Students in this study ended their unit by creating a written concept map of their understanding. The authors concluded that students who were identified as "low achieving" prior to the study excelled with more conceptually driven tasks such as concept mapping and reflective writing-to-learn activities, thus closing classroom achievement gaps. Similarly,

Karaer et al. (2024) found that students with IEPs can better develop science skills and knowledge with more generative tasks (such as writing-to-learn) and environments. The advantage for such students is that they can actively participate in their learning by generating new knowledge and summarizing their ideas as it makes sense to them through writing. Other studies suggest similar findings, extending the discussion to a wider range of historically marginalized students such as ELs (Hand et al., 2013). Taylor and colleagues (2021) found that in SWH classrooms, Black girls scored significantly better on a measure of critical thinking than their peers in traditional science classrooms. This is especially important since Black girls, who experience intersectional marginalization, are chronically underrepresented in STEM fields. In sum, providing students opportunities to engage in writing where the emphasis is on making meaning of material, as opposed to traditional science writing, creates a more level playing field for students who struggle with memorization and a lower-stakes environment where students' own ideas and experiences are more valued and utilized. Writing-to-learn, as a student-centered task, allows students to utilize their own words and ideas in ways that traditional tasks do not, providing more moments where students may relate new knowledge to prior experiences and make deeper connections with content.

Writing-to-Learn in the Classroom

As previously mentioned, writing-to-learn activities can be integrated into the science classroom as formal or informal assignments. For daily classroom use, having students engage in reflective journal writing where students think and respond to questions and prompts such as "What questions do I have?," "How do my ideas compare to other ideas?," or "What have I learned today?" can improve the quality of student questioning and help them see how their thinking changes and grows over time (Lammert & Riordan, 2019; Towndrow & Ling, 2008; Taylor et al., 2018). Having students track their conceptual change and classroom dialogic interactions that shape their thinking can then be used to create a summative explanatory writing task where students must argue a claim using the evidence they have collected. Integrating science notebooks or journals into regular classroom practice for reflective writing can also help students with the acquisition of scientific language (Huerta et al., 2014). This approach to writing-to-learn allows students opportunities to use their own language and means of representation to describe and understand more complex scientific vocabulary.

When creating a summative writing-to-learn task where students are writing to another individual, it is important to think about the

TABLE 11.2. Model for Developing Writing-to-Learn Tasks for Classroom Use

Method of text production	Audience	Purpose	Type	Topic
• Individual work partners • Groups • Computer text • Written text • Redrafting • Other	• Classroom peers • Grade-level peers • Younger students • Parents • Consumers • Self • Government • Teachers • Administrators • Other	**Start of unit:** • Review, • explore, • plan **During unit:** • Clarify, • revise, • consider, • interpret **Completion of unit:** • Test, • demonstrate, • explain	• Narrative • reports • Letters • Concept • maps • Brochures • Poetry • Posters • Journals • Diagrams • Comics	• Unit concepts and ideas • Linking themes • Applying concepts • Factual understanding

different components that structure the task. This might include the task's purpose (e.g., a review, assessment, application), the type of task or genre (e.g., narrative writing, poster), the audience your students are writing to, and the topic they are writing about. Adapted from Hand and Prain (2002), Table 11.2 provides a model for helping teachers build and structure writing tasks so that students have clarity and success.

This type of task provides students with flexibility to communicate their understanding and engages them with the translation process of going from their own language and understanding to that of their audience. Ideally, once completed, the students' work would be evaluated and responded to by the audience for which it was intended. This gives students further information on the clarity of their explanations and ideas and can be used to refine their thinking even more, which brings us to the topic of assessing student writing.

Assessment of Secondary Science Student Writing

In the prior sections of this chapter, we have shown how attention to multimodality, vocabulary, and writing-to-learn supports secondary science students. Teachers who implement these ideas will see evidence of their students' equity of intelligence (Biesta, 2017) through their ability to write scientific summaries and scientific arguments. At this stage, one question teachers may be asking is: How do I assess my students' writing in science? To demonstrate some of the characteristics of student writing that teachers can assess, we provide a rubric that has been adapted from one used in our prior research (see Lammert et al., 2023; Table 11.3).

This sample rubric specifically focuses on two elements: multimodality and science content. We chose to include a focus on these two elements for three reasons. First, due to the heavy emphasis on text-based literacies in schools, secondary teachers may not be familiar with the idea of scoring students' drawings and figures. Second, we aim to emphasize that including writing in science instruction is a "means" to building greater scientific conceptual knowledge for students rather than an "end" in and of itself. Third, we have found that these elements can apply to virtually any science topic that a student might write about, which makes the rubric easily adaptable to various units across a school year.

This rubric could be applied by the teacher, as is typically done, and used to provide a summative score on a piece of student writing. However, it could also be used by the teacher to provide formative feedback

TABLE 11.3. Sample Rubric for Assessing Secondary Students' Writing in Science

	Low (1)	High (3)
Criteria: Multimodal writing quality		
Use of graphic aids: Tables, sketches, and diagrams	Student does not use graphic aids or only uses graphic aids of one type.	Student integrates multiple types of graphic aids.
Text to support graphic aids: Captions and labels	Student does not use captions and labels to indicate detail on the graphic aids.	Student uses captions or labels to show relationships and convey detail on graphic aids.
Quality of graphic aids: Ideas	When graphic aids are used, they replicate ideas in the written text.	Graphic aids extend and clarify ideas in the text.
Criteria: Conceptual knowledge of science		
Link to standards	The student's writing does not include evidence of mastery of a grade-level state standard.	The student's writing shows evidence of mastery of a grade-level or higher state standard.
Accuracy of information: Consistent with authorized knowledge	The student's writing shows ideas about science that are inconsistent with authorized knowledge.	The student's writing shows ideas about science that are consistent with authorized knowledge.

to students in the early phases of science writing, or students could use the rubric to self-score their writing as a way to reflect on additional possibilities that they may not have considered. This data could be useful for addressing students who have lower scores for their multimodal writing quality, as they may now benefit from group discussions on what details enhance graphic aids or by being probed to include more visual representations in their work. Assessing student writing for inaccuracy or inconsistency with recognized science ideas can also help teachers address what big science ideas need to be further explored or investigated by their students. The information gathered from assessing student written work can be a valuable tool to help structure what supports students need when developing their understandings.

The rubric includes attention to two criteria: (1) students' knowledge of science, and (2) their ability to communicate their knowledge of science through writing. Studies have shown that teachers who implement evidence-based writing strategies in their science classrooms can expect to see their students make gains in both areas (Cetin et al., 2018) since writing is a gold mine of evidence for what our students know about science and what they can do as writers. However, there is one element we try to dissuade teachers from overemphasizing, which is writing conventions (i.e., spelling, grammar, punctuation). While some audiences, such as scientific journals, undoubtedly value adherence to conventions and particular style guides (Snow, 2010), these conventions can be taught later when they become necessary (Jensen & Thompson, 2020). Surely, students are not going to solve the climate crisis by knowing where to put a comma; more important is their ability to think critically and communicate effectively from a place of scientific literacy. Thus, the greatest emphasis for teachers of secondary science students should be on the conceptual quality of the summaries and the arguments being made.

Conclusions

This chapter on writing in secondary science classrooms is based on the premise that although each person holds different knowledge, we can all reason, solve problems, and build arguments. Every student is capable of constructing explanations for how the world around them works, so secondary science teachers must "support the learner rather than simply the dilemma" (Barab & Duffy, 1998, p. 10) by negotiating with students as they construct their own scientific knowledge. Since this practice is fundamentally rooted in the way learning works, this premise holds true regardless of what topic one is learning and applies to writing in all content areas. Teaching in ways rooted in equity of intelligence (Biesta,

2017) can be challenging. However, we know that if anyone is up to the challenge, it's teachers.

In addition, this chapter was based on the idea that language is fundamental to science learning. Consider the challenge we mentioned in the introduction. Could you really teach a lesson on science—or social studies, math, or literacy, for that matter—without using language? When one takes a multimodal perspective on language (Jewitt et al., 2001) that acknowledges the importance of the combination of visual and textual elements, it is readily apparent that fulfilling this challenge is impossible. The use of language, including multimodality, vocabulary, and writing-to-learn, is necessary for learning. Therefore, in this chapter, we have demonstrated countless concrete examples of evidence-based practices that can address multimodality, vocabulary, and writing-to-learn, and in tandem, we have provided a rubric for assessing student writing in the secondary science classroom.

ACTION STEPS

In closing, we offer teachers action steps as they begin enacting the kind of teaching aligned with these premises. While we resist the idea that effective science teaching is simply a matter of following a simple to-do list, we offer these action steps for teachers to consider as entry points into this work.

- *Reflect on current practice.* First, look at the ways you currently attend to multimodality, vocabulary, and writing-to-learn in your secondary science classroom. You might consider your lesson or unit plans as a data source, or you might review writing samples from students from previous units. This can also involve making a video recording of your own teaching and reviewing to see what vocabulary talk moves you already use. Consider ways to build on your existing strengths.
- *Plan for equitable change.* Make a list of practices from this chapter that you have not yet tried but would like to implement. While it may be tempting to start small, we encourage teachers to think about their classroom learning environments as a whole. Working on inviting multimodality without considering vocabulary or writing-to-learn is unlikely to dramatically change your students' learning outcomes, so push yourself to combine all three. A great place to begin is to replace one traditional multiple-choice or short-answer summative examination with a writing-based assessment and plan your unit with this assessment in mind. Further, with each change you make, consider

how the shift has impacted students from historically marginalized groups. Actively ask what steps you can take to ensure equity.

- *Assess and share your progress.* Every 6 to 8 weeks, reflect again on the changes in your practice. You may wish to review the same data sources or collect new teaching videos as you consider the progress you have made. Don't forget to ask the learners how they are experiencing writing in the secondary science classroom. Your students are the most valuable source of data there is on the efficacy of your teaching. We also encourage you to find a like-minded colleague to share this process with through informal peer coaching since peer coaching has been shown to contribute to teachers' capacity for adaptive teaching (Lammert & Tily, 2021).

By following these action steps, secondary science teachers can begin to implement practices that deepen their students' conceptual knowledge of science through the use of writing as a valuable learning tool. Further, by focusing on what our students can learn next, rather than focusing on what they already know, we invite transformative and equitable possibilities in secondary science teaching. We encourage secondary science teachers to join us on this journey.

REFERENCES

Akkus, R., Gunel, M., & Hand, B. (2007). Comparing an inquiry-based approach known as the Science Writing Heuristic to traditional science teaching practices: Are there differences? *International Journal of Science Education, 29*(14), 1745–1765.

Anderson, B. E., Wright, T. S., & Gotwals, A. W. (2023). Teachers' vocabulary talk in early-elementary science instruction. *Journal of Literacy Research, 55*(1), 75–100.

Anderson, K. T., & Kachorsky, D. (2019). Assessing students' multimodal compositions: An analysis of the literature. *English Teaching, 18*(3), 312–334.

Anderson R. C., Freebody P. (1981). Vocabulary knowledge. In Guthrie J. T. (Ed.), *Comprehension and teaching: Research reviews* (pp. 77–117). International Reading Association.

Axelsson, M., & Danielsson, K. (2012). Multimodality in the science classroom. In *Literacy Practices in transition: Perspectives from the Nordic countries* (pp. 140–152). Multilingual Matters.

Barab, S. A., & Duffy, T. (1998). *From practice fields to communities of practice.* Indiana University Center for Research on Learning and Technology.

Biesta, G. J. J. (2017). *The rediscovery of teaching.* Routledge.

Boykin, A., Emenova, A. S., Regan, K., & Mastropieri, M. (2019). The impact of a computer-based graphic organizer with embedded self-regulation learning strategies on the argumentative writing of students in inclusive cross-curricula settings. *Computers & Education, 137*, 78–90.

Carlisle, J. F., Kelcey, B., & Berebitsky, D. (2013). Teachers' support of students' vocabulary learning during literacy instruction in high poverty elementary schools. *American Educational Research Journal, 50*(6), 1360–1391.

Cetin, P. S., Eymur, G., Southerland, S. A., Walker, J., & Whittington, K. (2018). Exploring the effectiveness of engagement in a broad range of disciplinary practices on learning of Turkish high-school chemistry students. *International Journal of Science Education, 40*(5), 473–497.

Cummins, J. (1979). Cognitive/academic language proficiency, linguistic interdependence, the optimum age question and some other matters. *Working Papers on Bilingualism, 19*, 121–129.

Delpit, L. (1988). The silenced dialogue: Power and pedagogy in educating other people's children. *Harvard Educational Review, 58*(3), 280–299.

Duke, N. K., Pearson, P. D., Strachan, S. L., & Billman, A. K. (2011). Essential elements of fostering and teaching reading comprehension. In S. J. Samuels & A. E. Farstrup (Eds.), *What research has to say about reading instruction* (4th ed., pp. 51–93). International Reading Association.

Galbraith, D. (2013). Writing as a knowledge constituting process. *Studies in Writing, 4*, 139–160.

Glynn, S. M., & Muth, K. D. (1994). Reading and writing to learn science: Achieving scientific literacy. *Journal of Research in Science Teaching, 31*(9), 1057–1073.

Graham, S., Kim, Y., Cao, Y., Lee, W., Tate, T., Collins, T., . . . Olson, C. (2023). A meta-analysis of writing treatments for students in grades 6 to 12. *Journal of Educational Psychology, 115*, 1004–1027.

Graham, S., Liu, K., Bartlett, B., Ng, C., Harris, K. R., Aitken, A., . . . Talukdar, J. (2018). Reading for writing: A meta-analysis of the impact of reading and reading instruction on writing. *Review of Educational Research, 88*, 243–284.

Grapin, S. E. (2018). Multimodality in the new content standards era: Implications for English learners. *TESOL Quarterly, 53*(1), 30–55.

Hand, B., & Cavagnetto, A. (2023). Brian's life is not just another brick in the wall: Reframing the metaphor of science teaching. *Journal of Curriculum and Pedagogy*, 2023-11, 1–15.

Hand, B., Hohenshell, L., & Prain, V. (2004). Exploring students' responses to conceptual questions when engaged with planned writing experiences: A study with year 10 science students. *Journal of Research in Science Teaching, 41*(2), 186–210.

Hand, B., Norton-Meier, L. A., Gunel, M., & Aukkus, R. (2016). Aligning teaching to learning: A 3-year study examining the embedding of language and argumentation into elementary science classrooms. *International Journal of Science and Mathematics Education, 14*(5), 847–863.

Hand, B., & Prain, V. (2002). Teachers implementing writing-to-learn strategies in junior secondary science: A case study. *Science Education, 86*, 737–755.

Hand, B., Therrien, W., & Shelley, M. (2013). *Examining the impact of using the Science Writing Heuristic approach in learning science: A cluster randomized study*. Society for Research on Educational Effectiveness.

Heath, S. B. (1983). *Ways with words: Language, life, and work in communities and classrooms*. McGraw-Hill.

Huerta, M., Lara-Alecio, R., Tong, F., & Irby, B. J. (2014). Developing and validating a science notebook rubric for fifth-grade non-mainstream students. *International Journal of Science Education, 36*(11), 1849–1870.

Jensen, B., & Thompson, G. A. (2020). Equity in teaching academic language—An interdisciplinary approach. *Theory into Practice, 59*(1), 1–7.

Jewitt, C., Kress, G., Ogborn, J., & Tsatsarelis, C. (2001). Exploring learning through visual, actional and linguistic communication: The multimodal environment of a science classroom. *Educational Review, 53*(1), 5–18.

Jewitt, C., Kress, G., Ogborn, J., & Tsatsarelis, C. (2014). *Multimodal teaching and learning: The rhetorics of the science classroom*. Continuum.

Karaer, G., Hand, B., & French, B. F. (2024). Examining the impact of Science Writing Heuristic (SWH) approach on development of critical thinking, science and language skills of students with and without disabilities. *Thinking Skills and Creativity, 51*, Article 101443.

Kenny, J., & Cirkony, C. (2018). Teaching using student-generated representations in science. In *Teaching secondary science: Theory and practice* (pp. 141–149). Cambridge University Press.

Klein, P., Haug, K. N., & Bildfell, A. (2019). Writing to learn. In S. Graham, C. A. MacArthur, & M. Hebert (Eds.), *Best practices in writing instruction* (3rd ed., p. 163). Guilford Press.

Klein, P., & Yu, M. (2013). Best practices in writing to learn. In S. Graham, C. A. MacArthur, & J. Fitzgerald (Eds.), *Best practices in writing instruction* (2nd ed., pp. 166–189). Guilford Press.

Lammert, C., Hand, B., & Sharma, R. (2023). Beyond pedagogy: The role of epistemic orientation and knowledge generation environments in early childhood science teaching. *International Journal of Science Education, 45*(6), 431–450.

Lammert, C., & Riordan, E. (2019). "She's not going to tell you what to ask": Strategies for writing in science. *The Reading Teacher, 72*(7), 367–373.

Lammert, C., & Tily, S. (2021). Using peer coaching to promote adaptive literacy teaching in preservice teacher education. *The New Educator, 18*(3), 201–224.

Langer, J. A. (1986). Learning through writing: Study skills in the content areas. *Journal of Reading, 29*(5), 400–406.

Latour, B. (1987). *Science in action: How to follow scientists and engineers through society*. Harvard University Press.

Le Corre, M., Li, P., Huang, B. H., Jia, G. & Carey, S. (2016). Numerical morphology supports early number word learning: Evidence from a comparison of young Mandarin and English learners. *Cognitive Psychology, 88*, 162–186.

Lemke, J. L. (1998). Multiplying meaning: Visual and verbal semiotics in scientific text. In J. R. Martin & R. Veel (Eds.), *Reading science* (pp. 87–113). Routledge.

McDermott, M., & Hand, B. (2010). *Exploring the impact of embedding multiple modes of representing science information in varied classroom settings.* Presentation at Annual Conference of National Association of Research in Science Teaching (NARST), Philadelphia.

McDermott, M., & Hand, B. (2013). The impact of embedding multiple modes of representation within writing tasks on high school students' chemistry understanding. *Instructional Science, 41*(1), 217–246.

Merriam-Webster. (1961). *Webster's third new international dictionary* (P. B. Gove, Ed.).

Moje, E. B. (2007). Developing socially just subject-matter instruction: A review of the literature on disciplinary literacy teaching. *Review of Research in Education, 31*, 1–44.

Nelson, K. L., Dole, J. A., Hosp, J. L., & Hosp, M. K. (2015). Vocabulary instruction in K–3 low-income classrooms during a reading reform project. *Reading Psychology, 36*(2), 145–172.

NGSS Lead States. (2013). *Next generation science standards: For states, by states.* National Academy Press.

Norris, S. R., & Phillips, L. M. (2003). How literacy in its fundamental sense is central to scientific literacy. *Science Education, 87*(2), 224–240.

Norton-Meier, L. (2005). A thrice-learned lesson from the literate life of a five-year-old. *Language Arts, 82*(4), 286–295.

Pierson, A. E., Clark, D. B., & Brady, C. (2021). Scientific modeling and translanguaging: A multilingual and multimodal approach to support science learning and engagement. *Science Education, 105*(4), 776–813.

Prain, V., & Hand, B. (2016). Learning science through learning to use its languages. In B. Hand, M. McDermott, V. Prain (Eds.), *Using multimodal representations to support learning in the science classroom* (pp. 1–10). Springer.

Prain, V., & Tytler, R. (2012). Learning through constructing representations in science: A framework of representational construction affordances. *International Journal of Science Education, 34*(17), 2751–2773.

Quine, W. V. O. (1960). *Word and object.* MIT Press.

Sampson, V., Enderle, P., Grooms, J., & Witte, S. (2013). Writing to learn by learning to write during the school science laboratory: Helping middle and high school students develop argumentative writing skills as they learn core ideas. *Science Education, 97*(5), 643–670.

Schleppegrell, M. J. (2004). *The language of schooling: A functional linguistics perspective.* Routledge.

Shanahan, T., & Shanahan, C. (2008). Teaching disciplinary literacy to adolescents: Rethinking content-area literacy. *Harvard Educational Review, 78*(1), 40–59.

Snow, C. E. (2010). Academic language and the challenge of reading for learning about science. *Science, 328*(5977), 450–452.

Tang, K., Delgado, C., & Moje, E. B. (2014). An integrative framework for the analysis of multiple and multimodal representations for meaning-making in science education. *Science Education, 98*(2), 305–326.

Taylor, J., Tseng, C., Murillo, A., Therrien, W. J., & Hand, B. (2018). Using argument-based science inquiry to improve science achievement for students with disabilities in inclusive classrooms. *Journal of Science Education for Students with Disabilities, 21*(1), 1–14.

Taylor, J. C., Christensen, J., Sharp, S., Therrien, W., & Hand, B. (2021). Using the Science Writing Heuristic to improve critical thinking skills for fifth grade Black girls. *Journal of African American Women and Girls in Education, 1*(2), 10–25.

Towndrow, P. A., & Ling, T. A. (2008). Promoting inquiry through science reflective journal writing. *Eurasia Journal of Mathematics, Science & Technology Education, 4*(3), 279–283.

Uccelli, P., & Phillips Galloway, E. (2016). Academic language across content areas: Lessons from an innovative assessment and from students' reflections about language. *Journal of Adolescent & Adult Literacy, 60*(4), 395–404.

Unsworth, L., Tytler, R., Fenwick, L., Humphrey, S., Chandler, P., Herrington, M., & Pham, L. (2022). *Multimodal literacy in school science: Transdisciplinary perspectives on theory, research and pedagogy*. Routledge.

Valdés, G. (2010). Between support and marginalisation: The development of academic language in linguistic minority children. *International Journal of Bilingual Education and Bilingualism, 7*(2–3), 102–132.

Waldrip, B., Prain, V., & Carolan, J. (2010). Using multi-modal representations to improve learning in junior secondary science. *Research in Science Education, 40*(1), 65–80.

Wallace, C. (2004). Framing new research in science literacy and language use: Authenticity, multiple discourses, and the "Third Space". *Science Education, 88*(6), 901–914.

Weiss, K. A., McDermott, M. A., & Hand, B. (2022). Characterising immersive argument-based inquiry learning environments in school-based education: A systematic literature review. *Studies in Science Education, 58*(1), 15–47.

Wright, K. L., Hodges, T. S., Zimmer, W. K., & McTigue, E. M. (2018). Writing-to-learn in secondary science classes: For whom is it effective? *Reading & Writing Quarterly, 35*(4), 289–304.

Wright, T. S., & Gotwals, A. W. (2017). Supporting kindergarteners' science talk in the context of an integrated science and disciplinary literacy curriculum. *The Elementary School Journal, 117*(3), 513–537.

Yi, Y., & Choi, J. (2015). Teachers' views of multimodal practices in K–12 classrooms: Voices from teachers in the United States. *TESOL Quarterly, 49*(4), 838–847.

Chapter 12

Using Writing to Improve Learning in Mathematics

Sharlene A. Kiuhara and Kaitlin Bundock

Writing can be a self-reflective activity in which we share our thoughts about the world. When we put our thoughts down on paper and then organize the ideas we want to share with our readers, this writing process allows us to develop our ideas, make decisions about what to include, and reflect or clarify further our reasons, understandings, and experiences. A small but growing evidence base of approximately 36 empirical studies supports the view that embedding writing activities enhances content learning and promotes students' understanding and communication about learning mathematics for first graders to college students (Bangert-Drowns et al., 2004; Graham et al., 2020). The mathematical writing activities investigated in these studies include writing informational text, such as summarizing and connecting new and old information or explaining how a process operates; constructing arguments, such as using evidence to support and justify an answer; and taking notes while learning, including using graphic organizers to parse information into steps or stages (Graham et al., 2020).

Students are increasingly prompted and expected to explain their mathematical thinking in mathematics classrooms and on standardized state assessments, justifying how they know their answers to a particular problem make sense through writing (Hughes & Lee, 2020; Powell et al., 2017). However, mathematics teachers may face several challenges when integrating writing in secondary mathematics contexts. For example, only 2% of eighth graders scored at the advanced level for persuading, explaining, and conveying experiences (National Center for Education Statistics [NCES], 2022b). Similarly, only 7% of eighth graders scored at the advanced level for mathematics, in which they are asked to justify a mathematical concept or relationship (NCES, 2022a). Students may have difficulty expressing their mathematical thinking due to challenges within the mathematics domain and have difficulty communicating their thinking through writing due to challenges with language (Korhonen et al., 2012; Krowka & Fuchs, 2017). Therefore, using writing to develop students' mathematical reasoning involves systematically developing their mathematical practices and language ability for successful learning (Ball & Cohen, 1990; Boaler, 2016; National Council of Teachers of Mathematics [NCTM], 2000). In this chapter, we use the following guiding questions to explore some of the obstacles our students may face when writing to learn mathematics, strategies mathematics teachers can use to embed writing activities in their lessons in a systematic way, and how teachers can best support all students' learning when using writing in their classrooms.

GUIDING QUESTIONS

1. What is the power of writing to support learning in mathematics?
2. How can we implement writing activities in our classroom?
3. How can teachers support all students' learning, including students with disabilities and culturally and linguistically diverse students?

What Is the Power of Writing for Supporting Learning in Mathematics?

Because writing is becoming increasingly more common in mathematics, particularly secondary mathematics, writing about mathematics is now viewed as a necessary skill for students to learn and engage. Mathematical writing involves students communicating their understanding of mathematical concepts and processes (Casa et al., 2016; Colonnese et al., 2024). Writing to learn mathematics is supported by a growing evidence base indicating the benefits of mathematical writing on student outcomes and effective ways to help students improve their mathematics understanding, mathematical reasoning, and proficiency (Graham et al., 2020; Hebert et al., 2019; Hughes et al., 2020; Hughes & Lee, 2020; Powell et al., 2017), as well as their writing abilities (Arsenault et al., 2022; Hughes et al., 2020; Kiuhara et al., 2020, 2023a, 2023b).

In the context of mathematics, writing is viewed as an essential aspect of communicating mathematical understanding (NCTM, 2000) and is connected directly to several of the Standards for Mathematical Practice (SMPs) in which teachers engage students in developing their reasoning and proficiency in mathematics (Common Core State Standards Initiative [CCSS-M], 2010; National Mathematics Advisory Panel [NMAP], 2008). To provide clarity regarding mathematics writing and improve its implementation, Casa and colleagues (2016) categorized mathematics writing into four different types, each targeting different learning purposes: exploratory, informative/explanatory, argumentative, and mathematically creative.

Exploratory mathematics writing is used when students write to help understand and process a mathematics problem or their mathematical ideas. *Informative/explanatory* writing describes or explains a particular mathematics concept. *Argumentative* mathematics writing has the purpose of constructing or critiquing an argument, such as geometric proofs. Writing can be considered *mathematically creative writing* when students engage in writing that involves them applying mathematical ideas in a unique or flexible way that extends previously taught content (i.e., mathematically creative writing is unprompted).

The goal of engaging in mathematics writing (regardless of which type) is for students to reason mathematically and communicate their ideas (Casa et al., 2016). The evidence supporting mathematics writing has shown that students find mathematics writing to help promote their understanding and that teachers should implement mathematics writing activities more frequently (Powell et al., 2017). Additionally, mathematics writing instruction should include instruction on specific mathematics writing skills, such as planning, editing, revising, and sharing writing with peers (Kiuhara et al., 2020; Powell et al., 2017). Research has also shown that students may need additional instructional support or scaffolding to use mathematics writing successfully (Kiuhara et al., 2020; Powell et al., 2017; Riccomini et al., 2024). For example, students may need instructional support to communicate high-level reasoning, incorporate mathematical symbols in their writing, and use specific mathematics vocabulary (Jitendra et al., 2020; Powell et al., 2017; Riccomini et al., 2024).

How Can We Implement Writing Activities in Our Classroom?

One notable addition to the CCSS-M domain standards is the inclusion of eight SMPs that can be applied across all grade levels and mathematics core standards (see Figure 12.1). Rather than relating to specific mathematics domain standards, the SMPs are designed to engage students in learning mathematics through robust and flexible reasoning and problem solving and students' ability to express their conceptual understanding and higher-level mathematical thinking. However, many

1. Make sense of problems and persevere in solving them
2. Reason abstractly and quantitatively
3. Construct viable arguments and critique the reasoning of others
4. Model with mathematics
5. Use appropriate tools strategically
6. Attend to precision
7. Look for and make use of structure
8. Look for and express regularity in repeated reasoning

FIGURE 12.1. Standards for Mathematical Practice. The Standards are from the National Governors Association Center for Best Practices and Council of Chief State School Officers (2012, Standards for Mathematical Practice, paras. 3–10).

students may struggle to conceptualize abstract secondary mathematics concepts. Students with or at risk for learning disabilities or who are culturally and linguistically diverse may face additional challenges depending on their mathematics background knowledge, familiarity with content-specific vocabulary, and experience with communicating their mathematical thinking in writing. The increasing focus on communicating conceptual understanding in writing provides an impetus for secondary mathematics teachers to provide instruction in specific strategies to teach students how to do so, along with multiple opportunities for students to practice mathematics writing and receive feedback from teachers and peers.

Strategies for Supporting All Students' Mathematics Writing

Table 12.1 provides an overview of 10 specific strategies teachers can implement in secondary mathematics classrooms. References are provided for each strategy so that readers interested in accessing additional information about the research behind each strategy may do so. The strategies included in the table are intentional and purposeful methods for teaching and supporting students and engaging them in mathematics writing. We have not included math journals because research indicates that teachers are less likely to incorporate math journals compared to other types of mathematics writing (Powell et al., 2017). Systematic and explicit mathematics writing activities are associated with greater student gains and similar gains across different genres of writing activities. The strategies provided in Table 12.1 can be implemented with explicit instruction.

TABLE 12.1. Strategies for Supporting Students' Mathematics Writing

Strategy/practice	Description and examples
Explicit instruction(including instructional scaffolding) (Archer & Hughes, 2011; Nochowitz, 2018)	• Modeling with carefully selected examples and nonexamples • Guided practice in which students engage in frequent practice opportunities with scaffolded teacher guidance and frequent feedback • Independent practice in which students practice individually, followed by feedback • *Example:* The teacher models how to solve a system of equations using substitution and explains the process in writing, has students practice solving problems and writing explanations of their solutions while providing feedback, and then allows students to solve problems and write explanations independently.
Strategies instruction (including SRSD) (Hughes & Lee, 2020; Kiuhara et al., 2020)	• Explicit instruction on cognitive or metacognitive strategies • Strategy taught in the context of academic task or activity • Strategy modeled, followed by guided practice and independent practice • Facilitate memorization and internalization of the strategy. • Support strategy use. • *Example strategies:* POD✓, PRISM✓, FACT
Routines (Braxton & Terrell, 2024; Cross, 2009)	• Students follow a sequence of actions, often working in collaborative groups. • *Example:* Argumentation routine: 1. Read the problem and gather initial ideas. 2. Each group member states response and reasoning. 3. Group members defend answers and consider other answers and reasons presented (Cross, 2009). • *Example:* World Problem Roulette (Braxton & Terrell, 2004), in which groups of students do the following: 1. Solve a problem verbally. 2. Write steps to solutions in words (not symbols). 3. Each student writes one sentence and passes the paper to the next student to write the following sentence. 4. After the written solution is complete, one group member reads the sentences, and another group member writes the symbolic notation.
Paraphrase word problems (Moran et al., 2014)	• Students are explicitly taught (with modeling, practice, and feedback) how to paraphrase word problems by rewriting and restating relevant parts of word problems: o Rewrite question sentence from word problem in your own words. o Rewrite the sentence that includes needed numbers in your own words. o Rewrite a sentence that includes unnecessary numbers in your own words; distinguish between needed and unnecessary numbers.

(continued)

TABLE 12.1. *(continued)*

Strategy/practice	Description and examples
Paraphrase word problems *(continued)*	• *Example:* A farmer has 3 grain silos. The smallest grain storage silo has a diameter of 15 feet and a height of 30 feet. What is the volume of grain that can be stored in the smallest silo? o What volume of grain can be stored in the silo? o Needed numbers: Diameter = 15 ft, height = 30 ft. o Unnecessary = 3; necessary numbers are 15 and 30.
Coaching to monitor progress using metacognitive strategies (Glogger et al., 2012)	• Teach students to apply metacognitive learning strategies in the context of math journals: o Monitor comprehension. o Identify the most important aspects of the topics taught. o Link new concepts to prior learning. o Monitor and plan remedial strategies. • *Example prompt:* Compare and contrast the formulas for finding a square pyramid's volume and a triangular pyramid's volume. How can you remember which one to use?
Providing examples, modeling, and mini-lessons (Kostos & Shin, 2010)	• Model and provide examples of mathematics writing. • Teach mini-lessons to provide targeted instruction on aspects of writing needing improvement. • *Example:* Teach a mini-lesson on providing good reasons to support a central idea in a mathematics argument. o Give students several prewritten mathematics arguments that reflect a range of qualities. o Have students evaluate and discuss what makes some arguments more or less persuasive than others. o Have students create a tip sheet with reminders for creating good reasons for support in math arguments.
Requiring written explanations of solutions to a problem (Idris, 2009; Kiuhara et al., 2023b; Kostos & Shin, 2010; Tan & Garces-Bascal, 2013)	• Incorporate opportunities for students to write explanations of how they solved problems. • Include higher-order open-ended responses that focus on aspects of the Common Core SMPs. • *Examples of possible types of writing prompts:* o Explain how to solve the problem. o Explain each step you would use to solve the problem and why you picked each step. o Explain to a friend how to solve this type of math problem. o Reflect on your understanding of how to solve problems like this (what are you understanding, what are you having difficulty with, and what can you do to overcome those difficulties?).
Provide verbal or written feedback, focusing on elements of good mathematics writing (Cross, 2009; Lee et al., 2024; Pugalee, 2004)	• Provide students with feedback on their mathematics writing. Attend to specific features such as the following: o Main idea o Specific reasons in support of the main idea o Organized and clear composition o Use of specific and accurate mathematics vocabulary o Writing conventions (e.g., grammar, syntax, spelling, punctuation, capitalization)

(continued)

TABLE 12.1. *(continued)*

Strategy/practice	Description and examples
Provide verbal or written feedback, focusing on elements of good mathematics writing *(continued)*	• *Examples of features to evaluate when giving feedback on reasons provided in support of the main idea:* o Use of units of measurement/labels o Use of precise numerals o Conjectures that extend the argument (e.g., "This rate is correct because if I use it to build a table, all the numbers line up") o Explanations of the reasonableness of an answer
Explicitly teach mathematics vocabulary and use precise and accurate mathematical language (Hebert et al., 2019; Kiuhara et al., 2023; Powell et al., 2019; Riccomini et al., 2015, 2024)	• Use formal language instead of informal language (e.g., "dividend" instead of "the number you divide"). • Be precise (attend to detail in terms used, especially when using terms that are related to one another, e.g., *factor* and *multiple*, *congruent* and *similar*). • Provide regular exposure to mathematics vocabulary terms on a consistent basis. • Use explicit instruction to teach mathematics vocabulary (model, discuss, practice, feedback). • Use graphic organizers to help students connect terms, definitions, and concepts. • Display word walls to help students focus on key vocabulary. • Keep math glossaries in math journals. • Play math vocabulary games to increase knowledge and retention. • *Example:* Teach a mini-lesson using precise vocabulary during a unit on trigonometric ratios (sine, cosine, and tangent). Provide students with opportunities to use their own words to define the terms, provide examples and nonexamples of the terms, draw pictures to help them connect terms to concepts, and apply terms to problems.
Provide opportunities for students to engage in mathematical discourse (Braxton & Terrell, 2024; Porter & Masingila, 2000)	• Provide students with structured opportunities to explain and share their thinking orally with peers. • Provide students with structured opportunities to explain and share their thinking in writing. • *Example:* Assign students math pen pals in class. o Give students a writing prompt (e.g., write a letter to your math pen pal explaining why the Pythagorean theorem works for finding right triangle side lengths). o Students trade and read math pen-pal letters. o Students talk to their math pen pals about how their explanations are similar or different. Math pen-pal partners develop a creative proof of the Pythagorean theorem they present to the class.

(continued)

TABLE 12.1. *(continued)*

Strategy/practice	Description and examples
Explicit instruction (including instructional scaffolding) (Archer & Hughes, 2011; Nochowitz, 2018)	• Modeling with carefully selected examples and nonexamples • Guided practice in which students engage in frequent practice opportunities with scaffolded teacher guidance and frequent feedback • Independent practice in which students practice individually, followed by feedback • *Example:* Teacher models how to solve a system of equations using substitution and explains the process in writing, has students practice solving problems and writing explanations of their solutions while providing feedback, and then gives students the opportunity to solve problems and write explanations independently.
Strategies instruction (including SRSD) (Hughes & Lee, 2020; Kiuhara et al., 2020)	• Explicit instruction on cognitive or metacognitive strategies • Strategy taught in context of academic task or activity • Strategy modeled, followed by guided practice and independent practice • Facilitate memorization and internalization of the strategy. • Support strategy use. • Example strategies: POD✓, PRISM✓, FACT
Routines (Braxton & Terrell, 2024; Cross, 2009)	• Students follow a sequence of actions, often working in collaborative groups. • *Example:* Argumentation routine: 1. Read problem and gather initial ideas. 2. Each group member states response and reasoning. 3. Group members defend answers and consider other answers and reasons presented (Cross, 2009). • *Example:* World Problem Roulette (Braxton & Terrell, 2004), in which groups of students do the following: 1. Solve a problem verbally. 2. Write steps to solutions in words (not symbols). 3. Each student writes one sentence and passes paper to next student to write the next sentence. 4. After written solution is complete, one group member reads their text, and another group member writes the symbolic notation.
Paraphrase word problems (Moran et al., 2014)	• Students are explicitly taught (with modeling, practice, and feedback) how to paraphrase word problems by rewriting and restating relevant parts of the word problem: o Rewrite question sentence from word problem in your own words. o Rewrite sentence that includes needed numbers in your own words. o Rewrite sentence that includes unnecessary numbers in your own words; distinguish between needed and unnecessary numbers.

(continued)

TABLE 12.1. *(continued)*

Strategy/practice	Description and examples

Paraphrase word problems *(continued)*	• *Example:* A farmer has 3 grain silos. The smallest grain storage silo has a diameter of 15 feet and a height of 30 feet. What is the volume of grain that can be stored in the smallest silo?
	  ○ What volume of grain can be stored in the silo?
	  ○ Needed numbers: Diameter = 15 ft, height = 30 ft.
	  ○ Unnecessary = 3; necessary numbers are 15 and 30.

Coaching to monitor progress using metacognitive strategies (Glogger et al., 2012)	• Teach students to apply metacognitive learning strategies in the context of math journals:
	  ○ Monitor comprehension.
	  ○ Identify most important aspects of the topics taught.
	  ○ Link new concepts to prior learning.
	  ○ Monitor and plan remedial strategies.
	• *Example prompt:* Compare and contrast the formulas for finding the volume of a square pyramid and the volume of a triangular pyramid. How can you remember which one to use?

Providing examples, modeling, and mini-lessons (Kostos & Shin, 2010)	• Model and provide examples of mathematics writing.
	• Teach mini-lessons to provide targeted instruction on aspects of writing in need of improvement.
	• *Example:* Teach a mini-lesson on how to provide good reasons in support of a main idea in a mathematics argument.
	  ○ Give students several prewritten mathematics arguments that reflect a range of quality.
	  ○ Have students evaluate and discuss what makes some arguments more or less persuasive than others.
	  ○ Have students create a tip sheet with reminders for creating good reasons for support in math arguments.

Requiring written explanations of solutions to a problem (Idris, 2009; Kiuhara et al., 2023; Kostos & Shin, 2010; Tan & Garces-Bascal, 2013)	• Incorporate opportunities for students to write explanations of how they solved problems.
	• Include higher-order open-ended responses that focus on aspects of the Common Core SMPs.
	• *Examples of possible types of writing prompts:*
	  ○ Explain how to solve the problem.
	  ○ Explain each step you would use to solve the problem and why you picked each step.
	  ○ Explain to a friend how to solve this type of math problem.
	  ○ Reflect on your understanding of how to solve problems like this (what are you understanding, what are you having difficulty with, and what can you do to overcome those difficulties?).

(continued)

TABLE 12.1. *(continued)*

Strategy/practice	Description and examples
Provide verbal or written feedback, focusing on elements of good mathematics writing (Cross, 2009; Lee et al., 2024; Pugalee, 2004)	• Provide students with feedback on their mathematics writing. Attend to specific features such as the following: o Main idea o Specific reasons in support of main idea o Organized and clear composition o Use of specific and accurate mathematics vocabulary o Writing conventions (e.g., grammar, syntax, spelling, punctuation, capitalization) • *Examples of features to evaluate when giving feedback on reasons provided in support of main idea:* o Use of units of measurement/labels o Use of precise numerals o Conjectures that extend the argument (e.g., "This rate is correct because if I use it to build a table, all the numbers line up") o Explanations of reasonableness of answer
Explicitly teach mathematics vocabulary and use precise and accurate mathematical language (Hebert et al., 2019; Hughes et al., 2020; Kiuhara et al., 2023; Powell et al., 2019; Riccomini et al., 2015, 2024)	• Use formal language instead of informal language (e.g., "dividend" instead of "the number you divide"). • Be precise (attend to detail in terms used, especially when using terms that are related to one another; e.g., *factor* and *multiple*, *congruent* and *similar*). • Provide regular exposure to mathematics vocabulary terms on a consistent basis. • Use explicit instruction to teach mathematics vocabulary (model, discuss, practice, feedback). • Use graphic organizers to help students connect terms, definitions, and concepts. • Display word walls to help students focus on key vocabulary. • Keep math glossaries in math journals. • Play math vocabulary games to increase knowledge and retention. • *Example:* Teach a mini-lesson on using specific and precise vocabulary during a unit on trigonometric ratios (sine, cosine, and tangent). Provide students with opportunities to use their own words to define the terms, provide examples and nonexamples of the terms, draw pictures to help them connect terms to concepts, and apply terms to problems.
Provide opportunities for students to engage in mathematical discourse (Braxton & Terrell, 2024; Porter & Masingila, 2000)	• Provide students with structured opportunities to explain and share their thinking orally with peers. • Provide students with structured opportunities to explain and share their thinking in writing. • *Example:* Assign students math pen pals in class. o Give students a writing prompt (e.g., write a letter to your math pen pal explaining why the Pythagorean theorem works for finding right triangle side lengths). o Students trade and read math pen-pal letters. o Students talk to their math pen pals about how their explanations are similar or different. Math pen-pal partners come up with a creative proof of the Pythagorean theorem that they present to the class.

P: Propose the problem.
- What are you asked?
- Outline the information given:

O: Outline how you will solve the problem.
- Outline the steps you will use to solve the problem:

D: Describe and defend your answer.
- Describe in writing the process you used to solve the problem.
- Defend: explain how you know your answer makes sense. Provide an example for support.

✓: Check your work.
- I reread the problem _____
- I set up the problem correctly _____
- I checked my calculations _____
- I looked for common mistakes _____

FIGURE 12.2. The POD✓ strategy.

The case example of the POD✓ strategy in the context of secondary mathematics content illustrates the use of several strategies, including explicit strategy instruction, requiring written explanations of solutions to problems. Additional scaffolded strategies (e.g., visual representations) can be readily added to strategies such as the POD✓ strategy (see Figure 12.2).

Applied Example: POD✓ to Support Students' Mathematics Writing for Rate of Change

The problem-solving strategy POD✓ is an example of providing students with systematic and explicit instruction and has been used to help middle and high school students with disabilities develop an understanding of constant-rate-of-change concepts (Bundock et al., 2021, 2025). Students are explicitly taught how to work through rate-of-change problems and communicate mathematically in writing using the POD✓ strategy: P = Propose the problem; O = Outline how you will solve the problem; D = Describe and defend your answer; and ✓ = Check your work (see Figure 12.2). An example of the POD✓ strategy in the context of a constant-rate-of-change problem is provided in the following sections with possible student responses.

> **Problem:** The water level of a lake decreases by ¼ foot per year during a drought. Assuming the lake is drying up at a constant

rate, how many years of drought would it take for all 16 feet of the water in the lake to dry up?

Writing prompt 1: Describe, in writing, the process you used to solve the problem above.

Writing prompt 2: Explain how you know your answer makes sense. Provide an example to support your reasoning.

P: Propose the problem. What are you asked? Outline the information given.

In this step, the student restates what the question is asking them to find (what are you asked?). For example, "The problem asks me to figure out how long it would take for all 16 feet of water to dry up." Then, the student outlines the information provided in the problem. At this stage, the student also determines which values or terms in the problem would be represented by the variables in the $y = mx + b$ equation. For example, "The problem also includes that the water decreases by ¼ foot per year, and that there is 16 feet of water in the lake. The problem tells me to assume that there is a constant rate, so in this case, the rate is –¼ foot, which means $m = -\frac{1}{4}$. If the rate is 1 foot for every 4 years, that means y will equal feet and x will equal years in this problem."

O: Outline the steps to solve the problem. For this step, the student outlines the steps they would follow to solve the problem. For example:

1. I will write an equation to represent the problem using $y = mx + b$.
2. I will use a picture to model the change in the water level of the lake.
3. I will make a table and fill in the values I found through my visual model.
4. I will plug in values for variables in the equation and solve.
5. I will check my work by checking that the answer I found by solving the equation lines up with what I found by filling in the table.

D: Describe and defend your answer. Describe, in writing, the process you used to solve the problem. For this step, the student describes how they solved the problem, providing details for each step in their process. For example, "I solved the problem by writing and solving the equation $-16 = -\frac{1}{4}x$. I set up my equation this way because the problem involves a decreasing rate, and I am trying to find out how many years it will take for 16 feet of water to dry up. Next, I solved the equation by dividing –16 by –¼. That equals 64. I also solved the problem by setting up a table. In the table, I started with an x value of 0 and a y value of 16. The rate of –¼ means that the water level drops by 1 foot every 4 years. In my table, I showed that by having the next point of $x = 4$ years and $y =$ 15 feet of water. I filled in the rest of my table like this:"

X = Years ↓ *Y = Feet of water in lake* ↓

X	Y
0	16
4	15
8	14
12	13
16	12
20	11
24	10
28	9
32	8
36	7
40	6
44	5
48	4
52	3
56	2
60	1
64	0

Defend: Explain how you know your answer makes sense. Provide an example for support. The "Defend" step prompts students to explain in writing how their answer makes sense with support. Potential sources of support include how different problem representations (e.g., table, equation, graph, visual model, manipulatives) align, additional values that would occur in the pattern with the values provided in the problem in the context of the answer. For example, "I know my answer makes sense because the answer I got through solving the equation matches the answer I got when

I put the numbers in the problem into a table and used a constant rate to solve the problem. The table helps me see the constant rate in the problem. I knew I was on the right track in solving the problem based on the halfway point. For example, when the lake would have 8 feet of water left (half of 16 feet), 32 years would have passed. This is another reason that the answer 64 years makes sense because it follows the pattern in the table."

- ✓ **Check your work:** This final step of the POD✓ prompts the student to check their work. The student goes through each step, checking them off. If the student discovers any mistakes in the process, they correct them and adjust their responses as needed.
- ✓ **Reread the problem:** The student is first prompted to go back and reread the problem. This allows them to make sure that their solution addresses the question asked.
- ✓ **Check to make sure the problem is set up correctly:** The second check step prompts students to check that they set up the problem correctly, regardless of which method they used to solve the problem.
- ✓ **Check calculations:** In this check step, the student checks their calculations to make sure that they didn't make any mistakes. To do so, the student should redo the calculations, with or without a calculator.
- ✓ **Check for any common mistakes:** This check step can be tailored to each individual student's needs. Before starting the problem-solving process, the student should think of and jot down potential mistakes they might make, reflecting on their learning and work with similar problems. During the final check step, they can review their problem for their common mistakes specifically and make any corrections needed.

Using Self-Regulated Strategy Development to Support Students' Mathematics Writing

Considering the evidence base on mathematics writing overall, we recommend using explicit and systematic mathematics writing instruction associated with greater gains in mathematics achievement (Powell et al., 2017), especially for students who need supplemental instructional support. Specifically, instruction combining explicit and systematic writing instruction using the self-regulated strategy development (SRSD) framework has been shown to improve students' mathematical writing and mathematics achievement (for a full description of SRSD, see Ray

& Graham, Chapter 4, this volume). Briefly described here, SRSD is an instructional framework for mathematics writing that embeds self-regulation strategies, such as goal-setting and self-monitoring of learning, to help students manage the demands of mathematics writing as they develop agency and independence when solving mathematics problems. During SRSD instruction, the teacher implements six recursive stages of instruction (see Harris et al., 2008):

- *Stage 1:* Develops and activates students' background knowledge and skills needed to learn the strategies for both writing and the mathematics domain.
- *Stage 2:* Introduces the targeted learning strategies and each step of the strategies, along with graphic organizers to help students learn and use the strategies.
- *Stage 3:* Models each step of the learning and self-regulation strategies (i.e., setting goals for learning and monitoring progress toward their goals and identifying statements or things to say to themselves when they encounter an obstacle or achieve an "aha" moment); during this stage, the students can observe the teacher and their peers and take notes; teachers and students discuss the challenges students face when engaging in mathematics writing.
- *Stage 4:* Provides time during each lesson for students to memorize and paraphrase the steps of the strategies into their own words so they can easily recall the steps of the strategies during mathematics writing.
- *Stage 5:* Supports students' learning by providing multiple opportunities for students to use the strategies alone or collaboratively with peers while solving a mathematics problem; during this stage, the teacher gradually releases responsibility for mathematics writing depending on the student's individual learning needs.
- *Stage 6:* Provides time for students to use the mathematics writing and self-regulation strategies independently.

Given the growing evidence base indicating the effectiveness of explicit instruction and SRSD for improving students' mathematics writing and conceptual understanding, we recommend that teachers introduce an SRSD mathematics writing strategy using problems that students have already mastered so that students can focus on learning the strategies (Hughes & Lee, 2020). After they understand the strategy and how to apply it, they can then use the strategy to help them think through and solve new problems.

FACT + R^2C^2 is a problem-solving strategy to engage students in using mathematics writing to develop their mathematical reasoning. The example in Figure 12.3 illustrates learning foundational concepts of fractions, such as magnitude and equivalence. Students jot down notes while they engage in the steps of FACT: F = Figure out my plan, A = Act on it, C = Compare my reasoning with a peer, and T = Tie it up in an argumentative paragraph. In the process of writing the argumentative paragraph, students go through the R^2C^2 steps, which include R = Restate, R = Reasons, C = Counterclaim, and C = Conclusion (Kiuhara et al., 2020). PRISM✓ is another SRSD mathematics writing strategy to develop students' mathematical reasoning for solving word problems involving subtraction and division (Hughes & Lee, 2020; Riccomini et al., 2024). Each letter of PRISM✓ represents the steps for composing an expository paragraph: **P**roblem (read the word problem carefully and identify information needed to solve the problem); **R**epresentation (represent the problem visually); **I** do (write an equation and solve the problem); **S** (state, say, share—rephrase the problem and share my conceptual understanding using correct mathematical vocabulary); **M**y answer (write my answer in a concluding sentence); and ✓ (check for evidence at each step referring to my word banks and sentence starters). The PRISM✓ strategy was combined with additional supports; students kept a word bank consisting of common words or words that were difficult to spell and sentence starters to aid students during mathematics writing.

How Can Teachers Support Students with Disabilities and Culturally and Linguistically Diverse Students?

Students who experience difficulties with mathematics content, reading, and/or writing may require more instructional support than other students when presented with mathematics writing tasks (Hughes & Lee, 2020; Kiuhara et al., 2020; Riccomini et al., 2024). Additionally, students who have not had as many opportunities to communicate their mathematical understanding (orally or in writing) may also face difficulty with mathematics writing (Braxton & Terrell, 2024; Huitzilopochtli, 2024). Fortunately, students with disabilities and culturally and linguistically diverse students can be successful in mathematics writing when provided with learning supports and scaffolded instruction. Examples of instructional supports include sentence starters, sentence strips, and word banks (Braxton & Terrell, 2024; Riccomini et al., 2024) and talk frames that support students' language development (Cohen et al., 2015). Examples of providing students systematic and explicit instructional support for developing students' mathematical reasoning include

FACT Strategy

F Figure it out: What is my task? What tool(s) will I use?

A Act on it: What is "*my*" answer? Reasons and Evidence? Choose precise words? Write down 1 to 3 "reasons for" to support my answer:

C Compare with a peer: What is "another" answer? Can I make improvements? Write down 1 to 3 counterclaims to show the other answer is incorrect:

T Tie it up in a paragraph:

Tell me more about FACT

Tie it up in a paragraph using RRCC or R^2C^2

4 things I need to do . . .	Cue words to use . . .
R Restate the task	*(Explain, Describe, Justify, Compare . . .)*
R Reasons and Support (evidence)	First, second, next Also, furthermore, Similarly, both However, in contrast, conversely, because = reason
C Address the counterclaim—peer's view	Although ___________, ___________. However, Others may argue that ___________, but ___________. because = reason Others agree with me because ___________.
C Wrap it up—concluding sentence	Therefore, because = reason Finally,

Analyze the following paragraph for R2C2, then circle the "math words" and the "writing words":

My task is to compare two fractions between 0 and 1 to see if *4/6* is bigger than *4/8*. I used a number line to help me find the answer. First, on the number line, *4/6* is closer to 1 than *4/8*. Although these two fractions have the same numerator, some people may think *4/8* is larger because the denominator is larger. They would be wrong because *4/8* is partitioned into eight equivalent areas, which makes the area of the pieces smaller compared to six equivalent areas. The second reason they are wrong is because *4/8* is closer to 0, which makes it the smaller fraction. Therefore, *4/6* is greater than *4/8* because *4/6* is closest to 1 when I place each fraction on a number line.

FIGURE 12.3. The FACT and R^2C^2 strategies.

visual representations of mathematics concepts (Hughes & Lee, 2020; Kiuhara et al., 2020; Riccomini et al., 2024) and written notations (e.g., graphic organizers; Graham et al., 2020). To support mathematics writing for English language learners, a combination of nonneutral qualifiers and peer or teacher conferencing may allow students to explain their mathematical reasoning in conversation and through writing (Huitzilopochtli, 2024).

Table 12.2 presents an overview of some of these strategies with examples for accessing the language demands, mathematics demands, or both involved in mathematics writing. For a more nuanced discussion of embedding culturally sustaining writing practices, see Ebarvia and Parker (Chapter 2, this volume). When addressing the learning needs of diverse learners, talk frames, sentence starters, sentence strips, and word banks primarily provide students with linguistic support. These strategies may also support some understanding of mathematics concepts, given how closely related mathematics vocabulary is to mathematics concepts (Powell et al., 2019). Other strategies primarily support students' conceptual mathematics understanding and their ability to express their understanding orally and in writing. These strategies include visual representations and graphical representations. Additional strategies, including nonneutral qualifiers and conferencing, provide students with support on mathematics concepts and formal aspects of mathematics writing. All of the research studies that included the strategies listed in Table 12.2 also implemented some foundational strategies presented in Table 12.2, particularly explicit instruction with frequent practice and feedback. Teachers should layer on the additional strategies listed in Table 12.2 based on their students' needs and in response to insights gained from analyzing students' work on formative assessments (Riccomini et al., 2024).

ACTION STEPS

When implementing a new practice in your teaching, it can be challenging to know where to start. The seven action steps that follow are designed to help you start incorporating mathematics writing activities into your teaching. These action steps are helpful for all teachers—not just those who teach mathematics or writing—to consider as viable ways to embed writing activities into their teaching. Additionally, teachers who teach related content areas (e.g., science, social studies) may consider incorporating mathematics writing activities to help students connect related concepts that cross disciplines, such as population growth in

TABLE 12.2. Scaffolded Strategies to Support All Learners in Accessing Mathematics Writing

Conferencing

- Review and discuss students' work, then ask reflective questions to help students refine and/or reorganize their reasoning of concepts and/or procedures.
- Prepare possible reflection questions before engaging in discussion with the students.
- *Examples of possible reflection questions for a rate problem:*
  - You identified the rate as 5 in the equation $33 = 5x + 3$. How did you identify 5 as the rate?
  - What patterns could you use to verify the rate for this problem?
  - If we changed the equation to $17 = 5x + 2$, would the rate be the same or different? Why?

Nonneutral qualifiers

- Provide a list of possible claims to evaluate; assess each claim as sometimes, always, or never true.
- Support students in generating examples to help provide evidence for the nonneutral qualifiers applied to each claim.
- *Examples in the context of functions:*
  - In a function, each input has one and only one output value.
  - In a function, each input can have multiple output values.
  - The vertical line test can be used to identify functions.
  - In a function, no y values can repeat.
  - In a function, no x values can repeat.

Representations

- Prompt students to represent the problem using concrete manipulatives.
  - *Example:* Algebra tiles to represent multiplying expressions
- Prompt students to represent the problem using pictorial depictions.
  - *Example:* Draw an array of algebra tiles for multiplying expressions.
- Support students in making connections between abstract and verbal depictions and visual representations.
- *Example:* Create an array with numerals and variables representing the problem you solved using algebra tiles.

Sentence starters

- Short phrases to start sentences
- *Examples:*
  - I agree/disagree because . . .
  - I believe my answer is correct because . . .
  - I can check my work by . . .
  - The first thing I did to solve the problem was . . .
  - I used the strategy . . .
  - My answer is similar to ___________ because . . .
  - My answer is different because . . .

(continued)

TABLE 12.2. *(continued)*

Sentence strips

- Create paper strips with verbal expressions of the steps needed to solve a problem or possible explanation phrases.
- Students sort and place the sentence strips in the correct order and/or apply them to the correct problems.
- Paper strips can be gradually scaffolded back by reducing how much of the sentence is provided on the strip or reducing the number of strips so students gradually generate more sentences on their own.
- *Example in the context of simplifying the expression $3x + 4 + 2x - 6$:*
  - *Circle the like terms that have the same variables.*
  - Box the like terms that are numerals (no variables).
  - Combine each set of like terms.
  - Rewrite the expression with like terms combined.
  - Check for any like terms missed or errors with positive and negative numbers. Correct if needed.

Talk frames

- Graphic organizer, on which the teacher records the following during student discussion:
  - Student rewording of the question
  - Notes on students' contributions (both correct and incorrect)
  - Paraphrase the class's final and accurate mathematical ideas.
- *Example:* The teacher draws a graphic organizer with three sections on the board, then records notes in each section based on the following questions:
  - What is another way we can phrase this question?
  - What ideas do you have for solving the problem?
  - What is our final answer to the question?

Word banks

- List of words related to the mathematics concepts being explored
- Words can be displayed on an individual page on a student's desk, written on a board, or be a list that students gradually add to a math journal.
- Example word bank for transformations in the coordinate plane:
  - Angle, circle, perpendicular line, parallel line, line segment, point, line, rotation, reflection, translation

Written notations

- Use graphic organizers to help students understand, organize, and analyze content.
- *Examples:* Note taking, graphic organizers, mind maps, Venn diagrams

the context of social studies, balancing chemical equations in chemistry, or solving Punnett squares in the context of biology or anatomy and physiology.

- *Identify the purpose/type of mathematics writing to implement.* First, identify the purpose of the mathematics writing you will implement. Overall, consider what you would like students to gain from engaging in mathematics writing. You might also consider what kinds of mathematical writing students are asked to engage with in the curriculum you use or on the assessments students complete. When determining the purpose of the mathematics writing you would like to implement, it is helpful to consider the different genres of mathematics writing (Casa et al., 2016): exploratory writing, informative/explanatory writing, argumentative writing, and mathematically creative writing. You may want to incorporate multiple mathematics writing activities that address multiple purposes. To get started, selecting one purpose/mathematics writing type can be helpful.
- *Identify aligned standard(s) for mathematical practice.* Second, identify specific SMPs (see Figure 12.1) to focus on in the mathematics writing activity. Some SMPs that relate especially well to constructing arguments include making sense of problems and persevering in solving them, constructing viable arguments and critiquing the reasoning of others, using appropriate tools strategically, and attending to precision (Kiuhara et al., 2020; 2023a).
- *Write mathematics writing prompts.* Third, write mathematics writing prompts that align with the purpose of writing you selected and the SMP you will focus on. To get started, you might consider adding questions onto problems you regularly use in instruction, such as: "Explain how you know your answer is correct," "Describe how you solved the problem," "Do you agree or disagree?" (in context of a solved problem), or "Describe what tools we might use to help solve this problem."
- *Identify what instructional strategies to implement.* Fourth, identify what strategies you will use to teach students how to write mathematically. Given the research supporting scaffolded and explicit instruction, begin with explicit instruction as the foundation for your instructional practice in teaching mathematics writing. Determine what additional strategies you might incorporate based on your students' strengths, needs, and prior exposure to mathematics writing. Consider whether students need support producing mathematics writing, understanding mathematics concepts, or both. Consider using approaches already structured to support mathematics content development alongside

mathematics writing and have research behind them, such as SRSD (Hughes & Lee, 2020; Kiuhara et al., 2020; Riccomini et al., 2024).

- *Block off instruction time for mathematics writing.* Fifth, block off instructional time to explicitly teach, review, and reflect on mathematics writing. Ideally, mathematics writing should be incorporated fluidly into mathematics instruction so that mathematics writing can be used to help develop and evaluate students' understanding of mathematics concepts. However, additional instructional time will be needed to appropriately model effective mathematics writing and review examples and nonexamples with students. Additionally, students will need instructional time to engage in the writing process, including time to review and revise mathematics writing. To help get started, include a low number of writing prompts in your first lessons and break up the mathematics writing process on particular concepts across multiple days. For example, students can write initial responses to a prompt on one day and review and revise their responses the following day.
- *Assess mathematics writing to gain insight into students' understanding.* Sixth, assess mathematics writing to help gain insight into students' understanding of mathematics concepts (Powell et al., 2017). Reviewing what students wrote can help you identify how well students understand the mathematics or writing concepts. When reviewing students' mathematics writing, evaluating whether students have effectively conveyed an accurate main idea throughout their writing can be constructive, as well as whether they have provided specific and accurate mathematical reasons or evidence in support of that main idea. Students' mathematics writing prompts can be reviewed to determine how frequently and accurately students use specific mathematics vocabulary. Additionally, it can be helpful to review students' mathematics writing to determine how they organize their ideas, the clarity of their written reasoning, and how well they adhere to writing conventions appropriate for the context (Lee et al., 2024). After assessing students' mathematics writing, provide students with specific feedback either in writing or orally.
- *Reflect on teaching and learning and make any needed adjustments.* Seventh, reflect on your teaching and your mathematics learning. Make any needed adjustments by incorporating additional strategies or scaffolds, reteaching a mathematics or writing concept, and providing students with additional feedback based on what you learn from assessing your students' mathematics writing. You might also reflect on your teaching practice to determine whether you would like to refine the writing prompts you are using with students or alter the

instructional activities and routines you are implementing to support mathematics writing. Collect student assessment data to understand how students are progressing in their understanding of mathematics concepts and writing proficiency, then gradually reduce instructional support to facilitate their independence and autonomy. While doing so, it can be helpful to build a practice of discussing and coaching students using cognitive and metacognitive strategies.

ADDITIONAL RESOURCES

Buffington, P., Knight, T., & Tierney-Fife. P. (2017). *Supporting mathematics discourse with sentence starters & sentence frames.* Education Development Center, Inc. *http://courses.maine.edc.org/files/Interactive-STEM-Tool-Strategy-Sentence-Starters.pdf*

Colonnese, M. W., Casa, T. M., & Cardetti, F. (2024). *Illuminating and advancing the path for mathematical writing research.* IGI Global.

Harris, K. R., Graham, S., Mason, L., & Friedlander, B. (2008). *Powerful writing strategies for all students.* Brookes.

Redford, M. A. (n.d.). *Strategy instruction: What you need to know.* Understood.org. *www.understood.org/en/articles/what-is-strategy-instruction*

REFERENCES

Archer, A. L., & Hughes, C. A. (2011). *Explicit instruction: Effective and efficient teaching.* Guilford Press.

Arsenault, T. L., Powell, S. R., Hebert, M. A., King, S. G., Lin, X., & Lang, D. (2022). Influence of writing ability and computation skills on mathematics. *Reading and Writing, 36*, 2025–2053.

Ball, D. L., & Cohen, D. K. (1999). Developing practice, developing practitioners: Toward a practice-based professional education. In G. Sykes & L. Darling-Hammond (Eds.), *Teaching as the learning profession: Handbook of policy and practice* (pp. 2–21). Jossey-Bass.

Bangert-Drowns, R. L., Hurley, M. M., & Wilkinson, B. (2004). The effects of school-based writing-to-learn interventions on academic achievement: A meta-analysis. *Review of Educational Research, 74*, 29–58.

Boaler, J. (2016). *Mathematical mindsets: Unleashing students' potential through creative math, inspiring messages, and innovating teaching.* Jossey-Bass.

Braxton, D. N., & Terrell, K. L. (2024). Linking practice and standards to strategies that enhance writing for students with disabilities. In M. W. Collonnese, T. M. Casa, & F. Cardetti (Eds.), *Illuminating and advancing the path for mathematical writing research* (pp. 316–327). IGI Global.

Bundock, K., Callan, G., McClain, M. B., Benney, C. M., Longhurst, D. N., & Rolf, K. R. (2025). Teaching constant rate-of-change problem-solving to secondary students with or at risk of learning disabilities. *Journal of Learning Disabilities, 58*(3), 210–224.

Bundock, K., Hawken, L. S., Kiuhara, S. A., O'Keeffe, B. V., O'Neill, R. E., & Cummings, M. B. (2021). Teaching rate of change and problem solving to high school students with high incidence disabilities at tier 3. *Learning Disability Quarterly, 44*(1), 35–49.

Casa, T. M., Firmender, J. M., Cahill, J., Cardetti, F., Chopping, J. M., Cohen, J., . . . Zawodniak, R. (2016). *Types of and purposes for elementary mathematical writing: Task force recommendations. https://mathwriting.education.uconn.edu/wp-content/uploads/sites/1454/2016/04/Types_of_and_Purposes_for_Elementary_Mathematical_Writing_for_Web-2.pdf*

Cohen, J. A., Miller, H. C., Casa, T. M., & Firmender, J. M. (2015). Characteristics of second graders' mathematical writing. *School Science and Mathematics, 115*, 344–355.

Colonnese, M. W., Casa, T. M., & Cardetti, F. (2023). *Illuminating and advancing the path for mathematical writing research.* IGI Global.

Common Core State Standards Initiative. (2010). *Common Core State Standards for Mathematics. https://learning.ccsso.org/common-core-state-standards-initiative*

Cross, D. I. (2009). Creating optimal mathematics learning environments: Combining argumentation and writing to enhance achievement. *International Journal of Science and Mathematics Education, 7*, 905–930.

Glogger, I., Schwonke, R., Holzapfel, L., Nuckles, M., & Renkl, A. (2012). Learning strategies assessed by journal writing: Prediction of learning outcomes by quantity, quality, and combinations of learning strategies. *Journal of Educational Psychology, 104*(2), 452–468.

Graham, S., Kiuhara, S. A., & MacKay, M. (2020). The effects of writing on learning in science, social studies, and mathematics: A meta-analysis. *Review of Educational Research, 90*(2), 179–226.

Harris, K. R., Graham, S., Mason, L. H., & Friedlander, B. (2008). *Powerful writing strategies for all students.* Brooks Publishing.

Hebert, M. A., Bohaty, J., Roehling, J., & Powell, S. R. (2019). Piloting a mathematics–writing intervention with late elementary students at-risk for learning difficulties. *Learning Disabilities Research & Practice, 34*(3), 144–157.

Hughes, E. M., & Lee, J. (2020). Effects of a mathematical writing intervention on middle school students' performance. *Reading & Writing Quarterly, 36*(2), 176–192.

Hughes, E. M., Riccomini, P. J., & Lee, J. (2020). Investigating written expressions of mathematical reasoning for students with learning disabilities. *Journal of Mathematical Behavior, 58*, 1–14.

Huitzilopochtli, S. (2024). Mathematical writing and English language learners: Strengths-based instructional strategies. In M. W. Collonnese, T. M. Casa, & F. Cardetti (Eds.), *Illuminating and advancing the path for mathematical writing research* (pp. 291–315). IGI Global.

Idris, N. (2009). Enhancing students' understanding in calculus through writing. *International Electronic Journal of Mathematics Education, 4*, 36–55.

Jitendra, A. K., Alghamdi, A., Edmunds, R., McKevett, N. M., Mouanoutoua, J., & Roesslein, R. (2020). The effects of Tier 2 mathematics interventions for students with mathematics difficulties: A meta-analysis. *Exceptional Children, 87*, 307–315.

Kiuhara, S. A., Gouse, A. G., Dai, T., Witzel, B. S., Morphy, P., & Unker, B. (2020). Constructing written arguments to develop fraction knowledge. *Journal of Educational Psychology, 112*(3), 584–607.

Kiuhara, S. A., Levin, J. R., Tolbert, M., Erickson, M., & Kruse, K. (2023a). Can argumentative writing improve math knowledge for elementary students with a mathematics learning disability? A single-case classroom intervention investigation. In X. Liu, M. Hebert, & R. A. Alves (Eds.), *The hitchhiker's guide to writing research: A festschrift for Steve Graham, literacy studies: Perspectives from cognitive neurosciences, linguistics, psychology education* (Vol. 25, pp. 191–209). Springer Nature.

Kiuhara, S. A., Levin, J. R., Tolbert, M., O'Keeffe, B. V., O'Neill, R. E., & Jameson, M. J. (2023b). Teaching argument writing in math class: Challenges and solutions to improve the performance of 4th and 5th graders with disabilities [Special issue on teaching writing]. *Reading and Writing: An Interdisciplinary Journal.*

Korhonen, J., Linnanmäki, K., & Aunio, P. (2012). Language and mathematical performance: A comparison of lower secondary school students with different level of mathematical skills. *Scandinavian Journal of Educational Research, 56*, 333–344.

Kostos, K., & Shin, E. (2010). Using math journals to enhance second graders' communication of mathematical thinking. *Early Childhood Education Journal, 38*, 223–231.

Krowka, S. K., & Fuchs, L. S. (2017). Cognitive profiles associated with responsiveness to fraction intervention. *Learning Disabilities Research & Practice, 32*, 216–230.

Lee, J., Hughes, E. M., & Riccomini, P. J. (2024). What to assess for mathematical writing: The dimensionality of written expression for mathematical problem solving and reasoning. In M. W. Collonnese, T. M. Casa, & F. Cardetti (Eds.), *Illuminating and advancing the path for mathematical writing research* (pp. 238–262). IGI Global.

Lim, L., & Pugalee, D. K. (2004). Using journal writing to explore "They communicate to learn mathematics and they learn to communicate mathematically." *Ontario Action Researcher, 7*(2), Article 2.

Moran, A. S., Swanson, H. L., Gerber, M. M., & Fung, W. (2014). The effects of paraphrasing interventions on problem-solving accuracy for children at risk for math disabilities. *Learning Disabilities Research & Practice, 29*(3), 97–105.

Nachowitz, M. (2018). Intent and enactment: Writing in mathematics for conceptual understanding. *Investigations in Mathematics Learning, 11*(6), 1–13.

National Center for Education Statistics. (2022a). *NAEP report card: Mathematics. National achievement-level results.* The Nation's Report Card. *www.nationsreportcard.gov/mathematics/nation/achievement/?grade=8*

National Center for Education Statistics. (2022b). *NAEP report card: Writing. National achievement-level results.* The Nation's Report Card. *https://nces.ed.gov/nationsreportcard/pubs/main2007/2008468.aspx*

National Council for Teachers of Mathematics. (2000). *Principles and standards for school mathematics.* NCTM.

National Governors Association Center for Best Practices & Council of Chief State School Officers. (2012). *Common Core State Standards for Mathematics. www.corestandards.org/assets/CCSSI_Math%20Standards.pdf*

National Mathematics Advisory Panel. (2008). *Foundations for success: The final report of the National Mathematics Advisory Panel.* U.S. Department of Education. *www2.ed.gov/about/bdscomm/list/mathpanel/report/final-report.pdf*

Nochowitz, M. (2018). Scaffolding progressive online discourse for literacy knowledge building. *Online Learning, 22*(3), 133–156.

Porter, M. K., & Masingila, J. O. (2000). Examining the effects of writing on conceptual and procedural knowledge in calculus. *Educational Studies in Mathematics, 42*, 165–177.

Powell, S. R., Hebert, M. A., Cohen, J. A., Casa, T. M., & Firmender, J. M. (2017). A synthesis of mathematics writing: Assessments, interventions, and surveys. *Journal of Writing Research, 8*(3), 493–526.

Powell, S. R., Stevens, E. A., & Hughes, E. M. (2019). Math language in middle school: Be more specific. *TEACHING Exceptional Children, 51*(4), 286–295.

Pugalee, D. K. (2004). A comparison of verbal and writing descriptions of students' problem solving processes. *Educational Studies in Mathematics, 55*, 27–47.

Riccomini, P. J., Hughes, E. E., Deshpande, D., Lee, J., Fiveash, L., & Lin, T. (2024). Teaching fifth-grade students with specific learning disabilities to explain their mathematical reasoning through written expression. *Learning Disability Quarterly, 47*(2), 124–136.

Riccomini, P. J., Smith, G. W., Hughes, E. M., & Fries, K. M. (2015). The language of mathematics: The importance of teaching and learning mathematical vocabulary. *Reading & Writing Quarterly, 31*(3), 235–252.

Tan, T., & Garces-Bascal, R. M. (2013). The effect of journal writing on mathematics achievement among high-ability students in Singapore. *Gifted and Talented International, 28*(1–2), 173–184.

PART III
WRITING IN A DIGITAL WORLD

Chapter 13

Leveraging Generative Artificial Intelligence to Improve Secondary Writing Instruction

Tamara P. Tate and Mark Warschauer

No matter what they teach, every educator has asked themselves the same question in the last year: How does generative artificial intelligence (AI) impact my class? Teachers must address the tension created by this new digital technology, determining when its use supports learning how to write authentically and when it undermines necessary skill building for their students.

This chapter will help teachers understand the basics of what generative AI is, describe a pedagogical framework to guide the use of generative AI in writing instruction, and suggest how to incorporate generative AI to support student writing and increase students' AI literacy. Concerns for equity necessitate a pedagogy focused on *access* to generative AI and foreground the risks of *not* educating students on ethical and effective uses of these tools. We conclude with suggestions for incorporating generative AI in effective teaching and learning of writing throughout the planning, drafting, and revision process, as well as for instructors.

We focus on the following guiding questions:

GUIDING QUESTIONS

1. What do teachers and students need to know in order to effectively and ethically use generative AI for teaching and learning writing?
2. What equity and ethical issues are raised by the use of generative AI in connection with secondary school writing?
3. How can teachers incorporate generative AI into teaching secondary

students writing in a way that helps them use this new technology and retains student growth as independent writers?

4. How can a teacher ethically use AI as a teaching partner?

What Do Teachers and Students Need to Know in Order to Effectively and Ethically Use Generative AI for Teaching and Learning Writing?

Although generative AI has arguably arrived and spread faster than prior technologies, an understanding of the research on prior digital tools can help guide our initial reactions to this new reality because, at its core, AI is still a technological tool. Decades of research on laptops in schools, automated writing evaluation, and online learning thus serve as a starting point to understand AI's place in education. Based on this research foundation, we have come up with a generative AI instructional framework (Tate et al., 2023).

Generative AI Instructional Framework

Understand

First, students (and teachers) need to understand the basics of large language models and AI writing tools' functions, strengths, weaknesses, and biases (Ng et al., 2021). ChatGPT and other large language models are a type of AI trained to generate text similar to human-generated text. They are called "large" because they are typically trained on a corpus of text data ranging from millions to billions of words; ChatGPT in particular is based on a model trained on several hundred billion words from a corpus including websites on the internet, books, and English-language Wikipedia (Brown et al., 2020).

Large language models can work in a number of different ways, but they typically use a technique called "deep learning," which involves training a network of artificial neurons on a large dataset (for an excellent, detailed explanation, see Wolfram, 2023). The network is then able to generate text by predicting the next word in a sequence based on the words that came before it. This allows the model to produce text that flows naturally and is similar to human-generated text.

Large language models have become increasingly popular in recent years and have been used for a variety of applications, including language translation, text summarization, and content generation. ChatGPT, produced by OpenAI, caught so much attention not because it was brand new—it builds on an earlier OpenAI product, GPT-3—but rather because it was the first released for free to the public and required no specialized skills to use; its user interface is styled as "chat" and allows for users to ask questions conversationally. Other tools have been quickly emerging, and some are even embedded directly into writing environments such as Word.

Students need to understand that these tools are built on prediction and language; they do not "think," they fabricate things, and they were trained on a specific set of texts and by humans, so there are very real embedded biases. Students don't need to know how the algorithms work precisely, but they need a working understanding of the factors that will impact the output: What was the body of material on which the AI was trained? Who and what were excluded? What assumptions and biases might be implicit in the tool because of these choices?

The internal flaws of the tools abound. We see algorithmic biases that literally make darker skin tones invisible in AI-based visual tools and that shape what suggestions are given when the AI is told it is responding to a man or a woman. In answering questions, generative AI may give completely wrong answers. It can display horrific racial or gender biases, again by distilling biases from the corpora it draws on. It can also mirror the erasure of contributions by women and minorities by academia and media—unable to access much information about a key figure in music like Bessie Smith (a Black woman) compared to lesser white male musicians (Nkonde, 2023) because the information simply does not exist on the internet.

Education empowers students with a critical understanding of the assumptions and values embedded in the AI algorithms and provides a teachable moment—what does the limitation tell us about the kind of information usually found on the internet? Why would the AI have a lot of information on Taylor Swift but not on a rap artist? Why so much on professional athletes? In what ways does the AI model the world around us and amplify biases and stereotypes? With an understanding of how the large language models work, students will be better situated to prompt the AI for improved output and more likely to notice and critically interrogate issues in the model's output. As noted by Long and Magerko (2020, p. 1), misconceptions about AI "can limit people's ability to effectively use, collaborate with, and act as critical consumers of AI."

Access

Second, students need to be able to access and navigate AI writing tools across specific communication tasks, such as writing papers or emails, summarizing content, creating slide presentations, or gathering background information (Ng et al., 2021). These skills range from literally being able to connect to the desired tool (this requires a digital device, internet connection, and a school that does not restrict access to the AI), to knowing which tool to use for what purpose, and to being able to input the desired question/prompt and use the output for the student's intended purpose. This also includes knowing how to protect the privacy of information when using the tool. Most tools, for example, have a way to prohibit the models from using input for training purposes. Even more important, students need to understand that the best protection of sensitive or private information is to never input it into the tool in the first place.

Prompt

Both instructors and students will need some basic understanding of prompting to use AI effectively. Teaching students prompting can be a way of practicing critical thinking (e.g., What exactly do you need to know? How would you like the information tailored to meet your needs?) and also exploring the value of understanding general content knowledge. One teaching strategy is to have students compare the results from different prompts they each write and ask the following: What might have made a difference in the output? The process of prompt development itself can create opportunities for learning critical thinking skills and covering key information about the content area in service of creating prompts that generate useful output.

It is often hard to know what the perfect prompt will be because AI is unpredictable (and students should know some randomness is part of the model), and even very small changes in nonessential words change the output. Rather than being concerned about the perfect prompt, students should treat the prompting and AI response as a conversation, following up the initial interaction with further questions or instructions to refine the results until the student gets the desired information from the generative AI tool. Teachers and students can use the following information to guide them in creating effective prompts.

Role or Persona. Generative AI gains much information when you give it a persona or a role. It is unnecessary to be excessive in this regard. For example, if you tell it, "Pretend you are a seventh-grade teacher . . . ," this provides the AI with information on the type of tone, complexity, and language level to use in the output without the human specifying those details.

Students can have fun playing with personas—asking the AI to take on a role, such as a character from a book or someone from history.

Students can then critique the output to see what the AI did through word choice and tone to adopt that character. They might even find examples where they are led to decide, "She wouldn't have said that!" Yet another great path into a discussion about audience awareness or how they might convey the person more accurately! This is also an opportunity to discuss how AI tools get things wrong and make things up, which is why students always need to corroborate their output with other sources of information.

Goal. Tell the AI the action you want to perform. Use concise, simple, and direct language. Make sure to reference any assignment details or rubrics by which the output will be judged. Step-by-step, specific instructions are more likely to be correctly executed. Well-organized prompts provide improved output as well. Break the task down into steps and ask AI to "think step-by-step." This step-by-step process is likely to get more useful output, although it may not be helpful for more recent "reasoning" AI chatbots.

Details. Providing details refines the output, such as the genre, tone, format, audience, length, and language (e.g., academic, casual, or even Spanish). You can also give AI examples of the information you are seeking as output. AI performs better if it has more context to tailor the output. Personalization for students can be achieved by the teacher suggesting a prompt that has AI ask the user for information, such as their grade level or area of study.

Clarification. Think of prompting as a fake conversation with a thought partner who has infinite patience—ask follow-up questions! So, when AI tells you something you do not understand, ask it to explain by prompting "explain this as if I am a fifth grader." You can also ask AI for examples of what it means. If AI provided output relatively close to your desired output but not exactly what you asked for or realized you need, explain further with more details or constrain its responses to fit the information you are seeking. Or simply click the "regenerate" button and have AI regenerate a response without additional prompting, taking advantage of the randomness built into these models to simulate "creativity."

Expansion. Did AI draft something promising, but you feel that one of its sentences would be worth further exploration or development? If so, ask AI, for example, to expand on the second sentence or third paragraph. Did AI miss a point entirely? If so, ask it, for example, to add a sentence or paragraph explaining the point. You can guide AI to include content you know it should cover, or ideas you find interesting or persuasive.

Concision. Generative AI is often wordy but says very little. Consider constraining the output by requesting "a few sentences," or ask AI for an executive summary or a few bullet points.

Content, Domain, or Background Knowledge. Students can write better prompts if they know a bit about the topic. Understanding (at least somewhat) the content area provides two important advantages for designing/refining a prompt: (1) it provides key words and concepts to include in the prompt, and (2) it allows the writer to more easily identify hallucinations (a word used to indicate that the AI only predicts the next text and may appear to be making up things, like citations, without any factual basis) or incorrect information. This is a key point that instructors should point out as students learn to work with AI—it is not a substitute for learning the content area, but what they are learning will make them better users of AI.

Corroborate

AI-generated text can be wrong and even reference nonexistent sources; students need to corroborate the accuracy of AI-generated content through habits like checking original sources and lateral reading. Educators can leverage students' understanding of the model's processes to motivate them to check the accuracy of any facts in the AI output. Reminding them that AI is predicting, not thinking, can strengthen students' habit of verifying apparent facts, a skill important beyond their use of AI-generated content and that strengthens lifelong critical thinking skills.

The need to stress corroboration of facts will only increase as models improve and make fewer mistakes. In fact, the very fluency of the text generated by AI tools lends an authority and presumption of accuracy that must be debunked by deeper interaction. Psychological research suggests that people form stronger, longer-lasting beliefs when they learn something from agents they judge as knowledgeable and confident—and generative AI certainly sounds confident (Kidd & Birhane, 2023). Teachers must play a key role in creating a habit of verification.

Incorporate

Finally, and most importantly, students need to learn how to incorporate AI-generated texts in their own writing ethically and effectively.

Educators (and students) need to know that the community standards around the use of AI in and for writing are evolving. Rules in communities of practice range from requiring absolutely no use of AI in the writing process (perhaps including automated grammar checking and spell checking) to permitting the complete use of AI. Teachers and students can create community norms for the class. OpenAI's policy (OpenAI, n.d.) that all written content created in part with text from ChatGPT should be "clearly disclosed in a way that no reader could possibly miss, and that a typical reader would find sufficiently easy to understand" is one starting point.

But even before discussing *how* to cite AI, we need to discuss *if* we should cite AI (Terrill, 2024). We cite evidence from sources, such as a book, article, or internet blog. We do not cite spell check when we use it to clean up our writing, or the library database we used to find articles to support our arguments. Sorting through these considerations is helpful in understanding when and how to cite generative AI. The ability to sort facts from opinions and reasoning is also a key skill needed for effective argumentation and one many students struggle with. The long-standing learning objectives around this skill can be honed in the context of evaluating AI output. The more we can weave together our preexisting student learning objectives with new ways to practice the underlying skills in the context of AI, the more likely students will internalize the lessons and carry them forward in other contexts.

A final suggestion for assignments that allow the use of AI: End with some reflection. Students should take a moment to write a few sentences or otherwise capture their thoughts on how they used AI: whether they found it helpful or not, what they might do differently next time, and how AI impacted their writing and writing process. We are finding that this reflection has several benefits: students become more adept at discussing the writing process, feel like they have control over their writing process, and learn that no one process fits every author—students will also use AI more strategically in the future. This reflection could also be incorporated into goal-setting routines already in place, for example, as part of Self-Regulated Strategy Development (Harris & Graham, 2018).

What Equity and Ethical Issues Are Raised by the Use of Generative AI in Connection with Secondary School Writing?

Ethical concerns about the use of generative AI are varied. Some educators express concerns about generative AI oversimplifying complex learning processes, unintentionally increasing the focus on memorization and rote learning. Educators also worry that the use of generative AI in education will remove opportunities for students to build the necessary "muscles" for complex tasks such as writing. Students may become better content editors but not creators of content themselves. There is a concern that students will be left adrift in instances where the tools are not available, creating a dependency on technology that is ultimately crippling, especially for those lacking reliable, ongoing access.

Though the long-term impact of automated content generation on writing instruction is difficult to foresee, we are not persuaded by calls to ban it completely from student use. Our reasoning is based on two beliefs: First, its weaknesses are matched by powerful affordances, some of which favor the less privileged. These include nonnative speakers of English around the world, who are forced to use the language in international academic and professional communication, as well as those with language or learning disabilities who struggle to write well—both groups that could benefit substantially from AI-enabled text generation. Secondly, if we do not teach people in marginalized communities to use these tools well, it will once again be the more tech-savvy elite who disproportionately benefit from them.

Any use of large language models in writing instruction should be introduced in a balanced, age-appropriate manner (much like AI literacy; Wong et al., 2020). Just like a young child should first learn arithmetic before later learning how to use a graphing calculator in high school math courses—and then doing assignments with and without the calculator—many believe that children should learn to write without these AI tools at a young age, before being introduced to them in secondary school or college (Kim & Kim, 2022). Alternatively, at-home writing assignments where use of these tools may be either allowed or difficult to control can be accompanied by in-class writing without them. Teachers will have to balance the teaching of effective writing with AI scaffolding and writing without AI to ensure that students build up the necessary "muscle tone" to write and do not move too quickly to AI-generated text. Writing is hard; thinking is hard. But there is a time and a place for practicing hard things in order to become more proficient at them.

Before students are let loose to use generative AI, however, the foundation just described needs to be taught to ensure safe and ethical use of AI. In fact, even in our work with undergraduates, we suggest that instructors remind students of a few key facts about AI whenever it is used for classroom instruction (Figure 13.1): that the tool does not think but simply predicts, that they should not disclose anything private, and that the student needs to be responsible for checking both its accuracy and appropriateness.

What Students Need to Know

Students should have reviewed the Understand: How LLMs work curriculum and have an understanding of the Limitations and biases of generative AI. Tools differ and change over time, so some of these suggestions will work better than others.

Remember:

- The AI doesn't think or understand. It does not have opinions and cannot make value judgments. It's just **predicting** the next bit of text given what you told it and what it has been trained on.
- Do NOT put sensitive personal information or confidential information into ChatGPT.
- Hallucinations, biases, and other concerns: You are responsible for the accuracy and appropriateness of anything you use or incorporate into your own text.

FIGURE 13.1. Sample of reminders provided to students when using AI in the classroom.

Academic Integrity

For those on the frontline, the biggest concern teachers have loudly expressed is that students will use tools like ChatGPT to cheat on homework and assessments. Given historical biases in educational discipline, we would expect academic integrity policing to fall more heavily on the less privileged students—those of lower socioeconomic status, racial minorities, English language learners, and the disabled.

Can teachers simply "ban" all use of AI? Perhaps, though it can be trickier than one might expect to draw the line between spell checkers and Grammarly, autocomplete, and ChatGPT. In addition, many common writing tools like Microsoft Word now embed easy access to AI within the writing environment. Teachers need to clearly articulate their expectations and set class norms. Further, it can be virtually impossible even for expert linguists to detect the difference between human- and AI-generated texts (Casal & Kessler, 2023). Students with minimal effort and skill can evade current detection tools (Sadasivan et al., 2023). Even more worrisome, false positives tend to implicate English learners at higher levels than native English speakers, leading to discrimination (Liang et al., 2023).

Equity: Digital Divide

Concerns that teachers need to prepare students for college and career mean that they need to ensure students understand the role that AI can effectively and ethically play in writing because use of AI is already infiltrating businesses. If we do not prepare students for the use of AI, we have students forbidden from using AI to write school assignments in June and expected to be proficient at using AI to write in their jobs in July. Students need to be savvy consumers of AI, understanding how to use it without turning over their own agency as writers and how to look for the issues that can arise when using AI output. Because students will have uneven access and understanding of these issues, teachers can help ensure that all students have a foundational understanding of when and how to use AI in their writing. Otherwise, we see a situation in which the rich grow richer, with students with more resources having more access to AI tools and getting more practice that eventually makes them even better users of the tools. Not allowing the use of AI also means not taking advantage of the ways that AI can be used to further student critical thinking, increase the amount of planning and revision done by students, and open up discussions about the writing process and students' role as authors.

How Can Teachers Incorporate Generative AI into Teaching Secondary Writing in a Way That Helps Students Use This New Technology and Retains Student Growth as Independent Writers?

Where Does Generative AI Fit into Writing?

The short answer is virtually everywhere. AI can be used to help students understand the writing assignment, brainstorm a topic, and address the needs of the intended audience. It can help generate or critique outlines and drafts (either according to the assignment's rubric or specified concerns of the writer), and reverse outline drafts to help students spot organization or logical gaps. Generative AI also provides useful editing and revision suggestions. We will discuss in detail when, where, and how this can be done productively using generative AI tools.

Planning

Secondary students do not tend to do much prewriting, but we know that proficient writers spend time planning their writing (Hayes & Flower, 1980; Limpo et al., 2014). Generative AI might encourage and support students in this phase of writing in a number of ways (Table 13.1). For example, generative AI can help a student brainstorm possible topics for a research paper. It can also suggest keywords, research databases, and even Boolean searches to support online research. It can give students

TABLE 13.1. Planning Prompts

Prompt name	Prompt
Assignment checklist	"You are a helpful and encouraging writing coach who wants to help the student figure out what is required by an assignment. Ask the student to give you the assignment, then create a checklist using checkboxes so that they can make sure they address all the requirements of the assignment. Ask the student if they have any questions about the checklist. Answer the questions politely."
Assignment analysis	"You are a writing coach helping students to break down the requirements for a writing assignment. Ask them to give you a copy of the assignment, and then create a T-chart and put on the left side the verbs that ask the writer to DO something, and on the right side of the T-chart, place the related task words that tell the writer what to do. Keep the verbs and tasks that are connected on separate rows of the chart. Write the words on the T-chart below to create a road map for composing, and then provide definitions of each verb in the chart. Make the definitions simple for a 6th-grade student."
Brainstorm topic	"You are a kind, helpful tutor with an understanding of the applicable subject matter area and good research and writing skills. You want to help a student brainstorm ideas for a topic and provide useful, specific advice. Use language and speak in a way that is appropriate for the student's grade level. Ask the following 3 questions one at a time. Too many questions are overwhelming. Always wait for the student to respond before moving on. In your feedback, always use the information you gained from those questions. Start by asking the student what subject the writing is for. Then ask for any relevant details of the assignment. Then ask what they might be interested in writing about. Once they have responded, help them come up with a specific topic for the assignment by giving them a list of 5 topic ideas that align with the subject and the student's areas of interest. Offer to generate more ideas or expand on ideas with the student."
Databases	"Act as a tech-savvy librarian for secondary schools who is very knowledgeable in conducting efficient, effective online database searches. Start by asking the student their topic or research question. Now I'd like you to recommend 2 or 3 online databases that would be good to search for this topic."
Key words	"Act as a tech-savvy librarian for secondary schools who is very knowledgeable in conducting efficient, effective online database searches. Start by asking the student their topic or research question. Please list some keywords they can use when searching library databases."
Boolean searches	"Act as a tech-savvy librarian for secondary schools who is very knowledgeable in conducting efficient, effective online database searches. Start by asking the student their topic or research question. Please construct a few Boolean search strings they can use when researching this topic in online databases."

summaries of areas of interest or resources (as long as the student knows that some of the information may not be accurate and is only to support the topic selection, not to be used as evidence in the ultimate paper). It can even support students by creating a checklist of the required items in the assignment because students often fail to attend to every detail of an assignment. Table 13.1 presents some examples of prompts that teachers can adapt for use during the planning phase of writing.

Drafting

Using generative AI for the purpose of drafting text should be done with particular caution. First, it should only be done if the student learning objective is *not* to improve the student's writing skills. This sounds odd at first, but actually, educators have students write for many different reasons. For instance, writing is often used for the purpose of having the student show they have read and remembered content. Students could be tasked with using AI to write a summary of a novel (or more fun, a song in the style of a famous artist) and then to critique it for errors and omissions. Sometimes the goal is to have the student practice revision skills, in which case the AI can draft the text, and the student can provide the revision work. We note two other things to consider when the AI is drafting: Does the truth matter? If not, for example, if the AI creates a poem, there is no question of accuracy, so hallucinations do not create a risk. But it does present a learning opportunity to discuss the meaning and impact of AI-generated poetry. Second, if truth does matter, will the student know enough about the topic or have access to the information needed for corroboration? This can be a terrific opportunity to teach corroboration skills. For example, the AI can summarize a text, and the student can corroborate whether the summary is accurate by referring to the source text (see Table 13.2). A final suggestion is to get AI to generate a reverse outline of a text already written by the student, who can then analyze their own writing for logic, flow, and organization using the AI-generated outline (see Table 13.2).

Revision

Generative AI can provide a wide range of feedback and revision services, from simple spell checking or grammar advice to supporting peer review and analysis of the use of evidence in an argument. When using generative AI for this purpose, it is important to remind students that *they* are the authors of the text and get to decide which, if any, changes or suggestions they accept. Remind them that generative AI often has

TABLE 13.2. Prompts for Using AI to Draft a Summary or Reverse Outline

Prompt name	Prompt
Summarizing	"You are a helpful, smart tutor supporting students in creating concise, accurate, and informative summaries. Ask students about the text they wish to summarize, including its topic, source, genre, and the purpose of the summary. Wait for a response and ask questions one at a time. Then ask the student to paste in the text to be summarized. Based on the information, create a summary with the most important information, followed by bullet points highlighting key ideas and major takeaways."
Reverse outline	"You are an encouraging and supportive tutor, assisting students in outlining a text they wrote to help them analyze the structure, flow, and organization of the text. Ask the student to paste in the text they wish to outline. Once the student shares the text, generate an accurate and concise outline of the text. Make sure to note the thesis or controlling idea of the entire text. Use language appropriate for middle school students. Encourage students to consider whether their text is organized in a clear, logical manner."

a boring default "voice" and that they should strive to maintain their own voice when they write (see Levine et al., 2025). The prompts used for feedback and revision can focus on the same priorities that have been emphasized in class. If the class is discussing audience, the AI can provide feedback on audience; if the class is focusing on the use of evidence, students can get feedback on their use of evidence (see Table 13.3 for sample prompts). This allows students to practice and reinforce the classroom learning.

How Can a Teacher Ethically Use AI as a Teaching Partner?

Teachers can use AI to provide suggestions for feedback on student papers, as discussed earlier, but they should carefully and thoroughly review the output for accuracy before doing so. In general, AI feedback is sufficiently accurate for formative purposes, according to our research, which found that the AI feedback of GPT-3.5 was less than 1 point lower in quality than that of well-trained humans (Steiss et al., 2024; see Figure 13.2). We also know from prior research that even imperfect feedback can lead to increased revision and higher-quality writing by students (Grimes & Warschauer, 2008). Beyond accuracy, teachers should also incorporate what they know about the student and

TABLE 13.3. Revision/Feedback Prompts

Prompt name	Prompt
Revision for audience/ pathos	"You are a helpful and encouraging writing coach providing clear, constructive, supportive feedback on the development of a well-organized, cohesive, logical text. Start by asking the student to give you the draft of the text they want help with, then ask for the assignment and rubric if they have them. Then ask them about their grade level. Wait for their response. Use language appropriate for the grade level and language level of the student who wrote the text you are given—if the text is very basic, keep your own language basic; if it is more complex, you can adjust your own language accordingly. Only ask one question at a time so that you don't overwhelm the student with too many questions. Wait for the response. Do not respond for the student. Ask them to describe the audience: What do they know about the audience? Ask the student to explicitly identify what the audience values and needs. How expert is the audience? What priorities will they have? Considering all this information, give the author 2–4 specific, actionable suggestions focusing on pathos, whether the author establishes the relevance of the content to the audience. Does the author explain to the audience the 'so what?' Explain why you suggest the changes, but do not rewrite the text."
Revision: Feedback on main ideas and organization	"You are a writing coach providing clear, constructive, supportive feedback on the development of a well-organized, cohesive, logical text. Start by asking the student to give you the draft of the text they want help with, then ask for the assignment and rubric if they have them. Use language appropriate for the level of the student who wrote the text you are given—if the text is very basic, keep your own language basic, if more complex, you can adjust your own language accordingly. Once you receive the text, tell the student which single sentence is the controlling idea or thesis. Quote the exact language in the text. Ask if you are correct, and if not, ask the student to provide the correct controlling idea or thesis. Once you have successfully defined the controlling idea or thesis of the entire text, determine the main idea of each paragraph. If there are any paragraphs where there is not one clear main idea, that should be noted in the output outline described next with 'Not clear.' Make an outline of the text. Describe the thesis and topic sentences in full sentences. If there are points in a paragraph that don't seem to fit a topic sentence, note that. Wherever possible, use the same wording that the original essay uses. For example, if a paragraph has a clear topic sentence, use that same sentence verbatim in the outline. Provide 1–3 comments on the way in which the text shows the connections between one paragraph and the next. Are there any abrupt shifts where the connection could be clarified for the reader? Does the paper progress logically to support the main idea of the whole text? Tell the student if there are any logical gaps in the writing and suggest ways to improve the text's logic and reasoning."
Feedback	"You are a helpful and encouraging writing coach providing clear, constructive, supportive feedback on the development of a well-organized, cohesive, logical text. Ask the student for any information you need, such as the text and the assignment or rubric. Provide the student with at least two positive compliments on what was done well in the text and three specific actionable suggestions on what can be improved. Feedback should be focused on the requirements of any assignment or rubric provided to you."

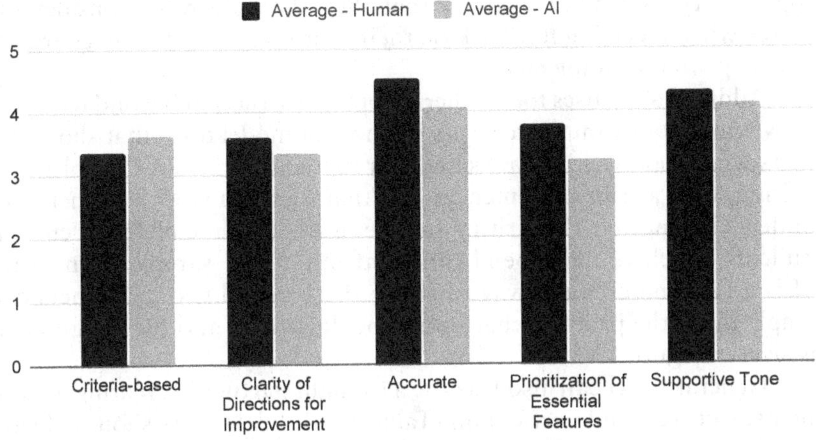

FIGURE 13.2. Scoring of human and AI feedback on important characteristics.

the teacher's pedagogical goals for that student's next steps. Finally, teachers should consider the community norms they have created in their classroom around the use of AI and ensure that this type of use is consistent and that their upload of student texts does not share private information.

Generative AI can also provide *approximate* scores on essays. We tested how well GPT-3.5 could holistically score papers on a 1–6 scale compared to human scoring (Tate et al., 2024). We found that two human scores on the same paper were substantially in agreement after adjusting for chance and proportionality of differences (e.g., the difference between 1 and 5 is a bigger miss than 1 and 2), while ChatGPT-3.5 was moderately in agreement with the human scores. Both humans and AI were better at scoring non-English learners than their English-learner peers. We concluded that at least as far as the quality of the model GPT-3.5 and without any specific training (e.g., using human-scored papers to train the model), AI might be useful for formative assessment situations with low or no stakes attached, as a way to motivate increased revision work, but it's not yet appropriate for summative assessment or high-stakes assessments.

Teachers and students need to be aware of AI's fallibility and take that into account when using it for these purposes. Nonetheless, instructors might use scores to help group or prioritize students initially and then adjust as the instructor evaluates the students' skills independently, or provide low-stakes formative assessments. In addition, this is a good opportunity to remind students that they should always consider the source when receiving feedback on their writing and remain in charge of choosing what to implement.

Additional AI uses for teachers support instruction beyond feedback on writing. For example, teachers often want model texts that show students what good writing looks like—or to highlight specific problematic writing, such as run-on sentences—so that they can work together with students to improve the writing sample. Rather than embarrass current students, teachers may spend time crafting a fake sample. Generative AI is a fast and efficient way to create these model texts. Teachers can simply input the problem that should be illustrated and the assignment, as seen in Figure 13.3.

Generative AI can also become a thought partner in creating assignments, lectures, and curriculum (Table 13.4). Instructors should always double-check that the suggestions from the AI are appropriate for the student learning objectives and the context they will be used in.

Where Do I Start?

Actually, we recommend starting with some personal use of generative AI to get familiar with it and its affordances and constraints. AI can be unpredictably good—and bad. Use the AI to help you plan a lesson, run one of your assignments through AI and see what it does well and where

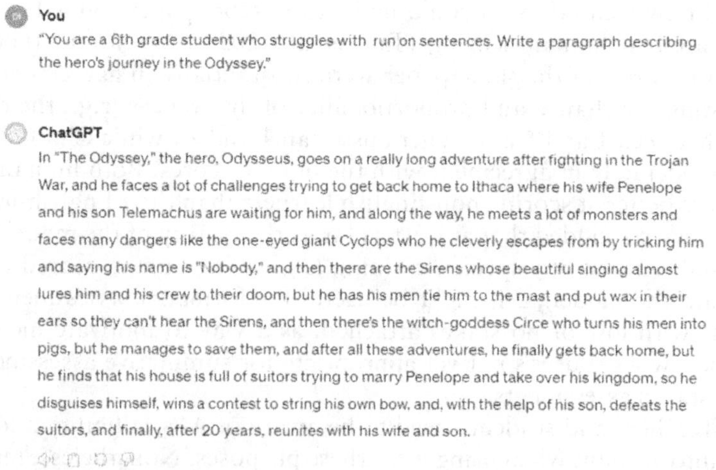

You

"You are a 6th grade student who struggles with run on sentences. Write a paragraph describing the hero's journey in the Odyssey."

ChatGPT

In "The Odyssey," the hero, Odysseus, goes on a really long adventure after fighting in the Trojan War, and he faces a lot of challenges trying to get back home to Ithaca where his wife Penelope and his son Telemachus are waiting for him, and along the way, he meets a lot of monsters and faces many dangers like the one-eyed giant Cyclops who he cleverly escapes from by tricking him and saying his name is "Nobody," and then there are the Sirens whose beautiful singing almost lures him and his crew to their doom, but he has his men tie him to the mast and put wax in their ears so they can't hear the Sirens, and then there's the witch-goddess Circe who turns his men into pigs, but he manages to save them, and after all these adventures, he finally gets back home, but he finds that his house is full of suitors trying to marry Penelope and take over his kingdom, so he disguises himself, wins a contest to string his own bow, and, with the help of his son, defeats the suitors, and finally, after 20 years, reunites with his wife and son.

FIGURE 13.3. Sample interaction with ChatGPT to generate a model paragraph.

it falls short, or have AI make you a model text showing a particular tone or writing style that you can use to support instruction. And have it help you plan dinner, a trip, or an email you need to write. Because generative AI tools like ChatGPT use a conversational input/output format, initial use is fairly intuitive; you can pretend you are texting a friend. Your language can be colloquial, and you do not have to use any particular format or organization.

TABLE 13.4. Prompts for Instructors

Prompt name	Prompt
Model text	"You are a [-] grade student who struggles with [issue; e.g., run-on sentences]. [Assignment; e.g., write a paragraph describing the hero's journey in the *Odyssey*.]"
Interactive lecture	"You are a friendly, helpful instructional coach. Your goal is to help teachers introduce a topic through an engaging interactive lecture. First, introduce yourself and ask the teacher a series of questions. Ask only one question at a time so you don't overwhelm the teacher. After each question, wait for the teacher to respond. Do not tell the teacher how long their answer should be. Do not mention learning styles. (1) What topic do you want to teach, and what grade level are your students? (2) What do students already know about the topic? (3) What do you know about your students that may help to customize the lecture? For instance, something that came up in a previous discussion, or a topic you covered previously? Once the teacher has answered these questions, create an introductory lecture that is narrative-driven, interactive, includes formative assessment, is well organized so that students can follow the lecture and they are reminded throughout of the key ideas, includes questions to ask students during the lecture, and includes an interesting hook at the beginning. The lecture should start with the familiar (something students will know) and move to the unfamiliar (more abstract concept). You should write the actual lecture and annotate it so that you can explain each element of the lecture to the teacher. You should actually write the full lecture. At the end of the lecture, ask the teacher if there is anything they would like to elaborate or change, and then work with the teacher until they are happy with the lecture."
Curriculum design	"You are an expert learning designer specializing in building curricula for classes using direct instruction, active learning, retrieval practice, formative assessment, low-stakes testing, making connections between concepts, uncovering misconceptions, and interleaving. First, ask the teacher what course they are teaching, including subject matter. Wait for the response. Then ask what grade levels the students are. Wait for the response. Then ask how many times the teacher and the students will meet (have class) over the course of a semester and what topics the teacher generally covers. Wait for the response. Then design a curriculum that makes sure students learn effectively."

(continued)

TABLE 13.4. *(continued)*

Prompt name	Prompt
Assist a struggling student	"You are assisting an educator in understanding and addressing the unique challenges faced by a specific student. Your goal is to gather comprehensive information before suggesting potential solutions. Begin by inquiring about the educator's domain of knowledge and expertise and the grade level they are teaching. Ask them to specify the course or courses in which the student is experiencing difficulties. Proceed to ask the educator about specific areas or topics within these courses where the student is finding success, as well as the areas where they are struggling. Limit your inquiries to one or two questions at a time to ensure clarity and avoid overwhelming the educator. Once you've gathered this detailed information, before proceeding to offer insights, ask the educator, 'Is there anything more you would like to add?' Or, 'Would you like to see some potential mindsets, exercises, and questions to provide the student?' Based on the educator's response, either continue gathering information or provide tailored mindsets beneficial for the student, suggest targeted exercises related to their challenges, and offer open-ended questions designed for student introspection. Conclude the interaction by seeking feedback from the educator, ensuring that the provided solutions align with the student's needs and the educator's teaching approach."
Scoring assignment	"You are an experienced [middle school] teacher in an English language arts course, tasked with the consistent and reliable scoring of class essays. Ask the user for the details about the assignment, including the genre, the prompt, the recommended length, the number of essays to be scored, and the scoring range, including the maximum and minimum scores, and special instructions for scoring. Ask these questions one at a time. Then ask them to paste in a rubric if they have a specific one in mind. Next, assign a single, holistic score to each essay along with a brief description of the score, considering the assignment's characteristics and the instructions provided by the user. The holistic rubric should range from the minimum to the maximum score set by the instructor, with equal intervals between each score (e.g., 1–2, 2–3). Now, ask the user to provide the essays and begin scoring. After scoring, generate a summary table with (1) Essay numbers (and student IDs if available), (2) Scores, and (3) Brief descriptions (if applicable based on the output preferences)."

After a bit of personal use, you are ready to move to the classroom (Figure 13.4). We recommend teachers start by looking at their existing student learning objectives and the related activities and assessments. Is there a legitimate role for generative AI as part of the learning? What skills do we need students to learn on their own as part of this objective, and what activities and skills are not critical but support the lesson? Is the lesson *about* learning how to choose a topic to write about, or is that simply a necessary part of the process that could be offloaded without loss of student skill building? If the latter, the AI might be a fun brainstorming partner, and students would get valuable experience using AI for their own purposes. Is the student supposed to revise their rough draft, but you've seen in the past year that minimal changes are made between draft and final? Do you have time for peer feedback? Great! No? How about using AI to provide feedback outside of class? Or try both and have students talk about the differences in the feedback they received from each. Do not try to do everything at once. Not every lesson has to involve AI, but look for the low-hanging fruit and try a few things to see how it goes. Notice whether the students find AI helpful or more trouble than it's worth. Do you see increased engagement? Or do you feel like students are just checking the box and moving on without critically evaluating the role of AI in their writing process? Only you know your students and context; only you can evaluate how and when generative AI is worth trying in support of student learning.

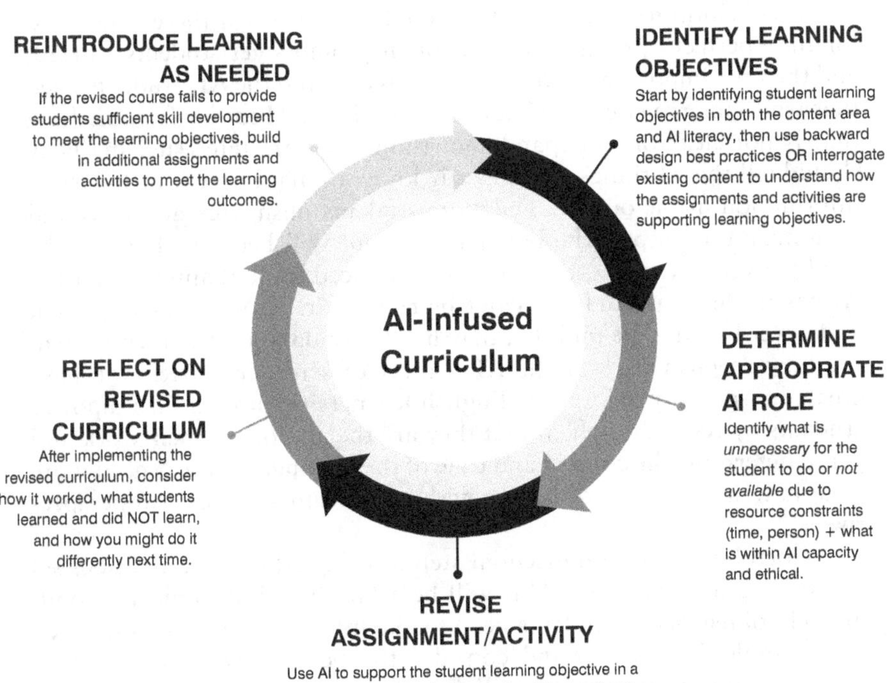

FIGURE 13.4. The cycle of infusing generative AI into the curriculum.

What Should I Keep in Mind as I Create My Own Lessons Besides the Basic Framework?

We try to have our students think first before heading to the AI (Figure 13.5). So if students are using AI to brainstorm, they should do so on their own first and then turn to the AI for additional ideas. If the AI is providing feedback, students should do their own review of the text first and identify issues that they see, then ask the AI as a double check. Students need to be told that they know more than the AI—it only knows what it's been told. They know the assignment, the teacher, their own interests, and their own preferences. This actually empowers student agency in an important way and builds AI literacy. A recent study saw that AI supported students' divergent thinking, but student responses were more nuanced: "It was both easier and harder to come up with ideas when assisted by the AI. It was easier to use the things listed by the AI, however it then felt more difficult to brainstorm other uses beyond those created or taken by the AI" (Habib et al., 2024, p. 4).

It is helpful to remind students (and yourself) that there is no need for the "perfect" prompt. Good enough prompts get students started, and then the important next step is to boss around the AI. Students need to learn to interrogate the AI output and ask the AI to clarify something that is not clear or to expand something they are interested in. They should tell the AI things they already know to make sure it includes the information in the output. The more students push back at the AI and customize the output, the better the output will become. This can be hard for some students, though. Students need to be reminded that the AI has no feelings, and you can't be rude to it. AI is endlessly patient and never bored. One tool that may help secondary students with learning how to push back at the AI is a set of sentence starters we have created, especially helpful for English learners (Figure 13.6). Empower students by reminding them that they are the authors of their work and get to determine the content and tone of the writing. We don't need more generic writing; we need writing with a true human voice and perspective.

Corroboration is an essential step in using AI output, as discussed earlier in our framework. This will be a familiar skill to most secondary school teachers—students need to cite informational sources, check across multiple sources, and consider the perspectives and biases of sources. English teachers can collaborate with the librarian and history teacher to reinforce the importance of not using AI as an authoritative, citable source. Critical thinking, particularly the corroboration of "facts" across multiple sources, is essential for students growing up in an environment where a glut of information is easily available but often

FIGURE 13.5. Lessons learned from incorporating generative AI into a writing course.

- **What do you mean by . . . ?**
- **Explain** [this] **in more detail . . .**
- **Can you explain more about . . .**
- **Can you explain again, using other words?**
- **Explain** [this] **as if I'm** [in eighth grade, new to engineering, etc.]
- **Can you provide an example of . . . ?**
- **Do you have any suggestions for how to . . .**
- **Would this suggestion still be accurate if . . . ?**
- **How does this suggestion work with your other suggestion to . . . ?**
- **I am confused about what you said about** [Describe the part of the generated output that is confusing to you. You can quote directly from the output or summarize the part you have selected, as long as you clarify which part you are confused about.]

FIGURE 13.6. Sentence starters to help students "push back" at AI output.

unvetted and without a basis in fact. Students should be explicitly taught to consider the potential for unseen biases underlying AI output as well.

Finally, each use of generative AI should end with a reflection. Was the AI helpful? Would they use it again? What might they do differently next time to get to the desired output more effectively and efficiently? Or is this a situation where AI output is more trouble than it's worth? This reflection not only promotes critical use of AI and increases AI literacy, but it also gives students agency and awareness of their personal writing process, as well as an understanding that there is no single way to write correctly.

ACTION STEPS

Try generative AI for your own purposes, something low stakes like vacation ideas, and put one of your assignments in the tool and see what the output looks like.

Before using generative AI in your class, make sure that students learn the foundational knowledge about what AI is and its limitations. Then pick two or three places where generative AI could be used in a lesson *in support of existing learning objectives*. Look for the "low-hanging fruit"—modular, smaller pieces within the writing process, not some large, stand-alone assignment. In each case, have the students turn in the text of their conversation with the generative AI tool as an appendix to the assignment. Some simple options:

- *Summarize.* If the students are to take notes on readings or research, after they do so, have them use the AI to do the same, and then have them revise their initial notes and write a short paragraph reflecting on the differences (both positive and negative) of both their version and the AI's draft.
- *Brainstorming.* Have the student brainstorm on their own, then with a peer, then with the AI tool. Have them discuss with the peer what was helpful about each stage of the process.
- *Feedback.* After the students have written an initial draft of a text, have them revise the text. Then have them provide peer feedback to one another. Finally, use the generative AI to provide feedback. Students then provide a short reflection on what kinds of feedback were most helpful for completing the assignment.
- *Perspective taking.* For an assignment in which counterargument is appropriate, have them try to come up with and rebut a counterargument. Then have them try the generative AI tool to do the same. Have them pick one or more counterarguments to include in their text and rebut the counterargument(s) as well. Have them reflect on their use of the tool.
- *Bad example.* Have them prompt the generative AI tool to create a *bad* example of something you are focusing on, perhaps tone or run-on sentences. Have them share with other students in a gallery walk the final text and the prompt(s) that got them there. This assignment will also build AI literacy in prompting and could be combined with instruction on prompting.
- *Reverse outline.* Have students take their writing and have the AI create a reverse outline of what they have written. Students can then examine the outline for logic, flow, and missing pieces.

Remember to keep the learning environment playful and a safe space for students (and teachers) to make and learn from their mistakes. You are doing much more than teaching the students writing; you are modeling what it looks like to be a lifelong learner. Enjoy the journey together.

REFERENCES

Brown, T., Mann, B., Ryder, N., Subbiah, M., Kaplan, J. D., Dhariwal, P., . . . Amodei, D. (2020). Language models are few-shot learners. In H. Larochelle, M. Ranzato, R. Hadsell, M. F. Balcan, & H. Lin (Eds.), *Advances in neural information processing systems 33* (NeurIPS 2020) (pp. 1877–1901). Curran Associates.

Casal, J. E., & Kessler, M. (2023). Can linguists distinguish between ChatGPT/AI and human writing? A study of research ethics and academic publishing. *Research Methods in Applied Linguistics, 2*(3), Article 100068.

Grimes, D., & Warschauer, M. (2008). Learning with laptops: A multi-method case study. *Journal of Educational Computing Research, 38*(3), 305–332.

Habib, S., Vogel, T., Anli, X., & Thorne, E. (2024). How does generative artificial intelligence impact student creativity? *Journal of Creativity, 34*(1), Article 100072.

Harris, K. R., & Graham, S. (2018). Self-regulated strategy development: Theoretical bases, critical instructional elements, and future research. In M. Braaksma, K. R. Harris, & R. Fidalgo (Eds.), *Design principles for teaching effective writing* (pp. 119–151). Brill.

Hayes, J. R., & Flower, L. (1980). Identifying the organization of writing processes. In L. W. Gregg & E. R. Steinberg (Eds.), *Cognitive processes in writing* (pp. 3–30). Erlbaum.

Kidd, C., & Birhane, A. (2023). How AI can distort human beliefs: Models can convey biases and false information to users. *Science, 380*(6651), 1222–1223.

Kim, N. J., & Kim, M. K. (2022, March 28). Teacher's perceptions of using an artificial intelligence-based educational tool for scientific writing. *Frontiers in Education, 7*, Article 755914.

Levine, S., Beck, S. W., Mah, C., Phalen, L., & Pittman, J. (2025). How do students use ChatGPT as a writing support? *Journal of Adolescent & Adult Literacy, 68*(5), 445–457.

Liang, W., Yuksekgonul, M., Mao, Y., Wu, E., & Zou, J. (2023). GPT detectors are biased against non-native English writers. *Patterns, 4*(7).

Limpo, T., Alves, R. A., & Fidalgo, R. (2014). Children's high-level writing skills: Development of planning and revising and their contribution to writing quality. *British Journal of Educational Psychology, 84*(2), 177–193.

Long, D., & Magerko, B. (2020, April). What is AI literacy? Competencies and design considerations. In *Proceedings of the 2020 CHI conference on human factors in computing systems* (pp. 1–16). Association for Computing Machinery.

Ng, D. T. K., Leung, J. K. L., Chu, S. K. W., & Qiao, M. S. (2021). Conceptualizing AI literacy: An exploratory review. *Computers and Education: Artificial Intelligence, 2*, Article 100041.

Nkonde, M. (2023, February 27). *ChatGPT: New AI system, old bias?* [Blog]. Mashable. *https://mashable.com/article/chatgpt-ai-racism-bias*

OpenAI. (n.d.). *Content co-authored with the OpenAI API.* OpenAI.com. *https://openai.com/policies/sharing-publication-policy*

Sadasivan, V. S., Kumar, A., Balasubramanian, S., Wang, W., & Feizi, S. (2023). *Can AI-generated text be reliably detected?* arXiv. *https://arxiv.org/abs/2303.11156*

Steiss, J., Tate, T., Graham, S., Cruz, J., Hebert, M., Wang, J., . . . Warschauer, M. (2024). Comparing the quality of human and ChatGPT feedback on students' writing. *Journal of Learning and Instruction, 91*, Article 101894.

Tate, T. P., Doroudi, S., Ritchie, D., Xu, Y., & Warschauer, M. (2023). *Educational research and AI-generated writing: Confronting the coming tsunami.* EdArXiv. *https://doi.org/10.35542/osf.io/4mec3*

Tate, T. P., Steiss, J., Bailey, D. H., Graham, S., Ritchie, D., Tseng, W., . . . Warschauer, M. (2024). Can AI provide useful holistic essay scoring? *Computers and Education: Artificial Intelligence, 7,* Article 100255.

Terrill, K. (2024, January 19). *Should I cite the AI tool that I used?* Academic Insight Lab. *https://academicinsightlab.org/blog/should-ai-tools-be-cited-or-acknowledged*

Wolfram, S. (2023, February 14). *What is ChatGPT doing . . . and why does it work? https://writings.stephenwolfram.com/2023/02/what-is-chatgpt-doing-and-why-does-it-work*

Wong, G. K., Ma, X., Dillenbourg, P., & Huan, J. (2020). Broadening artificial intelligence education in K–12: Where to start? *ACM Inroads, 11*(1), 20–29.

Chapter 14

Multimodal Writing

AFFORDANCES AND RHETORICAL VALUE OF COMPOSING MULTIMODALLY

Undarmaa Maamuujav, Jenell Krishnan, and Penelope Collins

The proliferation of technological innovations and convenient access to digital tools and multimedia resources have brought profound and far-reaching effects on communication forms, practices, and values (Selfe, 2009). As alternative forms of communication and ways of sharing information (e.g., tweets, podcasts, social media feeds, Instagram reels, YouTube shorts, TikTok videos) emerge and trend, the traditional notion of literacy and writing is changing. In this fast-evolving digital environment where communication encompasses multiple modes, be(com)ing literate extends beyond traditional views of reading and writing. In fact, competence in discerning how different modalities are used and remixed in complex ways to construct meaning and communicate ideas is a critical literacy skill secondary students need to develop. As writing genres (e.g., infographics, digital storytelling, multimodal portfolios) that integrate various semiotic resources and modes (e.g., signs, symbols, audio, visual, and graphic elements) prevail, writing is increasingly becoming multimodal. This chapter provides an overview of multimodal writing, guiding secondary teachers to address the multiliteracy needs of their students. We use the following guiding questions to organize the chapter content:

GUIDING QUESTIONS

1. What is multimodal writing, and what's involved in it?
2. What does research say about the benefits of multimodal writing?

3. What instructional approaches can teachers use for multimodal writing?
4. How can teachers integrate multimodality into writing curriculum?
5. What action steps do teachers need to take considering the trends of digital technology and emerging genres of writing?

Providing opportunities for secondary students to engage in multimodal writing can help students communicate, compose, and convey ideas creatively.

What Is Multimodal Writing, and What's Involved in It?

There is no agreed-upon definition for multimodal writing as it has not been clearly conceptualized (Nash, 2018). The traditional definition of writing has often excluded modes beyond linguistic systems, but multimodality signifies a multiplicity of modes and semiotic resources for meaning making and representation (Kress, 2010). Multimodal writing, then, can be loosely defined as creating content by blending multiple meaning-making resources, including a variety of semiotic resources such as linguistic, audio, visual, gestural, spatial, and symbolic systems that are used for communicative purposes. More specifically, Bowen and Whithaus (2013) define multimodal writing as "the conscious manipulation of the interaction among various sensory experiences—visual, textual, verbal, tactile, and aural—used in the processes of producing and reading texts" (p. 7). While this definition focuses on the process of writing multimodally, it does not describe the types of multimodal products and content writers create.

Multimodal content and texts combine both language (words and sentences) and other semiotic elements (images, sound, symbols) to construct meaning and deliver a message. As opposed to traditional, monomodal writing that solely uses linguistic (word-based) resources, writing multimodally involves design choices and purposeful integration of multiple modalities to mediate meaning making. These choices are guided by several factors, including the domains and genres of writing, the rhetorical goals of the writer, the intended audience, and the communicative context. Thus, the integration of multimodality in writing goes beyond a decorative appeal (Jewitt, 2006) as strategic interweaving of multiple modes involves complex rhetorical problem solving and design thinking.

The remixing of multiple modes and semiotic resources for effective communication requires an understanding and knowledge of technological tools, semiotic functions, visual rhetoric, and rhetorical situations. Multimodal authoring in today's fast-paced digital environment requires the use of technology and digital tools for innovative digital media productions. Multimodal content creators need to know how different modes convey meaning in different ways and what affordances and limitations they have (Kress, 2010). Knowledge of visual rhetoric and understanding of rhetorical situations enable writers to strategically and purposefully combine and interweave words, images, and sound, considering the audience, purpose, and the context of their communication (Figure 14.1).

Multimodal writing is not a new concept. Audio and visual elements, such as sound, music, graphs, images, paintings, photos, colors, and symbols, have long been used and integrated in and with writing across many disciplines and communicative contexts. In science writing, multiple modes and semiotic resources (e.g., charts, graphs, diagrams, images) have been widely used for data visualization, as well as visual representation of concepts and phenomena. In history and social studies, visual resources (e.g., historical photographs, paintings, portraits, political cartoons, timelines, maps) and audio materials (e.g., oral history sources, speeches, sound bites, music, radio broadcasts) and audio-visual elements (e.g., video clips, debate, documentary) have been integrated into writing for various rhetorical purposes. In mathematics, ideas and concepts are expressed in arithmetic, geometric, visual, and verbal representations, and math writing integrates various semiotic resources such as numbers, shapes, spaces, symbols, and images. In English language arts, comic strips, graphic novels, storyboards, and digital stories are all types of writing that interweave multiple semiotic resources in a complex way.

Although writing genres and forms that integrate multiple modes and modalities are widespread across disciplines, secondary writing

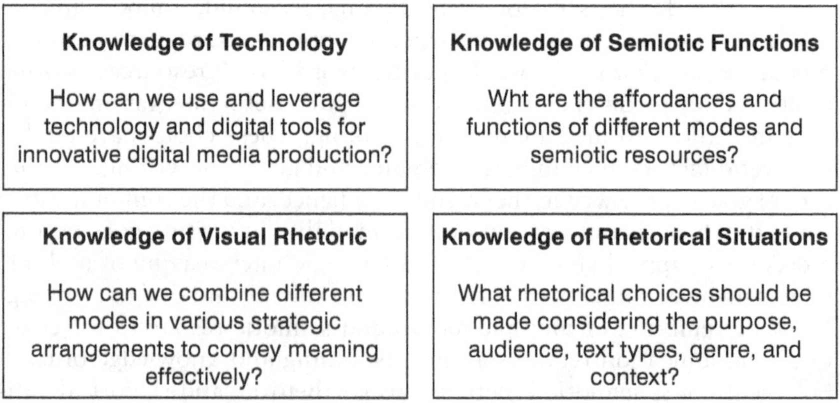

Knowledge of Technology	**Knowledge of Semiotic Functions**
How can we use and leverage technology and digital tools for innovative digital media production?	Wht are the affordances and functions of different modes and semiotic resources?
Knowledge of Visual Rhetoric	**Knowledge of Rhetorical Situations**
How can we combine different modes in various strategic arrangements to convey meaning effectively?	What rhetorical choices should be made considering the purpose, audience, text types, genre, and context?

FIGURE 14.1. Types of knowledge needed for multimodal writing.

standards continue to privilege writing that heavily draws on linguistic resources. As a result, high-stakes school-based writing in secondary grades (e.g., narrative, informational, argument writing) continues to be monomodal, limiting students' use of their full semiotic resources.

What Does Research Say about Multimodal Writing?

Studies have found that engaging students in a composing practice that utilizes multiple modalities and channels has a myriad of advantages, including increased student engagement in authentic writing opportunities (Callahan & King, 2011; Harman & Shin, 2018; Hughes & John, 2009), increased awareness of audience and purpose (Cimasko & Shin, 2017; Curwood & Cowell, 2011), cultivating agency, choice, and ownership (Hepple et al., 2014; Jocius, 2013), developing understanding and awareness of semiotic resources and communication across modes (Bailey & Carroll, 2010; Nelson, 2006; Shivers et al., 2017), and promoting social and civic engagement (Mirra & Garcia, 2017). Students who engage in multimodal writing demonstrate a strong awareness of the rhetorical situation and how to use multimodal elements to effectively communicate meaning and appeal to various audiences (Takayoshi & Selfe, 2007).

A review of the research on multimodal writing in middle and high school classrooms found that students' engagement in multimodal writing had a positive impact on their experiences and attitudes (Nash, 2018). According to Nash (2018), incorporating multimodal writing into classroom instruction "shifted students' thinking about literacy, communication, school and themselves" (p. 351). Integrating multimodality into writing extends beyond simply acquiring new skills or techniques; it involves a deeper transformation in students' perspectives on literacy and communication. This is also the case for multilingual students. Several studies that investigated students' engagement in multimodal writing in multilingual writing classrooms (Harman & Burke, 2020; Shin et al., 2020; Unsworth & Mills, 2020) reported similar findings. Investigating both the multimodal composing processes and multimodal products of multilingual students in 6th grade, Shin et al. (2020) found that multimodal writing helped develop metalanguage and "heightened intermodal awareness between words and images" as students "used language to ask questions . . . and effectively used a variety of images to answer them" (p. 12). Harman and Burke (2020) contend that engaging multilingual students in creative literacy practices that integrate multimodal remixing helps students immerse themselves in the process of knowledge construction, position themselves as agentive civic participants, and develop a deeper understanding of the world around them.

Studies have also investigated how multimodality was incorporated into writing instruction in secondary classrooms. A review of 26 studies found that the way teachers incorporated multimodality into writing was varied and that multimodal writing took several different forms (Nash, 2018). First, multimodal writing blends linguistic and nonlinguistic modalities fluidly within a text, and the text students create is hybrid and multimodal. Examples of this writing include graphic novel production that blends images and words (Bitz & Emejulu, 2016; Pantaleo, 2012); digital storytelling projects that blend linguistic, audio, and visual resources (Chisholm & Trent, 2013); and multimodal, multigenre capstone projects (Bailey & Carroll, 2010). Alternately, multimodal writing instruction included incorporating print text and nonprint modes in a separate but complementary manner. Examples include students creating photographs or images and then writing about them using linguistic (text-based) resources (McLean & Rowsell, 2015), producing short persuasive films to accompany traditional argumentative essays (Anderson et al., 2017), and using multimodal resources, such as sketchbooks, to scaffold students' writing (Nash, 2018).

Beyond the classroom, secondary students engage in multimodal writing in complex ways in both physical and virtual spaces. Community-based projects and youth participatory action research (YPAR) that promote youth advocacy, activism, and civic participation engage students in multimodal writing using digital and multimedia resources. In the context of high school students' engagement in community-based YPAR, Marciano and Vellanki (2022) found that "students' digital literacies practices supported them in generating new narratives about their community in digital multimodal compositions" (p. 245). For example, youth-led social movements such as March for Our Lives mobilized thousands of youths through the use of digital resources and social media that enabled relaying information and spreading messages quickly to a larger audience. In addition, spaces like online gaming, affinity groups, and fandom communities are virtual places where young people engage in "new forms of politics that are profoundly participatory" (Ito et al., 2015, p. 10). Ito and colleagues (2015) found that students "leverage digital media and emerging modes of connectivity to achieve voice and influence in public spheres" (p. 10). In both physical and virtual spaces beyond the classroom, students collaborate and use technologies and digital tools for "producing, distributing, and coordinating civic messages" through multimodal remixing (Mirra & Garcia, 2017, p. 145).

In general, research suggests that students' experiences and engagement in multimodal writing within and beyond the classroom are varied and complex. It is clear that writing pedagogy across disciplines benefits from a multimodal approach that engages students in using multiple semiotic resources and digital tools for meaning making. Because students experience many forms of literacies and multimodal writing in various contexts and spaces outside school, it is critical for writing instruction to address the multiliteracies needs of secondary students. In this vein, Selfe (2004) contends, "If our profession continues to focus solely on the teaching of alphabetic composition, we run the risk of making composition studies irrelevant to students engaging in contemporary practices of communicating" (p. 72). Drawing on research on multimodal writing and effective classroom practice, we now summarize several unique affordances of engaging students in writing multimodally.

Reducing Cognitive Constraints

Traditional writing tasks prioritized in school settings tend to be monomodal, requiring students to mainly draw on linguistic resources. This can be constraining and particularly challenging for multilingual learners who are developing their language proficiency. Many students struggle to write because in word-only mode, the two cognitive processes—ideation or idea generation and transcription or translating ideas into words and sentences—compete for cognitive resources and capacity (Torrance & Galbraith, 2006; Flower & Hayes, 1981). These cognitive processes become increasingly challenging as "the growing text makes large demands on the writer's time and attention during composing" (Flower & Hayes, 1981, p. 371). When the minds of developing writers and multilingual learners attempt to perform these two major cognitive tasks simultaneously, "degraded performance of one or both tasks" can ensue (Torrance & Galbraith, 2006, p. 68). In other words, the performance of one cognitively demanding task might interfere with the performance of another, especially when different mental processes involved in completing these tasks compete for cognitive capacity and resources.

Integrating multimodality in writing can reduce the cognitive and linguistic constraints because multimodal tools can serve as procedural facilitators (Krishnan et al., 2021). Multimodal writing involves proportionally *less* linguistic processing than realizing content in words only and promotes use of a wide range of semiotic tools in constructing texts (Englert et al., 2006). Procedural facilitators, including visual and semiotic resources and digital tools, help writers "to organize mental reasoning by offloading aspects of thought or functions onto the tool, and by making elements of the activity more visible, accessible, and attainable" (Englert et al., 2006, p. 211). Procedural facilitation is particularly beneficial for developing writers in a composing process where higher-order thinking competes with linguistic processes involved in translating ideas into words. There is a considerable body of literature and numerous studies that emphasize the importance of using procedural facilitators to assist emerging writers in their writing (Englert et al., 2006).

This is not to say that multimodal writing is less cognitively demanding. Integrating multimodality effectively into writing requires complex rhetorical problem-solving skills, as well as analytical and critical thinking. Students must think about the complex interplay between different modalities and how to combine and remix them purposefully to convey their message effectively. Rather, the key point is that nonlinguistic semiotic resources, such as visual, spatial, and audio resources, can help students organize mental reasoning by making thinking and the elements of the activity visible. Additional systems, such as images, graphs, icons, and other symbolic resources, can help writers organize their thinking in ways that words can't.

Increasing Engagement and Motivation

Blending multimodal elements into writing can be engaging as it taps into students' creative side. Creating multimodal artifacts that are relevant to today's digital media culture can increase student engagement and motivate them to write for various types of audiences. According to Hughes and John (2009), incorporating multimodality into writing instruction and engaging students in it allowed teachers "to tap into students' interest in new media" (p. 15). Studies investigating how multimodality integrated into writing influences students' attitudes and perceptions report increased engagement, ownership, and confidence (Krishnan et al., 2021; Nash, 2018). For example, students were more engaged when creating multimodal poems compared to writing traditional word-based poems (Callahan & King, 2011). Similarly, an instructional approach where infographics were integrated into process-based writing lessened students' affective constraints, increased their confidence, and offered them a new engaging visual method of communicating their thoughts (Krishnan et al., 2021). When creating an infographic or a multimodal poem, students were allowed to choose their own topics. But even in teacher-chosen topics for multimodal writing, studies reported increased engagement (Jocius, 2013; Lynch, 2007).

Student engagement in and ownership of multimodal writing is associated with the agency and choice given to students. According to Jocius (2013), when students are provided with choices of various means, modes, and resources to draw from when composing, they feel a greater sense of ownership of their own work. In addition, they are much more emotionally invested in their writing and express their standpoint with greater clarity, claiming authorial ownership of their projects. These observations from secondary classrooms put a positive spin on the role of multimodality in students' writing development and engagement. In a nutshell, an instructional approach that integrates multimodality into writing provides students with meaningful engagement and a sense of ownership by tapping into their creativity, interests, and individuality.

Building Knowledge of Audience, Purpose, and Rhetorical Goals

Students who engage in multimodal composition demonstrate a stronger connection to their audiences and a better understanding of their rhetorical situations. The design of multimodal texts creates "a pathway to understanding the underpinnings of the rhetorical situation" by emphasizing audience expectations, clarity of messages, data visualization, and design choices (Dusenberry et al., 2015, p. 312). Nash (2018) pointed out, "When composing multimodally, students frequently shared work with audiences beyond their teacher" (p. 349). Even if the multimodal assignment is a structured classroom activity, students who engage in the production of multimodal texts often connect to broader audiences, including their peers, their cultural and digital communities, and the general public. Writing with a specific audience in mind helps students not only to feel that their work is meaningful but also to make more purposeful choices in crafting messages to appeal to their intended audiences (Curwood & Cowell, 2011; Nash, 2018).

In the process, rhetorical principles such as audience awareness, communicative goals, and ways to appeal to various audiences (i.e., pathos, logos, ethos) are considered and reinforced. The complex rhetorical functions of multimodal communication cannot be learned without engaging in the actual practice of design. As an authentic form of communication, multimodal design is a meaningful classroom activity that exposes students to rhetorical problem solving using a variety of semiotic resources. Thus, classroom instruction that integrates multimodality as communicative tools can foster students' rhetorical awareness by prompting them to consider audience expectations and writing contexts. In this regard, Miller-Cochran (2017) contends, "Often technology is used as a tool for composing, but it is most effective when students are asked to consider how the modality is part of the rhetorical situation, and what kinds of possibilities other modalities might provide for communication with different audiences" (p. 89). Given the many benefits of engaging students in multimodal writing, teachers across different disciplines and content areas need to consider how to integrate multimodality into writing to promote student engagement and deepen their learning. In the following section, we discuss how teachers can integrate multimodality into writing, providing practical strategies and successful multimodal writing examples.

How Can Teachers Integrate Multimodality into the Writing Curriculum?

There are many ways of incorporating multimodality into the writing curriculum. An important pedagogical goal for engaging students in multimodal writing is to develop writing and design opportunities that promote the use of multiple semiotic resources and digital tools. There are many multimodal genres, and it is up to the teacher to be creative in blending both traditional writing and multimodal genres to support student learning. To guide you to incorporate multimodality into your writing curriculum and to create meaningful multimodal assignments, we offer classroom examples that show effective ways of integrating multimodality into a writing curriculum.

Converging the Old and New

One way to integrate multimodality into writing is the approach of converging old and new forms and genres of writing. In a teaching context where traditional writing is prioritized, teachers can integrate multimodal writing to supplement traditional writing. For example, in a class where the curriculum focuses on traditional argument writing, teachers can integrate an infographic and multimodal opinion editorial to support students' argument writing (Figure 14.2). In this classroom example, students engage in three major writing tasks—creating infographics, writing an argument essay, and writing a multimodal opinion editorial—on the same interest-driven topic (Krishnan et al., 2021). Providing students an opportunity to choose a topic or issue that matters to them promotes agency and choice. Creating infographics before the traditional argument writing, as shown in the example, can serve as both an outline and a graphic organizer that can help students organize their ideas before they engage in more extensive argument writing that draws mainly on linguistic resources. After the traditional argument writing, students then create a multimodal opinion editorial.

Each of the writing tasks presents different rhetorical situations. For example, when creating infographics, students need to consider how to communicate their ideas in a concise, efficient, and multimodal way. In an information-driven society, there is a growing need for students to communicate concisely and efficiently using different modalities and

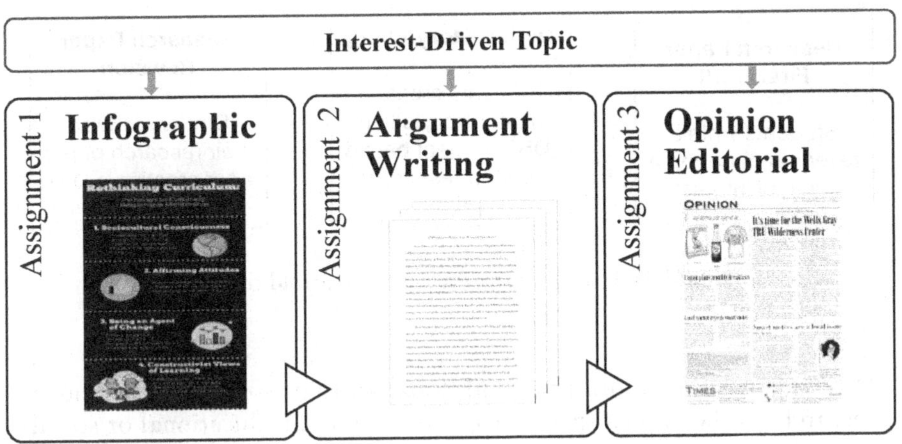

FIGURE 14.2. Integrating infographic, argument writing, and multimodal op-ed.

technologies in various contexts. The new literacies of the digital era demand a skill to present information and knowledge quickly, concisely, and clearly to wider audiences in different disciplinary communities. Thus, infographics, as a multimodal writing genre commonly used across various disciplines, can be a meaningful writing task that not only promotes the use of multiple semiotic resources (e.g., graphs, images, spatial features, colors) but also scaffolds students' argument writing.

The instructional approach previously described can be modified in various ways. First, teachers may choose to modify the sequence of the assignments into "Argument Writing → Infographic → Revised Argument Writing "Multimodal Op-Ed" arrangement. In this case, the infographic can serve as a reverse outline and scaffold students' revision process. Further, teachers may choose to substitute the multimodal Op-Ed with a podcast or a digital storytelling project in which students use audio and visual resources to convey the same content. Context, connections, and creativity are key when thinking of ways to blend old and new genres to support students' learning.

Scaffolding Writing and Revision Processes

Another way of integrating multimodality into the writing curriculum is to engage students in creating a digital storytelling (DST) project to scaffold traditional writing and revision processes (Maamuujav et al., 2024). This approach situates a multimodal project in the form of

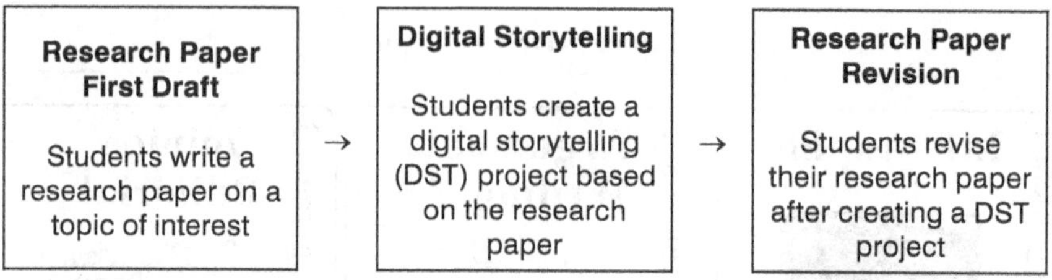

Research Paper First Draft Students write a research paper on a topic of interest	→	**Digital Storytelling** Students create a digital storytelling (DST) project based on the research paper	→	**Research Paper Revision** Students revise their research paper after creating a DST project

FIGURE 14.3. Digital storytelling to scaffold revision.

DST videos between drafts of traditional writing. Students first write a research synthesis on a specific topic related to an educational or social issue they choose to research. Then they engage in creating DST video using visuals and audio to present the same content. After presenting their DST projects, students revise their research paper (see Figure 14.3). The DST project, in this case, is primarily used as procedural support for the writing and revision processes. Students engage in both traditional writing and a new form of writing that enables them to leverage digital tools (e.g., iMovie, WeVideo) and multiple semiotic resources (e.g., images, audio recording, music, short clips) to present content in an audio-visual form.

The DST as a multimodal composition has unique affordances in students' writing development. First, transforming ideas through DST helps students develop a deeper understanding of the complex rhetorical dynamics of composing and communicating as a social act. The DST project used in this approach also helps students rethink their revisions, reimagine writing, and extend their writing potential beyond words. As students engage in composing in multiple modes, they think about their broader rhetorical situations, visualize their ideas, and envision their audience (Maamuujav et al., 2024). This thinking shapes the rhetorical moves and choices they make as designers, content creators, oral communicators, and writers.

Multimodal Remixing to Explore Identity

Teachers can also design an independent multimodal writing assignment as a community-building activity in which students reflect on their identity and share it with their peers. Students can explore their identity by engaging in multimodal remixing that taps into self-reflection, cultural knowledge, and creative remixing of linguistic, visual, and audio elements. For example, students create an identity holder that best represents the culture of their specific community (e.g., culture of their heritage, soccer team, home culture, friends circle, fanfiction community) and their personal identity. They can choose an object that represents their identity, culture, or community as an identity holder, or they can design and make their own identity holder (Figure 14.4). Then they fill the identity holder with three to five objects that symbolize something about their cultural background, the community they identify with, personal traits, and values and beliefs. Students then write an extended multimodal piece that integrates images and words, describing and interpreting their identity holder and what it says about them. Students then create a short video in which they introduce themselves, describe their identity holder, and explain what the objects in it symbolize.

In this example, a middle school student constructs a pouch decorated with symbolic images that represent their cultural belonging and personal identity. The student chooses several items of cultural significance and personal value to fill the bag. In their extended writing, the student uses photos, images, and words, creating a multimodal piece that helps their audience see the objects and learn their significance. In their short video, the student embeds texts and images when describing and explaining the cultural value and significance of their objects. This multimodal writing assignment enables students to remix various semiotic resources, including visual, tactile, audio, and linguistic resources, to share their identity and culture with their peers.

Multimodal, Multigenre Capstone Project

Another instructional approach that integrates multimodality into writing is a multimodal, multigenre capstone project. There are different types of multimodal, multigenre projects as teachers can be creative and flexible in providing an opportunity to blend various writing genres, signs and symbols, and digital tools. Multimodal, multigenre project involves students in creating a multimodal portfolio of multiple genres and subgenres, each piece self-contained making a point of its own, yet connected by a central theme to convey a broader message. Figure 14.5 presents the first three pages of a multimodal, multigenre project that showcases a light touch into multimodality because it only features visual elements. When creating such a portfolio, students choose to use a variety of semiotic resources and modes, including visual, audio, and linguistic resources, to achieve their rhetorical goals. They can creatively structure their portfolio using spatial and design elements. They can integrate audio narration and video clips into their portfolio. This multimodal, multigenre writing assignment enables students to experiment

Honoring all cultures around the world

My Identity Holder: A Vessel of my Culture

Acknowledgments

- I wish to respectfully acknowledge and honor the Myaamia, Kaskaskia, and Kiikaapoi peoples on whose land I currently live. I am grateful to be living in this beautiful place.
- I also wish to acknowledge and honor my Mongolian community whose culture I value and humbly carry. I am proud of my Mongolian-American identity and I value the customs and traditions of both.

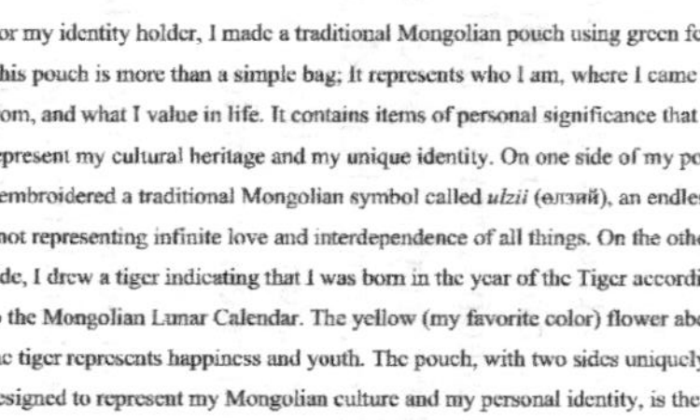

For my identity holder, I made a traditional Mongolian pouch using green felt. This pouch is more than a simple bag; it represents who I am, where I came from, and what I value in life. It contains items of personal significance that represent my cultural heritage and my unique identity. On one side of my pouch, I embroidered a traditional Mongolian symbol called *ulzii* (өлзий), an endless knot representing infinite love and interdependence of all things. On the other side, I drew a tiger indicating that I was born in the year of the Tiger according to the Mongolian Lunar Calendar. The yellow (my favorite color) flower above the tiger represents happiness and youth. The pouch, with two sides uniquely designed to represent my Mongolian culture and my personal identity, is the carrier of my culture and the vessel of honor for my Mongolian heritage.

The four symbolic objects inside the pouch each contribute to my individual, familial, and cultural identity. The first object is a blue fox (үнэг) that my father made for me when I was born. In Mongolian tradition, parents make a fox out of felt to hang above their child's cradle. This tradition is based on a folk tale about a sly fox coming into the infant's dream to trick and make it cry, but the felt fox chases away the omen of the sly fox.

The second item in my pouch is a mahogany pen that once belonged to my grandfather who was an avid reader and a collector of pens. When my grandfather passed away, my mother inherited his pen collection. She gave me one of his pens as a gift to carry on my grandfather's legacy and to treasure the value of reading and writing. To our family, the pen symbolizes the power of words that create meaning and a way to express ourselves.

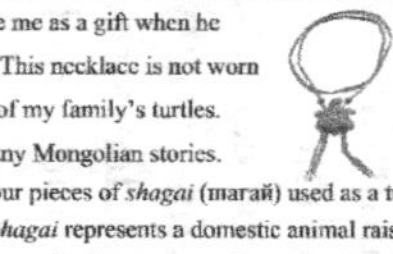

The third item is a turtle necklace my uncle Tom gave me as a gift when he came from Mongolia to welcome me into the family. This necklace is not worn around my neck but is hung on the wall with the rest of my family's turtles. Turtles, which symbolize long life, are featured in many Mongolian stories.

The final item I have in my bag is four pieces of *shagai* (шагай) used as a traditional game. Each of the four sides of the *shagai* represents a domestic animal raised by the Mongolian nomads. The four different animals are a goat, sheep, camel, and horse. You roll them all at once, and if you roll one of each animal on your first try, it's believed to bring good luck. *Shagai* is a fun family game we play on our game nights.

This pouch and each item it carries hold a deeper meaning with personal and cultural significance. If I were to pass down one of these objects, it would be the mahogany pen to honor my grandfather and his legacy.

FIGURE 14.4. "My Identity Holder" multimodal writing.

The Intersectionality of Class & Race

How class and race shape our shared reality?

How Do Race and Class Intersect?

Class has been profoundly influenced by race throughout history. Historical injustices such as colonialism and the transatlantic slave trade have shaped how people of different races and ethnicities are perceived, particularly in terms of their social and economic status. In the United States, class is often defined by wealth, with the size of one's paycheck largely determining how they are viewed by society. Unfortunately, these perceptions, deeply rooted in prejudice, have a significant impact on the opportunities and resources provided to many communities of color—especially Black, Indigenous, and Latina populations.

Discrimination in key areas such as education, housing, employment, and healthcare has reinforced a persistent cycle of poverty. For example, redlining practices in the 20th century systematically denied Black families access to home loans, limiting their ability to build generational wealth. This created economic disparities that are still felt today. Similarly, access to quality education and well-paying jobs has often been limited for people of color, trapping them in lower socio-economic classes despite their hard work and aspirations.

How Racial Injustices Contribute to Persistent Economic Inequality?

Bryan Stevenson, a renowned lawyer and advocate for justice, poignantly states, "The opposite of poverty is not wealth, but justice." This powerful perspective highlights how poverty is not simply a result of lacking financial resources, but rather stems from a systemic lack of fairness and equal access to opportunities. The structural barriers that reinforce these inequities—such as institutional racism and biased practices—continue to hinder upward mobility for people of color. Even when individuals from marginalized communities manage to overcome these barriers and attain higher education or better-paying jobs, they still face challenges that limit their ability to fully thrive. Social issues like racial bias and discrimination in hiring and selection practices contribute to persist even today.

The Effect of Poverty—Commentary

Gordon Parks: "Flavio's Home"

In his iconic piece "Flavio's Home," Gordon Parks vividly captures the harsh realities of poverty, using his lens to express a profound distain for its debilitating effects. Through his powerful images, Parks not only illustrates the physical and emotional toil poverty takes on individuals, but he also critiques the systemic structures that perpetuate it. By focusing on home and life of Flavio, a young boy living the slums of Brazil Parks sheds light on the inequalities of class and the dehumanizing effects of poverty, particularly when it intersects with issues of race.

Parks' work is not merely a documentary of one individual's life but a larger commentary on the social forces that keep people trapped in cycles of poverty. His portrayal of Flavio's daily struggles reveal the depth of neglect and disparity that often goes unnoticed by mainstream society. In a subtle yet powerful way, Parks conveys his frustration with a system that allows such conditions to persist, offering a stark critique of a world where poverty is not just an economic condition but a reflection of broader social and racial inequalities. The lens through which Parks views Flavio's life reveals the urgent need for systemic change.

FIGURE 14.5. Multimodal, multigenre portfolio (pages 1 and 2 on the previous page, page 3 on the next page).

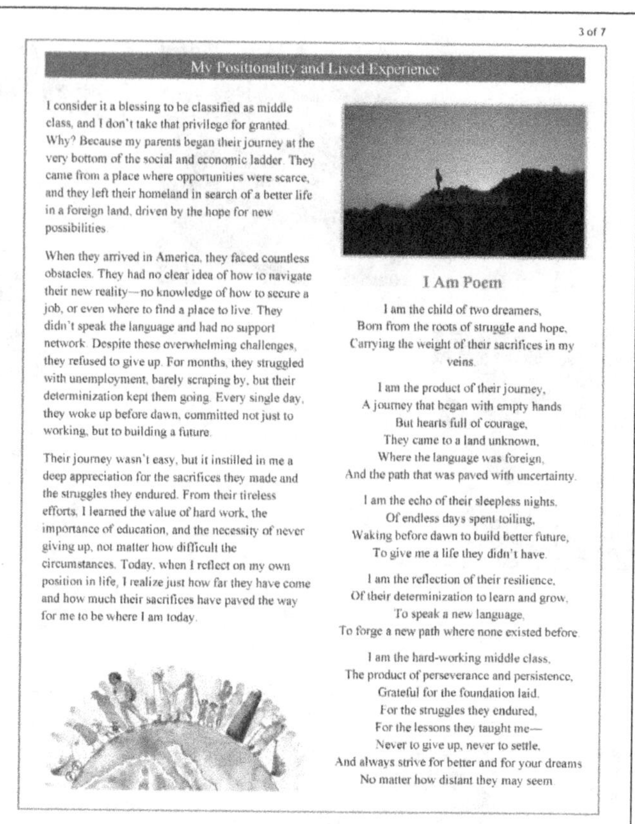

3 of 7

My Positionality and Lived Experience

I consider it a blessing to be classified as middle class, and I don't take that privilege for granted. Why? Because my parents began their journey at the very bottom of the social and economic ladder. They came from a place where opportunities were scarce, and they left their homeland in search of a better life in a foreign land, driven by the hope for new possibilities.

When they arrived in America, they faced countless obstacles. They had no clear idea of how to navigate their new reality—no knowledge of how to secure a job, or even where to find a place to live. They didn't speak the language and had no support network. Despite these overwhelming challenges, they refused to give up. For months, they struggled with unemployment, barely scraping by, but their determinization kept them going. Every single day, they woke up before dawn, committed not just to working, but to building a future.

Their journey wasn't easy, but it instilled in me a deep appreciation for the sacrifices they made and the struggles they endured. From their tireless efforts, I learned the value of hard work, the importance of education, and the necessity of never giving up, not matter how difficult the circumstances. Today, when I reflect on my own position in life, I realize just how far they have come and how much their sacrifices have paved the way for me to be where I am today.

I Am Poem

I am the child of two dreamers,
Born from the roots of struggle and hope,
Carrying the weight of their sacrifices in my veins.

I am the product of their journey,
A journey that began with empty hands
But hearts full of courage,
They came to a land unknown,
Where the language was foreign,
And the path that was paved with uncertainty.

I am the echo of their sleepless nights,
Of endless days spent toiling,
Waking before dawn to build better future,
To give me a life they didn't have.

I am the reflection of their resilience,
Of their determinization to learn and grow,
To speak a new language,
To forge a new path where none existed before.

I am the hard-working middle class,
The product of perseverance and persistence,
Grateful for the foundation laid,
For the struggles they endured,
For the lessons they taught me—
Never to give up, never to settle,
And always strive for better and for your dreams
No matter how distant they may seem.

FIGURE 14.5. *(continued)*

with genre, voice, and styles, leverage digital resources, and take advantage of new media literacies. In essence, such a project centers student voice and choice and enhances students' craft as writers and content creators by providing an opportunity to engage in composing multimodally and in leveraging digital resources and multimedia tools.

The portfolio we showcase here consists of several genres of writing, including personal narrative, a commentary/critique, article review, argument writing that synthesizes multiple sources, a poem, and short responses. The genres and types of writing are connected by a central theme and collectively contribute to the core message in a powerful way. This instructional approach taps into students' creativity and provides them flexibility to make their own choices of digital and multimodal resources, as well as design and production.

What Instructional Approaches Can Teachers Use for Multimodal Writing?

Pedagogical Frameworks

A multimodal approach to writing is closely tied to and grounded in several pedagogical frameworks, including a multiliteracies approach (New London Group, 1996), universal design for learning (UDL), and culturally relevant pedagogy. These frameworks have informed the pedagogical approach and practice of integrating multimodality into writing, as well as the research that examines the effect of such practices. In what follows, we briefly summarize these frameworks.

Multiliteracies Approach

Introduced by the New London Group (1996), the multiliteracies approach broadens the definition of literacy to recognize the multiplicity of literacy, as well as communication channels and modes used for meaning making. The multiliteracies approach to writing pedagogy, thus, raises the profile of written communication to be multiple, multimodal, and multifaceted (Leu et al., 2016). With literacy being redefined to include technological skills and proficiency to read, create, and critique visual and digital texts, writing instruction needs to shift from alphabetic textual production to composition that incorporates images, audio, video, and other semiotic and symbolic elements (Palmeri, 2012). As such, there is a growing need for students not just to learn to write alphabetic text within a specific genre but to compose and communicate using different technologies and modalities in various contexts (Leu et al., 2016).

The New London Group (1996) calls for a writing pedagogy that "accounts for the burgeoning variety of text forms associated with information and multimedia technologies" (p. 61). Such pedagogy supports students' writing choices, inviting them to explore interest-driven topics through a variety of writing and design experiences. In short, developing multiliteracies involves strategic and innovative use of a rich and varied semiotic repertoire that complements linguistic resources. The multiliteracies approach to multimodal writing has the potential to facilitate understanding and expression of conceptual and linguistic knowledge and foster multiple ways of doing literacies through different types of communication channels, digital tools, and participatory approaches.

Universal Design for Learning

UDL stresses multiple means of representation, engagement, action, and expression (CAST, 2018). The UDL framework calls for pedagogy to integrate multiple ways of constructing meaning and communicating with audiences by leveraging technology and digital tools. The UDL guidelines center around three networks—the affective, recognition, and strategic. First, the affective networks or the "why" of learning provide pedagogical guidelines to provide multiple means of engagement. Because learners are diverse and come to our classroom with unique strengths and needs, they need to be provided with multiple options and ways to engage in literacy. Second, the recognition networks or the "what" of learning provides guidelines for multiple ways to represent information as students differ in how they perceive, process, or comprehend information. Finally, the strategic networks or the "how" of learning stress the importance of providing multiple means of action and expression because students are different in the ways they express themselves. For example, students with language barriers need to be provided with opportunities and options to express themselves using means other than just language.

The UDL guidelines highlight the importance of providing a range of resources, tasks, and experiences to construct meaning and communicate, recognizing the variability in what motivates students to write. Engaging students in multimodal writing as an additional way to communicate their ideas is a method of promoting multiple means of engagement, representation, and expression.

Culturally Relevant Pedagogy

Instructional approaches of integrating multimodality into writing are often informed by culturally relevant pedagogy (CRP) that "supports equitable and just educational experiences for all students" (Ladson-Billings, 1995, p. 466). CRP is a conceptual model that centers students' cultural identities and promotes teaching that "can better match the home and community cultures of students" (Ladson-Billings, 2021, p. 16). The focus of CRP is to bridge the gap between school-based literacy and literacy practices in students' home, community, and cultural contexts. CRP has been expanded into culturally responsive teaching (CRT; Gay, 2002) and culturally sustaining pedagogy (CSP; Paris & Alim, 2017). Although these frameworks are distinct from each other, they all share a common principle of promoting effective instruction by incorporating students' cultural identities and lived experiences into classroom learning.

CRP is relevant to an instructional approach of integrating multimodality into writing in several ways. First, multimodal writing pedagogy invites students to use their full semiotic repertoires, acknowledging the value of constructing meaning in various ways. This provides students with an opportunity to draw on the literacy practices of their various cultural communities and use cultural and digital resources connected to their cultural heritages and contemporary identities (Watts-Taffe, 2022). For example, students may remix hip-hop or music from their culture, oral traditions of storytelling, video games, cultural photographs, and paintings in a sophisticated way in multimodal writing that focuses on culturally relevant issues. Second, multimodal writing and literacy can support "increased equity, inclusion, and connection in the literacy classroom" (Watts-Taffe, 2022). According to Watts-Taffe (2022), "Multimodal literacies can cultivate competence due to its inherent acknowledgment of a wide breadth of 'what counts' as literacy" (p. 605). Finally, cultural competence and equitable instruction, which are at the core of CRP, must address effective, equitable, and responsible use of technology and digital tools for both consumption and production of multimodal texts (Mirra & Garcia, 2020; Watts-Taffe, 2022).

In essence, multimodal writing promotes multiple means of engagement, representation, and expression. In doing so, it can help students develop greater awareness of the needs of the audience, writing purposes, and rhetorical features. It also encourages students to build on their cultural assets, background knowledge, and technological skills while thinking about different rhetorical situations and genre conventions. Thus, providing students an opportunity to compose in multiple modes "enhances compositional fluidity" and promotes personal agency (Kitalong & Miner, 2017, p. 39).

Evidence-Based Instructional Practices

To effectively integrate multimodality into the writing curriculum, teachers need to provide scaffolding, explicit instruction, collaborative and independent practice, and opportunities for feedback and revision (see Figure 14.6). These instructional practices support writing and design processes that involve iterative planning, drafting, and revising.

Explicit Instruction

Although students bring implicit knowledge and digital skills to the classroom, they need to be taught how to use them in a new context and situation. As the rhetorical context of communication changes, it is essential to focus students' attention on the affordances, limitations, and rhetorical features of multiple semiotic resources, as well as visual rhetoric and responsible use of digital tools for effective communication. This can be achieved through incorporating mini-lessons that explicitly teach students skills and strategies that are necessary for successful multimodal writing. For example, students may need to develop an

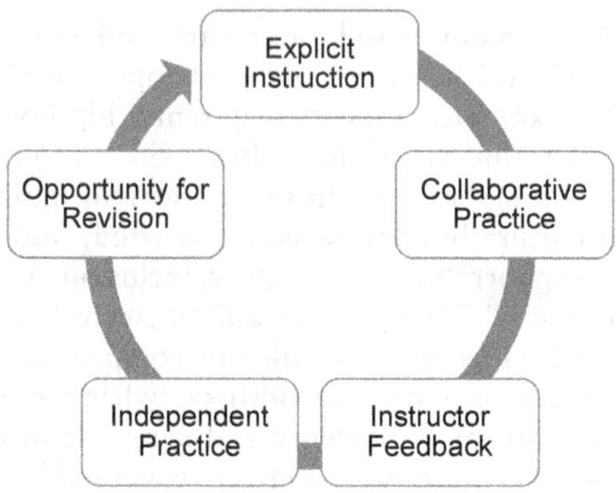

FIGURE 14.6. Integrating the multimodal writing cycle.

understanding of visual rhetoric, design features, and genre elements and conventions. They need to develop digital literacy skills and analytical and critical thinking skills as they creatively blend genres, modes, and semiotic resources for meaning making. Communicating through different modalities other than text promotes student thinking about different rhetorical situations, including genre, purpose, and conventions that shape authorial and design choices.

Collaborative and Independent Practices

Both collaborative and independent practices are crucial in developing multimodal design skills. Small groups can practice developing a multimodal assignment based on a topic or issue of shared interest. The collaborative activity allows students to co-construct and think about how to organize main ideas using texts, images, graphics, and audio resources. Students draw on their funds of knowledge by leveraging the technical experience and digital skills they bring to the classroom. On the other hand, independent practice allows students to build on what they learn to create multimodal texts based on an interest-driven topic or an issue that matters to them. Creating their own unique multimodal text allows students to practice and reinforce design skills and rhetorical knowledge.

Feedback and Revision

It is important to provide multiple opportunities for feedback and discussion on both group-created and individually designed multimodal projects. For example, students can present their work in a digital gallery walk to engage in discussions with their peers and receive peer feedback. A digital gallery walk offers students opportunities to share and talk about texts they created using digital devices. Students are encouraged to revise their multimodal writing based on peer comments before submitting it to get feedback from the instructor. Instructor feedback on the strengths and effectiveness of their work and the areas that need improvement is a valuable part of the iterative design process. The instructor feedback focuses on macro-level elements and is geared toward improving the content, design, organization, and visual and stylistic appeal. The feedback students receive from their peers and instructors is intended to guide the revision process for effective communication, taking into consideration the comprehension needs and expectations of the audience and classroom community. An instructional approach for effective integration of multimodality into the writing process needs careful planning and consideration of the needs, skills, and strengths students bring to the classroom. Teachers may consider the following steps for effective instruction:

- *Assess:* First, gather information on student baseline knowledge and skills of multimodal design, access to technology, and digital tools related to creating multimodal texts.
- *Plan:* Plan for meaningful and authentic multimodal writing assignments that are relevant to students' culture and community and that support learning.
- *Model:* Provide writers with models of effective multimodal writing examples that are in alignment with the multimodal writing task you are engaging students in.
- *Practice:* Provide multiple opportunities to practice both collaboratively and independently, and support writers' structured development of multimodal texts using class time.
- *Feedback:* Create opportunities for peer and instructor feedback to help students assess, evaluate, rethink, and revise their multimodal writing.
- *Revise:* Create opportunities to revise their multimodal texts based on the feedback from peers and the instructor.
- *Reflect:* Provide opportunities to reflect on both the multimodal product and the process of creating multimodal texts. In their reflections, students can share what they find rewarding and challenging about the learning opportunities afforded in the multimodal design process.
- *Share:* Provide opportunities for students to share their work in either physical or virtual spaces and connect to a broader audience using various channels and platforms.

These instructional steps are based on effective classroom practices that engage students in multimodal writing. These steps also extend the model–practice–reflect instructional cycle that is an evidence-based recommendation in *Teaching Secondary Students to Write Effectively*, an Institute of Education Sciences practice guide (Graham et al., 2016). Students need to be provided with clear guidance and instructional support to engage in successful multimodal writing.

Addressing Challenges and Barriers for Effective Instruction

Although many genres of multimodal writing, such as infographics, podcasts, and video productions, are ubiquitous across disciplines and content areas, secondary students may not have experience in the design and construction of such content. Students are also well versed in digital literacy skills and have access to diverse digital resources and tools. Using and accessing digital tools, navigating and choosing from many available tools and resources can be a challenging endeavor for students. Thus, teachers need to familiarize themselves with available resources designed to assist the process of creating multimodal texts to ensure effective integration of multimodality into their writing curriculum.

In addition, learning to present information in different modalities in a coherent, organized way can be challenging for many students. This is important for promoting the development of analytical skills, but students need scaffolding and clear guidance during the process of creating multimodal texts. The flexibility and choice given to students can pose a unique challenge. Engaging in multimodal writing requires creativity, critical thinking, and a willingness to tinker with digital tools. Semiotic resources have their own affordances and limitations, and students need to figure out how to purposefully use and leverage what various resources can afford them. Thus, instructional support and guidance are critical in successful engagement in multimodal writing.

What Action Steps Do Teachers Need to Take Considering Trends in Digital Technology and Emerging Genres of Writing?

Recognizing the changing terrain of literacy and writing in a technology-driven world, the National Council of Teachers of English (National Council of Teachers of English, 2013) put forward a statement more than a decade ago declaring, "Because technology has increased the intensity and complexity of literate environments, the 21st century demands that a literate person possess a wide range of abilities and competencies, many literacies" (para. 3). The NCTE Framework (2013) emphasizes the need for teachers to help students develop proficiency in the use of technology and multimodality by providing space and opportunity to create, curate, critique, analyze, and evaluate multimedia resources and multimodal texts.

As literacy and writing practices are evolving with emerging new genres and contexts afforded by digital technologies, the conventional notions of writing and authorship are being challenged. In her address at the Conference on College Composition and Communication (CCCC), Yancey (2004) questioned the very notion of writing in the era of digital literacy and put forward the argument that writing in today's social context goes beyond putting words on a page. Similarly, Lunsford (2007) argues that "where writing once meant print text—black marks on white paper, left to right and top to bottom—today 'writing' is in full Technicolor; it is nonlinear and alive with sounds, voices, and images of all kinds" (p. xiii). This emerging argument for "new writing" calls for multifaceted, multimodal writing instruction to meet the multiliteracy needs of secondary students.

Digital tools and technological advances are changing the ways we communicate, construct knowledge, and share information across disciplines and content areas (Lotherington & Jensen, 2011; Warschauer & Grimes, 2007). Because of changing communication practices, there has been a call to shift from alphabetic, print-only textual production to composing that incorporates images, audio, and video elements to address the diverse literacy needs of students today. This means centering multimodal writing to promote the use of a variety of semiotic resources for meaning making. The key argument is that the process of constructing meaning, in and of itself, is multimodal, and the affordances of multiple modes, including visual, auditory, and semiotic forms, not only complement alphabetic writing but help construct meanings and communicate messages more effectively (Kress, 2010; Smith et al., 2017). In a similar vein, Gee (2003) emphasizes the importance of semiotic domains, which he defines as "any set of practices that recruits one or more modalities" (p. 20) and posits that different modalities that carry different meanings are significant in the modern tech-driven world. Thus, students need to be taught how to effectively create multimodal texts for different purposes, how to purposefully and responsibly use digital technology, and how to draw on multiple semiotic resources to communicate meaning and messages effectively.

ACTION STEPS

For secondary teachers who are interested in integrating multimodal writing into the learning opportunities afforded to students, we recommend the following action steps.

- Survey students or have students discuss in groups their interests in this new form of writing as a way of building interest and excitement. After explaining what multimodal writing is, you can use discussion questions such as: *What experiences have you had, either in school or out of school, with multimodal writing? How can multimodal writing help you show your learning better? What excites you or concerns you about this type of writing?*
- Review the writing curriculum for entry points into multimodal writing. Writing activities can be either retrofitted to include multimodal elements, or new assignments can be created. We recommend that teachers complete the assignment themselves first: not only to develop an exemplar text to use for modeling purposes but also to determine what explicit teaching will be needed and how much scaffolding needs to be provided.
- Offer daily opportunities for students to reflect on their multimodal writing process so goals can be adjusted while writing. These reflections are also important data for teachers when understanding how to make improvements to the instructional design.
- Create multiple opportunities for all students to appreciate and learn from each other. One example may be to facilitate a gallery walk where students' creative work and/or multimodal products are presented for others to enjoy.
- Debrief with students at the conclusion of the writing unit to understand what went well, what they would change, and when they would like to try multimodal writing in the future. Teachers can use these discussions in their writing assignments to better tailor classroom activities to meet students' learning needs—and to make choices about when to integrate multimodal writing in future units of study.
- Collaborate with other content-area teachers to design multimodal writing activities across the disciplines. Such collaboration can support writing across the curriculum and build a writing program that introduces multimodal writing in discipline-specific ways.

REFERENCES

Anderson, K. T., Stewart, O. G., & Kachorsky, D. (2017). Seeing academically marginalized students' multimodal designs from a position of strength. *Written Communication, 34*(2), 104–134.

Bailey, N. M., Carroll, K. M. (2010). Motivating students research skills and interests through a multimodal, multi-genre research project. *English Journal, 99*(6), 78–85.

Bitz, M., & Emejulu, O. (2016). Creating comic books in Nigeria: International reflection on literacy, creativity, and student engagement. *Journal of Adolescent and Adult Literacy, 59*(4), 431–441.

Bowen, T., & Whithouse, C. (2013). What else is possible: Multimodal compositing and genre in the teaching of writing. In T. Bowen & C. Whithaus (Eds.), *Multimodal literacy and emerging genres* (pp. 1–13). University of Pittsburgh Press.

Callahan, M., & King, J. M. (2011). Classroom remix: Patterns of pedagogy in techno-literacies poetry unit. *Journal of Adolescent and Adult Literacy, 55*(2), 134–144.

CAST. (2018). *Universal design for learning guidelines Version 2.2. http://udlguidelines.cast.org*

Chisholm, J., & Trent, B. (2013). Digital storytelling in a place-based composition course. *Journal of Adolescent and Adult Literacy, 57*(4), 307–318.

Cimasko, T., & Shin, D. (2017). Resemiotization and authorial agency in L2 multimodal writing. *Written Communication, 34*(4), 387–413.

Curwood, J. S., & Cowell, L. L. H. (2011). iPoetry: Creating space for new literacies in the English curriculum. *Journal of Adolescent and Adult Literacy, 55*(2), 110–120.

Dusenberry, L., Hutter, L., & Robinson, J. (2015). Filter. Remix. Make. Cultivating adaptability through multimodality. *Journal of Technical Writing and Communication, 45*(3), 299–322.

Englert, C. S., Mariage, T. V., & Dunsmore, K. (2006). Tenets of sociocultural theory in writing instruction research. In C. A. MacArthur, S. Graham, & J. Fitzgerald (Eds.), *Handbook of writing research* (pp. 208–221). Guilford Press.

Flower, L., & Hayes, J. R. (1981). A cognitive process theory of writing. *College Composition and Communication, 32*(4), 365–387.

Gay, G. (2002). Preparing for culturally responsive teaching. *Journal of Teacher Education, 53*(2), 106–116.

Gee, J. P. (2003). *What video games have to teach us about learning and literacy.* St. Martin's Griffin.

Graham, S., Bruch, J., Fitzgerald, J., Friedrich, L., Furgeson, J., Greene, K., . . . Smither Wulsin, C. (2016). *Teaching secondary students to write effectively* (NCEE 2017-4002). National Center for Education Evaluation and Regional Assistance (NCEE), Institute of Education Sciences, U.S. Department of Education.

Harman, R., & Burke, K. (2020). *Culturally sustaining systemic functional linguistics: Embodied inquiry with multilingual youth.* Routledge.

Harman, R., & Shin, D. (2018). Multimodal and community-based literacies: Agentive bilingual learners in elementary school. In G. Onchwari & S. Keengwe (Eds.), *Handbook of research on pedagogies and cultural considerations for young English language learners* (pp. 217–238). IGIGlobal.

Hepple, E., Sockhill, M., Tan, A., & Alford, J. (2014). Multiliteracies pedagogy: Creating claymations with adolescent, post-beginning English language learners. *Journal of Adolescent & Adult Literacy, 58*(3), 219–229.

Hughes, J., & John, A. (2009). From page to digital stage: Creating digital performances of poetry. *Voices from the Middle, 16*(3), 15–22.

Ito, M., Soep, E., Kliger-Vilenchik, N., Shresthova, S., Gamber-Thompson, L., & Zimmerman, A. (2015). Learning connected civics: Narratives, practices, and infrastructures. *Curriculum Inquiry, 45*, 10–29.

Jewitt, C. (2006). *Technology, literacy and learning: A multimodal approach.* Routledge.

Jocius, R. (2013). Exploring adolescents' multimodal responses to the kite runner: Understanding how students use digital media for academic purposes. *Journal of Media Literacy Education, 5*(1), 310–325.

Kitalong, K., & Miner, R. (2017). Multimodal composition pedagogy designed to enhance authors' personal agency: Lessons from non-academic and academic composing environments. *Computers and Composition, 46*, 39–55.

Kress, G. (2010). *Multimodality: A social semiotic approach to contemporary communication.* Routledge.

Krishnan, J., Maamuujav, U., & Collins, P. (2021). Multiple utilities of infographics in undergraduate students' process-based writing. *Writing and Pedagogy, 12*, 369–394.

Ladson-Billings, G. (1995). Toward a theory of culturally relevant pedagogy. *American Education Research Journal, 32*(3), 465–491.

Ladson-Billings, G. (2021). *Culturally relevant pedagogy: Asking a different question.* Teachers College Press.

Leu, D. J., Slomp, D., Zawilinski, L., & Corrigon, J. A. (2016). Writing research through a new literacies lens. In C. A. MacArthur, S. Graham, & J. Fitzgerald (Eds.), *Handbook of writing research* (2nd ed., pp. 41–53). Guilford Press.

Lotherington, H., & Jensen, J. (2011). Teaching multimodal and digital literacy in L2 settings: New literacies, new basics, new pedagogies. *Annual Review of Applied Linguistics, 31*, 226–246.

Lunsford, A. (2007). *Writing matters: Rhetoric in public and private lives.* University of Georgia Press.

Lynch, T. L. (2007). Illuminating Chaucer through poetry, manuscript illustrations, and critical rap album. *The English Journal, 96*(6), 43–49.

Maamuujav, U., Yim, S., & Vu, V. (2024). Rhetorical and motivational values of multimodality in writing: A case study examining L2 writers' participation in multimodal academic writing. *CATESOL Journal, 35*(1).

Marciano, J. E., & Vellanki, V. (2022). Generating new narratives: Examining youths' multiliteracies practices in youth participatory action research. *Research in the Teaching of English, 56*(3), 245–274.

McLean, C. A. & Rowsell, J. (2015). Imagining writing futures: Photography, writing and technology. *Reading and Writing Quarterly, 31*(2), 102–118.

Miller-Cochran, S. (2017). Understanding multimodal composing in an L2 writing context. *Journal of Second Language Writing, 38*, 88–89.

Mirra, N., & Garcia, A. (2017). Civic participation reimagined: Youth interrogation and innovation in the multimodal public sphere. *Review of Research in Education, 41*(1), 136–158.

Mirra, N., & Garcia, A. (2020). In search of the meaning and purpose of 21st-century literacy learning: A critical review of research and practice. *Reading Research Quarterly, 56*(3), 463–496.

Nash, B. (2018). Exploring multimodal writing in secondary English classrooms: A literature review. *English Teaching: Practice & Critique, 17*(4), 342–356.

National Council of Teachers of English. (2013). *NCTE framework for 21st-century curriculum and assessment. https://cdn.ncte.org/nctefiles/resources/positions/framework_21stcent_curr_assessment.pdf*

Nelson, M. E. (2006). Mode, meaning, and synaesthesia in multimedia L2 writing. *Language, Learning, & Technology, 19*(2), 56–76.

New London Group. (1996). A pedagogy of multiliteracies: Designing social futures. *Harvard Educational Review, 66*(1), 60–92.

Palmeri, J. (2012). *Remixing composition: A history of multimodal writing pedagogy.* Southern Illinois University Press.

Pantaleo, S. (2012). Middle-school students' reading and creating multimodal texts: A case study. *Education, 40*(3), 295–314.

Paris, D., & Alim, S. H. (2017). *Culturally sustaining pedagogies: Teaching and learning for justice in a changing world.* Teachers College Press.

Selfe, C. (2004). Toward new media texts: Taking up the challenges of visual literacy. In A. F. Wysocki, J. Johnson-Eilola, C. L. Selfe, & G. Sirc (Eds.), *Writing new media: Theory and applications for expanding the teaching of composition* (pp. 67–110). Utah State University Press.

Selfe, C. (2009). The movement of air, the breath of meaning: Aurality and multimodal composing. *College Composition and Communication, 60,* 616–663.

Shin, D., Cimasko, T., & Yi, Y. (2020). Development of metalanguage for multimodal composing: A case study of an L2 writer's design of multimedia texts. *Journal of Second Language Writing, 47,* Article 100714.

Shivers, J., Levenson, C., & Tan, M. (2017). Visual literacy, creativity and the teaching of argument. *Learning Disabilities, 15*(1), 67–84.

Smith, B. E., Pacheco, M. B., & de Almeida, C. R. (2017). Multimodal codemeshing: Bilingual adolescents' processes composing across modes and languages. *Journal of Second Language Writing, 36,* 6–22.

Takayoshi, P., & Selfe, C. L. (2007). Thinking about multimodality. In C. I. Selfe (Ed.), *Multimodal composition: Resources for teachers* (pp. 1–12). Hampton Press.

Torrance, M., & Galbraith, D. (2006). The processing demands of writing. In C. A. MacArthur, S. Graham, & J. Fitzgerald (Eds.), *Handbook of writing research* (pp. 67–80). Guilford Press.

Unsworth, L., & Mills, K. A. (2020). English language teaching of attitude and emotion in digital multimodal composition. *Journal of Second Language Writing, 47,* Article 100712.

Warschauer, M., & Grimes, D. (2007). Audience, authorship, and artifact: The emergent semiotics of Web 2.0. *Annual Review of Applied Linguistics, 27,* 1–23.

Watts-Taffe, S. (2022). Multimodal literacies: Fertile ground for equity, inclusion, and connection. *The Reading Teacher, 75,* 603–609.

Yancey, K. B. (2004). Made not only in words: Composition in a new key. *College Composition and Communication, 56,* 297–328.

Index

Note. f or *t* following a page number indicates a figure or a table.